ALSO BY GÖTZ ALY

Why the Germans? Why the Jews?:
Envy, Race Hatred, and the Prehistory of the Holocaust

Into the Tunnel:
The Brief Life of Marion Samuel, 1931–1943

Hitler's Beneficiaries:
Plunder, Racial War, and the Nazi Welfare State

Architects of Annihilation:
Auschwitz and the Logic of Destruction
(with Susanne Heim)

Europe Against the Jews

1880–1945

EUROPE AGAINST THE JEWS

1880–1945

GÖTZ ALY

Translated by Jefferson Chase

Metropolitan Books
Henry Holt and Company   New York

Metropolitan Books
Henry Holt and Company, LLC
Publishers since 1866
120 Broadway
New York, NY 10271
www.henryholt.com

Metropolitan Books® and ▥® are registered trademarks of
Henry Holt and Company, LLC.

Library of Congress Cataloging-in-Publication Data

Names: Aly, Götz, 1947– author. | Chase, Jefferson S., translator.
Title: Europe against the Jews : 1880–1945 / Götz Aly ; translated by
    Jefferson Chase.
Other titles: Europa gegen die Juden
Description: First edition. | New York : Metropolitan Books ; Henry Holt
    and Company, 2020. | Includes bibliographical references and index.
Identifiers: LCCN 2019038047 | ISBN 9781250170170 (hardcover) |
    ISBN 9781250170187 (ebook)
Subjects: LCSH: Antisemitism—Europe—History—19th century. |
    Antisemitism—Europe—History—20th century. |
    Jews—Persecutions—History—19th century. |
    Jews—Persecutions—History—20th century. | Holocaust, Jewish
    (1939–1945) | Europe—Ethnic relations.
Classification: LCC DS146.E85 A4913 2019 | DDC 305.892/40409041—dc23
LC record available at https://lccn.loc.gov/2019038047

Our books may be purchased in bulk for promotional, educational, or business use. Please contact your local bookseller or the Macmillan Corporate and Premium Sales Department at (800) 221-7945, extension 5442, or by email at MacmillanSpecialMarkets@macmillan.com.

First Edition 2020

Designed by Kelly S. Too

Printed in the United States of America

1 3 5 7 9 10 8 6 4 2

CONTENTS

Europe Against the Jews

1880–1945

Introduction

More than two million Eastern European Jews emigrated to America between the early nineteenth century and 1914 in increasing waves, looking for security and better lives. Whereas Polish, Italian, Chinese, or German families tended to send out young men in advance, Jews often sold everything they had, packed up their entire families, and headed off into the unknown, never to return to their former countries. They were not just seeking fairer prospects; they were fleeing collective persecution. Israel Zangwill, the son of Jewish-Russian emigrants who left for Britain and the man who coined the phrase "melting pot," described their situation. "The Italian or Chinese [who emigrated to the US] secretly plans to come home again with the money he's made. But what home does the Jew have to return to? He has burned all his bridges. Often he was made to flee without a passport. He cannot return."

In the summer of 1907, the United States was rocked by an economic crisis. Within weeks, 300,000 Italian immigrants returned to their home country. Speaking to an audience in London that year, Zangwill asked them to imagine what would happen if "300,000 Jews came back" to Europe.[1]

Some thirty years later, Germany and Poland demonstrated exactly what would happen. In the summer of 1938, the Polish government in Warsaw issued regulations stripping Jews of their Polish citizenship if they had been living abroad for more than five years. In response, at the end of October, German police arrested 17,000 Polish Jews, brought them to the Polish border, and forced them across. Although Poland was their home country, they were not welcome. In the eyes of many, they were Jews and nothing but. For days, Polish and German border patrols herded the deportees back and forth. Finally, they were interned in hastily constructed, closely guarded camps on the Polish side. The largest camp, with space for more than eight thousand men, women, and children, was built near the Neu-Bentschen/Zbąszyń border crossing between Frankfurt an der Oder and Poznan. It remained in operation until the summer of 1939.

A deportee from Berlin, the violinist Mendel Max Karp, wrote of conditions there: "The place is strictly cordoned off by police, and there are police checks at the train station. Only refugees over the age of sixty-five are allowed to travel further on into Poland. The rest of us are left to find our own way of escaping this cage, and since that is only possible with an entry visa to another country, we are desperately awaiting help from the outside." Karp, who had been born in 1892 in the Austrian village of Ruszelczyce, Galicia (which became part of Poland at the end of World War I), had family in Germany.[2] He sent this plea for help to his cousin, Gerhard Intrator, who had been a legal clerk in Berlin and who had fled to the US in 1937. Ever since, Karp had tried repeatedly to follow in his footsteps, to no avail.[3]

In mid-November, two weeks after Karp sent his letter, the Polish government cut food rations for the camp inmates. At the same time, it called on Washington, London, and the League of Nations in Geneva to make other countries admit the deportees who had been driven out of Germany. On what grounds? The Polish ambassador in London, Count Edward Raczyński, argued that although these people might still possess Polish passports, they had "no other connections" to Poland. A bit later, Raczyński's deputy, Count Jan Baliński-Jundziłł, warned the British Foreign Office that while Poland had so far been able to tamp down actions against Jews, it could not do so forever. If the community of Western nations didn't help out by accepting the deportees, Poland would have "only one way of solving the Jewish problem—persecution."[4]

Thanks to international intervention and agreements reached between Germany and Poland, Max Karp was granted permission to return to Berlin from the Zbąszyń camp on June 29, 1939—although German authorities demanded that he leave the country for good within two months. He planned to emigrate to Shanghai, and his American relatives raised the money to pay for his passage. By the end of August, Karp had gathered everything he needed: an undated ticket paid for in dollars, identification papers full of official stamps and seals, and an extension of his residence permit granted by the Gestapo covering the time until he was able to depart. But it was too late. The Second World War began on September 1. On September 13, Berlin police took Karp into custody and interned him as a stateless Eastern European Jew in the Sachsenhausen concentration camp. There he was given the number 009060 and put in what was known as the small camp, together with other people in his situation. On January 27, 1940, he died or was killed. The exact circumstances of his death are unknown.

His death certificate was filled out by a Brandenburg city official named Otto Griep, who wrote that Karp had succumbed to the flu "according to the written notification of the Sachsenhausen camp commandant." Sachsenhausen didn't yet have its own death registry. It also lacked a crematorium, so Karp's body was cremated at the Baumschulenweg facility in Berlin. Karp's aunt, Rachel Intrator, had his ashes buried at the Jewish Cemetery in the Weissensee district of Berlin in the grave of his mother, Anna Karp.

The story of Mendel Max Karp's life and death embodies European hostility toward Jews in many respects. The German government persecuted him, deprived him of his livelihood as a musician, turned him into a door-to-door tinker, and forced him to the border. The Polish government stripped him of his citizenship and then refused to take him in. In the end, it was Germans and not Poles who murdered Karp, but the Polish government bore responsibility for lowering his chance of survival.

GERMAN CULPABILITY, EUROPEAN COLLABORATION

The deportations and murders of the Holocaust were the result of German initiative. Germans controlled the bureaucratic operations, detaining people, sending them to ghettos, and confiscating their possessions. Germans developed the technology of the genocide. They organized the mass executions and death camps. They unleashed the violence against the Jews in the states that were occupied by Nazi Germany or allied with it. There is no question that the ultimate culpability rests with the Hitler regime.

Nonetheless, the genocide could not have been carried out solely by those who initiated it. When we examine the daily practices of persecution in various countries, we cannot fail to note the ease with which German occupiers were able to enlist local nationalist, national-socialist, and anti-Semitic movements to serve their ends. Without at least passive support in those countries, without the help of administrators, police, state officials, and thousands of non-German helpers who all played a role in the atrocities, Hitler's monstrous project could not have been realized with such breathless speed. There is no way we can comprehend the pace and extent of the Holocaust if we restrict our focus to the German centers of command.

On learning of Hitler's plan to wage war on the Soviet Union, Romanian dictator Ion Antonescu, for example, saw an opportunity to rid his country of its Jewish population. "Romania needs to be liberated from this entire colony of bloodsuckers who have drained the life essence from the people," he remarked. "The international situation is favorable, and we can't afford to miss the moment."[5] Like many others, Antonescu wanted to exploit the exceptional historical situation that Germany had brought about, the collapse of moral and legal standards in so many parts of Europe.

In his monumental history of the Holocaust, *Nazi Germany and the Jews*, Saul Friedländer points out that not a single social group in Europe showed solidarity with the Jews persecuted between 1939 and 1945. He concludes: "Thus Nazi and related anti-Jewish policies could unfold to their most extreme levels without the interference of any major countervailing interests."[6] My book deals with a similar dynamic but locates it in the prehistory of the genocide. It attempts to understand how, why, and in what forms anti-Semitism increased in post-1880 Europe to the point that the architects of genocide were able to find support for the Final Solution in nearly all the countries occupied by or allied with Germany.

That support was a major topic at the Wannsee Conference, originally convened to discuss deporting German Jews from the country. The head of the Reich Main Security Office, Reinhard Heydrich, had already issued invitations for December 9, 1941, and then cancelled the meeting on short notice, offering no explanation but promising that new invitations would be forthcoming. The conference was rescheduled for January 20, 1942, and in the interval, German leaders expanded its scope. Now on the agenda was the "final solution of the *European* Jewish question."[7] At the meeting, Heydrich explained what the regime had in mind and called for constructive cooperation through the "coordination of the lines of leadership." He expected resistance in some but not all occupied and allied countries.

"Dealing with the problem in individual countries will encounter certain difficulties with regard to general attitudes and outlooks," the conference minutes record Heydrich saying. "In Slovakia and Croatia, the matter won't be all that difficult because the core questions have already been given solutions. In Romania, too, the government has already appointed a commissioner for Jewish affairs. In Hungary, it will be necessary to impose an official to deal with the Jewish question sometime soon." Heydrich added that he would be personally negotiating with his Italian counterpart. With regard to occupied and Vichy France, he reported optimistically, "the detention of all Jews for deportation will most likely proceed without great difficulties." Heydrich defined the disenfranchisement, expropriation, and social isolation of Jews either by or with the help of the respective national governments as the "core" preconditions that would facilitate the Final Solution project. As for the occupied parts of the Soviet Union, he referred to the successful experience of German troops who had already worked with Romanian, Ukrainian, Latvian, and Lithuanian helpers to murder 800,000 Jews.

Deputy Undersecretary Martin Luther of the German Foreign Ministry also addressed the willingness of specific countries to arrest Jews and deport them to the east, cautioning that "difficulties could arise if the problem were pursued in greater depth, for instance in the Nordic countries." For that reason he advocated putting off the Final Solution in those countries that "would not be of great significance anyway given the low numbers of Jews there." As for Southeastern and Western Europe, Luther, too, saw "no major difficulties." Adolf Eichmann's minutes record the view espoused by Gauleiter Alfred Meyer (from the Occupied Territories Ministry) and State Secretary Josef Bühler (from the German Civilian Administration in occupied Poland) that Germans themselves "would have to take certain preparatory measures for the Final Solution in the occupied territories so as to avoid unrest among the populace."

The fifteen men at the conference understood that "preparatory measures" referred to the already ongoing construction of gassing facilities and experiments with different methods of mass murder. In late March 1942, a short time after the conference, Joseph Goebbels noted: "An extremely barbaric procedure that cannot be described in more detail will be employed, and there won't be a lot left of the Jews."[8]

That was the plan. Its execution turned out to be somewhat varied. In Belgium, 45 percent of the country's Jews were delivered to the German invaders, but there were great regional variations. In Flemish Antwerp, local police collaborated in rounding up 65 percent of the city's 30,000 Jewish inhabitants. In Francophone Brussels, only 37 percent of the city's 22,000 Jews were captured because the authorities and the Jews' gentile neighbors were significantly less cooperative.

In Hungary, with the help of the state rail company, some 20,000 gendarmes deported 437,402 Jews to Auschwitz between May 15 and July 9, 1944. Germans only took over responsibility for the transports after the trains crossed Hungary's Slovakian border. Those condemned to die were mostly traditional, Yiddish-speaking Jews from the Hungarian provinces, whom the politicians and the people of Budapest contemptuously referred to as "Galicians." In early July 1944, Eichmann ordered the deportation, previously postponed, of some 150,000 well-assimilated Budapest Jews. In this case, however, the Budapest government refused to cooperate. Forced to rely on his staff alone, the best Eichmann could do was to arrange for three trains to transport Jews who had already been confined to a ghetto before he himself returned to Berlin. Without Hungarian assistance he could achieve little. For this reason most of Budapest's Jews survived.[9]

Romania, an ally of the Reich, fought alongside Germany against the Soviet Union. Protected and encouraged by Germans, and receiving occasional help from the SS's infamous Einsatzgruppe D, Romanian police, militiamen, and soldiers murdered or drove to their deaths at least 250,000 Jews in the areas Romania occupied: Moldavia (Bessarabia), Transnistria, and Bukovina. Yet the same government protected the majority of the 315,000 Jews in Romania proper. As of 1943, Romania also offered shelter to Jews who had fled there from German-occupied areas.[10] In Bulgaria, too, the government left the 48,000 Jews living in the center of the country untouched. But Bulgarian police sent more than 11,000 Jews from Thrace and Macedonia, which Bulgaria controlled in 1941, to the German-occupied parts of Poland, and those people were murdered in Treblinka.

In Salonika, Greeks helped Germans deport 45,000 Jews to Auschwitz, where almost all of them were killed. But more than two-thirds of the 3,500 Jewish residents of Athens escaped falling into German hands as a result of both Greek refusal to cooperate and direct help. Unlike the Jews of Salonika, the Jews of Athens were assimilated. Moreover, the north of Greece, which had only been annexed in 1942, was considered by both ordinary Greeks and their government disputed territory that needed to be Hellenized.

These different histories and outcomes introduce the main questions of this book. First, I will examine why Jews who were integrated into mainstream society had markedly better chances of survival than those who dressed in traditional clothes or spoke Yiddish or Ladino. Second, I will look at the extent to which Nazi-allied and -occupied countries supported Jewish deportations as a means of ethnic cleansing on the disputed national borders of their relatively young states. Third, I will ask how the anti-Semitic campaigns of the first half of the twentieth century were connected to general policies of ethnic homogenization. Following on from that, I will explore whether a number of European governments, including those that collaborated with Nazi Germany, approved or at least tolerated the deportation of Jews in the hope that their own, newly nationally defined populations would benefit economically. Taken together, these separate lines of inquiry will attempt to explain how a combination of both positive and negative motives—national renewal and anti-Semitism—made the "removal of the Jews" desirable and encouraged people to participate or at least look the other way.

Nationalism had spread throughout Europe in the late nineteenth century but took on special force after the First World War. When the victorious powers met in Paris in 1919 and 1920 to create the nation-states we still know today and to draw thousands of miles of new European borders, it occasioned a problem unknown in the former continental empires: What to do with minorities within these just-formed nation-states? The people defined by the new national seats of government as minorities had every reason to fear discrimination, while the majority population enjoyed governmental protection and privileges. For this reason, England, France, and the US pushed through a number of treaties and agreements to protect European minorities in 1919–20, but these yielded a host of bitter quarrels and failed to stanch the spread of nationalism throughout Europe.

This nationalism also resulted in efforts by various states to facilitate ethnic homogenization and disadvantage minorities to the benefit of their majorities—be they Poles, Slovaks, Magyars, Ukrainians, Croats, or Romanians. Discriminatory measures included constraints on economic opportunities and citizenship rights, mandatory assimilation, displacement, and forced resettlement. France's resettlement of Germans from Alsace-Lorraine between 1918 and 1923 and the compulsory "transfers" of hundreds of thousands of people between Greece, Turkey, and Bulgaria immediately after the First World War were part of this European panorama. These two events affected Jews only tangentially, but they established the expulsion of minorities as an acceptable European political practice. In 1919, when French authorities began the *épuration*—cleansing—of the German population in Alsace-Lorraine, they came up with an easily applicable bureaucratic definition to decide who was an immigrant: the birthplace of a person's parents and, if necessary, his or her grandparents. This is similar to the definition of Jews later adopted under the Nuremberg laws in Nazi Germany. It was in anticipation of such persecution that the authors of the Paris Peace Treaty adopted protections for minorities, but they failed to consider that, as Hannah Arendt wrote, "whole groups of people would be undeportable because they had no right to reside in any country on earth."[11]

LONG BEFORE 1939, there were lively discussions in various European countries about how Jewish minorities "could be encouraged to emigrate." In 1921 and 1924, the US declared a moratorium on immigrants from Eastern Europe, particularly Jews. With this major escape route cut off, European countries wondered where they could send their unwanted Jews. How could they be removed? Ten years after the crises and civil wars that followed the First World War, the Great Depression created further internal divisions in the European community of nations. Anti-republican nationalism was on the march everywhere. Then, in 1933, the rise of Nazi Germany disrupted the fragile European order and set it on a path toward another major continental war. A number of European political parties, politicians, and electorates succumbed to fascism. They were seduced by the success of the authoritarian governments of Germany and Italy, their state-directed economic and social policies, their mobilization of normally lethargic populaces, their foreign-settlement initiatives, and the measures taken to boost the national majorities and discriminate against minorities, particularly Jews.

Because the forms of discrimination were often similar, it makes little sense to provide a history of anti-Semitism for each country. But my account also focuses on some European states more than others for the reason that some 85 percent of the six million Jews killed in the Holocaust came from Poland, Russia, Romania, Hungary, and the Baltic countries. Although relatively few Jews lived in Greece, I describe the development of anti-Semitism there in detail because Greece is a paradigm of a nation that unified slowly and through various forms of violence. It therefore offers instructive parallels with nationalism in other countries. France is representative of Western Europe. Despite the legal guarantees of equal rights, which had been codified in 1791 (albeit temporarily restricted under Napoleon), a modern form of anti-Semitism developed even there in the 1880s.

THE LONG HISTORY OF EUROPEAN ANTI-SEMITISM

Why choose the period from 1880 to 1945 for this study? The end point is obvious—1945 represents a clear break. There are several arguments for 1880 as a plausible starting point, if not an apparent watershed. It was around then that anti-Jewish sentiment notably increased. In 1874, Romanian politicians reversed laws intended to promote Jewish integration that had been promulgated ten years earlier. In 1882, harsh laws targeting Jews were enacted in Russia, including the Russian part of Poland, which had a huge influence on the events of the next thirty-five years. In the wake of the Russian pogroms from 1881 to 1884, large numbers of Russian, Polish, and Romanian Jews began emigrating to the West, particularly to the US.

At the same time, nationalist ideas began to take hold of the European masses. Originally democratic and emancipatory, these movements advanced militant programs that deified their own "native" nations and excluded other nationalities. Meanwhile industrialization was progressing, albeit at a varying pace, throughout most of Europe, bringing crises, general uncertainty, widespread poverty, and involuntary and voluntary mobility. In central and western Europe, where Jewish minorities had largely enjoyed legal protection since 1867 at the latest, some people came to feel that Jews had perhaps been granted too many rights and were threatening to outstrip Christian majorities thanks to their penchant for education, business acumen, and seemingly innate cleverness.

The Jewish national movement, Zionism, arose in response to the growing nationalism. Its representatives acted according to the notion that, if everyone else was defining themselves as exclusive nations, then Jews, like it or not, would have to do the same. The first significant Zionist manifesto, written by Leo Pinsker and published in 1882 in Berlin, bore the title "Autoemancipation: A Russian Jew's Warning to His Tribal Comrades." In Warsaw, Nahum Sokolov also published his first Zionist manifestos at precisely this time.

Moreover, 1880 was the year the term "anti-Semitism" first appeared. It originated in Germany but soon became part of the world's vocabulary. The term denoted a new type of anti-Jewish hostility, no longer based on religious prejudices and superstitions, which seemed outmoded, but on national, social, and economic arguments. These were supplemented by rationales, considered empirical and modern at the time, imported from anthropology, ethnology, biology, and population studies. The man who coined the word "anti-Semitism," Wilhelm Marr from Magdeburg, had been on the leftist fringe of the failed democratic revolution of 1848. "We are not equal to this foreign tribe," he fretted. For Marr and his rapidly growing ranks of followers, "quick, clever Israel" was the opposite of the plodding, indolent German. Jews, who were "spreading like weeds thanks to their talent," were the antithesis of the Christian Germans with their "ethical gravity," and who on average were developing far more slowly. Marr's contemporary, the Berlin pastor Adolf Stoecker, repeatedly saw in Jewish ambition the reason for "the exacerbation of the social question." In 1882, the first "International Anti-Jewish Congress of Anti-Semites" took place in Dresden.[12]

Such new ideas, which were connected to contemporary crises, made the nonreligious anti-Semitism of the 1880s politically viable in modern, secular states. Political parties could either combat it or co-opt its aims into their own platforms. It was no accident that the tumultuous and infamous two-day session of the Prussian parliament at which the body debated the so-called Jewish question happened in November 1880. For all these reasons, it made sense to begin this investigation in 1880. Similarly, Simon Dubnow chose to begin the tenth and final volume of his great *World History of the Jewish People* (1929) in the year 1880.

METHODOLOGY

For the most part I have drawn from printed source materials. These are divided into three groups. The first consists of contemporary documentation, polemics, and informal records that appeared shortly after the incidents depicted, such as "The Pogrom in Lemberg," compiled by the Jewish witness Joseph Tenenbaum. Theodor Herzl's pamphlet "The Jewish State" also belongs to this category. I consider such texts important because the authors did not know how history would turn out and did not feel compelled to consider events in light of the Holocaust.

The second group contains wider-ranging and more detailed accounts of events written with some historical perspective. They include the comprehensive and nuanced investigative report "Jewish Pogroms in Russia," written in German and published in London in 1910; the book *La Campagne antisémite en Pologne*, edited by Leo Motzkin and published in Paris in 1930, which contains texts presented to the League of Nations to substantiate complaints; the many scholarly works on and collections of source material concerning anti-Semitic subject like the Dreyfus Affair; and individual memoirs. For the reason cited above, here too I prefer works written prior to 1939.

More recent editions of documents and scholarly studies form my third group of resources. Following the epochal shift of 1989–90, a diverse body of literature has appeared on the history and persecution of the Jews in particular European states. Again, I concentrate primarily on material written before 1939.

I am well aware that Jews were French, Polish, or Greek citizens, and that distinctions between Jews and their countrymen are artificial and risk replicating the anti-Semitic perspective. But for the sake of economy, I am forced to use them. Historians must always live with the conceptual framework of the time about which they write. Readers should rest assured that I am not disputing anyone's citizenship when I write of the measures aimed at the Jews of Salonika, for example. I mean Greek citizens of the Jewish faith. A similar caveat applies to phrases like "Jewish businesses" referring to commercial enterprises that belong to a person of the Jewish faith, which are a useful bit of shorthand. How to refer to Jews collectively is a tricky issue. Anti-Semites spoke of "the Jews" and acted accordingly. This identity, to some extent imaginary, is one of the subjects of this book. It goes without saying that there were rich and poor, Zionist and anti-Zionist, atheist, converted, and nationally assimilated Jews as well as those who strictly maintained their linguistic, religious, and cultural particularity. Sometimes different categories apply simultaneously. In fact, the variety of behaviors among Jews was one of the characteristics that especially enraged their enemies.

The collective concepts of European nationalism are likewise problematic: Germans, Poles, Greeks—all these terms are false insofar as many individuals and subgroups thought and acted differently. Conversely, there are many common reductionist phrases that help conceal individual responsibility: "anti-Semitic mob," "the Nazis," "Romanian fascists," or the "German," "Slovakian," or "Hungarian regime." Anti-Semitism did not just cast its spell over "National Socialists." People from all walks of life took part in stealing the property of Jews. The twentieth-century European governments didn't impose anti-Semitism dictatorially. They adopted it to expand their base.

In this sense I consider the topic of European hostility toward Jews only one of many perspectives necessary to understand that history. This book is about the rise of a modern European anti-Semitism, not about resistance to anti-Jewish discrimination and persecution. Nor do I consider my attempts, here or in my other works, to analyze the crimes committed under Hitler to be comprehensive answers to the questions of how and why. Rather, they strive to make a phenomenon that has often been declared beyond understanding a bit more intelligible.

Perhaps they will help us learn how to prevent similar horrors from happening in the future.

Historians must investigate the preliminary stages and contemporary conditions that lead to certain historical developments. They research the interests and behavior of the many people involved and try to depict them as political processes so that readers can imagine and comprehend the actions of individuals and groups. The attempt to contextualize a crime unique in the history of humankind, using historical means, will always run into obstacles. It will necessarily remain fragmentary, and every answer will give rise to further questions. But one thing is certain. Anyone who wants to understand the many conditions that made the Holocaust possible should not separate the worst genocide of the twentieth century from the continuum of German and European history.

1

Prophets of Future Horrors

Numerous social and political currents were shifting in Europe in the decades before and after 1900. The national-democratic movements weren't yet victorious, but they were developing and spreading while the large European empires showed the first signs of crumbling. In the nations of Central Europe, Jewish minorities achieved legal equality, encouraging the belief among national majorities that Jews enjoyed superior privileges to everyone else. Communism, which had arisen as a theory in nineteenth-century Western Europe, became a practical reality in Russia in 1917. Although themselves enemies, both socialists and nationalists fought against liberalism, which had been the political force driving the social and economic changes of the nineteenth century. Both were either skeptical of or hostile toward individual liberties, free trade, and the free-market economy. Terms like liberalism and individualism became insults. Nationalist, socialist, and national-socialist concepts of equality were gaining popularity, with their adherents wearing standardized uniforms and brandishing identical symbols. These groups prioritized the internal homogeneity and solidarity of their own particular collectives above everything else, drawing strict distinctions between themselves and other groups, which they defined, in one form or another, as their enemies.

The dawning twentieth century opened up previously unimaginable possibilities, wealth, and opportunities for many of Europe's underprivileged. Everywhere, governments tackled the problem of illiteracy and hastened to expand school and university systems. Barriers between social classes were lowered, and people were encouraged to better themselves socially. Technological and medical achievements were part of this liberation. The results could be sudden leaps up the social ladder or profound declines. Seen as a whole, Jews in Europe were one of the groups that took advantage of the new possibilities. They not only sang the words of the traditional labor movement hymn: "No saviour from on high delivers / Our own right hand the chains must shiver." Jews lived them—with great inventiveness and daring.

Every transition from one century to the next gives rise to predictions, and none occasioned more than the year 1900. Despite the Belle Époque's seeming peace and calm, old certainties were rapidly disappearing, and increasing numbers of people came to feel that the future entailed serious risks. Jews during this period thought critically and realistically about their future, while self-proclaimed adversaries and friends also sought to redefine Jewishness for the modern world. Theodor Herzl turned the anti-Semitic nightmare scenarios of his day into powerfully worded dreams of a Jewish state. "If you really want it," he told his followers, "then it is no fairy tale."

Zionism: "We Are One People!"

While working as a newspaper correspondent in Paris in late 1894, Herzl was able to closely observe the Dreyfus trial, in which the Alsatian military captain Alfred Dreyfus, a Jewish member of the French general staff, was convicted on false evidence of passing military secrets to Germany and exiled from France for life. "The popular organism has been afflicted with the Dreyfus disease," Herzl wrote, adding that cries of "Death to the Jews" had echoed in the streets of Paris. Because the case was ostensibly about military secrets, the public was excluded from the trial. Like other reporters, Herzl had to make do with scraps of information gathered outside the military court. He did so in a brilliant, no-frills style that remains exemplary even today. His report about the public degradation of Dreyfus, carried out in the courtyard of the École Militaire on the dreary winter morning of January 5, 1895, appeared that afternoon in the Viennese newspaper *Neue Freie Presse*.

"Several minutes after nine, Dreyfus was led out," wrote Herzl. "He wore his captain's uniform. Four men brought him in front of the general, who said: 'Alfred Dreyfus, you are unworthy of bearing arms. In the name of the French people, I strip you of your rank. The verdict has been carried out.' Dreyfus then raised his right hand and said: 'I swear and declare that you are degrading an innocent man. Vive la France!' At that very moment, drum rolls began. The military bailiff began to tear off the decorations, which had previously been loosened from Dreyfus's uniform. Dreyfus maintained his calm demeanor."[1]

It shook Herzl to the core that "even in the France of the Great Revolution," an assimilated Jewish officer who should have been equal under the law and who had been promoted to captain could be stripped of his rank. Herzl empathized with Dreyfus as a disrespected Jew and a defenseless individual victim of a collective defamation.

Working independently of the existing Jewish nationalist associations, Herzl composed his manifesto, *The Jewish State*, during his final two months in Paris. Intoxicated by his vision for the future, he allowed himself little respite while writing. "My only relaxation in the evening was going to hear to Wagner's music," he wrote. "Especially *Tannhäuser*, an opera that I can listen to as often as it is performed."

The Jewish State—A Political Manifesto

Viewed from the Zionist perspective, Jews constituted a nationality rather than a religious community. This was a new idea. Instead of civic integration and legal emancipation for individuals, Zionists pushed for the collective emancipation through the creation of a Jewish state. In so doing, Zionism offered an alternative model for how Jews could react to political realities. The Zionist movement founded in Basel in 1897 aimed at bringing Jews together to form an independent nation that would then become a sovereign member of an increasingly nationally organized world of peoples and states.

Coming in the wake of a number of literary predecessors, Herzl's manifesto, *The Jewish State: An Attempt at a Modern Solution to the Jewish Question*, established itself as a work of lasting significance. Published in 1896, it examined how Jewish national desires had become dormant, only to reawaken in recent years. In the preface to the German edition of the pamphlet, Herzl had a simple explanation for the reemergence: because "the earth resounds with calls to act against Jews."[2]

Herzl began by admitting that he would not be able to describe the state of which he dreamed. He also expressed some self-doubt: "Am I ahead of my time? Is the suffering of Jews not yet great enough? We will see." Herzl, who would die at the age of forty-four, eight years after the publication of his programmatic work, had no way of suspecting how many doors, borders, and harbors would be closed to Jews and how much horror would descend upon them before the state of Israel was created in 1948.

Given this, two retrospective questions are of particular interest to us today. How did Herzl perceive the anti-Jewish agitation and violence of his day, roughly half a century before the Holocaust? And why did he consider the liberal path of cultural coexistence and progressive assimilation a failure? Prior to the publication of his pamphlet, Herzl himself had long been a believer in assimilation. But by 1896, he stressed that resentment, envy, and hatred toward Jews was not a local but a global threat, wherever Jews "lived in visible numbers."

"In Russia Jewish villages are burned to the ground," Herzl wrote. "In Romania, a few Jews are killed. In Germany, they are beaten on occasion. In Austria, the anti-Semites terrorize the entirety of public life. In Algeria, itinerant preachers spew hatred. In Paris, the so-called better society closes ranks to keep Jews out." Herzl could not see any signs that things could get better. In his view, the culturally nationalist zeitgeist was leading to the creation of more or less homogeneous

nations. "Everywhere we have made honest attempts to subsume ourselves in the life of the people around us and to preserve only the faith
of our fathers," Herzl wrote by way of summarizing his own life as
well. "But this is not allowed."

Herzl avoided expressing outrage. He engaged in no tub-thumping
about injustice, human rights, equality before the law, or even the worst
violations of the simplest commandments of civilization, enlightenment,
and humanity. He accepted the challenge of the anti-Semitism all around
him and defined it as a question of power versus impotence. From this
vantage point, it was imperative for Jews to no longer be subjected to
national majorities that could arbitrarily decide who was a foreigner.
Herzl considered it a truism that "we" (the pronoun he used when referring to Jews as a collective) could only escape by also regarding "ourselves" as a nation and forming a corresponding state. For this vision to
become reality, Jews would need a territory, preferably Palestine, and an
effective military. He painted a picture of this modern state with police,
tax authorities, statistics, and diplomacy, organized around a rational,
secular construct of laws and institutions. Religion did not serve as a
constitutional basis. It was the cultural framework that would bring
together all Jews, no matter how different their ways of life.

Herzl urgently warned Jews against getting lulled into a false sense
of security in times of decreased persecution or economic or social
prosperity among what he called the "host peoples," writing: "The
longer anti-Semitism is in coming, the crueler the outbreak will be."
From his experiences in Budapest, Vienna, Berlin, and Paris, Herzl
had become only too well acquainted with the main reason hostility
toward Jews could quietly grow. "The infiltration of immigrant Jews,
attracted by the illusion of security, together with the rise in social class
among established Jews proved a potent combination and encourages
upheaval," he wrote. Herzl predicted that there would be nationalist
revolutions directed against Jews in precisely those countries where
they seemed to have little to fear and to be decently well integrated.
As we now know, Herzl was accurately describing the repressed but
no less malevolent anti-Semitism that was coming to a boil not just in
Germany, but also in France and Hungary.

Herzl understood the project of a Jewish state as the necessary anti-
dote to two millennia of intense suffering that, while horrific, contained a lesson for the future. "Whole branches of Jewishness can die
and fall to the ground, but the tree lives," Herzl wrote. In his view,
Zionists and anti-Semites were tacitly working hand in hand, the latter
by forcing Jews to gather their strength and take their destinies into
their own hands. With good leadership and sufficient force of will, they
could succeed in transforming themselves from passive, abused historical objects, who were at best tolerated, into active historical subjects.
Herzl believed in historical determinism, prophesying that "the world
needs a Jewish state," which would arise in a "council of the world's
civilized nations." The reason why was simple: "We are one people."

Between Revolution and the "Terrible Power of Money"

Socially and economically, *The Jewish State* picked up on the great misery and opportunities of the industrial age. In Herzl's eyes, the furious
pace of technological progress and the constant development of new
commodities were important factors driving the new hostility toward
Jews. What had created this hostility, he asked rhetorically. "The entrepreneurial spirit." What was the opposite of that spirit? "Sedentary"
work. What was a typical example of such work? "The farmer in his
field who stands on exactly the same spot as his ancestors stood one
thousand years ago." This "historical category," Herzl believed, would
quickly disappear because the "agrarian question" was essentially a
"question of machinery," and ultimately American-style progress would
win out over the European cult of the land. Consequently, he approved
of the fact that European Jews didn't allow themselves to be "converted into farmers."

The anti-Semitic stereotype of rag-trading Eastern European Jews
ready to pour across the Prussian border and work their way upward
more quickly than sluggish Christian natives was familiar from the
political writings of the ultraconservative historian Heinrich von Treitschke. Herzl, however, described such people sympathetically as an
incipient Jewish proletariat "thrown to and fro by political pressure

and economic need, from place to place, country to country." Poor Jewish immigrants from Galicia, Western Russia, and Romania were rejected by socially established Jewish citizens who feared that their co-religionists from the east would fan the flames of anti-Semitism anew. The affluent gentlemen of the Friendly Society of German Jews also considered Yiddish, a "German-Jewish jargon," a "degraded" parody of their own educated language and an offense to the ear.[3]

This sort of upper-middle-class smugness was foreign to the politician Herzl. His affinities with Marxist thought led him to tailor his Zionist project to the needs of the poorest of the poor and to count on their desire to put their crushing poverty behind them. He promised them upward mobility, a thoroughly modern economy, and a social-welfare state of the first order. Herzl repeatedly put forward the idea of the Jewish nation as a "seven-hour land," going the unsuccessful demands of the Social Democratic movement for an eight-hour workday one better.[4] But Herzl also thought the state should take a hard line toward anyone unwilling to work: "Beggars will not be tolerated. Those who refuse to do anything voluntarily will be sent to the workhouse."

At the center of the utopia presented in *The Jewish State* is what Herzl's Zionist predecessor Leo Pinsker (1821–1891) called a vision of collective "auto-emancipation." Like Herzl, Pinsker had long placed his faith in assimilation, and because of this conviction he had founded a society to support the advancement and education of Russia's Jews. But he ultimately changed his mind in the face of increasing Judeophobia, which he came to consider an immutable fact of life that left its victims with no choice but to find a territory of their own where they could happily live independently.[5]

According to Herzl's plan, the gradual, controlled emigration of Jews would benefit their former homelands by allowing for the "internal migration of Christian citizens into the posts vacated by Jews" and "an unprecedentedly peaceful rise of the [Christian] masses to prosperity." State governments would also profit from a slow, controlled exodus of Jews. The Jewish Company, which would administer the assets Jews left behind, would offer large-scale properties to the governments in question at favorable terms. Governments would be able to sell the assets they had acquired so cheaply to private buyers and use the revenues generated for "specific social improvements on a large scale." This amounted to a redistribution of assets. Herzl combined the Jewish and the social questions so as to solve the former while alleviating the latter. As we will see, the ideas of most anti-Semites ran in similar, if far more militant directions. They, of course, demanded that the Jews disappear sooner rather than later, no matter how, so that jobs and economic opportunities would become available.

Read retrospectively, *The Jewish State* contains alarming diagnoses and recommendations about how to avoid the impending catastrophe. Herzl compared the potential effects of Jewish emigration on the general (Christian) standard of living to the redistribution of assets during the French Revolution. The difference, he emphasized, was that the latter was the result of a breakdown of law and order, a state of anarchy and rivers of blood. His project, he emphasized, aimed to create peaceful, legal procedures for separating Jews and Christians. He urged his supporters not to equate traditional religious narrow-mindedness with the anti-Semitism of his day, since he understood the latter as the immediate consequence of Jews' economic and legal emancipation, which had turned them into "terrible competition" for both the traditional and newly ambitious Christian middle classes. Conversely, such anti-Semitism meant that while members of the well-educated Jewish middle class could rise into the capitalist bourgeoisie, they were barred from certain careers, and there were ceilings on their advancement. Jews, for instance, were not allowed to become civil servants or serve in the military. Unable to pursue their ambitions and often living in a materially precarious situation, overeducated Jews formed an "academic proletariat" that tended toward socialism.

Herzl himself distinguished between "money Jews" and "intellect Jews." Amid the tensions in the decades around 1900, he predicted that Jews would follow the two major ideas of progress at the time, bourgeois liberalism and revolutionary socialism. On the lower end of the wealth spectrum, they provided "the staff sergeants of all the revolutionary parties," while at the upper end, their "terrible power of money" was shooting to the skies. This pair of insights led Herzl to anticipate anti-Semitic political parties' later conviction that Jews were the crux of societal turmoil: "The social battle in any case had to be fought on our backs because we occupied the most prominent positions in both the capitalist and socialist camps."

The extent to which Adolf Hitler was determined to wage exactly this battle can be gauged from a speech he gave twenty-six years after Herzl's manifesto. From the outset he depicted "the Jew" as doubly threatening, as a simultaneously plutocratic and Bolshevik monster. In Hitler's view, one arm of this monstrosity was strangling the middle classes and enslaving farmers and workers to big money, while the other arm unleashed communism, destroying every form of social order, ethics, and religion and clutching greedily at all the assets upright, hardworking people had legitimately earned. "Jewry has made a step of political genius," Hitler said in 1922. "This capitalist people, which created the most unscrupulous form of human exploitation the world has known, understands how to seize the leadership of the fourth estate." Just as Herzl predicted, Hitler accused Jews to trying to further radicalize the proletariat, the members of this new fourth estate, while simultaneously making capitalism even more inhumane. "While Moses Kohn braces his shareholders so that they react as inflexibly and hostilely as possible to the demands of their workers, his brother, the labor leader Isaak Kohn, is at the factory stirring up the masses." In the Nazi view, the two worked together to seduce the German people "into destroying their own economy and trapping themselves all the more inevitably in the [Jewish] race's golden manacles—eternal interest slavery."[6]

THE FATHER OF A STATE

A man of his era, Herzl assumed there were empty spaces on earth where Europeans could do whatever they wanted. In this spirit, he created the profile of the "land taker" and described the migration to be organized by the Jewish Company as a "replanting." He titled one section of *The Jewish State* "Our Human Material." He was also at ease with the term *Volksgemeinschaft* (people's community), which later became a Nazi favorite. At the same time, he hoped that his great project would be realized with a minimum of violence. In his last will and testament, he advised the Jewish people: "Make your state so that the stranger feels at home among you."

The idea of founding a new state was hardly outlandish at the time. Belgium had only existed since 1830, California, as such, since 1850. Bulgaria, Romania, and Greece were gradually formed in multiple stages of expansion. In 1905 Norway broke away from Sweden, in 1917 Finland split from Russia, and in 1922 Ireland became independent from Great Britain. The list doesn't even include the many states that would arise from the disintegration of the Hapsburg, Russian, Ottoman, and various other colonial empires. Migrations of large masses of people weren't unusual either. In 1896 alone, the year *The Jewish State* was published, 2.3 million Europeans emigrated overseas.

Blinded by the ethos of colonialism, Herzl wasn't particularly concerned with what would happen to the Arabs who lived in Palestine. The holy sites of Christianity were to be protected, he wrote—he didn't mention the holy sites of Islam. In fact he hoped that attacks by the great imperial powers on the Ottoman Empire would further his own project, which was very much conceived in a European spirit. "If a portion of the Oriental question is solved by solving the Jewish question," he proclaimed, "this would certainly be in the interests of all civilized people everywhere." After visiting Palestine for the first time, Herzl noted: "We will need to expropriate private property in these territories. We'll try to transport the penniless population across the border by finding work for them in transit countries, but we shall deny them all work in our own country. The propertied population will come over to our side. The job of expropriation as well as the removal of the poor must be carried out gently and carefully. Property owners should be made to believe that they've cheated us, that we've paid more than the land's actual value. But we won't sell anything back to them."[7]

Herzl was a strict, though not autocratic, disciplinarian and an obsessive yet pragmatic believer in a utopia that seemed neither attainable nor desirable to the majority of Central European Jews at the time. As the "father of the state," as he described himself, he was pursuing a mission "given to him by the highest necessity." When he died in 1904, obituaries referred to him as "our deceased leader," someone who had been able to give a diasporic people a concrete form and who would go down in history as a "new Moses."[8]

Herzl attracted few followers, and not much progress was made toward establishing Jewish settlements in Palestine. Around 1882, some 35,000 Jews lived in Ottoman-ruled Palestine. By 1914, in the wake of pogroms in Russia and thanks to the incipient Zionist movement, that number had grown to 90,000. In 1917, Palestine became a battleground for Turkish-German battles. In 1920, due to war, forced resettlement, and people fleeing hunger and disease, only 58,000 Jews still lived in Palestine, which was now under British mandate.[9] The majority of Western European Jews would continue to regard the Zionist idea as a phantasm of a lunatic, blowhard, or swindler. During his lifetime, many rabbis spoke out against Herzl in their synagogues. His editor at the assimilationist *Neue Freie Presse* forbade him from using the word "Zionism," and Austrian satirist Karl Kraus made fun of him in a pamphlet titled "A Crown for Zion." In his later years, Herzl couldn't enter Vienna's Burgtheater without people in the audience murmuring sarcastically, "His Majesty has appeared!"[10]

Among the early anti-Semitic proponents of forced Jewish resettlement in Palestine, Germany's Paul de Lagarde and Heinrich Class and the Hungarian politician Győző Istóczy particularly stand out. In his 1853 essay "Conservative?" Lagarde argued for the relocation of the approximately two million Jews who lived under German and Austrian rule. "It is impossible to tolerate a nation within our nation," especially since Germans were "a much too delicate material . . . to withstand these Jews who have been steeled by Talmudic discipline."[11] But because resettlement required "hard work" and a determined leader, Lagarde had doubts about its prospects, writing, "There is no such leader."

In the summer of 1878, following the recent Russo-Turkish war, representatives of the great European powers came together for the Congress of Berlin to discuss the "Oriental question" and redefine national borders and spheres of influence. At the same time, on June 24, Istóczy, who was a delegate, presented a draft resolution to the Hungarian parliament. "This lofty house," it read, should declare that the Jewish people's "cherished original homeland Palestine" would be restored either as an autonomous, "appropriately enlarged" province of the Ottoman Empire or "alternately as an independent Jewish state." Istóczy had a reputation as a determined and influential anti-Semite. The aim of his initiative was to remove the Jews, "who are so dangerous to Christian civilization," from Europe so that they could serve as the bearer of culture "amidst the Semitic tribes related to it." Like Herzl after him, Istóczy defined Jews as a national people.

Istóczy thought it inevitable that Muslims would disappear from Southeastern Europe, leaving only Jews as a "foreign element . . . one that will be fully isolated" in the Christian Occident. With that, he put his finger upon a point that would prove particularly pivotal for twentieth-century anti-Semitism. The more other national minorities were driven out, the more delicate the position of remaining Jews would become. Policies of resettling or expelling minorities in general were part of the context of growing European anti-Semitism. In societies that had been culturally homogenized, Jews like those in Salonika stood out as a final nonnational group that refused to be integrated, replaced, or driven away.

With demagogic enthusiasm, Istóczy enjoyed demonizing Jews, who, he claimed, were bent upon "achieving domination over the people of Europe and forcing them into the yoke of slavery." To this end, Jews employed "demonic skill" and encouraged "disproportionally high birth rates" and "mass immigration." Istóczy turned Jews' statistically demonstrable resistance to cholera and other epidemics, as well as their greater longevity, into an accusation, asserting that the differences showed that they "studiously avoided" heavy physical labor. Jews also benefited from "the advantages of wealth."[12] (In fact, thanks to Jews' better hygiene and moderation in eating and drinking habits, Jewish longevity greatly exceeded that of Christians. Jewish women did not have more children than Christians, but the infant mortality rate in Jewish families was around 25 percent lower.)[13]

In his pamphlet "On the German War Goal," written in the intoxication of military victory and initially only circulated privately, the leader of the Pan-Germanic League, Heinrich Class, also warmed to the idea of resettling Jews in Palestine. In September 1914, he argued that the Russian Empire should be broken up and Poland, the Baltic states, and Ukraine placed under German control. Inspired by visions of imperial grandeur, he discussed the idea he considered "most important" in the preface to the published version of the pamphlet in 1917: the notion that "previously foreign territory should be acquired without its previous inhabitants," indeed, if possible "without people."

It was in this context that Class turned his attention to Jews, arguing that as many as possible should be deported to Russia, even though it was to be drastically reduced in size. But he made another suggestion, one he considered even better and claimed Eastern European Jews would welcome if they understood "that the path to the west was no longer open." Germany's ally the Ottoman Empire, he proposed, should offer Palestine as a "national Jewish state." This, in Class's eyes, was a way to "seize the Jewish problem by the roots." No matter how the mass resettlement was approached, he argued, it would be born of "a serious necessity that should be acknowledged by everyone." Waves of Jewish immigration should not be allowed "to break over Germany" nor should "Jews be allowed to remain in such great masses in the new German territories to the east since they would present an extreme danger to the development of those areas."

Class spelled out in 1912 why the Jews represented such a threat to German claims and aspirations in the gigantic empire of which he dreamed. Jews, he believed, enjoyed "the advantage of education" and "talent," which had granted them impressively rapid social and economic success in Germany. The Christian majority—Lagarde, Istóczy, and Class all argued—required special protection because it was "only able to orient itself slowly and clumsily." Because they were so sluggish, Class proposed, "whole classes" of Germany "have still never become equal" to the demands of the times.[14]

In Russia, which Class hoped to transform into a German colonial space, the writer Maxim Gorky sent a questionnaire to his readers in 1915 concerning the "Jewish problem." One respondent answered that the "congenital, cruel, and consistent egoism of the Jews is everywhere victorious over the good-natured, uncultured, trusting Russian peasant or merchant." Another proposed that while equal rights were of course desirable, "great caution" was required lest "the ignorant Russian people . . . pass into Jewish slavery." A third suggested that "Jews should be given a separate colony, or they'll reduce Russia to nothing." A fourth went even further, writing: "My Russian opinion is that all Jews should be wiped off the face of the Russian Empire and that's the end of it."

Gorky summarized the results of his poll as follows: "In the final analysis, whatever nonsense anti-Semites may talk, they do not like the Jew because he is obviously better, more dexterous, and more capable than they are."[15]

"The Jew must be burned alive!"

Within the space of twenty-seven years, between 1881 and 1908, 1,550,000 Jews emigrated from the Russian Empire, 305,000 from Austria-Hungary, and 100,000 from Romania. Of these two million people, 190,000 found a new home in Britain, but the overwhelming majority, 1,750,000, resettled in the US. In 1914, the number of Eastern European Jews who had received American citizenship since 1881 broke the two million mark. Between January and August 1914 alone, 102,600 Russian Jews left their "stepmotherland" and tried to gain entry to the US.[16]

As we have seen, very few of the Jews who went overseas ever returned to the countries from which they came. The situation was different with other Europeans. Between 1908 and 1925, having been disappointed in the US, 57 percent of Italian émigrés returned to their former homeland, along with 40 percent of Christian Poles, 64 percent of Hungarians, 67 percent of Romanians, and 55 percent of Russians. By contrast 95 percent of Jewish emigrants stayed permanently. Moreover, whereas other émigrés were predominantly young men seeking work and adventure, Jews relocated to the US with their entire families.[17]

In his short 1912 book, *The Future of the Jews*, German sociologist Werner Sombart, an adherent of the Social Democratic movement, posed a question that was soon to become urgent. What would happen if the avenues for migration abroad were closed off? Citing the never-ending phenomenon of pogroms and other untenable conditions of his day, Sombart concluded that the situation of the Jews in Eastern Europe would grow even more intolerable if they did not migrate in great numbers.[18]

Conditions of life for Jews in Russia had been declining since 1863, but now they took a dramatic turn for the worse. The abolition of serfdom had opened the door to capitalism, economic freedom, the creation of a proletariat, loss of tradition, and competition for social status. Already existing hostility toward Jews increased and led to frequent pogroms. In response, hoping to pacify the Christian majority and distract attention from their own inability and that of the Christians to modernize the country's economy and society, Russian lawmakers imposed additional economic restrictions on Jews.

Like Herzl, Sombart didn't spend time condemning the measures taken in Russia as unjust or wrongheaded. He accepted them as facts of life, treating the future of Eastern European Jews as "a problem of accommodation, provision and, more precisely, of settlement and resettlement." Sombart assumed that economic misery and pogroms would persist, but that regular emigration would make them less explosive. "But what if this release valve were to be closed?" he asked. Emigration to the US might have helped to stabilize the situation in Russia. Despite relatively high birth rates, the number of Galician Jews, for example, declined by some 17,000, to 793,360, between 1900 and 1908. "The bitterest privation," wrote Sombart, had forced tens of thousands of people "to leave their homeland and try their luck abroad."[19]

Hope for Zionist Success

In the early twentieth century, there were many reasons to assume that the US and Britain would soon close the escape routes open to poor Eastern European Jews. In Britain, for example, Sombart identified the rise of what he called "social anti-Semitism." In the summer of 1911, he wrote, there had been "crass excesses" against Jews in Wales. Meanwhile, American politicians were advocating that all immigrants be required to prove a certain level of wealth and that "all economic undesirables" be refused entry into the country.

In the late nineteenth century, the US had begun to restrict its once liberal approach to immigration—at first cautiously, then more resolutely. An 1875 law banned prostitutes and convicts from entering the country. In 1882, regulations were imposed on Chinese immigration, and that same year a tighter law came into force barring people who represented a danger to the general prosperity of the community. In 1913, congressmen in Washington debated legislation to prevent illiterates from entering the country.

Authorities also began interpreting existing legislation more strictly. Customs officials turned away more and more people at the border as undesirable and ordered them to be returned to Europe at the cost of the ocean-liner companies. Under the regime of New York Immigration Commissioner William Williams, which began in 1909, the winds blowing over Ellis Island were increasingly frosty. Williams concluded his annual report for 1910 with the words: "The time has come when it is necessary to put aside false sentimentality in dealing with the question of immigration and to give more consideration to its racial and economic aspects and in deciding what additional immigrants we shall receive, to remember that our first duty is to our country."[20]

Sombart's analysis led him to conclude that the fundamental economic misery of Eastern European Jews needed to be approached, "without a lot of contemplation," as a present and future political problem requiring a solution. The entire world faced the task of finding territory suitable for accommodating these five million impoverished people. Should that territory turn out to be Palestine, all the better. But the main thing was to commence this process of colonization "systematically and energetically . . . with the sole initial, practical and sober goal of creating humane living conditions for the greatest possible number of Jews." Sombart concluded his rumination with the statement: "May the optimists among the Zionists be proven right on the path they've suggested we follow so that a solution can be found to at least one part of the 'Jewish question': the fate of the Eastern European Jews."[21]

Hardly had they been founded than the barely organized Zionist groups concluded in 1903, the year of the large-scale Kishinev pogrom, that they would have to lobby for "a secure Jewish homeland," in which millions of Jews could live "in a Jewish setting" without anti-Semitism. "If this homeland is not created," Zionists in 1903 warned, "hundreds of thousands of Jews" could soon be delivered up, defenseless, to poverty and even murder because "they cannot get out of their country as the last remaining release valves—England and America—have been blocked."[22]

In his 1908 pamphlet, "Emigration and Immigration—A Word on the Plight of Jewish Emigres," the German author Eugen Doctor described in lurid detail the growing popular anti-Semitic hatred in Russia, Russian Poland, and Romania. For that reason, he argued, Jews were fleeing en masse to other European countries and overseas. But once there they were again forced to compete against ordinary people, and then "the sort of societal hatred developed that they had just fled." Doctor was thus skeptical of the "old theory" of America as a cure-all. Jewish immigrants, he claimed, "no longer knew where they should tread or lay their heads." If nothing happened and no territory for Jewish settlement was opened up, the situation in Russia and Romania would "come to a boil." Doctor concluded: "One fine day, even this constellation will be swept away, and all we'll have will be the revival of the old refrain: 'The Jew must be burned alive.'"[23]

From Popular Hatred to Popular Murder

Amid the Belle Époque's celebration of progress and the rise of the bourgeoisie, a handful of Jewish authors warned that Europe was facing an extremely violent century to come. In 1882, Viennese journalist Isidor Singer predicted that while the causes of this violence would have nothing to do with Jews, Jews would nevertheless be affected with particular severity. Singer suspected that in the not-too-distant future, ruthless battles would erupt between "Germanity and the Slavic world," soon expanding into a conflict between Europe and "an Orient undergoing terrible turmoil." All of Europe would take up arms, and in the "long-feared European war . . . Jews would doubtlessly receive the deepest and most painful wounds." To support his prognoses, Singer argued that such a war would inevitably lead to the "collapse of the Russian Empire," exacerbating the "rage of the mob" across the entire continent, loosening "the bonds of law and order" throughout Western Europe and allowing "unruly elements" to gain the upper hand. Should that happen, there would be no one left to oppose "the nearly ineradicable resentment of Jews arising from only the basest forms of envy and greed."

As Singer knew, anti-Semitism in Germany had been reined in somewhat after the outbreaks of 1880, but even then, some thirty years before the start of the First World War, there were reasons not to trust the calm. In the twentieth century, Singer envisioned, protracted warfare would encourage minority populations to think in absolute terms of friends and enemies and to search for scapegoats. Singer's vision was based on his experience of history and humanity. "Are we really so sure," he concluded, "that if the German people have stood armed on battlefields in Russia or France for days and years, anti-Semites at home won't raise their voices even more and renew their shrill battle-cry: 'Down with the Jews?'"[24]

In his 1897 book *Culture and Humanity*, a diagnosis of its era, the obscure Bavarian author Siegfried Lichtenstaedter, a Jew, dismissed the Christian, Occidental idea of respecting human life as a "great lie." Seen clearly, European imperialism inevitably led to the destruction of allegedly uncivilized peoples. "Beating, robbing, destroying, burning, and murdering take up a major part of the working strength of European officials, officers, merchants, and travelling researchers," Lichtenstaedter remarked. The author briefly alluded to the "great mass butchering" with which Russia put down the aspirations to liberty of the Tartars and other Muslim peoples, the "gruesome deeds of shame" that had disgraced French rule in the Northern Vietnamese province of Tonkin, the slaughter of "probably more than 100,000 peaceful Turkish and Bulgarian Muslims" by Russian and Bulgarian soldiers around 1877, and the bloodthirsty methods employed by the Dutch to reinforce their rule over the Malaysian peoples. "The destruction of the [human] species is one of the most noteworthy manifestations of civilization, by which I mean modern civilization," he concluded.

Lichtenstaedter repeatedly asked himself what the twentieth century was likely to bring. He predicted "an unanticipated growth and strengthening of the Russian Empire." He also believed there would be a battle between the European and Far Eastern peoples. That conflict, he wrote, would mobilize the strength of other peoples, "bringing it to bear heavily." "Under certain circumstances," he added, those people would include "even the least respected races, whose only purpose thus far had been to be exploited by Europe."[25]

One year later, in 1898, Lichtenstaedter published a pamphlet titled "The Future of Turkey: A Contribution to the Solution of the Oriental Question." In it, he analyzed the power vacuum and the Christian-Muslim tensions that the great European powers encouraged within the disintegrating Ottoman Empire. In 1895 and 1896, the separatist ambitions of Armenian revolutionaries, inspired by European nationalism, had resulted in "the Turkish carrying out large-scale massacres of Armenians." The Turkish people, Lichtenstaedter wrote, lived in fear of "being subjected to the rule of the Russians, the Armenians, or the Greeks." The author blamed the nationalist and religious tensions within Turkey on "the whisperings of European theoreticians" and the interests of imperialist powers, specifically Russia and Great Britain, who actively tried to inculcate European Greeks and Armenians with nationalist ideas.

In response to the threat of further genocides, Lichtenstaedter suggested persuading the "Christian populations" to emigrate from the Ottoman Empire. As a practical alternative, he advocated immediately founding a "new mother country" for Greeks and Armenians "at another location," possibly in America or Australia, where they would be surrounded by Christian neighbors. Although he acknowledged that his suggestions would be "called inhumane," Lichtenstaedter stressed that time was running out. "In twenty years, it will be too late," he wrote.

Lichtenstaedter maintained no illusions about nationalists' true motives. Of the ongoing Greek "battle for liberation" on Crete, which was heavily supported by France, Russia, and England, he remarked: "The 'freedom fighters' are pursuing a very specific goal: to steal the land possessed by Muslim populations. There's no reason to expect that Cretan Christians will voluntarily hand back these territories to the Muslims." European philo-Hellenism may have become muted in recent years "because the Greeks exceeded the normal level of allow-able dishonesty by far too great a margin." But Lichtenstaedter pre-dicted that the situation would swing round again: "If in the next three to five years the Greeks will refrain from deceiving their credi-tors again, which is possible, if not probable, Europe will shower them with love even more greatly than before, which will of course come at the cost of the Turks."[26] That was precisely what happened in the First Balkan War against Turkey in 1912, in the Paris-Sèvres agreement of 1920, and during the Greek war of aggression against Turkey's Anato-lian heartland from 1919 to 1921.

In 1901 and 1903 Lichtenstaedter published a two-volume work he described as a history of the future. Consisting of fictional govern-mental declarations, newspaper articles, and parliamentary protocols, it ended in 1945 and was titled *The New World Empire—A Con-tribution to the History of the Twentieth Century*. For the year 1910, he predicted that Italian troops would land in Tripoli and that there would be a major war in the Balkans, that "flashpoint of Europe," over the unresolved Macedonian and Albanian questions. In the process, the Christian states of Bulgaria and Greece would play a special role in the battle against Turkey. Lichtenstaedter cited from the fictional "widely read" people's newspaper in Sofia, which had early on raised a "fiery cry" to expel "the Turkish enemy from the civilized corridors of Europe." On January 12, 1910, snatches of fictional conversation would echo from the Greek Chamber of Deputies: "Leonidas ... spirit of Achilles ... traitors ... rights with no statute of limitations ...

Hellenism . . . fatherland . . . subjugated brothers . . . barbarians . . . liberty . . . death."[27]

As things actually turned out, Italian troops occupied Tripoli in 1911, not 1910, and Italy officially annexed Libya a short time later. The Second Balkan War was waged from 1912 to 1913. Greece tried to annex parts of Turkey, Bulgaria, and Albania during this period. Peace initiatives had little effect, and the German ambassador in Athens reported that Greek paramilitaries "have been guilty of the most unprecedented cruelties against Muslims, massacring these unfortunate people en masse."[28]

For 1912, Lichtenstaedter had envisioned a "gruesome" massacre of Armenians by Muslims in the East Anatolian city of Erzurum.

For June 23, 1939, Lichtenstaedter imagined a newspaper article with the headline "Marvelous Solstice Celebration Among German University Students." The festivities were so "suffused by German racial feeling" that the students excluded everyone associated with "outmoded, foreign, Jewish, or feminine" thinking. "Authentic German" activities were taking place at the venue, a tavern called "Zum deutschen Blitz" (The German Thunderbolt): "There were indescribable cheers," ran the fictional report, "as people began singing the latest militant German song 'When a Parasite People Threaten Us.'" Several Czech and Slovenian ruffians grinned mockingly, the article adds, whereupon they were "punished in appropriate fashion."

Another entry foresaw German leadership declaring on October 2, 1939, that its patience had run out and war was now inevitable. The reason given was "the most recent violent incidents" perpetrated by an "ignorant, brain-washed Slavic mob." The imagined declaration then warned the "Slavic population" that "he who sows the wind will reap a whirlwind" and reassured everyone else that this punitive action would not affect Germany's friendly relations with Russia. (This presaged Nazi Germany's invasion of Poland and the Ribbentrop-Molotov pact that saw the Third Reich and the Soviet Union partition Germany's eastern neighbor.) Lichtenstaedter also anticipated Germany's annexation of Austria, although he predicted it in April 1940 rather than

March 1938. His German Reich chancellor declares: "We extend our hand to beloved old brother tribes by sending parts of our army to the Austrian border." Lichtenstaedter wrote of an agreement with the Russian government about "the drawing of ethnic borders." (This actually took place in August 1939.) The final entry was just as unerring. On October 1, 1945, a "Russian commissioner for the administration of the liberated Western Slavic countries" would take up work in Prague and, on January 1, 1946, issue an "edict of tolerance for the liberated Western Slavic countries." According to its paragraph 3, school instruction in all these countries would henceforth be carried out in Russian as a means of combating "the disastrous fragmentation of the Slavic cultural world." Additionally, the edict required that all printed material was to be published in Russian using the Cyrillic alphabet. Anyone violating these ordinances would be "deported to the Arctic islands of Novaya Zemlya and lose all benefits and amenities."[29]

Lichtenstaedter was born in the Bavarian town of Baiersdorf in 1865, the son of leather trader Wolf Lichtenstaedter and his wife, Sophie, née Sulzberger. He got a degree in Oriental studies and law and later worked as a high-ranking official in the Bavarian tax authority. He regularly published political essays, often under a pseudonym, and articles on Jewish religious subjects, which were banned. On June 6, 1942, Munich police deported the seventy-seven-year-old to the Theresienstadt concentration camp, where he died exactly six months later.

On January 1, 1901, Russian historian Simon Dubnow wrote in his diary: "We are entering the twentieth century. What will it bring for us—for humanity and especially Jews? To judge from the final decades of the past century, it's possible that humanity is heading toward a new Middle Ages full of terrible wars and national conflicts. But one's soul resists believing that."[30] Dubnow achieved recognition as the author of a ten-volume World History of the Jewish People. He was born in 1860 in the Belarussian shtetl Mstsislaw as the son of a wood seller. Unwilling to live in Bolshevik Russia, he went into exile in Berlin in 1922. In 1933, he fled Nazi Germany for Riga, the Latvian capital. When the Germans conquered that city in the summer of 1941, they forced him along with all other Jews into a ghetto. On December 8,

1941, the eighty-one-year-old was murdered as part of a "mission," in which soldiers from the German Einsatzgruppe A and their helpers in the Latvian police shot to death 25,000 Jews within a single week.[31]

Zionists, notorious anti-Semites, and their Jewish and gentile critics used many of the same basic arguments for the creation of a Jewish territory. In the age of European colonialism, all sides supported a Jewish settlement in the Earth's supposedly "empty spaces." From the Jewish perspective, such projects were based on assumptions that wider economic, social, and military conflicts in the twentieth century would particularly endanger Jewish minorities. Such conflicts included the increasing economic competition between Jews and gentiles, the rapid rise of xenophobic nationalism, and the imminent closing off of overseas emigration.

The Jewish prognosticators did not talk about races or racism, but rather about the coming reality as they saw it. They all assumed that time was running out and that Jewish assimilation had failed. While their motivations may have differed, they all felt loyal to their people and thought it should finally be elevated into a homogeneous nation at peace with itself. To that end, the Jews needed to receive a territory on which they could found a state of their own.

2

The Sluggish Versus the Ambitious

As a young professor, the German natural scientist Carl Vogt became a supporter of the 1848 revolution and was sent as a radical democratic deputy to the National Assembly in Frankfurt. After trying to incite a popular uprising in southwestern Germany in 1849, he fled to Switzerland. Later, from his post at the University of Geneva, he watched anti-Semitism spread throughout Germany and Europe.

In late 1880 and early 1881, in three articles for the *Frankfurter Zeitung*, he expressed his outrage at the "entirely repulsive" yet growing ideology in Germany. Vogt wrote of anti-Semites' "impotent jealousy," their "base greed," and the "fury of the intellectually backward at the greater intelligence of an older and deeper civilization." Vogt's ire was prompted in particular by the anti-Semitic agitation of Heinrich von Treitschke and the Protestant pastor Adolf Stoecker. He tried to enlighten Germans about the positive Jewish characteristics he had observed "everywhere in the same fashion." Jews, he wrote, were "hardworking, intelligent, frugal to the point of miserliness, mild-mannered, disinclined to violence or crime against other people and not prone to drunkenness."

In 1885, when asked by the Viennese journalist Isidor Singer about the underlying causes behind anti-Semitism, the Dutch physiologist Jacob Moleschott answered: "Everywhere Jews rank among the best doctors, the most influential writers, and the wealthiest and best-educated merchants because they have been restricted to these areas, the only ones in which they have been allowed to achieve anything, yet people wonder why there are so many excellent Jewish doctors and journalists. They resent rich Jews and reject and envy their Oriental splendor, acting as if all religion were in jeopardy whenever a clever remark by a witty Jew burns holes through a thousand ignorant words from Messers Stoecker and Treitschke." When the same question was asked of Vogt, he responded: "In my estimation, the answer to the question has nothing to do with religion, but with the instinctive hatred of the untalented for the gifted, the poor for the rich, and the sluggish for the ambitious."[1]

The agrarian engineer Eugenio Righini, who lived in the northern Italian city of Ferrara and who also worked as a journalist, concealed his own anti-Semitism behind a scientific tone and a variety of objectivistic embellishments. But the observations of Italian society he published in his 1901 book, *Antisemitismo e semitismo nell'Italia politica moderna*, supported the insights gleaned from German culture by Vogt and Moleschott. These three men—as well as a number of others, including the pathologist Rudolf Virchow, historians Theodor Mommsen and Johann Gustav Droysen, industrialist Werner Siemens, and banker Ludwig Bamberger—all identified envy and greed as the central causes of anti-Semitism. It was a point the pro-democracy journalist Ludwig Börne had made as early as 1821.[2] Righini proposed that although Jews were no more intelligent than the Christians around them, they were much better at applying their abilities. Their capacity for getting things done, their focus on goals, and their determined but flexible desire to get ahead irritated others, in particular "their economic competitors." Righini wrote, "This tension gives rise to envy, and envy is the deepest, most general, and perhaps most important reason for anti-Semitism."

A pro-democracy nationalist, Righini was at the time the chairman of the local socially integrative trade union *società operaia*. No doubt with a tinge of regret, he concluded that anti-Semitism in Italy "was definitely widespread but weakly developed and without goals."[3] Around 1900, Italy had some 34 million inhabitants, of whom a tiny minority—just 43,000—were Jews. These Jews lived well-integrated lives in cities such as Rome, Milan, Florence, Turin, Livorno, and Ferrara. They were allowed to become officers in the military and hold state positions, theoretically right up to the office of prime minister. Active anti-Semitism had little chance of thriving in Italy, wrote Dubnow in 1929.[4] Neither Italian university students and merchants nor small business people and nationalists were particularly hostile to Jews. The illiberal anti-Semitism propagated by Pope Pius IX (1792–1878) had only a faint echo in Italian society.[5]

The situation was completely different in countries where Jews represented a greater percentage of urban populations and posed serious competition to gentiles. Fear and inability to confront the challenges of modernity drove the majority populations of both Russia and Romania to nip Jewish emancipation in the bud. Around the same time, in 1880, massive economic boom-and-bust cycles helped give rise to envy, jealousy, and xenophobia throughout Europe, even in France, whose comparatively small Jewish population had enjoyed legal equality for ninety years. There, too, social movements, not governments, called for an end to "Jewish predominance" in certain career sectors. In Greece, governmental forces encouraged hatred for Jews because they wanted to "cleanse" their territories of competitors and people viewed as foreigners. That, of course, was beneficial to the national majority. Let us now examine these four exemplary situations: Russia, Romania, France, and Greece.

JEWS AND RUSSIAN MISERY

Before the First World War, Russia extended westward to the border of the German Empire, encompassing large stretches of what would later become Poland. Moldova, Finland, Estonia, Latvia, Lithuania, Belarus, and major portions of Ukraine were at the time also parts of Russia. According to an 1897 census, 125 million people lived in this gigantic nation. Of them, 5,216,000 (4.2 percent) identified with the Jewish faith—they represented half the entire world Jewish population. Almost without exception, their native language was Yiddish. Because of their linguistic distinctiveness, Russia considered Jewish people a nation unto itself within the state. In 1906, German Zionist Arthur Ruppin praised this situation as "the only case of a European state officially according Jews the character of a nation."

Originally, Jews primarily settled in the territory of the former Kingdom of Poland and Lithuania. During the nineteenth century, driven by material privation, many migrated to Novorossiya, those parts of the Ottoman Empire that had been gradually conquered by the Russian army: southern Ukraine, Crimea, and later Transnistria and Moldova (Bessarabia). The major anti-Jewish pogroms of 1881 and 1882 put an abrupt end to this semivoluntary internal migration. As was often the case, officials, police, and officers had encouraged the outbreaks of violence. It was they who turned loose *pogromshchiki*, only reining them in after several days of brutality. The initial justification for the violence in the spring of 1881 was the assassination of Tsar Alexander II, which was carried out not by a Jew but by a Christian student.

In any case, most of these Jews lived in poverty, scraping by as peddlers, artisans, factory workers, and day laborers. In 1883 and 1884, a commission chaired by the Baltic-German Count Konstantin von der Prahlen studied the living conditions of these people and reported back to Tsar Alexander II: "Almost nine-tenths of the total Jewish population are a mass of people whose existence is secured by nothing and who live day in, day out in misery under the worst conditions. All other castes and classes of the populace live in better conditions than the Jews."[6]

State-Sanctioned Pogroms and Legal Discrimination

Balta, a city in the south of the administrative region of Podolia, provides an example of Jews' pitiable lack of legal protection and opportunities for defense. Of the city's 32,000 inhabitants, 80 percent were Jews, but despite constituting most of the population, they were still subject to savage acts of terror. In mid-April 1882, a pogrom raged for three days, during which a mob destroyed more than a thousand houses and three hundred businesses, robbing, pillaging, and raping. Forty-two Jews were murdered and 121 seriously injured. Clearly, for the Christian minority to get away with such brutality, they would have needed state accomplices.

Kiev (today Kyiv, Ukraine) had also been the scene of mass rapes, murders, plunder, and arson. An eyewitness report from the aftermath in the suburb of Predmestje described what happened during the pogrom of May 1881:

"On the right side of the street, nothing more can be seen of the fifteen one-story brick houses but scattered bricks and charred wood. Mr. Bornspolski suffered the worst of it. He led me through his warehouse and home. Every door and window had been smashed, every piece of furniture chopped up, the strings had been ripped out of the piano, then bent and cut, and the stone walls bore the traces of attempts to destroy them as well. The courtyard was full of broken household items and bed feathers. The cellar was burned out after a mob of about 150 people, bolstered by 500 workers from the sugar factory across the street, had literally rolled around in alcoholic spirits. The soap and lighting factory behind were destroyed, too. Bornspolski had rented out part of his building to a Christian druggist. Police officers had sat drinking vodka with the man. B.'s losses have been estimated as at least a hundred thousand rubles."

The author of the report then visited the synagogue on Dmiyevka Street—here too, "nothing had escaped destruction." In the outlying district of Salomenka, the mob had murdered three people. As the crowd approached, the wife of a certain Mordecai Wienarski had fled to the attic with her children but in her panic had left one behind. What had the "leaders of these dehumanized" people done when they stormed the house? "They seized the child by his little legs and purposely slammed him to the ground. He died instantly. All of this happened in plain view of military officers. The poor woman told me the story with tears in her eyes. And while I stood there in the bright sunlight, the laughter and chatter of the soldiers, loitering or sitting by the windows, echoed across the street and made her story all the more terrible. I could hardly believe that in this place, in the light of day, despite a barracks full of soldiers and military men in the streets, a three-year-old child had been murdered in such barbaric fashion."[7]

Despite the hundreds of similarly shameful occurrences, Russia didn't pass any new laws to protect those who had been persecuted. Instead, it enacted legislation that further curtailed Jews' already scant rights. Interior Minister Nicolay Pavlovich Ignatyev, a Pan-Slavist to the core, was the man responsible for this. He justified the draconian new laws, which were named after him, as a means of protecting the Christian majority and thereby preventing future unrest. The "fundamental, indeed sole reason" for the pogroms, he claimed, was economic: "In the past twenty years, Jews have gradually taken over trade and commerce, acquired extensive property by purchase or lease and, relying on their internal solidarity, have tried everything to plunder the people, in particular the poorer classes." For that reason, Jews had themselves to blame for "protests that have taken on the unpleasant form of violence." After the government had pursued the ringleaders of the pogroms, it now had a duty "to immediately issue strict ordinances aimed at correcting the unjust relationship between the general populace and the Jews and to preserve the former in the face of the harmful activity of the latter."[8]

Isaak Rülf, a rabbi in the Prussian town of Memel (today Klaipėda, Lithuania), tried to provide material help and publicize the plight of his coreligionists in neighboring Russia. Rülf characterized Ignatyev as a "coarse, heartless barbarian in the costume of a diplomat," a man permeated "with envy and rage, like many of his comrades, at the skill, grace and superiority of Jews." Born of feelings of inferiority, Rülf wrote, the anti-Jewish laws and nationalism Ignatyev encouraged in Russia were two sides of the same coin. Suddenly catchphrases about the "decayed and rotten West" were becoming increasingly popular, while the "rugged, authentic Slavic people" were celebrated as a group who were destined for "world domination" and who were now justly demanding "Russia for Russians" after many years of foreign exploitation. Courting the favor of the masses, Ignatyev demanded that regional and district officials answer leading questions such as: "To what extent has the economic activity of the Jews had a harmful effect on the living conditions of the original population?" The governor general of Kiev, the man responsible for the May 1881 violence, promoted Jewish emigration as the sole way of protecting the Christian populace from the "harmful consequences of the economic activity of Jews, their tribal separateness and their religious fanaticism."[9]

Although rulers and ruled may have been at odds in autocratic Russia, anti-Semitism could be used to weld "the logic of the state and the impulses of the people into a powerful unity." Such was the conclusion of the Austrian Zionist Berthold Baruch Feiwel, when he analyzed the consequences of the anti-Semitic symbiosis between people and state. Feiwel wrote: "Almost organically a common view of Jews established itself in the entire populace. It was drenched in both brutality and the sort of violence that articulates itself in a thousand small details of everyday life and that has gradually become a general Russian trait encompassing all classes of the people."[10] Feiwel put his thoughts to paper in 1903, directly after the pogrom of Kishinev, which we will examine shortly.

Even before the outbreak of pogroms, Russian politicians and officials had harassed and denigrated Jews with specially formulated ordinances, laws, and arbitrary administrative measures. After the Ignatyev Laws (also known as the May Laws) of 1882, Jews were essentially prohibited from residing anywhere but special settlement districts, the so-called Pale of Settlement, that were in effect giant ghettos. They included the ten governorates of the former Kingdom of Poland and the governorates of Bessarabia, Vilnius, Vitebsk, Volhynia, Grodno, Yekaterinoslav (Dnipropetrovsk), Kiev, Kovno (Kaunas), Minsk, Mogilev (Mohilev), Podolia, Poltava, Tauris (Crimea plus its hinterlands), Cherson, and Chernigov. On average, Jews made up 10 to 18 percent of the population in those places, although they numbered up to 30 percent in certain individual districts like Białystok. The Russian government had issued residence edicts as early as 1804 to keep "ur-Russia" free of Jews.

Of the 5.2 million Jews in the Romanov Empire, around 200,000 enjoyed the privilege of living wherever they wanted. In some cases, this right was either expanded or restricted according to local needs. That tended to benefit Jews with certain careers and levels of income: master tradesmen, graduates of Russian universities with higher degrees, physicians, and merchants of the highest order. But before merchants could choose their own places of business or residence, they were subject to five years of personal tax at high rates ranging from 500 to 15,000 rubles annually and then ten years of direct tax running from 5,000 to 15,000 rubles paid directly to the state treasury office. Even after those fifteen years had elapsed, this privileged class was still required to pay a special annual levy of 500 rubles. In other words, Jews had to purchase their freedom of movement every year by paying a special tax—although because of the horrendous sums required, few could afford this means of escaping the difficult living conditions in the districts where Jews were forced to live.[11]

The new laws also prohibited Jews from moving out of cities to the countryside even within the settlement districts, even though conversely they could be expelled from the country to urban areas. There were few cities in Russia, and few Christian Russians resided in them. As a result, Jews made up the majority in the urban centers of nine governorates: Minsk (59.1 percent), Grodno (58.3), Siedlce (53.7), Kiev (53.5), Vitebsk (52.7), Mogilev (52.5), Kielce (51.3), Volhynia (51), and Radom (50.6). With the exception of Crimea (where the number was less than 25 percent), their proportion of urban inhabitants in the rest of the governorships ranged from 25 to 50 percent. On average, 38.5 percent of the urban inhabitants of the settlement regions were Jewish. Their density was highest in Berdichev, with 78 percent. Overall, 94 percent of Russian Jews lived in cities, compared with only 7.4 percent of all Russian Christians.

The Ignatyev Laws and subsequent ordinances banned Jews from purchasing or leasing plots of land, required them to close their businesses on Sunday, and imposed special taxes on kosher meat, rental income, and inheritances. On January 28, 1884, Russia's Council of Ministers shut down the Jewish trade school in Žitomir on the grounds that "in the cities and areas of the southwestern Pale, Jews already represent the majority of artisans and are hemming in the development of artisanship among the basic population." A Jewish trade school was thus, in the absence of a comparable Christian one, an undesirable weapon Jews could use to "exploit the base population." To undermine the position of Jewish merchants the state exempted gentile cooperatives from taxes. Armed with this advantage, the cooperatives tried to attract customers with the slogan, "Don't buy from Jews!"[12]

A government order of March 28, 1891, compelled Jewish tradesmen, mechanics, and other skilled laborers to leave Moscow. Including their family members, this measure affected ten thousand Muscovites who had previously been allowed to reside in the city because of the head of the family's special skills. They were now to be replaced by gentile tradesmen and mechanics. To increase opportunities for gentiles, Kiev had already expelled Jewish plasterers, masons, stonecutters, carpenters, stucco workers, carters, gardeners, servants, unskilled laborers, and butchers, together with their families, in 1885. An edict of June 11, 1892, prohibited Jews from directly electing representatives to the local council, as gentiles did. Within the Pale, administrators determined which Jews would be admitted to communal parliaments, and their numbers were never allowed to exceed 10 percent. In 1893, the Russian state made it a criminal offense for Jews to use Christian names.

These special laws, together with the pogroms either tolerated or directly unleashed by the state, achieved their desired effects. Masses of Russian Jews began emigrating. Some 880,000 of them left for the US between 1880 and 1904. All told, some 1,150,000 Jews fled Russia within the space of fifteen years, with conspicuous peaks coming after the pogroms of 1890–91 and 1903–05. But as common as emigration was, it was not enough to counteract the growth in Russia's Jewish population—there were around 85,000 more Jewish births than deaths in the country annually.[13]

The average émigré to the US came from a poor artisan family, arrived there with only $8.70 to his name, and resettled his whole family. That made Russian Jews the poorest of all the immigrant groups, although they could count on the assistance of relatives who had already settled in the US. In the words of one historian, unlike other migrants, they were most likely to receive a "welcome reception." The density of social relations among the East European Jews subsidized both passage and settlement. The result was a system of serial migrations of extended families that allowed even the poorest of the poor to pack up their scant belongings and flee their homeland, where they had few to no rights.[14]

1903: The Kishinev Pogrom

Around 1900, 120,000 people lived in Kishinev (today Chișinău, Moldova), part of the Black Sea region called Bessarabia. Their numbers included some 30,000 Russians, 20,000 Romanian-speaking Moldovans, and 50,000–60,000 Jews. Kishinev was known as "the wealthy center of one of the most blessed Russian swaths of land." Farmers benefited from the fertile soil, and Jews, too, suffered far less privation than elsewhere, although they were not permitted to own property or participate in banking and finance. They did, however, control trade and artisanship, since Moldovans "were neither talented nor hardworking enough" to market the products of their labor. For that, they needed Jews who were long tolerated by the "sluggish and epicurean" majority—that, at least, was the impression of the authors of a report drawn up in 1910 by a commission of the Zionist Relief Fund in London and titled "Anti-Jewish Pogroms in Russia." The report went on to note that Christians in affluent Kishinev had not taken part in pogroms like those that flared up throughout southern Russia from 1881 to 1883, turning deaf ears to the common calls to "Smite the Jews!"

Although Kishinev prospered in the twenty years prior to 1903, and although there was neither an economic depression nor a failed harvest, on April 5 of that year, which marked both the final day of

Passover and Easter Sunday, all hell broke loose. The primary document of the carnage for this and other subsequent pogroms was the 1910 report, which encompassed more than eight hundred pages and was published, with some delay, not in English but in German, the language most commonly spoken by the intended audience.[15]

Around noon on that spring day, several youths began attacking Jews. Police dispersed but did not arrest the attackers. That afternoon a crowd of men suddenly appeared at the city's Novy-basar market. They were all wearing red shirts, fashionable holiday wear for Russian workers at the time, and shouted without interruption "Death to the Jews! Strike down the Jews!" They divided themselves up into twenty-four groups of ten to fifteen men and went on rampages throughout various city districts.

"They began hurling stones at houses in such numbers and with such force that they not only smashed windowpanes but shutters," the report read. "Then they tore the doors and windows from their hinges, entered Jewish houses and apartments, and smashed and destroyed all the furniture and household effects. Jews were forced to turn over all their jewelry, money and everything they had of value to the thieves. Even the slightest act of resistance led to them being bashed over the head with broken pieces of furniture. The looting was particularly heavy in the warehouses. Goods were either stolen or tossed out into the street and destroyed. A large crowd of Christians—members of the 'intelligentsia,' state officials, seminarians and others—trailed in the marauders' wake. Ladies from the 'best society' accepted clothing, donning silk coats and wrapping themselves in fine material where they stood. The looters themselves did much the same. They got drunk on spirits, put on the jewelry they had taken and dressed up in stolen clothing. On Gostinnaya Street, a shoe warehouse was plundered. The marauders threw away their old shoes and pulled on new ones. The police officers in attendance joined in. All polished boots were handed over to the police."

In their frenzy, "with a kind of lust," the plunderers and marauders hacked everything they didn't steal into tiny pieces, throwing tables out the windows and ripping apart pillows, together with cushions they had cut open, so that the feathers "swirled like snow." While several hundred people actively took part in the pogrom, the rest of the city inhabitants attended a Sunday concert or strolled around, saying to one another, "At least we can enjoy a nice walk without having to breathe in that Jewish smell." While the attackers raged through the side streets, "the elegant world rode past in carriages enjoying the spectacle of such uncontrolled destruction." The report added: "Christians were standing calmly in the doorways of their houses. Smiling, they watched the *pogromshchiki* go to work and helped out wherever they were needed." An engineer named Baginsky, for instance, showed the furious and soon bloodthirsty mob "which were the Jewish and which the Christian warehouses." At 5 p.m., the first person was murdered. "The plunderers descended upon a tram where a Jew was present and yelled to the other passengers 'Throw the Jew out to us!' The man was pushed out, and such terrible blows rained on his head from all sides that his skull broke open and his brains seeped out."

Policemen out on patrol were indifferent to this spectacle. Later, the police chief rode through the streets, where he was surrounded by plunderers wanting to know whether they were allowed to kill Jews. The police chief said nothing. "His silence was the decisive factor," the report concluded. "Those who had organized and led the orgy of violence had restrained themselves a bit. Now they and the other Christians recognized that they had nothing to fear from the police and that Jews were completely at their mercy." The following day, high schoolers, theology students, and government officials marked Jewish homes with white chalk. Workers and bourgeois joined those who had wreaked such mayhem the day before. "Messengers were sent to nearby villages inviting the farmers to come to the city and help plunder Jewish homes and businesses. They were told to bring large sacks."

In the end, forty-nine Jews were murdered in Kishinev. People from all segments of society—"soldiers and police, officials and priests, children and women, farmers, workers and vagabonds"—participated in this mass crime. Groups of plunderers, brawlers, and murderers quickly expanded from ten or twenty to eighty to one hundred people. "The murderers raped women, one after another, in front of their husbands and children," the Zionist Relief Fund report explained. The most disturbing passages described in gruesome detail how individuals, all of them named, were humiliated, abused, tortured, and killed out in the open for all to see.

The mob stormed synagogues with "especial rage." In one, the intruders murdered the beadle as he tried to protect the Holy Scriptures. The Torah was torn from its ark and the parchment ripped to shreds, which were then given to Christian children who immediately "sold them for a few kopeks as a 'souvenir of Kishinev.'" The report adds: "Many people betrayed Jewish tenants who had lived in their houses for ten years or more to the marauding bands. It happened that Christians called out to Jews, promising protection, sometimes in return for money, only to beat them and join in the looting and destruction, when the raging mob arrived. People who had been employed by Jewish businesses for years themselves encouraged the bands of attackers to attack Jews."

Fresh troops arrived and declared martial law, whereupon the situation calmed down. But within the space of a few hours all legal, moral, religious, and civic norms had been shattered, and in a savage frenzy, tens of thousands of people had "suffocated every human feeling" and "blurred all lines of gender, education, age, caste and class distinction." Seemingly out of nowhere, envy, greed, and brutality had exploded in Kishinev on April 5, 1903. It was an "abrupt, terrible catastrophe during an era in which pogroms were considered things of the past." Even worse, this pogrom was "the first in a long chain of misfortunes . . . that would befall Russian Jews" in the two years that followed. Kishinev itself experienced more days and nights of looting, destruction, and murder starting in October 18, 1905. Twenty-nine Jews were murdered, although the international public took little notion of this further mayhem. During the revolutionary turmoil of 1905, 656 pogroms took place in Russia, with some locations seeing multiple outbreaks of violence.[16]

In 1906 Wilhelm Münz, the rabbi of the town of Gleiwitz in Silesia, struggled to find words to describe how Jews had been butchered. In an open letter to world leaders, he wrote that people were dying "because they're Jews" and that the "guardians of the law"—government officials, police, and soldiers—had become "murderers of the law." As a result, "the horrible work of systematically prepared human butchery has been able to spread with unfettered wildness throughout the country."[17] Contemporaneous literature shows how accurate he was. Six years before the first Kishinev pogrom, the archreactionary, government-supported newspaper *Besarabez* was founded. It was the only regional newspaper in the area and was heavily influenced by Russified Moldavan finance official Pavel Krushevan. The highest ranking censor in the district, Vice Governor Ustrugov, authorized the paper and himself wrote articles hostile to Jews under a pseudonym. In 1903, in St. Petersburg, Krushevan was one of the people responsible for the notorious anti-Semitic pamphlet, "The Protocols of the Elders of Zion."

In the autumn of 1905, on the margins of the public agitation of Lenin and Trotsky, occurred the bloodiest pogrom by far. Christian inhabitants of Odessa had already launched pogroms in 1821, 1859, 1871, 1881, and 1900. The city had rapidly expanded during the nineteenth century, and new inhabitants poured in, bringing with them problems that prompted crises. From 1850 onward, Jewish merchants succeeded in gradually taking over the export of grain, a significant trading sector in the port city. Some Jews also became prominent bankers and stockbrokers. Greek merchants who made their homes there felt they were being pushed to the side and launched the pogrom of 1871 because they were "losing the competition over trade monopolies."[18]

The majority of Odessa businesses and factories may have remained in Christian hands, and most Jews may have been poor, but Odessa's Russian inhabitants became convinced that they were being exploited by Jews nonetheless. Day laborers, the jobless, and port workers, who were particularly susceptible to economic ups and downs, accused Jews of pushing down wages. "Several years ago, there was one Jew for every hundred Russian coachmen," one carriage driver lamented. "But ever since the rich Jews have given the poor ones money [to buy or rent a horse and wagon], there are more Jewish carriage drivers than you can count." Odessa's Jewish population did, in fact, increase by a factor of ten, from 14,000 to 140,000, between 1860 and 1900. As a proportion of the general population, Jews went from 14 to 35 percent in that period.

The 1905 pogrom was preceded by revolutionary unrest among workers. In June of that year, protesters at the port set fire to wooden shacks, soldiers fired into the crowd, and by the following morning 2,000 people had been killed. On October 18, large numbers of demonstrators once again convened. Initially, they chanted "Down with the autocracy," "Long live freedom," and "Down with the police," but soon many protesters, mindful of the catastrophe during the summer, gravitated toward groups who were agitating for a proud, nationalistically defined Russian fatherland and who carried pictures of the tsar and not the red flags of socialist revolution. The character of the marches completely shifted, and dissatisfied day laborers, port, factory, and construction workers, small shop owners, salesmen, low-level employees, rubberneckers, and passersby joined in. Ethnically, the marchers were Russians, Ukrainians, and Greeks. Together they sang religious and nationalist songs. Vodka flowed. Once an initial shot was fired somewhere, the October pogrom in Odessa—the most virulent in what turned out to be fateful months for Russian Jews—began to run its course. The attackers were largely working class and had fought against the tsar's rule as recently as the previous June. According to police statistics, some 400 people, 300 of them Jews, were killed between October 19 and 21. Other serious estimates put the number of victims at double that.[19] Thousands of people were wounded or had everything they owned taken from them. At least 1,600 houses, apartments, and businesses were destroyed.

The violence was sparked by profound social inequalities and the general agitation created by the ebb and flow of the June protests. State tolerance of violence against Jews legitimized proletarian hatred for

Jewish grain exporters, who served as scapegoats for the economic crisis, working-class misery, and the dearth of decently paid work. Although port workers and day laborers had vented their anger and challenged state authorities in June by destroying harbor buildings, "in October the same workers directed their ire against Jews." The economic situation had not changed, but the political one was now different. Forces wanting to preserve state authority had regrouped and won a significant portion of the impoverished Christian working class back over to the nationalist cause.

A few months later, the chief executive of the Relief Association for German Jews, Paul Nathan, offered his summary of the acts of terror sponsored by the Russian state but carried out by ordinary people. Nathan's statistics were consistently conservative, but he still recorded anti-Jewish "butcherings," as he called them, in no fewer than 639 places in the eighteen months after the Kishinev pogrom. Nine hundred sixty-five people were killed (300 alone in Odessa), and 38,225 families "affected by these terrible events." In total, 162,700 people had been "plundered, wounded, abused and butchered in their home countries by their own fellow citizens," and it had happened with "the friendly assistance and even direct assistance of government bodies."

Jews' "long period of suffering" didn't end with this wave of violence, Nathan wrote in 1913. On the contrary, it was the start of "a new era of discrimination." Russian Jews remained unable to freely choose a trade, buy property, live wherever they wanted, or send their children to secondary schools and universities as a matter of course. They enjoyed no legal rights. At the mercy of all, they were repeatedly subjected to arbitrary acts of violence.

When Russian prime minister Pyotr Stolypin took office in 1906, it briefly seemed possible that the restrictions on Jews might be relaxed. But any such hopes were quickly dashed. By December 1906, after Nathan had met with Stolypin on numerous occasions, he wrote that all their discussions had come to nothing. Stolypin, Nathan reported, had spoken "in the most critical terms" about the entirely wrongheaded laws concerning Jews. But when asked why he didn't act on those beliefs, he had answered: "Because we cannot!"[20] At the same time that "the boldest speeches for liberty" were being held in the duma, a resigned Nathan wrote in the association's annual report, "organs of the government in the provinces continue doing whatever they want in concert with the Russian people and other criminal organizations of Russian bureaucracy."

Russia's leadership refused to consider Jewish emancipation because they feared provoking popular resistance and endangering public order. On January 23, 1907, when Tsar Nicholas II received a delegation from the "Real Russians Association," the leader of that group said: "I beseech you, oh mighty emperor, not to grant the Jews any rights. Otherwise they will rule over us." Every inch the monarch, Nicholas responded: "I will take that into consideration." Indeed, nothing was done to ease the situation of the Jews. Following the Russian example, a group of "Real Romanians"—"many of them descendants of a curious mix of races," as Nathan sarcastically noted—soon formed. In 1909, they set about terrorizing Jews in Turnu Severin, Fălticeni, and Bucharest.[21]

On August 19, 1907, Nathan once again sought out Stolypin but without getting any positive response. Ten days later, the Real Russians published their platform, according to which, as was the case in Romania, Jews were to be considered foreigners.[22] In April 1910, a delegation from the Russian Rabbis Conference secured an appointment with Stolypin. The latter kept the clergymen "waiting for a long time, listened to their petitions impatiently," and rebuffed them. "The improvement in the situation of Russian Jews is a matter for the distant future," he said, explaining that "the Jewish question touches upon general political and civic questions."[23]

WHAT HISTORICAL CIRCUMSTANCES bolstered anti-Jewish hostility in traditional Russia? In his book *Easter in Kishinev: Anatomy of a Pogrom*, Edward H. Judge writes of "the perceived ignorance and vulnerability of the Russian lower classes," whose reactions and sensitivities the tsars had no option but to take into account. Exacerbating the situation were the destabilizing effects of industrial modernity, which happened comparatively slowly in Russia but which was perceived as very rapid, as no less a writer than Anton Chekhov depicted in *The Cherry Orchard*. Other contributing factors were the end of serfdom (more threatening than empowering when serfs lacked money, land, or education), the abrupt growth in the population, and the hunger and increasing readiness to revolt among the rural poor. In *The Jewish Century*, American historian Yuri Slezkine proposed a distinction between western and eastern anti-Semitism: "Fin de siècle Hungary and Germany (and later most of Russia's western neighbors) contributed to the growth of political anti-Semitism by combining vigorous ethnic nationalism with a cautiously liberal stance toward Jewish social and economic mobility; late imperial Russia achieved a comparable result by combining a cautious ethnic nationalism with a vigorous policy of multiplying Jewish disabilities."[24]

A further aggravation was the location of the Pale where Jews were permitted to settle. Sited on the disputed margins of the tsarist empire, which had only been conquered in the late-eighteenth and early-nineteenth centuries, the territory was still the subject of fierce nationalist acrimony. The Pale included Latvia, Belarus, the Kingdom of Poland-Lithuania, which extended well into Ukraine, formerly Ottoman Transnistria, Crimea, and heavily Romanian Moldava. In the latter part of the nineteenth century, separatist movements would flourish in all these places. Increasing the potential for conflict, the western parts of the Russian Empire were industrialized far more quickly than the central and eastern ones. Nationalist striving for independence and pressures caused by unequal industrial progress often discharged themselves in hostility toward Jews.

AT THE CENTER of all the conflict was education. On December 5, 1886, Russia restricted the number of Jews allowed to study at the country's eight universities, setting different quotas for various institutions. The proportion of Jews in Moscow and St. Petersburg was capped at 3 percent; in Kharkov, Dorpat (Tartu), and Tomsk 5 percent; and in Warsaw, Kiev, and Odessa 10 percent. This drastically limited Jews' opportunities to educate themselves and improve their lot in life. Before the implementation of the new regulation, Jews had represented 11.7 percent of students in St. Petersburg, 10.1 percent in Moscow, 28.4 percent in Kharkov, 14.8 percent in Dorpat, 15.5 percent in Kiev, and 29.8 percent in Odessa.[25] If able to, young Jewish men hungry for knowledge went to Western Europe. One of them was the later president of Israel Chaim Weizmann, who studied chemistry in Darmstadt and Berlin.[26]

Even leftist constitutionalists in the duma followed the logic behind the discriminatory quotas. If Jews were allowed to develop without constraint, the reasoning ran, it would spell the end of the Russian people, who were deemed too immature "to resist the attacks of such a superior segment of the population."[27]

In July 1887, the restrictions on Jews studying at university were followed by corresponding ones for university-track middle schools that, together with academies, were the gateway to a higher education. Those limits were intended to ensure a "normal numerical relation of Jewish school pupils to pupils of the Christian confession" and set a cap of 10 percent on Jewish pupils in the cities of the Pale. Here we should recall that Jews often made up 38 percent and sometimes as much as 50 percent or more of the population of such cities.

Between 1870 and 1881, the proportion of Jews in middle schools in Odessa had risen from 19.2 to 35.2 percent and in Vilnius from 10.4 to 26.7 percent. Politicians violently throttled back young Jews' chances for education, among other things, because they sensed how well such edicts were received by "the Russian population at large" and how much the nationalist, imperial policies of Alexander III were greeted by "warm sympathies and moral support."[28] On educational policy as well, Russian state anti-Semitism proved an excellent means of provisionally plastering over the cracks in the social order.

No sooner had the education minister denied the majority of Jews access to middle schools than he turned his attention to the public specialized trade schools and academies. Again the justification was neither religious nor racial. The crucial element was the superior zeal for learning among all Jewish students, which to some extent originated in Jews' pariah status and was anchored in their bright minds and intellectual training. "The Jew always strives with all his might to be one of the best students in class and never to fail an exam," wrote the liberal former Russia Postal and Telegraph Minister Count Ivan Tolstoy in 1907. "This measure entails nothing other than seeing the overly strong drive of Jews for education as an anomaly." Having "encouraged Jews to attend educational institutions for twenty years," in 1886 the government was shocked "at the glorious results they had achieved." Tolstoy wrote, "Usually he doesn't have to repeat grades and finishes his studies in the regular time." By contrast, Christian pupils much more frequently had to repeat classes or were expelled for poor marks. For Tolstoy, that was the explanation why despite strict quotas, Jews ultimately made up "a conspicuously large number" of the students who received university-qualifying degrees.

That ran contrary to the intended result, so the educational administration of the Kharkov governorate carried out a representative study of the situation. The governor had reported "a significant rush of people of Jewish origins" spreading "materialistic views" and exercising "a by no means salutary influence" on the youth of Russia. The Education Ministry then formed a committee to investigate "the overcrowding of educational institutions by Jews." It recommended extending quotas to all places of learning that led to further education. Beginning in 1890, voluntarily or after state pressure, private educational institutions began to do precisely this. In 1901, the responsible minister reduced the quota from 10 to 7 percent in the Pale. The reduction wasn't enshrined in law. It was instituted administratively.[29] In 1911, the Russian Council of Ministers came up with another trick to lower the numbers of Jews in the higher ranks of schools. Quotas were no longer calculated on the basis of the number of young people enrolled in public high schools or middle schools, but also included children who studied at home or in private schools and went on to take university-qualifying exams. This additional hurdle led to the "near complete exclusion of knowledge-hungry Jewish young men from access to the necessary school qualifications."

Even those few who did obtain such qualifications were often barred from attending university. In 1912, some 3,000 Jews applied for university places in Russia, but only 350 matriculated. In 1913, there were an equal number of Jewish applications, with a mere 164 matriculations, and not a single one at the universities of Warsaw and St. Petersburg. The official reason was that the quota had been exceeded in previous years, and balance had to be restored.

Similar restrictions were put on professional schools. In 1882, even before the quota edicts of 1886 and 1887, the Russian War Ministry capped the proportion of Jewish military doctors at 5 percent and instituted a moratorium on hiring Jewish physicians throughout the Pale. The ministry also reduced the proportion of Jewish students at the military medical academy first to 5 and then to zero percent. An edict of March 3, 1882, barred Jews from auditing university lectures outside the Pale and on May 22 barred Jewish private tutors with higher degrees from working as private tutors there. The only universities inside the Pale were those of Warsaw, Kiev, and Odessa.

On June 7, 1885, the tsar ordered that the number of Jews at the Kharkov Technological Institute be reduced to 10 percent. In the fall of 1885, the Russian government denied almost all Jewish applicants admission to the Royal Music Conservatory, the courses of the renowned Fröbel Foundation for Pedagogy, and Russia's dentistry schools, which were all located outside the Pale. Moreover, as of 1889, Jews were no longer allowed to conduct military orchestras and were only permitted to make up at most 30 percent of the musicians. On January 27, 1887, a few weeks after the law restricting Jewish access to institutes of higher learning, the government had decreed that "Jews who studied in such institutions outside Russia do not belong to the privileged class of degree-holders free to live throughout the Empire, and thus they are not permitted to settle outside the Pale." On August 22, 1888, the theater academies of St. Petersburg and Moscow were completely forbidden to admit Jews. On February 13, 1889, the same prohibition was applied to the Dombrova Mining Academy. On October 6, 1893, the Russian medical administration imposed quotas of between 3 and 5 percent on Jewish apprentice apothecaries.

A law of November 8, 1889, required Jews to obtain express permission from the Ministry of Justice to open legal practices. In the following fifteen years, every single application was rejected, and only an isolated few licenses were granted thereafter. One of the men behind the law was the chairman of the St. Petersburg Lawyers Association, Vladimir Spasovich, otherwise a political liberal. But faced with the fact that half the young lawyers in St. Petersburg court district were Jews, he concluded against his usual political convictions: "We are dealing with a colossal problem, one which cannot be solved according to the rules of cliché liberalism."[30] Following the same logic, the Russian interior minister ordered on December 23, 1894, that Jewish veterinarians would no longer be eligible for the civil service. In the meantime, the number of Jewish brokers had been capped at a third on Russia's various stock markets. In 1890, a law was passed restricting Jewish participation in certain types of incorporated companies. That same year, a number of regional governors declared hundreds of market towns to be villages, in which Jews were forbidden to reside.[31]

The measures designed to protect the Christian majority slowed Jews' education-fueled upward social mobility somewhat. Nonetheless, talented Jews constantly sought to find alternative paths to circumvent the increasingly severe restrictions. In his memoirs, Simon Dubnow wrote of traveling to St. Petersburg to study in the summer of 1880 "with a forged certificate of artisan training that was intended to help me gain 'residence permission' in a capital, which was closed off to Jews." He succeeded in this aim with the help of the "unwritten Russian constitution"—bribes handed out to the relevant police officials. Large numbers of Jews paid off authorities in order to further themselves. In 1906, the sociologist and Zionist Arthur Ruppin would conclude that, despite all the barriers, none of the nationalities living within Russia in the past decades had made "anything like the progress concerning the acquisition of higher learning which Jews had."[32]

As early as 1882, during a trip through Russia, the rabbi of Memel, Isaak Rülf, observed that "the Jewish doctor or apothecary is infinitely harder working and more diligent than the Russian one." On his train journey from Vilnius to Minsk, he struck up a conversation with a salesman about the pogroms that had taken place the previous year. Rülf asked what had caused them. "The entire misfortune of the Russian Jew," he was told, "resides in the fact that he is infinitely superior, cleverer, more useful, more ambitious and more ethical than the Russian." That was why the charge was repeatedly leveled that "Jews were trying to push Christians aside everywhere and steal the bread from their mouths." As a result, the "so-called educated, higher classes" were susceptible to particularly virulent hatred of Jews. This deadly enmity was sparked by "the subjects of envy."[33]

The Polish-born social historian Arcadius Kahan, later on the faculty of the University of Chicago, wrote of the late tsarist period: "There was hardly an area of entrepreneurial activity from which Jewish entrepreneurs were successfully excluded. Apart from the manufacturing industries in the Pale of settlement, one could have encountered them at the oil wells of Baku, in the gold mines of Siberia, on the fisheries of the Volga and Amur, in the shipping lanes on the Dniepr, in the forests of Briansk . . . on railroad construction sites anywhere in European or Asian Russia, on cotton plantations of Central Asia, etc." Jews had also founded the leading Russian banks, even though the wielders of political power had always sought to keep them out of such positions. In 1911, Stolypin tried to drive Jews out of the bread trade. In 1913–14, laws came into force that denied Jews the right to sell or manage property and serve on the boards of incorporated companies. Ultimately, such measures too were only partially successful. In 1914, the government determined to its shock that in Russia's northwestern territories, only 8 percent of the employees of banks and incorporated companies were Russians, compared with 35 percent Jews, 26 percent Germans, and 19 percent Poles.[34]

Protectionism gave birth to further protectionism. One detail in particular speaks volumes about the effects of attempts to protect the majority. At first glance, it seems merely grotesque, but upon closer inspection it shows how central a motivator the Christian majority's shamefully concealed incompetence was. Because only small numbers of Jews were allowed to continue their educations at higher levels, the best and brightest of them grabbed the few places available. But the meritocratic principles used as educational selection criteria only highlighted the inferiority of those Jews' Christian schoolmates. To reduce what was perceived as a shameful gap in ability, in 1913 Russian authorities decreed that henceforth Jewish pupils would no longer be granted places at higher educational institutions on the basis of their grades but by lottery.[35]

Ultimately, the ever more variable and bureaucratically inflexible obstacles that were put in the way of Jews' desire to better themselves only achieved one thing. Instead of increasing Russian national pride and enlisting it as an integrative force to benefit the tsar's rule, they stoked hatred—all the more so when those supposed to be excluded managed to overcome such barriers. Despite being kept down in all these ways, Jews coped more ably with the new era than the majority of Russians. A thin but highly successful caste of Jewish merchants and bankers, entrepreneurs, engineers, and doctors shook up the country and earned good money in the process. They were granted privileges whenever it was in the government's interest—yet another source of hatred in the mainstream against Russia's Jewish minority, who were accused of exploiting simple, patriotic Christians.

PROTECTION FOR CHRISTIAN ROMANIANS

Notwithstanding the many myths of the Romanian people's long and glorious past, Romania only came into existence in 1859, when a group of aristocrats merged the principalities of Wallachia and Moldova. They soon made Bucharest the capital, established two chambers of parliament elected by census suffrage, confiscated church lands, and created a governmental administration based at least superficially on the French model.

Five years later, the new Romania abolished the last vestiges of serfdom. Yet because the power of the large landowners continued unbroken, the nominally liberated peasantry remained mired in poverty. As was also true in Russia, former serfs in Romania were largely unable to cope with their new freedom, deprived of resources and without entrepreneurial ability.[36]

According to the 1899 census, Romania had almost six million inhabitants, of whom 4.5 percent, or 266,000, were Jewish. Romanian Jews mostly worked as small-time merchants or independent tradespeople, for instance as bakers, carpenters, roofers, saddlers, clockmakers, tailors, tinsmiths, or masons. A minority of them were involved in the extremely tepid industrialization of the country. Around 1900, Jews owned around half of all glassmaking businesses and a third of the furniture and textile factories. In 1864, a year of massive reforms, Romania had introduced compulsory education and called upon Jewish communities no longer to teach their children at home but to send them to public schools. Inspired by the ideal of assimilation, the Romanian government hoped "to bring Jewish and Romanian young people in closer contact," since otherwise "the division of the nation" would persist. Jewish parents did as they were asked, but the state administration, which was poorly run, had difficulty convincing illiterate Romanians of the value of formal education. For that reason by 1880, Jewish pupils made up 11 percent of the total school population. In the cities that figure was often 30, 40, 50, or even 75 percent.

Success was quick to come. As one historian writes, Jewish children "entirely adopted the language and customs of the Romanian people," and before long assimilated Jews accounted for "a significant number of the doctors, engineers, authors and mathematicians" as well as the lawyers, financial administrators, and railway and telegraph project managers. The census documented how different Jewish parents, children, and young people were in their drive to educate themselves. That year, thirty-five years after compulsory education had been introduced, 82.7 percent of Romanians still classified themselves as illiterate.

Yet while Jewish assimilation seemed to be progressing nicely, Jews' legal situation remained precarious. They were still considered "foreigners" and "aliens" no matter how long their families had lived on Romanian soil. A 1864 law on military service enshrined this legal category. It said that along with Romanian citizens, "foreigners who reside in the country and do not enjoy any other nation's protection" were also subject to conscription. That was how Jews—foreigners who were not protected anywhere in the world—were officially described, and they were the only ones meant whenever there was talk about foreigners. In 1866, after lengthy debates, accompanied by serious acts of anti-Jewish violence, the Romanian parliament passed Article 7 of the country's constitution, which deemed that only Christians could gain Romanian citizenship. Meanwhile extra-parliamentary social movements were started to exert an influence on the country's lawmakers. An émigré to Lviv writing under the pseudonym S. Jericho-Polonius reported: "The first anti-Semitic outbreaks were inaugurated on the day Article 7 became law with the destruction of the grand, newly built synagogue in Bucharest. As usual, the national guard arrived too late on the scene—their mission consisted of nothing but watching over the ruins."[37]

Jewish School Pupils Become "Foreigners"

No sooner had Jewish pupils been integrated into public schools than journalists and parliamentarians began complaining that they had "assimilated too quickly and were too hungry for knowledge." In 1883, a spokesman for the Romanian Teachers' Association found that schools were "too full of Jews," so that there was no room left for Romanian children. At first, authorities attempted to redress this putative imbalance on the level of administrative policy. French observer Bernard Lazare wrote, "Contravening the law, teachers began to send Israelite pupils home under the pretext that individual schools were already full." But teachers also abused Jewish children and humiliated them in front of their peers, accusing them, for example, of tardiness because they had "helped their fathers in their usurious pursuits."

In the summer of 1887, the Romanian minister of education openly advised the principals of public schools to preferentially admit Christian pupils. Encouraged in this way, educators turned away thousands of Jewish youngsters. Six years later, these policies were written into law. Foreigners—that is, Jews—were henceforth only to be admitted to schools insofar as there was "space for them." Even when Jewish pupils were allowed to attend classes, their parents had to pay exorbitant special new school fees for foreigners—in cities those fees were double what they were in the countryside. In addition, there were foreigner-specific charges for getting documents and certificates stamped and for the administration of tests. Such discriminatory laws had the desired effect. In 1891–92 Jewish pupils represented 15.5 percent of the elementary school population, but ten years later that figure had declined to 5.5 percent—although part of this trend may have been due to better enforcement of compulsory education among Christian families.[38]

As they were making it as difficult as possible for Jewish children to attend grammar school, officials and lawmakers also tried to block the admission of Jewish young people to middle schools and university-track high schools. Discussions in parliament about the discriminatory laws concerning Jews and schools were mostly harmonious. One of the few deputies who spoke out against the legislation was the Anglo-phile, centrist economics minister Petre P. Carp, always a proponent of pragmatic compromise. On February 16, 1893, he was given the word on the floor at the Chamber of Deputies in Bucharest. The protocol reads:

> **Carp:** You complain today as you did ten years ago that we are being held down by the Jewish element. You say that our nation is under threat. I say: our nation will be under threat if you don't want to work the way the Jews do. Herein resides the solution to the Jewish question. Let's give the Romanian everything he has a claim to. Then tell him: you are beautiful, and you are great and strong, but you must know that you will lose all these advantages if you refuse to preserve them by working hard. That's what we have to tell the Romanian people. If we tell them that, if they get used to the sort of work they are not accustomed to . . . (cries of protest) . . .
>
> You say the Jews have to be gotten rid of. I understand your logic

as follows. The Romanian people are in danger. So either this particular element has to be driven out so that it doesn't pose a threat any
longer, or it will have to be killed. But since you retain this element in
the country and are unable to kill it, then the question arises: What is
in the best interests of the country? Is it better to have 200,000 igno-
ramuses, or is it better to have schools bring this foreign element more
in line with our character? You want this foreign population to be a
population of the uneducated, but then it truly does represent a danger for us. Or you want these foreigners to found their own schools.
But these will be better than ours because these persecuted people
work harder than everyone else. And then, the competition between
them and us in some other area will be terrible since the Jew will be
a foreigner with a foreign culture and not a foreigner with Romanian
culture . . . (interjections, interruptions)

Oh, I see, you want to go a step further and say: 'I'm not going to
give you permission to attend school!' Can you do this? No! Well, then,
if you don't drive them from the country or kill them or keep them in a
state of ignorance, and you're not able to prevent them from founding
their own schools, what results do you think you can achieve? You'll
achieve nothing at all! And in reality, for decades we've done nothing but institute measures and defend ourselves against them without achieving any practical results. You don't learn from experience.
You've drowned them, the Jews, in the Danube. You've done whatever
you wanted with them . . .

Calls: We object . . . you are denouncing our country . . . A Romanian
minister has no business talking like that. (noise)

Carp: With your permission, it is my duty to confront you with the
facts of the case. I've done nothing but cite the laws of this country
back at you. I have brought up the expulsion [of Jews] from rural communities. I have cited all the measures you yourselves have taken.[39]

The expulsion Carp mentions refers to the driving of Jews from
villages and smaller market towns, as had also happened in Russia. In
Romania, this took place on the authority of a general law enacted on

October 7, 1892. Parallel to the restriction concerning schools, state authorities erected barriers to Jews attending agricultural and technical academies, commercial and trade schools, and universities of all sorts. By this point, Jews could only gain admittance to institutions of higher education if "places were left open by the sons of Romanians," and the total number of Jews was capped at one-fifth. If Jews did manage to continue their studies, they were also subject to special, sometimes exorbitant fees, just as Jewish school pupils were. On principle, they were not eligible for scholarships or any forms of assistance.

On February 18, 1909, Paul Nathan complained that the Romanian state was "de jure or de facto closing off all access to public, tax-funded schools" to Jewish young people. Starting in 1893, Jews had been forced to use private money to reestablish their own schools, but before long they, too, were subject to arbitrary state repression. In 1899, the education minister prohibited Sunday instruction, and the government levied a special tax on every child "attending a private school that doesn't follow the public curriculum." By the 1900–1901 school year, only 0.8 percent of Romanian secondary-school students were of the Jewish faith.

Jews were barred from the civil service and the military and, while allowed to study law, prohibited from legal practice. For a time they were permitted to become doctors, if they could afford the horrendous special taxes slapped on Jews studying medicine. A sizable number of Romanian Jews concluded that it was better to study abroad and then return with diplomas and qualifications. But the Romanian government reacted promptly by amending the law to stipulate that only Romanians could practice medicine in Romania with a foreign diploma. As foreigners, Jews were excluded from this privilege. The law was soon also applied to engineers.

"The Last Remaining Slaves in Europe"

In other areas of economic life as well, nothing got better and a lot got worse for Jews. Between 1867 and 1875, the Romanian government had banned Jews from producing or selling tobacco and alcohol. Similar bans concerning matches and cigarette papers followed. According to a 1898 ordinance, attorneys found to be "foreigners" were to be permanently disbarred. Comparable regulations were imposed on apothecaries, doctors, veterinarians, druggists, stockbrokers, police, and members of the chambers of industry and trade. And on April 6, 1881, foreigners who endangered the "public order" or the "internal security of the state" faced being forcibly relocated within Romania or deported.

At the Congress of Berlin in 1878, in return for recognizing newly constituted Romania as a nation, the great European powers had demanded that it grant full rights to all residents of the country without regard to ethnicity or religion. But the leadership in Bucharest resolutely ignored those obligations. Until 1913, Romania naturalized only around a thousand Jewish families while the remaining 55,000 remained stateless, enjoying no official legal protection. Some 450 Jews worked as doctors, 35 as lawyers, around the same number as journalists, a handful as engineers, and two as professors. Jews were forbidden from selling wares door to door, owning more than four hectares of land, occupying official posts, trading at farmers' markets, or serving on the executive boards of trade guilds. Unlike "Romanians," as "foreigners" Jews didn't get treated for free in hospitals. Instead they were required to pay special fees for every day of medical attention.

When the electric tram in Jaşi was built, the city government brought in foreign workers because, according to the official justification, Romanians found the job too difficult and the government didn't want to hire Jewish laborers. The elected administrators of Bucharest behaved in similar fashion when they decided not to employ Jews in the construction of city streets and transport routes. In 1899, the minister responsible for railway administration had "Jewish track-layers, coachmen, carriers and workers driven from the workplaces and prohibited Jews from being hired to paint rail stations—since there were no Romanian workers in the region of western Moldova willing to do the work, laborers were brought in from Wallachia." If Jews were active politically or got involved in trade unions, they could be deported as "harmful foreigners" without further ado.

All told, such measures were intended to promote and protect a national middle class consisting of tradesmen, merchants, specialists, and university graduates who, it was hoped, would displace the Jewish competition. The fathers of these policies may have talked aggressively of "preventing the absorption of Romania by the Jews." But they hardly proceeded from an inner conviction in their own strength, as Lazare recognized: "People feared that the educated Jew would be superior to the Romanian, so he had to be humiliated to make him less dangerous." After a pogrom that raged in Bucharest in 1897, the Romanian interior minister characterized this act of terror as "a regrettable reaction against the over-elevation of the Jews." He made this statement after being questioned by the conservative deputy Alexandru Marghiloman, who wanted to know why police had done nothing to stop the violence.

As a result of the interplay of state and societal discrimination, by that juncture Jews represented only 4.2 percent of students at the country's universities. In 1910, Italian prime minister Luigi Luzzatti, who came from a Jewish family, called Romanian Jews "the last remaining slaves in Europe." In 1913, when Leon Trotsky, then still a journalist, went to view the battlefields of the Balkans, he came away with the impression that anti-Semitism had become a state religion in Romania. Trotsky wrote of the "final psychological cement that holds the thoroughly rotten feudal society together." He added: "The artisan, the shopkeeper, the restaurant owner and the doctor and journalist with them are enraged at competition from Jews. The lawyer, civil servant and officer are afraid that if the Jew has equal rights, he will snap up his customers or his position."

In 1902, Lazare concluded that, "as was the case everywhere, in Austria, Germany and France," anti-Semites in Romania gussied up their agenda with phrases taken from Christian anti-Judaism but pursued purely materialistic ends. "In reality, they do not distinguish their commercial and industrial interests from their religious prejudices and use the latter to advance the former." Lazare had nothing but bitter condemnation for Romanian socialists. In their earlier days, he wrote, they had advocated Jewish rights but then had allied themselves with the Liberals (centrist democratic nationalists), betraying their ideals or revealing their own fundamental lack of principles. "With members also engaged in the chase for jobs and wanting to enjoy their share of the state budget, the party gradually disappeared. Those who remained in the Socialist Party merged with the Liberals and became, like them, nationalists, protectionists and anti-Semites."

Enemies of Jews weren't content with getting parliaments and governments to pass anti-Semitic laws. They repeatedly engaged in destruction of property, larceny, and murder: in Bakău and Botşani in 1890; in Bucharest in 1897; in Iaşi in 1898 and 1899; in Drânceni in 1900; and then with special vigor during the peasant riots of 1907. On November 8, 1895, Christian community leaders founded the Anti-Semitic Alliance, which took the Archangel Michael as its patron and was organized as a kind of lodge. Among its first members and pioneers were influential politicians, including government cabinet member and later Prime Minister Take Ionescu (1858–1922), and political scientist Alexandru C. Cuza (1857–1947), who would go on to be minister of state.

This cross-party alliance, which defined itself as primarily "economic," was dedicated to "protecting the Romanian against the Jewish element," breaking Jewish "financial preponderance," and "paralyzing" Jewish influence in all other areas. According to its statutes, the group issued publications and held an annual congress of anti-Semites in the Romanian capital "in conjunction with all foreign anti-Semites' alliances." In article two of its constitutive document, the founders stressed the importance of driving Jews from Romania: "Because the Jewish element is incapable of assimilation, the alliance will oppose their being granted political rights. It will employ all allowable means that can help make the situation of Jews in Romania impossible and thereby encourage them to emigrate from the country."

On May 16, 1899, in Iaşi, a university city, the alliance demonstrated what this meant practically. An eyewitness report published a year later, on May 3, 1900, in Vienna's *Tagblatt* newspaper, described what happened:

A week in advance manifestos were posted calling upon the Christian populace to rise up, teach Jews a lesson and fly banners from their own homes so they could be recognized. Decorated with cockades and acting as official agents, the ringleaders went to surrounding villages, especially the suburb Ciurchi, whose inhabitants are known as larcenous rabble, and commanded the mob to turn up on May 16 in Circus Sidoli, armed with sticks, for a large-scale anti-Semitic meeting. There was no shortage of money and wine to elevate the mood of 'the people.' . . . The meeting commenced, hateful tirades were held, two ladies from the demimonde got up on stage to chant 'Down with the Jews' and 'Death to the Jews,' and then everyone marched through the city, led by a band playing gypsy music, the students carrying banners that read 'Down with the Jews' and 'Death to the Jews!' They were followed in wagons by the city prefect, the police prefect, the prosecutor, professors and high-level civil servants. After the mob had been sufficiently incited, the first stones began to rain down on Jewish houses. Gendarmes and police watched from both sides of the march, and they were stripped of their arms as soon as they gave a hint of calling for calm. A gendarme captain named Vrabie, who was naïve enough to take his job as a representative of public order seriously, had his skull split open before the eyes of the prosecutor. This was how the friends of Mr. Take Ionescu marched through the streets, demolishing and trampling everything in their path. Woe to the poor Jew who didn't succeed in fleeing to safety quickly enough. The following day, the city was a terrible sight. Rubble and ruins were everywhere as well as closed-up shops and terrified people discussing how they might save their very lives. This was the beginning of the general commercial decline.

In addition to the general mistrust of Jews, credit restrictions further darkened their economic prospects and left them with no choice but the "colossal mass emigration" the organized anti-Semites had hoped to provoke. Within a few months, by the end of May 1900, more than 10,000 Jews had left Romania, many for New York, although 2,500 went to Turkey, 2,000 to London and Paris, and several hundred each to Cyprus and other Central European countries. By 1914, a quarter of Romania's Jewish population had emigrated. The percentage of "foreigners" in the total population had declined from 4.5 to 3.3, and the Anti-Semitic Alliance celebrated its initial series of triumphs.[40]

FRANCE: DREYFUS AND THE AFTERMATH

Accused of libel, the renowned writer Emile Zola was called to answer for himself in front of a Paris court from February 7 to 21, 1898. His legal counsel was Georges Clemenceau, the later two-time French prime minister, who was then the editor in chief of the republican newspaper L'Aurore. At issue in the case was a Zola article titled "Lettre à M. Félix Faure," an open letter to the French president. It was published in L'Aurore with the headline "J'accuse . . . !" on January 13, 1898.

Filled with republican outrage, Zola had taken up the cause of a French Jew who had been convicted of treason and dishonorably discharged from the French military in 1894. Army captain Alfred Dreyfus had been imprisoned and left for dead on "Devil's Island," French Guiana. Zola demanded that Dreyfus be exonerated and the witnesses against him be convicted of forging documents and perjuring themselves. In Zola's eyes they were the real traitors to the French republic and the rule of law, having disgraced and condemned the impeccably loyal Dreyfus on trumped-up charges of betraying military secrets to France's archenemy, Germany. Zola also accused them of merging antirepublican themes with anti-Semitic ones, claiming that Catholic and royalist France had branded Dreyfus a traitor for the sole purpose of whipping up popular rage against a supposed enemy lurking within and thereby increasing support for the chauvinist and clerical reaction. Zola wrote: "It is a crime to poison the minds of the meek and the humble, to stoke the passions of reaction and intolerance, by appealing to that odious anti-Semitism that, unchecked, will destroy the freedom-loving France of the Rights of Man."[41]

No sooner had Zola published his article than French anti-Semites unleashed violent protests in fifty-five cities. They occurred in three waves over the course of several weeks, and "often the ones by students took the most extreme forms." The protesters destroyed Jewish-owned workshops and stores. Egged on by organizers, demonstrators in Paris chanted "Death to the Jews" and "Send Zola to Hell!" Graffiti reading "Never buy from Jews" and "France must belong to the French" were scrawled on walls. In French-run Algiers, there were also extended pogroms.[42]

On February 9, 1898, upon leaving the court building, Zola might have been "beaten to death like a dog, had he not been protected by a strong circle of police and had his horse not been such a good runner." On February 21, a criminal court sentenced him to a year in prison and a fine of 3,000 francs. After his sentence was upheld on appeal, Zola fled for a few months to England. It's worth remembering that while as a republican he adopted the cause of an unfairly persecuted Jew, as a pioneer of the naturalist novel he also didn't shy away from "quite unlikeable depictions" (Dubnow) of Jews in works such as *Nana* (1880) and *L'argent* (1891).

Colonel Marie-Georges Picquart, himself an officer of the French General Staff, took even greater risks than the world-famous novelist. Two years after the Dreyfus trial, Picquart, who had become the head of French military intelligence, was ordered to find further evidence to back up Dreyfus's conviction for treason. Picquart initially set about this task in the belief that Dreyfus's court martial had been completely aboveboard. After reading the secret dossiers on the case, however, he was disabused of that idea. Picquart discovered forged documents, and his investigation soon turned from Dreyfus to another officer, who was a well-known pleasure-lover and heavily in debt. The results of Picquart's investigation didn't sit well with his superiors. In the name of military fraternity, they cancelled the review of the Dreyfus case and transferred Picquart to another job.

But Picquart refused to go quietly, giving the results of his investigation to a notary for safekeeping and later writing a letter to the French prime minister offering to provide proof that the general staff had forged incriminating evidence against Dreyfus. Picquart established the foundation upon which Zola and his allies could launch their campaign and achieve a retrial of Dreyfus in 1899. Those proceedings only resulted in a pardon. It would take another seven years until Dreyfus was legally exonerated. He was then promoted to major and made a knight of the French Legion of Honor.

Picquart's superiors had transferred the troublesome officer, with his stubborn dedication to the truth, to Tunisia in 1896. They seem to have hoped Arab bandits would shoot him. Two years later, when that hadn't happened, they discharged him from the army and accused him of being the forger, sending him to prison for eleven months. Eventually, Marie-Georges Picquart was also rehabilitated. In 1906 he was promoted first to major general, then to war minister, serving in the first cabinet of Clemenceau. In 1899, writer Anatole France called Picquart a "gift" to the Third Republic.[43]

After twelve long years of internal struggles, France managed to overcome the shame of anti-Semitic intrigues within the military. Yet at the same time, in the Action Française political movement, antidemocratic, antimodern forces had found a new long-term vehicle. One of its leading thinkers, Charles Maurras, excoriated Dreyfus's rehabilitation as a "profound and general triumph of Jewish money." Maurras believed that the influence of a "chorus of Jewish ideas" went all the way back to the protagonists of the Protestant Reformation in 1517 and the French Revolution of 1789. As the Israeli historian Zeev Sternhell wrote, "Maurras made anti-Semitism into a pillar of nationalism" and of a biological notion of the French people "that grounded citizenship and national identity in history and ethnicity."[44] Two decades before Mussolini and Hitler, the Action Française developed a vision for a strict, authoritarian political order in which an ethnically defined people would feel liberated and socially secure. Confident nationalism and strong state leadership would be combined with the selling points of socialism to fight against Anglo-Saxon democratic liberalism. Protectionism would mitigate the consequences of technological progress. The slogan of the Action Française was "*Protectionisme, socialisme, nationalisme!*" The group's propaganda leaders suggested that their

enemies were backed by the "power of the Jews" and "Israelite finan-
ciers."[45] In 1906, with Dreyfus's exoneration, the republican spirit prevailed. But it was only a momentary comeback, a "triumph without a
future" that showed how fragile the democratic social order was even
in a country like France.[46]

Few Jews but More and More Anti-Semites

Out of France's total population of 40 million around 1890, there
were only about 70,000 Jews, 50,000 of whom lived in Paris. Most
were long-assimilated Sephardic immigrants. A small group of Ash-
kenazi Jews, to which Dreyfus belonged, came from the departments
of Alsace and Lorraine, which Germany had annexed in 1871. French
Jews had been granted full legal rights in 1791 and had participated in
the Industrial Revolution, the effects of which were milder in France
than in England, along with the rest of the French population. Unlike
in Germany, Jews were allowed to become civil servants, prefects,
and military officers. And almost uniquely in Europe, Jewish ministers served in the government, for example Adolphe (Isaac Moïse)
Crémieux and David Raynal in the Second and Third Republics. Thus,
the social and national conditions for a radicalization of the "Jewish
question" were lacking in France. In contrast to Germany and Austria,
Dubnow wrote, "the small handful of assimilated Jews provided far
less of a reason for silly talk about them gaining the upper hand economically and culturally."[47] So how could anti-Semitism nonetheless
take hold in France, the country of the great revolution?

   In 1892, after a few minor anti-Semitic publications had come and
gone, the newspaper La Libre Parole (The Free Word) commenced publication. Its motto was "France for the French!" and the publisher was
the popular author Édouard Drumont. In 1886 he had brought out his
major work, La France juive, which had gone on to become a long-
term best seller, attracting several hundred thousand readers in its first
year alone. As of 1892, the massive inflammatory tome had been available in a popular illustrated edition, and translations of the book
into languages such as German also sold well. By 1889, the German

translation was already in its sixth printing, and by 1945 there were more than 200 editions available worldwide.

Drumont was a Catholic monarchist who considered the French Revolution a misfortune that needed to be reversed posthaste. He characterized the 1889 Paris World's Fair, which celebrated the centenary of the Revolution, as a threatening internationalist invasion and the Eiffel Tower as a blasphemy of Babylonian proportions. "From its banal heights, it was intended to destroy the Paris of our fathers and our memories, the old buildings and churches of Notre Dame, the Arc de Triomphe, [the city's] piety, glory and honor," Drumont wrote.[48] Ever fond of dramatic images, he described how a Jewish tidal wave was rolling in from the east "from the area around Vilnius, the *vagina judeorum* so to speak." It had flooded Germany, "crossed the Vosges," and was now breaking over France.

Images of flooding were misleading. The truth was closer to a swelling stream. In the wake of the Russian and Romanian pogroms, 30,000 to 40,000 Jews had immigrated to France by the start of the First World War. Almost all of them moved to Paris. In 1914, they made up nearly half of all Jewish immigrants to the French capital. This group of Jews stood out because of their clothing, language, and customs. But as a group, they were also particularly ephemeral since many of them were only stopping off in Paris en route to the US.[49] Like Heinrich von Treitschke and Adolf Stoecker in Germany, Drumont developed his campaign at a time of economic and social upheaval and of Jewish migration from Eastern Europe. Drumont accused Jews of having no positive creative gifts and of being selfish, emotionless, lustful, avaricious, disrespectful, presumptuous, exploitative, craven, arrogant, argumentative, sly, treacherous, megalomaniacal, usurious, damaging to public morals, blasphemous, traitorous, and more. On the first pages of his book, Drumont attributed all these ugly characteristics to "the Semite"—itself a new, derogatory word. The author, who otherwise had nothing good to say about Germans or Protestants, imported the term "anti-Semitism" from Germany.

Drumont frequently ended his newspaper editorials with the slogan "Down with the exploiters and thieves!" In *La France juive*, he asked:

"Why would a Christian leader, a man of firm convictions and broad vision who considers matters not from a conventional perspective but looks at them directly—why would he not confiscate Jewish assets?" Drumont calculated the wealth of French Jews to be around five billion francs, and when he ran in a municipal election in Paris's seventh arrondissement in 1890 he promised: "With this five billion we will solve the social question—without any earthquakes and without violence."[50]

The roots of Drumont's ideas were in part traditionally leftist, and he described socialist Alphonse Toussenel, a disciple of Charles Fourier, as his "spiritual father." Toussenel had been one of the first Frenchmen to combine love for the common man and for democracy with hatred of Jews. In his 1845 book *Les Juifs, rois de l'époque*, he demonized Jews as a "nation within the nation," "speculators," "parasites," and "fraudulent wheeler-dealers." In 1941, the Nazi-friendly Vichy government honored Toussenel as a "pioneer" and a "*socialiste national antisémite*." One of his later disciples proudly claimed that "the Germans and particularly Dr. Goebbels would no doubt be amazed" to learn of "this French kindred spirit." Furthermore, a "direct line" could be drawn from "Toussenel's thought to Hitler's," even though in the 1920s the "young inmate of Landsberg prison," Hitler, was almost certainly unaware of Toussenel's ideas put forward eighty years earlier. In 1941, the author of an anti-Semitic and nationalist-socialist pamphlet would conclude: "Germany and France are so close to one another intellectually that they could join forces politically. If that were to happen, the Jew would have to leave Europe and Germans and French would be the joint lords of the continent."[51]

A number of early French socialists, including Pierre Leroux, Pierre Proudhon, Georges Duchene, and Auguste Blanqui, maintained fervent anti-Semitic attitudes. Gustave Tridon and Albert Regnard were both leaders of the Paris Commune and anti-Semites. Moreover, as historian Edmund Silberner has shown, in the years after 1871 "the most important writings with anti-Semitic tendencies came from the pens of socialists."[52]

Drumont was certainly not alone when he defamed Jews as "parasites on the economic body of the European peoples." But he was far more concerned with his home country's economy than any foreign ones. As was also true in Germany, the French government discontinued its free-trade policies in the 1880s, introducing protective tariffs first on metal and textile products and then, at the behest of various special interests, on a range of other goods. As in other countries, anti-Semitism in France was directed against Anglo-American economic liberalism. Espousing the slogan "*travail, famille, patrie*," French anti-Semites found supporters among all groups in French society. It was a short leap from class-spanning protectionism to state corporatism. This iteration of the socialist idea no longer aimed at combating capital as such but at politically restraining the market and freedom of competition. In times of crisis, the focus quickly switched to foreigners in general and Jews in particular. The resulting social order, which was considered new and just, required a strong state and, if necessary, a strong leader, who would be capable of resolving what was felt to be a painful conflict between economics and social welfare.[53]

In the same vein, article three of the statutes of the Ligue nationale antisémitique de France, which Drumont cofounded, demanded that the "moral and economic, industrial and commercial interests of our country must be defended with all means available." Drumont opposed "Jewish-modern civilization" and offered the following justification for why "the Jew" was a dangerous competitor and creator of unrest: "In an age in which people only live by their brains, he has the necessary boldness at his disposal, the boldness of mind." For reasons like this, Drumont and his followers insisted that Jews be pushed entirely out of French politics and their assets nationalized.[54]

The special-interest politics that dominated 1880s France reinforced the alliance between traditional agriculture and newly established industries. But protectionism in its various forms led to elevated domestic prices, economic stagnation, and a chronic negative balance of trade. As a result, industry, especially the textile trade, remained noncentralized and underdeveloped. To divert attention away from domestic economic problems and the fact that France was falling further and further behind, a succession of governments pursued colonial expansion. Tunisia was declared a protectorate in 1881, and Indochina and Madagascar followed in 1885 and 1890, respectively.

The extent to which protectionism, the resulting economic stagnation and anti-Semitism merged into one can be seen in the donation campaign Drumont organized in 1898 on behalf of a witness who had perjured himself testifying against Dreyfus. It raised 25,000 francs. Some 40 percent of those who donated were workers and artisans, primarily from the textile trade, while 29 percent were military men, primarily officers. Both groups felt under threat. French textile factories and manufacturers were in decline, while the French military had lost the war against Prussia in 1870 and was afraid of being stripped of influence by republicans. "The anti-Semitism Drumont represented," French historian Esther Benbassa writes, "united the divided forces of the nation, Catholics and workers, in the fight against the Republic, which was excoriated as capitalist, Jewified and of course anti-Catholic."[55]

Against the backdrop of this broad appeal, French socialists began to flirt with French anti-Semites. They considered the enemies of Jews as "useful assistants." Fearful of alienating their electoral base, they treated Drumont and his followers with kid gloves. In the words of Clemenceau, they "smiled at anti-Semitism because they believed that combatting Jewish capitalism would help them overcome capitalism as such."

Following this logic, the socialist group in the French parliament reacted to Zola's "*J'accuse!*" in a fashion not atypical of European socialists at the time. On January 13, 1898, the thirty-two deputies present unanimously called upon their followers and voters to remain neutral in the Dreyfus affair, citing two reasons. First, the reactionaries were using the conviction of a single Jew as an indictment of all Jews. But second, they argued, Jewish capitalists were exploiting Dreyfus's rehabilitation as a way of "washing Israel clean of all stains." The socialist deputies simultaneously warned against anti-Semitism while showing understanding for it: "In light of the involvement of the Jewish business world in all the scandals, certain segments of the populace, in particular from the petite bourgeoisie, think they are fighting against capital when they fight against Jewish power. These people are socialists *in spe*." That was the position of France's socialist press on January 20, 1898.[56] At the same time, Drumont reached out to socialists as incipient anti-Semites, writing: "Christian civilization nurtured labor, ennobling and honoring it in well-chosen words—Jewish civilization, led by capitalist Jews, exploits labor."[57]

By 1925, some 100,000 Eastern European Jewish immigrants had settled in France. Established French Jews were not well disposed toward them, fearing that their behavior, which was considered uncouth, would reflect badly on Jews as a whole and prompt further resentment.[58] Nonetheless, the time between Dreyfus's rehabilitation and the start of the Great Depression in 1929 was relatively calm. The First World War and France's victory over Germany temporarily drowned anti-Semitism in a wave of patriotic enthusiasm. Most Jewish immigrants from Poland, Russia, and Greece were integrated as they "rose into the middle classes." The second generation had already established itself in the free trades, the higher levels of administration, and the universities. As Benbassa wrote, "several immigrants' sons, for example André Citroën, who was born in 1878 in Russian-Poland Białystock, succeeded in spectacularly climbing the social ladder."[59]

SALONIKA: GREEKS VERSUS JEWS

Jews settled in Salonika in the first century BC. At the time, the port city was the center of the Roman province of Macedonia. Later Paul the Apostle preached in the synagogue there, trying to convince his reluctant listeners that the messiah was coming. In 1430, the Ottomans conquered the city. Fifty years later, expelled during the reign of Catholic King Ferdinand and Queen Isabella, thousands of Sephardic Jews fled there from Spain, Portugal, Sicily, and southern Italy.

These refugees brought with them their language, later called

Ladino, and modern techniques of textile production. Thanks to them, trade flourished, changing Salonika. The presence of a port and lots of surrounding land contributed to an upswing, as did the city's ethnic, linguistic, and religious diversity and its efficient division of labor between Turks, Bulgarians, Albanians, Greeks, and Jews. These groups may not have always coexisted in harmony—there were isolated outbreaks of violence and economic setbacks. But compared with the Christian persecution of Jews and the European anti-Semitism present elsewhere in nineteenth-century Europe, this four-hundred-year-long epoch can fairly be called peaceful.

In the latter half of the nineteenth century, Salonika's Jewish population had grown to more than 75,000—roughly one half of the city's residents. The port became a link between the Ottoman Orient, which was beginning to open up economically, and the West, in which capitalism was progressing by leaps and bounds. Jewish merchants and entrepreneurs, who were multilingual, internationally experienced, and privileged over Greek competitors by Ottoman authorities, flourished.[60] Jews made up the majority of the city's inhabitants, and Ladino, evolved from fifteenth-century Spanish, became a kind of lingua franca used by Greeks, Turks, Albanians, and foreigners. Jewish historian Joseph Nechama wrote: "The Turkish tram driver, the Greek waiter, the Gypsy bootblack will converse with you in the language of Cervantes when they conceive a doubt about your nationality."[61]

Jews dominated the port, the transport of goods, and the city's industrial development, trading in grain, flour and baked goods, cotton and textiles, tobacco and cigarettes, ore from the surrounding mines, construction materials, agricultural products, and farm equipment. In 1908, Greek competitors launched a failed boycott of Jewish fruit and vegetable dealers. But Jews weren't exclusively part of the economic bourgeoisie. They played a leading role in almost all segments of economic and social life. In 1913 they accounted for 300 master artisans, 40 apothecaries, 30 lawyers, 55 doctors and dentists, 10 journalists, 5 engineers, 1,105 self-employed merchants of various sizes, including bankers, 1,200 shop owners and grocers, and 2,200 unskilled workers.

Eight thousand Salonika Jews worked in sales, while the same number labored in the tobacco industry. There were 400 shipbuilders, 500
coachmen and truck drivers, 600 movers, 150 customs officials, and
some 200 waiters, servants, and street merchants. Jews ran twelve factories producing cloth and nine making textiles, four large mills (one
for jute), six industrial knitting factories, tanneries, and a cigarette-
paper factory.[62]

The Italo-Turkish War of 1911–12 imposed significant burdens
on Salonika. The city was hit by cholera and immediately thereafter
drawn into the Balkan conflict and the ensuing nationalism. Concepts
like Bulgarianization, Hellenization, and Turkification were on the rise,
and nationalist aggression challenged the city's tradition of diversity. In
early October 1912, the nascent, self-proclaimed Christian nations of
Montenegro, Bulgaria, Serbia, and Greece staged a successful uprising
against the tenuous rule of the Ottoman Empire, which was being continually attacked and worn down by the imperial powers of Europe.
Soldiers who had been whipped up into a nationalist frenzy committed
countless massacres of Muslims and Christians of other nationalities.
In 1911 and 1912 they drove out tens of thousands of people seen as
undesirable foreigners, including many Jews, who subsequently fled to
Salonika.[63]

The city of İştip (today Štip in Macedonia) is a case in point. Conquered by Serbs and Bulgarians, it had 25,000 inhabitants, 800 of
whom were Jews. Of the latter, everyone with the exception of six old
men and two younger ones fled. Two of the older men were murdered,
and all Jewish houses were looted and destroyed. Marauding Bulgarian and Serb Chetniks (self-proclaimed freedom fighters) burned down
the synagogue, twenty-four houses, and six warehouses. War correspondent Leon Trotsky reported that at noon on November 2, 1912,
"20 to 25 chetniks and highwaymen" had bashed in the skull of an
elderly Jew.

Seven hundred and ten Jews who fled İştip found refuge in Salonika, which was still under Ottoman control and thus safe. But on
November 9, 1912, Greek soldiers conquered the city, and allied Serbian and Bulgarian forces moved in as well. The Second Balkan War,

which commenced in June the following year, was begun by Bulgaria battling its former allies Greece and Serbia. The refugees in Salonika waited in pitiful conditions to return to their homes. In February 1913, after the guns from the first conflict fell silent, a delegation from the Union des Associations Israélites visited Macedonia to help Jews living there. The second war was already under way when the delegates wrote in their report that the "former Balkan allies have created a new situation" and "new and perhaps more serious afflictions" could be added to the ones Jews had already suffered. Two years later, in 1914, the German-Jewish Relief Association determined that repatriation remained impossible: "Those household goods or utensils that were spared or could be hidden in the first war were destroyed in the second war."

The Jews of Strumica, also in today's Macedonia, suffered a similar fate. There, too, Bulgarian militias went on larceny and murder sprees. On top of that, the new Christian authorities moved market day from Monday to Saturday, the Sabbath, in order to exclude Jewish competition. In a short time, the 650 Jews who had been doing "relatively well" were completely devastated and had to flee to Salonika as well.[64]

Unlike its Romanian neighbor, the Bulgarian government hadn't issued any anti-Semitic edicts or used the powers of state to stir up anti-Jewish hatred. On the contrary, it felt it had a duty to protect all peaceful citizens and "the culture that is of benefit to everyone." The number of anti-Semitic incidents was limited as a result.[65] It was only after Bulgarian wars of conquest met with little success that the desire to destroy things, see blood flow, and murder people erupted. The rampages were primarily directed against Muslims and secondarily against all "foreigners," including the small numbers of defenseless Jews who could not be expected to offer any resistance or take revenge. While the actual battles against the armed enemy might be won or lost, they were repeatedly accompanied by risk-free acts of violence against Jews by all sides in the conflicts. The ancillary terrorizing of Jews during wars and national-revolutionary fighting would recur in a number of twentieth-century multinational and civil wars.

In the course of the fighting, Greek troops seized much of what is today northern Greece. In so doing they doubled the square area of their nation, which was founded in a number of stages starting in 1830. The population rose from three to five million. Only a minority of people in the newly acquired territories spoke Greek, so plans were made from the beginning to Hellenize the region. But progress was slow. At the 1919 Paris Peace Conference, which yielded the Treaty of Sèvres, Greek prime minister Eleftherios Venizelos falsified statistics to suggest that the majority of people in these areas were Greek.[66]

For the urbane and economic core of New Greece, the issue of Hellenization had particular relevance. In 1912, Salonika's population of around 150,000 consisted of 27,000 Greeks, 33,000 Turks, 81,000 Jews, and 9,000 people of other nationalities. Two years later, Nechama still described Salonika as "a modern Babel of races, languages, faiths, customs, ideas and aspirations."[67] His description also applied to the whole of Thrace and Macedonia.

Decline as a Result of Greek Violence

In contrast to the Greek minority, Jews had good reason to want Salonika to remain under Ottoman domination during the Balkan Wars. As Maria Margaroni has argued, "neither the anti-Semitic attitudes of their Greek fellow citizens nor the financial disadvantages" gave Jews any incentive to join economically weak Greece or any hope that they "would feel at home in the new Greek 'fatherland.'"[68] With Salonika's annexation to a nation engaged in hostilities with all its neighbors, its economic heart, the port, went into steep decline. Cut off from its traditional trading partners, Salonika essentially disappeared from view. Greece's strict isolationism robbed the city of its basis for existence: open borders and the internationalism of a unique Ottoman-European, Muslim-Jewish-Christian metropolis, whose downfall was now sealed. The new borders after the First World War soon similarly deprived Trieste, Chernivtsi, Timişoara, Gdansk, and Łódź of their functions.

One reason for the passivity of Salonika's Jewish inhabitants was that they knew how violent Christian Greeks could be. During the wars for Greek independence from 1821 to 1829, Greeks had almost completely annihilated the Jewish communities of the Peloponnese, massacring both Jews and Turks and making them flee for their lives. The British consuls in Patras and Constantinople reported that thousands of Jews had been tortured or killed by Greek national fighters. A Jew who had fled to Corfu told of 5,000 Jews being butchered in Tripoli, the capital of the Peloponnese. That number may have been exaggerated, but what is certain is that after the Greek revolution, there were no Jews living there or in the other cities liberated by Greek nationalists. In 1821 Jewish residents had been "slaughtered en masse by enraged Greeks," in the words of Dubnow, and the revolutionary movement had meant nothing for Jews in Greece other than "a gruesome bloodbath." Some of those who had escaped being massacred fled to the Ottoman Empire, to Salonika, Constantinople, or Izmir, while others sought refuge on the British Ionian islands of Corfu and Zakynthos.

In the second half of the nineteenth century, as further parts of today's Greece gained their independence, Greeks committed further atrocities. A good example is Corfu, which had joined Greece in 1864. There, to cite Dubnow again, "hatred of Jews and mercantile envy coincided." Acts of terror recurred at odd intervals and forced many Jews to flee the island. On Easter in 1891, twenty Jews were killed in pogroms. Five thousand Jews lived on Corfu at the time, but by 1941 that number had shrunk to just 1,900. Pogroms also took place in Volos, Larissa, and Trikala in what is today central Greece, and hundreds of persecuted Jews fled to Salonika, while it was still under Ottoman rule, and to Izmir, Egypt, and Italy.

The regular Greek troops and paramilitaries who conquered Salonika in 1912 considered themselves liberators, but Muslims and Jews feared them and saw them as invaders. The Greek troops did everything they could to turn those fears into reality, and it was the Jewish community that suffered the most under them. Greek soldiers looted 400 Jewish businesses and more than 300 Jewish homes, raped more than 50 Jewish women, and arrested and extorted money from well-known Jews. They also murdered at least two Jewish men and massacred sixty Muslim civilians.[69] "No sooner had the victors marched in than scenes reminiscent of the Thirty Years War played out on Varda Street in the middle of the Turkish-Jewish Quarter," wrote the *Berliner Tageblatt*. "Who can tally up all the acts of violence, which were encouraged by the absence of gendarmes in the field? And there were fatalities as well—here and there you could see bodies lying on street corners. . . . What people said about this recalled the pogroms in holy Russia."[70]

Nechama described how the atmosphere had changed: "The Greeks in our region were jealous of our mercantile success and wanted to permanently displace us. They ignored the handful of Turks, whom they didn't consider serious competition, and proceeded directly to attacking Jews." Hamburg merchants received this concerned message: "The Greeks are demanding government support for their struggle against the preponderance of the Jewish element."[71] In Athens, Greeks insisted on an offensive, prohibited under Greek law, against Jewish commercial houses, which were highly regarded internationally for their reliability. The Greek burghers of Salonika immediately put these illegal measures into practice. The "general lack of personal protection," which seems to have been intentional, the absence of any guarantees under the law, and corruption among customs officials forced many Jewish and Muslim merchants to give up their businesses.[72] Every day, when the increasing numbers of Greek ships docked at the port, the first thing the vessels' captains asked was whether the dockworkers were Greeks or Jews. "They refused to hire Jewish workers. Jewish dockworkers were only allowed to unload non-Greek ships."[73]

In August 1917, a major fire destroyed the heavily Jewish center of Salonika, leaving some 45,000 Jews homeless. The Greek government made small compensation payments but forbade most victims from rebuilding their homes in this two-square-kilometer area of devastation. The government policy amounted to a mass expropriation, and Jews were the ones affected in 75 percent of the cases. Those left unhoused were quartered in hastily erected barracks and tents on the edge of town. The winter of 1918–19 was a hard one, and 1,569 Jews died within a month. Those who neither perished nor emigrated dispersed, the ruins of the city center were rebuilt in modern fashion, and the property affected by the fire was sold off at high prices to private buyers. The fire thus accelerated the massive increase in the city's Christian population and the emigration of thousands of Jews whose families had lived in Salonika for generations. They left for the US, France, Italy, and Alexandria, Egypt. When Germans occupied the city in 1941, roughly half of Salonika's Jews were still living in emergency accommodations.[74]

3

Peace, Civil War, Pogroms

For millions of Europeans, the official end of the First World War brought no peace. Bloody revolutionary, nationalist, and interventionist wars ravaged the former Russian Empire and demoralized the people who lived there. Hungarian and Romanian troops waged fierce battles over the future borders between their countries even as the Hungarian Republic of Councils was subjugated by counterrevolutionary forces. Yugoslavian soldiers attacked Kärnten, Austria, and Polish troops marched on Kiev. There were territorial conflicts in various spots between Germany and the newly created Polish state. Some 3,000 people died in the fighting in Upper Silesia. Those numbers may have been small compared to the millions of casualties in the national wars, revolutions, and counterrevolutions in Eastern Europe, but the internal outbreaks of violence and the wars over borders and against minorities that followed the 1918 armistice and the Paris peace agreements radicalized people and made them impatient for action.

Hundreds of thousands of people who had been declared personae non gratae left the territories Germany, Austria, Bulgaria, and Hungary had been forced to cede or otherwise lost. All too often they were driven from their homes. Two million people fled Russia for Western Europe, which itself was suffering from hunger, spiritual and material ruin, and a harrowing Spanish flu epidemic. Crises, insecurity, malnutrition, and the disintegration of law and order fueled hatred for Eastern European Jews.

The survivors of the Great War swept aside old social orders in Eastern, Central, and Southern Europe. They followed the principle of "self-determination of peoples"—an idea that initially sounded benevolently democratic but soon became a shrill call to arms. It had been popularized at the beginning of the First World War by the Russian revolutionaries Lenin and Trotsky. In September 1915, together with thirty-eight socialist delegates from eleven countries who met secretly in Switzerland's Zimmerwald Forest, they endorsed the nationalist cause "unanimously and enthusiastically." One passage from the "Zimmerwalder Manifesto," written by Trotsky, read: "The right of nations to self-determination must be the unshakable foundation of national relations."

NATIONAL SELF-DETERMINATION

No sooner had it taken power in late 1917 than the Bolshevik government in Russia proclaimed the right to national self-determination. In reaction US president Woodrow Wilson also adopted the concept, using it as the guiding political idea for his Fourteen Points, which were intended to lead to a just, lasting post-armistice peace. In January 1918, even as cannon were still firing on all fronts, Wilson presented his plan to Congress. He understood national self-determination in American terms: as a step toward national independence, modern, democratically legitimated constitutions, the rule of law and order, equitable relations between peoples and interests, and the constraint of violence between states and expansionist aggression.

In November 1918, as the war came to an end and the historic powers in St. Petersburg, Vienna, and Berlin collapsed, the "springtime of nations" so hotly anticipated by political strategists proceeded less peacefully than hoped. Wilson was not to blame. He put important issues on the agenda, ones that had long concerned Europe and the entire world and continued to excite people's passions: free trade, free passage for ships, radical, controlled disarmament, the "sincere welcome of Russia into the community of free nations," the creation of a Polish state, the territorial integrity of the Balkan countries, and the solidarity of the world's countries in a league of nations that would promote international peace by guaranteeing protection for all member states, particularly small ones pressured by larger neighbors.

Buoyed by such visions, Wilson told Congress on February 11, 1918: "'Self-determination' is not a mere phrase. It is an imperative principle of actions which statesmen will henceforth ignore at their peril." Yet the US president's British and French counterparts used the principle tactically to reduce the territories of Bolshevist Russia, the Ottoman Empire, Germany, and Austria-Hungary, decreasing their influence in favor of Britain and France's own interests. They thus supported self-determination for populations in Southern and Eastern Europe. In their minds, the principle didn't apply to colonial peoples at all.

Wilson's secretary of state Robert Lansing quickly recognized what sort of a genie his boss had released from its bottle. On December 30, 1918, he wrote in his diary: "The more I think about the President's declaration as to the right of 'self-determination,' the more convinced I am of the danger of putting such ideas into the minds of certain races. . . . The phrase is simply loaded with dynamite. It will raise hopes which can never be realized. It will, I fear, cost thousands of lives. What a calamity that the phrase was ever uttered!"

As a lawyer and constitutional expert, Lansing thought the concept, no matter how well meant, would lead to killings and violence and be put to unintended uses. He wondered what the effects of the word "self-determination" would be on "the Irish, the Indians, the Egyptians, and the nationalists among the Boers." What, he asked, if "the Mohammadans of Syria and Palestine and possibly of Morocco and Tripoli rely on it?" Moreover, how could it be "harmonized with Zionism, to which the President is practically committed?" All in all, the idea of self-determination seemed to Lansing to be completely incompatible with the political structure of a world built upon the idea of nationality.[1]

With the military collapse of the Central Powers, Czechs, Poles, Romanians, Ukrainians, and other peoples hastened "to draw the consequences from the principles Wilson proclaimed" and "make themselves free." That was how Joseph Bendow-Tenenbaum characterized the bitter fighting in late 1918 between nationalist Poles and equally nationalist Ukrainians over East Galicia, which had been under Austrian control. The Poles considered Lvov/Lviv as essentially Polish, the Ukrainians saw the city as totally Ukrainian, and the 70,000 Jews who lived there were caught between the fronts. In November 1918, seeing a Polish pogrom brewing, they sent a dispatch to Wilson pleading for help. In vain. A few days later, Jews were being murdered and robbed in the name of national self-determination.

In 1924, after the situation had calmed down somewhat and anti-Jewish discrimination had returned to its usual quiet form, the Jewish-German writer Alfred Döblin traveled to Poland. "Today's states are the grave of peoples," he wrote. The more or less arbitrarily formed new nations of Europe were "collective beasts" that taught the masses, "their subjects," the barbarism of nationalism rather than values. "It is impudent arrogance to blindly prioritize what is called national community ahead of everything else," Döblin wrote. "The freedom that is preached becomes hostile to other equally important freedoms in the way it is preached. I do not like the nation for its own sake."[2]

Zionists welcomed the idea of self-determination, which raised great hopes for a Jewish state. Encouraging them was a briefing prepared by Lansing for Wilson on September 21, 1918, to prepare him for future peace conferences. Its point eighteen read: "Palestine to be an autonomous state under a general international protectorate or under the protectorate of a Power designated to act as the mandatory of the Powers."[3] At the time around 700,000 people lived in Palestine: 568,000 Muslims, 74,000 Arab Christians, and 58,000 Jews. Within this protectorate-state, so conceived, Jews would be able to lead an autonomous existence. During a debate within Jewish circles, Lansing asked Chaim Weizmann, Britain's leading Zionist then visiting Washington, to sketch out a future Jewish community in Palestine, and Weizmann answered that it was his goal "to gradually form a Jewish nation in the same sense that France was a French and Britain a British one." Later, Weizmann added, "When Jews make up a large majority, the time will come to form a government, to push the country forward and turn our own ideals into reality."

Lansing didn't contradict this vision. On the contrary, he accepted the idea that in the medium term four to five million Eastern European Jews would be resettled in the "empty spaces" of Palestine. Weizmann returned triumphantly to London and announced that the US secretary of state together with political leaders from France and Britain supported him. On March 2, 1919, he assured the delegates of the American Jewish Congress: "In complete agreement with our government and our people, the Allied nations are unanimously of the view that the foundations of a Jewish community should be laid in Palestine." Representatives of defeated Germany, he went on, also supported the plan.[4] With that, the notion of a Jewish "national home" in Palestine was internationally recognized. It was a continuation and elaboration of the terse Balfour Declaration of 1917: "His Majesty's Government view with favour the establishment in Palestine of a national home for the Jewish people, and will use their best endeavors to facilitate the achievement of this object, it being clearly understood that nothing shall be done which may prejudice the civil and religious rights of existing non-Jewish communities in Palestine or the rights and political status enjoyed by Jews in any other country."

Along with the leaders and members of Zionist groups, anti-Semites were delighted with this vision—although they ignored the part of the declaration that supported Jews' civil and religious rights in every country of residence. They were simply happy at the prospect that Jews would soon begin to emigrate en masse. In 1917, for example, Greek prime minister Eleftherios Venizelos demanded the formation of a Jewish state for one reason only: "to de-Jewify and Hellenize" Salonika.[5] Driven by a far greater hatred of Jews, the early Adolf Hitler brusquely rejected the idea of a Jewish state. In 1926 in *Mein Kampf*,

he accused "Zionism" of trying to fool the rest of the world into thinking that Jews would be satisfied with such a state. In reality, Hitler
claimed, all Jews wanted was "an organization headquarters for their
international swindling and cheating with its own political power that
is beyond the reach and interference from other states."[6]

With their decision in 1920 to place Palestine under British mandate
and allow a homeland for Jews there, the delegates of the victorious
Allies in Paris laid the first cornerstone of what would later become
Israel. Germany laid the second one with the murder of six million
European Jews. It was only after the Holocaust that, on May 14, 1948,
David Ben-Gurion read out his declaration of the establishment of the
state of Israel in a Tel Aviv theater: "The catastrophe which recently
befell the Jewish people—the massacre of millions of Jews in Europe—
was another clear demonstration of the urgency of solving the problem
of its homelessness by reestablishing in Eretz-Israel the Jewish State,
which would open the gates of the homeland wide to every Jew and
confer upon the Jewish people the status of a fully privileged member
of the comity of nations. Survivors of the Nazi holocaust in Europe,
as well as Jews from other parts of the world, continued to migrate to
Eretz-Israel, undaunted by difficulties, restrictions and dangers, and
never ceased to assert their right to a life of dignity, freedom and honest toil in their national homeland."

DEPORTATIONS IN ALSACE, 1918–1923

One important precedent for mass resettlement was set by the French
administration in Alsace-Lorraine, which between 1918 and 1923
expelled large numbers of Germans and descendants of Germans who
had arrived in the two regions after the Franco-Prussian War. Their
stories are one example of ethnic cleansing in the first four decades
of the twentieth century. As states increasingly pursued the goal of
homogenization, they also came to view Jews as foreign elements
within the nation. Hannah Arendt, who herself fled Germany in 1933,
wrote of ethnically motivated displacements as having "specifically
modern features," including divorcing people from their homeland,

uprooting them socially, and stripping them of any political rights. In Arendt's eyes, this sort of treatment of people reached its apotheosis in the "murderous population policies of [Nazi] Germany." Nonetheless, while the Holocaust represents the apex of ethnic violence, it remains embedded within twentieth-century European history as a whole.[7]

With its age-old convolution of German, Alemannic, and French influences, Alsace-Lorraine was a culturally rich area. Residents had always had to deal with competing centers of power, and no matter who ruled over them, they maintained a pragmatic opportunism common to other European border and transitional areas. Cleverly, they stressed local patriotism and maintained distance from their perennially faraway, often bellicose masters. In 1871, Germany annexed most of Alsace and the northern, heavily industrialized half of Lorraine. On November 21, 1918, the two regions, which Paris had previously considered either imperial territory or eastern *départements*, were ceded back to France. From 1940 to 1944, they were once again made parts of Germany.

In November 1918, the venerable Alsatian rabbi of Strasbourg, Emile Levy, resigned to avoid having to greet French troops marching into the city—he had long since gotten rid of the accents over the "e's" in his first and last names. Inspired by German patriotism, he had himself transferred across the Rhine River in 1919 and became the rabbi of the Charlottenburg district in Berlin. In 1934, Levy fled Nazi Germany for Tel Aviv, where he died in 1953. By contrast, Harry Bresslau only left Strasbourg against his will when it was returned to France. He had taught medieval history at the university there since 1890. He owed his post to the liberal director of universities in the Prussian Ministry of Education, Friedrich Theodor Althoff. Althoff had been unable to get the respected Jewish scholar approved by the cliques at Berlin's universities and sent him to distant Strasbourg. Even today, Bresslau's *Handbook on the Study of Documents* is considered a classic among medieval historians.

On December 2, 1918, French police and soldiers hounded the seventy-year-old back to Germany, calling him a "pan-Germanist militant." But Bresslau, who was Albert Schweitzer's father-in-law, had never sympathized with the Pan-German League or similar nationalist associations. In his autobiographical sketches, composed in Heidelberg, he noted: "On Sunday, December 1, at 11 a.m., a gendarme brought the deportation order. The following day, at 3 p.m., on the orders of the commanding general, I was to appear at the bridge over the Rhine at Kehl. I was only allowed to take what I could carry. The question of furniture was to be settled at a later date. People of the same nationality who lived under one roof were allowed to accompany me, but they had no hope of being permitted to return. My wife immediately decided to go with me. That afternoon news arrived that every traveler could take 40 kilograms with them. The French would bring it to the Rheinbrücke. The next morning, I brought two hastily packed suitcases to the assigned collection point. I was afraid the French would search my luggage, so I left a number of papers behind that I would have liked to take with me."

That afternoon the first fifty people to be deported from Strasbourg arrived at the bridge. The commanding officer ordered the Germans to carry their own luggage; he forbade his men from offering any help. In the middle of the bridge, some soldiers relented and assisted the elderly Bresslaus in bringing their two suitcases, each weighing forty kilos, to the German side. Bresslau mentioned these details "in order to convey the unnecessary brutality" with which the French proceeded, although he "could be accused of nothing more than of being particularly unwelcome to the inventors of French propaganda because he had a lot of friends among Alsatians." It would take several years for Bresslau to be reunited with his furniture and his beloved library.[8]

France's Orderly Displacements

The fate suffered by the Bresslaus would be shared by at least 100,000 others in the months that followed. Deportees were usually only informed that they would have to leave France twenty-four hours before their departure, and they, too, were only allowed to take forty kilos of luggage, in some places less. Twelve *commissions de triage* with three members each decided who was to be driven out of the region. The ultimate aim was *épuration*, or "cleansing." The commission made their decisions on the basis of informants' denunciations and police and intelligence service dossiers. Their mission was to weed out all "suspects," "personae non gratae," and "pan-Germanists," in order to "cleanse Alsace-Lorraine from all the effects of the annexation." On January 24, 1919, French president Georges Clemenceau issued blanket orders to the committee members that "where and however the presence of Germans affected the public order, the threat is to be removed immediately."[9]

Clemenceau was not just worried about Francophobe German militarists, but also about leading Social Democrats and trade-union organizers, men who had been active in Strasbourg's revolutionary workers' and soldiers' councils before the region had been put under French control. Union and SPD activists were deported or detained, including several who had organized labor activities while Alsace-Lorraine was part of the German Empire. From the outset, Clemenceau used the policy of *épuration* to pursue social and political ends. He emphasized to committee members that they had a "duty" to get rid of superfluous German workers "so that the people of Alsace and Lorraine are not driven into unemployment."

To benefit demobilized French soldiers, it was ordered that German workers were to be the first to be fired in and around the city of Colmar. An anonymous informer reported that several Germans were still employed in the electrical plant in Turkheim—the letter writer demanded that "these undesirable people" be deported. On April 12, 1919, the local police commissioner wrote to the regional administrator: "I take the liberty of informing you that a number of *boches* [a pejorative term for Germans] are still at work on the construction sites of Munstertal, while Alsatians are sitting around on the streets looking for work."

Germans who were already unemployed were also put on the lists of "undesirables" because they represented a potential burden to the French social-welfare system. "To protect public hygiene," French officials drove German prostitutes into Germany. The same happened to "antisocial or degenerate elements," a category that included the unemployed Pole Maurise Feibusch, who was accused of doing black-market labor. The commissions soon ceased, however, to apply the category "undesirable" to specialists and other people whose skills could not be easily replaced.

This process of differentiation between people repeated itself in much harsher form in 1939 in German-annexed areas of Poland, Alsace, Luxembourg, and the Finnish-Russian border region of Karelia—and after 1945 in Carpathian Ukraine, Sudetenland, former eastern and southeastern Poland, Soviet-annexed East Prussia, Sieben-bürgen, and Banat. In these places, too, the ruling powers made exceptions for specialists and other essential workers. Wherever "foreigners" were displaced in Europe, the category "undesirable" was expanded and contracted to meet social and economic needs. As a rule, miners were usually allowed to stay in their homes, while members of the intelligentsia, shopkeepers, farmers, and the sick, the aged, and those branded as antisocial were made to disappear.

As was the case elsewhere when people were displaced, the expulsion of Alsatian Germans was justified as an act of punitive payback and accompanied by schadenfreude, vandalism, and larceny carried out by the majority. As Germans were being deported from Colmar, taking with them only what they could carry, a "corridor of hatred" formed along the sidewalks and "a respected woman in the town spit upon one man's frock coat." Youths pelted the Germans with small stones and horse dung and sang: "*Muss i denn, muss i denn zum Städtele erüs*" (Must I, must I, leave this little town). Families of Germans who had moved to Colmar anticipated deportation and began to make preparations. One of them, schoolteacher Wilhelm Schmitz, who was originally from the German Rhineland, took out an ad in the local paper reading: "Due to an impending move, an entire household up for sale cheaply. Everything in good condition. Bedroom, bureaus, make-up tables, armchair, chaise longue, chairs, beds, mirror, tables and pillows." Neighbors looted the furnishings of apartments deportees had been forced to leave behind. Even when there was no looting, French officials arranged "orderly" auctions to sell off the contents of people's homes at bargain prices, with the proceeds going to state coffers.[10]

Who was considered German and who was deemed French? The majority of the classifications according to the friend-or-foe schema in Alsace-Lorraine were not made by the *commissions de triage*. They were far too slow and were disbanded in late 1919. Officials at the residents' registry offices were far more efficient because they differentiated less between individual cases. On the basis of the residents' registry, they classified the 1.9 million people in the region using four groups: (A) full French, (B) partly French, (C) necessary or tolerated foreigners, and (D) Germans.

Class A identity cards were reserved for people of "pure heritage," whose parents or grandparents had all been born in the region or in France. In cases of doubt, people had to prove their lineage. A Class A identity card, bearing the tricolor, gave holders the right to travel, vote, and work; 1,082,650 people enjoyed these liberties.

Those who were the product of French-German "mixed marriages" fell into category B. The corresponding identity card bore two red stripes on the side. People in this group, of whom there were 183,500, were allowed to attain full citizenship if they proved their loyalty over the years. Until then, they lived as second-class citizens, always under threat of deportation.

Only 55,050 people, whose grandparents came from neutral or French allied countries, fell into category C. Almost all of them were workers who had come under German rule to Alsace-Lorraine to work in the mines or in industry. Their labor was still very much in demand, so they were given preferential treatment.

Group D encompassed 513,800 people of German heritage, or roughly one-fourth of the region's population. They had been born in Alsace-Lorraine, but their parents had moved to the area after 1870. The files drawn up for these people by French bureaucrats bore the heading "*purgatoire*."

These criteria meant that a man with German parents who was born in Alsace would be given the classification D while his French wife would be put in category A. The children would end up in group

B when they reached adulthood—minors were automatically given their fathers' classification. Along with difficulties in finding work and the constant threat of deportation, people in group D were economically disadvantaged in a number of other respects and were systematically robbed by the state insofar as they were forced to exchange money and other liquid assets in reichsmarks at the poor rate of 1.25 to 1 franc while the rate for everyone else was .74 to 1. (The Bulgarian government would do something similar with Jews in 1941, when they introduced the lev into annexed parts of Macedonia and Thrace.)[11] The French government also fired many Germans who worked in the public sector and the postal and rail services. They forced "halfbreeds" to move to other parts of France, restricted their freedom of movement and voting rights, and subjected them to police surveillance. But hardest hit were the people deported to Germany. By late 1919 they numbered around 100,000. Fifty thousand more were forced to return to Germany in the four years that followed. By 1926 there were also at least 575,000 people forced out of the territories Germany was required to relinquish after the First World War: Posen, Upper Silesia, and West Prussia. Among them were many Jewish-German families, who were put under enormous pressure to emigrate. Subjectively, of course they too felt like refugees.[12]

In France, those summoned before the committees as foreigners weren't allowed to view their files, which often contained denunciations by informants, nor were they permitted to introduce witnesses and evidence on their behalf. They had no legal counsel or any possibility of appeal. The witnesses for committees remained anonymous and didn't have to testify under oath.[13] Past quarrels, business competition, envy among colleagues, ambition, and plain treachery produced so many accusations that as early as December 1918 the police director of Strasbourg complained of being unable to deal with all the denunciations he was receiving in the mail.

At that juncture, France had suspended the principle of equality for all before the law of which it was otherwise so deservedly proud. Of the 1.9 million inhabitants of Alsace-Lorraine, 85 percent indicated that German was their native language. Under German rule, between

1871 and 1914, French had remained the official language in local government offices and schools wherever French native speakers were in the majority. It was only with the start of the First World War that French became the mistrusted language of the enemy. After the fighting stopped, victorious France was quick to try to Romanize the region. Strict centralizing rules were intended to eradicate the linguistic and cultural particularities of the inhabitants of the Franco-German border region and inculcate them with French nationalism once and for all. With the ethnic cleansing programs affecting many schoolteachers, the prefectures offered higher wages to attract teachers and superintendents from the French heartland. As a rule, these people spoke not a word of German. Yet they were charged with teaching classes in which less than 10 percent of the pupils spoke French.[14]

One Example, Many Imitators

Systematically and bureaucratically classifying masses of people within a larger populace on the basis of where their parents and grandparents had been born was something that had never before been done in Western Europe. France did not pursue this process of national sorting and expulsion to its ultimate conclusion. With the signing of the Treaty of Versailles, a milder pragmatism gradually won the upper hand. Beginning in the mid-1920s, the Third Republic naturalized people of German descent still living in the country, although they often had to pass a variety of individual tests. People with names like Karl Georg Görke became Charles Georges Goerké. School administrations were particularly strict in insisting upon the Romanization of names.

The twin ideas of selecting out certain groups for deportation and rigidly insisting upon a national language spread through Europe between the world wars. With the motherland of European republicanism having legitimized such methods, the newly founded and formed nation-states of the continent quickly stripped and denied people of citizenship because their parents and grandparents weren't Bulgarian, Greek, Romanian, Latvian, or Polish. Conversely, many older people lost their right to reside in the places their children or grandchildren did.

In the fall of 1935, Nazi Germany defined who was Jewish in what became known as the Nuremberg Laws. After considerable debate, the authors of the legislation decided that the crucial criterion was the religion of a person's grandparents—something that was relatively easy to determine. On October 3, 1940, when the Vichy government in France voluntarily proclaimed the *statut des juifs*, which brought its policies in line with the activities of the German occupiers, it was initially unclear who would be considered Jewish. But in a few weeks, leading civil servants agreed that individuals were members of the "Jewish race" if three of their four grandparents had been members of the Jewish religious community. That criterion was enshrined in law in the second *statut des juifs*, proclaimed on June 2, 1941. The commissioner-general for Jewish questions in Vichy France, Xavier Vallat, stressed that France was only following the example of "modern legislators" in Germany, Italy, Hungary, Romania, and Croatia, who had observed the same rule. Nonetheless, the procedure proved to be more difficult than in Germany since neither civil registrars' offices nor residential registries kept records of people's religion. On one score, the 1940 *statut des juifs* went even further than the Nuremberg Laws. It treated two "half-Jews" married to one another as "full Jews"—as Adolf Eichmann's representative in France, Heinz Röthke, noted with satisfaction.[15]

In May 1942, Hitler cited France as an example of how he wanted to impose ethnic categories, if necessary with brute force. A record of his monologues at mealtimes has him saying: "We can even learn a lesson from the way the French behaved in Alsace. Without the slightest regard for the generations of men who would have to suffer in consequence, they set to work to eradicate from Alsace every vestige and trace of German influence, thrusting brutally the customs and the culture of France down the throats of the inhabitants. Acting in the same way we will mercilessly wipe out bilingualism in these territories, and the radical methods to which we shall have recourse will themselves prove their efficiency, even among the population hostile to Germanization. We shall rapidly achieve a clear-cut situation, so that by the second generation, or at the latest by the third, these regions will have been completely pacified."

Hitler praised the "application of the most severe measures" begun in the summer of 1940 to expel natives of Alsace-Lorraine to France, scoffing, "we shall still have to get rid of a further quarter of a million of 'Frenchified' [sic] Alsatians." In contrast to the relatively orderly methods of the French, he cited a far more radical model of the brute force he wanted to apply to ethnic selection. Especially in eastern areas, Hitler proposed, his goals could only be achieved with Stalinesque procedures.[16]

The Germans retook Alsace-Lorraine in summer 1940 and deported 105,000 people between July and December. As a report put it, these were "mainly Jews, gypsies and other members of foreign races, criminals, antisocial people and incurable lunatics, in addition to French and Francophiles." These deportations were just the beginning. On September 12, 1940, Heinrich Himmler, head of the SS and the German police, decided upon "the future composition of the populace" in the "incorporated eastern regions," that is, the areas of Poland that Germany had annexed.

According to Himmler's decree, people living in these areas were to be divided into four groups: "A: members of the German people," that is, full Germans; and "B: people of German descent who needed to be educated to become full Germans and therefore only enjoyed German citizenship but not all the rights of members of the German Reich." They were generally to be resettled in traditionally German areas, if necessary, re-Germanifying them. Group C, in Himmler's definition, consisted of "valuable foreigners and renegade Germans whose German citizenship is conditional." Group D, the largest category, was made up of "members of foreign peoples who do not possess German citizenship." These close to eight million Polish men and women were to be "combed through" to separate out those who "represent a worthwhile addition for the German people." Himmler limited their number in advance to "one million people at the most."

On the basis of these categories, in the same edict, Himmler introduced a second, subsidiary classification system called the "German people's list." It divided up Germans and people worthy of being Germanified—more or less groups A, B, and C—into subgroups one through four and gave them various civic and social rights. Anyone who was "actively engaged" in the battle between German and Polish ethnicity or could at least show that he had "preserved his Germanity" was to go into subgroups one and two. "People of German descent who had formed connections over the years to Polishness . . . but on account of their behavior had the prerequisite conditions for becoming full members in the German ethnic community" were assigned to subgroup three. This subgroup also included "ethnically foreign" people who had married Germans—although only if in the opinion of German ethnicity experts the German part of the "mixed marriage" prevailed. That was the case if, for instance, a household conformed to German ideals of orderliness or had displayed a better-than-average desire to contribute to the collective. The fourth and final subgroup was reserved for ethnic renegades, "people of German descent who have completely gone over politically to Polishness."

The irreproachably German members of subgroups one and two were "to be deployed for the development of the East," while those in subgroups three and four "were to be educated through years of intensive training to become full-fledged Germans and made German citizens again." Members of subgroup four were given provisional German citizenship, as were "racially valuable foreigners (Ukrainians, Greater Russian, Belarussians, Czechs and Lithuanians)," and both were subject to police surveillance.

In line with Himmler's upper limit of one million, the people responsible for determining individuals' Germanity in the annexed Polish provinces added 977,000 people to subgroups one and two on the German people's list, giving them the status of reliable citizens; 1,928,000 were put in subgroups three and four. They were considered less reliable citizens, with too many Slavic influences, who needed to be subjected to a robust procedure of adaptation.

Werner Hasselblatt, an ethnic German from Latvia, described how the same criteria were used to distinguish between residents of the Baltic countries in 1942. As a delegate representing Latvia's German community, Hasselblatt had long functioned as a voice for reconciliation in European congresses on national minorities. But he went over to the other side, becoming the director of the special department of German Eastern Policy in Alfred Rosenberg's Ministry for the Occupied Eastern Territories in 1941. There he examined which Estonians, Latvians, and Lithuanians could be successfully Germanified. To that end, Hasselblatt developed a special Latin terminology, which he presented to Rosenberg's expert on racial issues, Erhard Wetzel. This vocabulary gave Himmler's criteria the sheen of classical-sounding respectability.

Hasselblatt distinguished between "*Homo genere et ingenio praestans*" (people of full value racially and personally), "*Homo germanisando dignus*" (those worthy of being Germanified), "*Homo germanisabilis atque germanisandus*" (those who could be Germanified and thus should be Germanified), and "*Homo germanisatus*" (those who had been Germanified). The recipient of this list, Wetzel, had made contact with Viktor Brack, the managing director of Hitler's Party Chancellery, and Eichmann after the "public" (and therefore "not to be approved of") mass shootings of Jews in Vilnius. On October 18, 1941, a satisfied Hasselblatt was able to inform his boss that both men approved of using gassing machinery in the future to get rid of "those Jews unable to work."[17]

In 1946, Sefton Delmer, the Berlin-born British journalist and Germany expert and critic, traveled to Mariánske Lázně, the city known in German as Marienbad, which had just been returned to Czech control. There he witnessed the deportations of Sudeten Germans—men, women, and children who all wore a large N pinned to their clothing. The N stood for Němec—Czech for "German." Delmer wrote that they were forced to wear this designation on their lapels exactly as Jews under the National Socialists had been made to wear yellow Stars of David. The deportees, he noted, were only allowed to take a maximum of fifty kilos of personal belongings with them.

Czech militiamen deported German-speaking Bohemians to Bavaria, not to gas chambers. Nonetheless, the sight of weeping women and children who begged him as an Englishman for help left Delmer teary-eyed himself, even as he reminded himself that these were the same people who had served Hitler as a fifth column as he tried to "wipe Czecho-slovakia off the map," to enslave the Czechs, to Germanify their children, and colonize the country with the help of Germanic supermen from the SS. Delmer was witness to a human tragedy unjustly visited upon certain people. Nonetheless, as a political thinker, he welcomed the decision of Czech president Edvard Beneš and his government to expel the Sudeten Germans.[18]

Nazi Germany radicalized the methods of classifying human beings to an unprecedented and previously unimaginable extent. German bureaucrats and population experts decided on the welfare and misery, life and death, of millions of people. That limits the validity of historical comparisons. Nonetheless, the comparatively harmless French beginnings, to which the French themselves soon put a stop, and other comparable processes should not be forgotten. They legitimized distinctions of this sort being drawn between human beings. They provided a model for far harsher and infinitely more violent repopulation projects and continued to exert influence long past 1945. The principle of sorting people according to ethnic, religious, bureaucratic, social, and economic perspectives, with the aim of deporting some of them, established itself in many parts of Europe after 1918. Leading politicians and commentators praised it as an ultimately useful if brutal tool for ensuring peace. They believed in all seriousness that the members of a national state were happiest when they lived together with people who were socially and historically as much like themselves as possible.

NEW FREEDOM, POLISH RAGE

While millions of Poles celebrated their freedom and a Polish republic was proclaimed on November 11, 1918, in Warsaw, pogroms, some of them major, erupted in villages and smaller and larger cities. In the six weeks following Polish national independence, there were at least 150 outbreaks of violence. Well over a hundred people were killed, the majority in Lviv. Israel Cohen, who traveled to Poland in January 1919 and composed a report for the Central Office of the Zionist Organization in

London, wrote that "in the euphoria of its long coveted independence, Poland ignited a wildfire of anti-Jewish extremism."

In their elation over the creation of a free, democratic Poland, three hundred representatives of the Jewish community in Kielce also held celebrations that day. In their minds, anything was better than the Russian rule the city had been under until 1914, and the word "republic" raised hopes of being freed from the tsarist special laws. But these Jews were badly mistaken. Led by provisional commandants, local militiamen stormed the Jewish events being held in the city theater. They herded the celebrants out of the theater and down the stairs through a gauntlet of people armed with sticks and bayonets. After that, they were pummeled by a mob. The violence lasted several hours, during which three members of the Jewish community were killed and more than one hundred injured. The following morning, farmers from nearby villages and residents of Kielce plundered the city's Jewish quarter. Police didn't intervene for six hours.

In the small Beskid Mountain city of Maszana-Doolna and the surrounding villages, Poles stole everything local Jews owned during the festive days of independence celebrations. On November 12, armed farmers stormed and looted the small West Galician city of Brzesko. To be able to take all they could they came in horse-drawn carts. Polish paramilitaries set several houses on fire and murdered eight Jews, throwing one of them in front of a moving train. Then, drunk and heavy with their spoils, they headed home.

In the neighboring city of Novy Wiśicz, anti-Jewish rioting was less wild. There crowds contented themselves with staging a barbaric spectacle, popular at the time, that was intended to show Jews who was boss. On November 27, under the command of a Polish officer, troops forced 132 Jewish men to strip bare in the city market place and whipped them. In the nearby Silesian city of Jaworzno on the German border, Christians terrorized their Jewish neighbors on November 5, 6, and 18. The ringleaders wanted to drive all Jews from the city within fourteen days, though they failed.

West of Krakow, in Chrzanów, the Polish population, freed from its oppressors, murdered two Jews on November 6 and went on a looting spree. The newly constituted city council demanded protection money in return for guaranteeing Jews' safety. The local authorities in the small West Galician city of Tuczempil near the southeastern border of today's Poland took a different tack. After four women, a child, and a young Jewish man on track to become an officer were murdered on November 15 and 16, Jews were allowed to raise a militia for self-defense.

The village of Grochów had only a single Jewish family, that of Aron Brochower, his wife, and their three sons. They were murdered by their neighbors on November 17. Similar crimes were committed in Lasi. There the only Jewish family—a shopkeeper, his wife, their daughter, and their grandchildren—died in a fire in their house, which local farmers had set. In Przemyśl on the San River, Poland's day of independence coincided with a victory over Ukrainian troops. The celebrations went on from November 11 to 13—at the cost of fifteen Jewish lives.[19]

The Freedom Pogrom in Lviv

Galicia and its capital, Lviv, were handed over to the Austrian monarchy as part of the first partition of Poland in 1772. In the fall of 1918, at the end of a world war that had been particularly hard on Galicia, the Hapsburg regime's troops withdrew, defeated. With no fanfare they retreated to Vienna, whereupon Poles and Ukrainians immediately sought to gain the upper hand and seize disputed territory. After a few weeks, the Polish side emerged victorious in Lviv and the surrounding area.

In 1918, Lviv had a population of 220,000, including 75,000 Jews. Tens of thousands of inhabitants had fled west when the Russian army took the city in 1914. They had lost everything they once possessed, so many of them didn't return home, staying on in Vienna or Moravia even after the city was retaken by the Austro-Hungarian army. In their stead, Jewish refugees from the eastern Galician cities razed by the Russians moved into the looted apartments. Lviv's historic Jewish community had been badly weakened by war, flight, and deprivation.[20]

A week after Polish troops captured Lviv, a well-organized pogrom was staged. It proceeded according to the "Russian model" but with "greater brutality," as observers from the Jewish Defense League attested. In contrast to several other Jewish organizations and the German Foreign Ministry in Berlin, the League was not known for exaggeration and checked its reports carefully. In their annual report for 1918, the authors tersely noted: "On November 22 and 23, and as a kind of aftershock on December 29, there were horrible outbreaks of violence in Lviv." Seventy-two Jews were murdered, 443 injured, "28 homes razed to the ground, 9 damaged by fire and between 4,000 and 5,000 families looted." The Polish soldiers, militiamen, and civilians who had taken part in the violence stole 11 million Austrian crowns in cash, 6 million worth of jewelry, clothing valued at 15 million, and 50 million in salable goods. (By comparison, the average weekly wage of an Austrian worker at the time was around 100 crowns.) The murder victims seem to have been partly targeted by profession. Thirty-six were merchants while ten were artisans.[21]

The most precise account was the one published in 1919 by the military doctor Joseph Tenenbaum, writing under the pseudonym Josef Bendow. He was a Jewish militiaman in Lviv, both a victim and a witness. In writing his report he called upon 800 pieces of testimony, which were recorded in the weeks after the pogrom. Recent historical studies based on police files and other sources that have become available support his fundamental points.[22] In 1920 Tenenbaum emigrated to the US. In 1936, he helped found the Joint Boycott Council, at the urging of the American Jewish Congress, which aimed to exert economic pressure on Nazi Germany.

Preceding the pogrom in the late autumn of 1918 were three weeks of constant fighting between Ukrainian and Polish nationalists. Knowing that they had much to fear from both sides, Jews proclaimed their strict neutrality. Nevertheless, in their hour of victory, the Polish "freedom fighters" turned reality on its head, claiming that Jews had covertly supported the Ukrainians and given them large sums of

money. With such statements, leading Polish military officers, politicians, and journalists essentially declared open season on Jews.[23] Lviv's
"liberators" spread rumors and laid the groundwork for the horror
to come. A high-ranking municipal administrator declared: "We will
take everything from the Jews, and poor Christian children will have
an abundance of everything." The organization and initiative for the
pogrom was the task of the military and the republican paramilitaries. Military and political leaders determined how long it would last
(forty-eight hours) and when it would start (at 4 a.m. on November
22). They saw the orgy of violence as a reward for troops who had
achieved the "heroic deoccupation" of Lviv. The military also had a
vested interest in filling their warehouses with food, shoes, cloth, and
the like. For their part, nationalist politicians welcomed the chance to
find an internal enemy and to consolidate identification with a newly
autonomous and free Poland by staging a bloody mass spectacle.

Tenenbaum wrote, "In the early morning hours, the terrified populace of the Jewish quarter heard the jeering and whistling of marching Polish soldiers accompanied by gunshots, harmonica playing, and
anti-Jewish curses and insults." The men of the Jewish self-defense
organization were disarmed, and machine guns and armored cars were
brought into position on the margins of the district. "This barrier was
intended to keep the people to be slaughtered from running in all directions and to show the pillagers the limits of where they could loot," so
that Christian businesses and homes were spared any damage.

Polish soldiers and paramilitaries ransacked the other buildings. If
doors were open, the troops used hand grenades. "Jew, hand over your
wallet!" they bellowed into rooms, seizing anything they could get their
hands on. "Lust for money was what gave the patriotic incitement its
individual stamp and greatest appeal," wrote Tenenbaum. "The Polish heroes rewarded themselves handsomely for their efforts and paid
themselves a splendid wage for their work as executioners." Whatever
the troops couldn't take away was destroyed or handed out to the
Polish mob. Following plans drawn up by the military leadership, the
marauders forced their way into Jewish businesses and warehouses.
Officers drove up in automobiles and helped themselves "in particular

to leather goods, cloth and food." Paramilitaries and Christian residents of Lviv had the run of smaller shops and workshops—even Red Cross nurses joined in, claiming they were "requisitioning items for the hospital." The well-organized soldiers brought canisters of petroleum in cars to start fires. They set individual buildings ablaze under the watchful eyes of officers, not neglecting to open all the doors and windows "so that air could better fan the flames." Having been informed in advance of what was to occur, officials at the city water company had cut off the water supply to the Jewish quarter.

Jews were burned to death in their houses after Polish troops nailed their doors shut from the outside. "The hordes of soldiers had stock answers to all pleas and entreaties: 'The Jews needed a good roasting. Today, there'll be Jewish bacon.' These and other inhumane taunts were the only consolation the poor victims received. Sometimes, promises of enhanced protection money moved hearts that remained stone deaf to pleading, and soldiers filled their wallets in return for allowing a Jewish family to slip through alleyways past the machine guns and armored cars. But others weren't susceptible to pecuniary arguments and went about their work as executioners immune to bribes—so that all that was left of unfortunate people was charred remains."

On the following morning, it was the synagogues' turn. At 10 a.m., incited and often intoxicated nationalist marauders stormed the synagogue on the edge of the city, stealing sacred items and destroying whatever they could. "You could see paramilitaries and women wrapped in the curtains of Holy Ark, horsing around and treading on the Holy Scripture." Then the burning of the city's oldest house of Jewish worship began. "Paramilitaries heaped the mutilated Torah scrolls in the middle of the synagogue, poured petroleum on the pyre and set it ablaze. . . . Two boys, David Rubinfeld and Israel Feigenbaum, who tried to save two Torah scrolls from the burning synagogue, were shot to death at the entrance. Several students were found dead, with Torah scrolls clutched to their chests." Following that, soldiers also burned down the city's Hasidic synagogue.

Amid such a reign of rage and terror, the Polish masters of the city organized a follow-up pogrom on December 29. Soldiers who had been recently transferred from Warsaw to Lviv claimed that they had been shot at. Led by a captain, they used explosives to blow open the doors of buildings near their barracks where Jews lived, ransacking and looting apartments. "The events of November 22, 1918, repeated themselves. Women and girls were abused, while men were beaten, taken away and interrogated in the Czacki School, before being beaten again and sent up before a court as suspects." No one was killed that night, but a number of people, "victims of a barbaric system of bad conscience," were left homeless.

"How did Polish society behave in the Jews' days of greatest need?" Tenenbaum asked in a separate chapter of his documentary report. As was the case with Russian pogroms, all of society, "nearly without regard to party affiliation, rank, or sex" in the new Poland took part in the violence. "The proud aristocrat," he wrote, "was of one mind with the common man, and the blackest reactionary with the reddest Marxist. Where the pogroms were concerned, there was a rare harmony of emotion and opinion on the otherwise so fissured political ground of Galicia."

The leader of the Polish social democratic movement, Ignacy Daszyński, had the audacity to try to rescue the new nation's honor by spreading the lie that the pogroms were "an act organized by Austrian Germans." Nonetheless, he couldn't bring himself to utter a single word of condemnation concerning the violence. The town's Women's Committee called for a return to calm and law and order, while claiming that "the Jews have taken a provocative stance." Equally devoid of human sympathy, the Roman Catholic Archbishop of Lviv, Józef Bilczewski, who was sanctified in 2005, refused to clearly condemn the larceny and murder: "If the Jewish people have incurred guilt in some way, the court of divinity and humanity will render a just verdict."

On the second day of the main pogrom, the *Kuryer Lwowski* newspaper ran the following fictional report: "The scum of society, many of whom were disguised in military uniforms, broke into businesses and plundered them. Paramilitary patrols intervened but prevention proved impossible." Why? According to the article, the flames from the rioting spread so quickly because of a lack of firemen. In fact, not a single fire fighter had tried to extinguish the blazes lit on Krakow Square. On November 28, the Polish news agency turned the facts upside down and reported that the damage had been done by a mixture of criminals freed from prison by Ukrainians and "Jewish plunderers." The report went on to claim that "the Polish military authorities moved immediately against the bandits and were soon able to quell the uproar." Other newspapers such as *Słowo Polskie*, *Trybuna Polska*, and *Ilustrowany Kuryer Codzienny* tried to obfuscate the Lviv murder and looting spree in similar fashion.[24] When news of the horrors became known outside Poland, foreign papers ran reports based on interviews with eyewitnesses, but Polish media immediately went on the counterattack. On December 5, the newspaper *Pobudka* (Call to Awaken), the central organ of the Polish military command, threatened: "The Jews should not forget that they rely on hospitality in Lviv and elsewhere and every provocation on their part will necessarily bring unforeseeable consequences."

Reports in Austrian newspapers were in the main accurate about what had happened, but one editorial represented a notable exception. It ran on November 29 in Vienna's *Arbeiter-Zeitung*, the main outlet of the Social Democratic Worker's Party of German Austria, and is a prime example of the sort of left-wing anti-Semitism that masqueraded as anticapitalist theory. The newspaper blamed the violence in Lviv on the "savage hatred" of the poor for "Jewish dealers and [war] profiteers." It added: "Once again, as is so often the case, Jewish proletarians have had to pay the price for what Jewish capitalists have done. . . . Jewish capitalist greed understood how to extract a healthy profit out of the misery of struggle, and poor, ignorant Polish proletarians had no other way of avenging the crimes committed against them than by attacking Jewish proletarians who were equally poor, innocent and as victimized by the great and rich as they themselves." But the historical facts contradict such pseudo-explanations. The Jews murdered in Lviv were largely merchants and self-employed people, and the large numbers of injured included 271 women and children, 124 merchants, and 5 workers.[25]

A Society Poisoned by Chauvinism

On December 12, 1918, the quartermaster of Polish troops stationed in Lviv published an official announcement in newspapers. It read: "Recently it has been documented that, contrary to the oath they solemnly swore to the military command, the Zionists have established very lively contact with the enemy and have prepared a common plan of attack." The previous day, to lend credence to what was an obvious lie, the army had arrested five Jews: Dr. Michael Ringel, Dr. Alexander Hausmann, Dr. Leon Reich, the editor M. A. Tennenblatt, and the staff physician Wilhelm Gabel. The Polish civil administration of Galicia sought to convince the English and French governments, both allies of Poland, that statements by the Jewish National Council in Poland and articles in the Jewish press about "allegedly planned anti-Jewish pogroms" were fabrications designed to provoke the Polish public "to an extreme extent." The real entities behind such propagandistic horror stories, Polish officials argued, were their former enemies in Berlin and Vienna. They wrote: "The relationship of the majority of Jews to the Prussians and the former Austrian government is too well known for us to overlook in whose interest this is happening."

In this atmosphere of suspicion, Jews, and in particular Jewish representatives, were subjected to constant verbal and written threats. A letter sent to the Jewish Relief Committee and cleared by Polish military censors read: "You should pack your things and move to Palestine by New Year's Day. Your entire wealth belongs to the Poles, but consider leaving as soon as possible because there are new pogroms on your doorstep, much bloodier and more serious ones." Reporting from Lviv, journalist Max Reiner described the general mood among Catholic and Polish residents: "No matter how many Poles I have talked to, they all found it natural to severely discipline Jews for their neutral stance in the battle against the Ukrainians."[26]

On November 28, 1918, the community buried its dead, bringing the remains of those killed directly to the city's Jewish Cemetery because "under the prevailing political conditions" a funeral procession was out of the question. "The entire multitude of mourners—40,000 souls—wept, wailed and almost perished in pain." Their despair was the expression of "the immense misery of a people who can be butchered without punishment or recompense."

The seventy-two people who were murdered and buried together in a common grave were: Josef Goldberg, Julius Goldberg, Michael Chewander, Toni Rad, Markus Kontes, Mendel Mandel, Moses Smoczak, Scheindlinger, Chaim Donner, Dawid Rubinfeld, Abraham Broder, Zygmunt Gorne, Genia Gorne, Jakób Hermann Schäfer, Salomon Spiegler, Leib Einschenk, Zygmunt Langnas, Izydor Mesuse, Salomon Langnas, Meschulem Frauenglas, Samuel Acker, Heinrich Dawid, Moses Agid, N. Silberstein, Moses Posner, Chaim Abend, Hania Necheles, Zalel Wildner, Majer G. Pordes, Hermann Bardach, Hermann Herbst, Adolf Grab, Mendel Hochberg, Rubin Hiss, Eliasz Sebel, Leon Einschlag, Jakob Neuer, Juda Leib Schnips, Nachmann Altmann, Leib Windmann, Klara Sonntag, Małka Riess, Izrael Feigenbaum, N. Tauber, Reize Berger, N. Herz Zuckermann, Marjem Ester Windmann, N. Wilner, Freide Jelles, Małka Kupferstein, Genia Turszynska, N. Brumer, Ignacy Rothberg, Mordche Zwickel recte Stern, Izrael Lipsker, Chane Menkes, Henryk Lewin, Moses Goldscheider, Meier Selig Peries, Schulem Mayer, Dawid Ennoch, Salomon Katz Sr., Salomon Katz Jr., Oskar Schwarzenberg, Rosa Finkelstein, Mechel Achtentuch, Berl Terten, Laura Krapp, Meilech Weiss, Johann Reiter, Benjamin Toth, and one man who was never identified.

Having no way of knowing what sorts of crimes against humanity lay ahead, Tenenbaum ended his chronicle with words of encouragement: "In its time of flourishing, Jewishness cannot be choked to death or be defeated no matter how great the brutality! No pogrom, no matter how terrible, can destroy Jewishness. It will survive all pogroms and those who incite them." Tenenbaum's words notwithstanding, the era of reunited, independent Poland began with months of violence against Jews, which recalled, in the words of Zionist Leon Chasanowitsch in 1919, "the most terrible and darkest times of the Middle Ages." He added: "Chauvinism poisoned the mind of Polish society and caused its conscience to ossify. Larceny and murder became tools in the political and economic struggle."[27]

Even as his account of the violence was going to press, Israel Cohen had to add a final section titled "The Latest Pogroms." In it he wrote of a "new cyclone" that had swept up Polish Jews and Jews subject to Polish authority in March 1919 in places like Szydłów, Paxanow, Stobnica, Dąbrowo Górnicza, Chmielnik, Busk, Wieluń, Częstochowa, Kalisz, Pinsk, and Lida.

In early March, Polish troops captured the Belarussian city of Pinsk, which had been held by units of the Bolshevik Red Army. Several weeks later, on the evening of April 5, 1919, Polish soldiers stormed a meeting of the Jewish Welfare Committee, which had been registered with city commanders, and arrested those in attendance on suspicions of Bolshevik activity. The soldiers then searched the Zionist People's Home for weapons, found none, and then arrested more Jews on the street. After robbing their prisoners of anything of value they had on them, the soldiers released the women, children, and elderly, herded the remaining thirty-four men into the Russian Orthodox church, stood them up against the wall, and mowed them down with machine guns. Three managed to survive, injured, and were shot to death the following morning immediately after they had shown signs of life. This mob of soldiers also locked twenty-six Jews in prison cells and demanded that Pinsk's Jews pay a collective fine of 100,000 rubles for fomenting "unrest." The major who commanded the troops, Jerzy Narbut-Łuczyński, later admitted making a "mistake." That error didn't damage his military career, however; he was made a brigadier general in 1924. No one was ever punished for the massacre.[28]

All the while, Poles, Lithuanians, Belarussians, and Ukrainians were all trying to gain the upper hand in the important city of Vilnius. In the end, on April 19, 1919, Polish troops succeeded in seizing control, after fighting street by street and suffering thirty-three casualties. None of the city's Polish civilians died in all the shooting but sixty-five Jews, including four women, were believed killed. During and after the fighting, Polish soldiers and city residents also plundered more than two thousand Jewish homes and businesses.[29]

MASS MURDER IN UKRAINE

In Ukraine, the end of the First World War in November 1918 brought not peace but two years of terror. More than fifteen hundred pogroms took place in this interval, and the number of victims reached the tens of thousands. Throughout Ukraine, Jews were burned alive in their homes, stabbed on the street in broad daylight, beaten and kicked to death, or gunned down. Entire families were murdered. No one was left behind to report what had happened to them. In comparison to earlier pogroms, writes historian Oleg Budnitskii, the violence was completely new in scope. The chapter of his book about the situation of Jews during the Russian and Ukrainian civil wars bears the title "In the Shadow of the Holocaust—The Pogroms of 1918–1920."[30]

As long as German and Austrian troops controlled large parts of Ukraine, they prevented random violence as far as they were able. But starting in late 1917 the German occupiers incited Ukrainian nationalism as a way of weakening the influence of Bolshevik Russia and gaining access to raw materials and grain. In April 1918, they established a puppet government in Kyiv. To give the regime the appearance of legitimacy, they dug up "from the depths of history the seventeenth-century Hetman Constitution." Hailed as a remnant of a heroic past, it recalled the bloody uprising led by Ukrainian national hero Hetman (Head of State) Bohdan Chmielnicki against Poles and Jews in 1648 and 1649. The head of the new Ukrainian state propped up by the Germans, Pavlo Skoropadskyi, even went by the title of "hetman." His men ran around in "Cossack hats with fur tails" and replaced the Russian "o" with a Ukrainian "i" in place names like Kharkov/Kharkiv and Lvov/Lviv. But while pushing the politics of national identity, they otherwise remained subservient to the Germans.[31]

With the withdrawal of the defeated Central Powers following the armistice agreement in Compiègne on November 11, 1918, various civil and interventionist wars broke out. Led by Symon Petliura, Ukrainian "social nationalists" deposed Skoropadskyi in December 1918. Petliura, who became the president of Ukraine, and his deputy and prime minister, Volodymyr Vynnychenko, seized power in Kyiv. They proclaimed a "people's republic of Ukraine," calling their regime a "directorate" and pursuing a strict anti-Russian course.

Back in 1905, taking their inspiration from the social democratic movements in Germany and Austria, the two leaders of the new Ukrainian nation had founded the "Ukrainian Social Democratic Labor Party," which from its inception tried to merge nationalist and social-welfare aims. Vynnychenko even translated major works by socialists Karl Kautsky and Ferdinand Lassalle into Russian. In December 1918, Petliura and his comrades emphasized the social-welfare goals of the revolution they had led. "The rebellion was not motivated as much by nationalism as by socialism and in part by Bolshevism," wrote Elias Heifetz, the first chronicler of the massacres of Jews that were about to commence. In the following months, during the fighting against Russians and Poles, the nationalist aspect of the movement came to the forefront, although socialism remained the main tool for mobilizing the masses. Both elements were used to justify robbing and murdering people who were not envisioned as being part of the Ukrainian state—first and foremost Jews.[32]

After some frenzied commando missions, military defeats, and loss of territory, Petliura's troops were driven from the country in late 1919. For several months, they tried to team up with Polish interventionists to retake parts of Ukraine, but such attempts were only temporarily successful. In March 1921, the Peace of Riga between Poland, Soviet Russia, and Soviet Ukraine ended the fighting and—for the time being—the dreams of many Ukrainians for an independent nation. Poles and Russians had joined together against them. Most of western Ukraine was given to Poland, and some smaller stretches of land to Romania and Czechoslovakia; the considerable rest, which had been conquered by the Red Army, was annexed by Russia and its successor, the Soviet Union.

The Scope and Sociology of the Pogroms

From late 1918 to the spring of 1921, Ukraine—one of the main European regions in which Jews had settled—became the central terrain for battling and marauding militias, bands of rootless men including deserters and former civilian home-front defenders. Whenever one or the other group would win a battle, there were hasty retreats and fresh attacks. Ukrainian nationalists, Polish invaders, Red and White Russians, and Black (anarchist) groups fought against and with one another. Meanwhile armed mobs spread destruction sometimes on one side, sometimes on the other. Without political goals, they were driven solely by avarice and bloodlust.

Between the unclear frontlines, which often changed on a weekly basis, were Jews who were only protected in rare cases by Red commissars or Polish officers. All the participants in the fighting treated them as fair game. The results were the worst pogroms in modern European history, carried out by tens of thousands of nationalist and socialist "freedom fighters."

We will never know how many Jews were murdered and how many of them, in particular women and children, starved or froze to death because their homes were burned down, all their belongings, provisions, and tools were stolen, their husbands and fathers were slaughtered, and external assistance couldn't reach them as the numerous battles were being waged under a multitude of flags. Estimates of the number of people directly murdered or injured so badly that they died soon thereafter range from 50,000 to 200,000. In any case, in 1923, chronicler Elias Tcherikover wrote of "a massive and lasting calamity for our people."[33]

In 1921, Heifetz published a preliminary, incomplete account, based on individual reports, of what had happened in Eastern Europe in 1919. According to his report, at least 372 Jewish neighborhoods had been destroyed in the preceding twelve months. In some places four, five, or even ten pogroms had taken place in quick succession. In scattered small cities, pogroms went on continuously for as long as it took to get rid of the Jewish population entirely and to completely plunder or destroy their assets. In Ukraine alone in 1919, Heifetz confirmed on the basis of verified eyewitness reports that at least 30,500 Jews had been murdered. But "this figure," he added, "does not by any means give an accurate idea of the actual number of persons who perished." Neutral observers had been unable to reach many places and regions, including Western Volhynia, Volhynia, and the southern part of the Cherson governorate. Heifetz assumed that at least 70,000 civilians had lost their lives in anti-Jewish violence within a year in Ukraine.

It wasn't until Nahum Gergel's 1928 essay "The Pogroms in the Ukraine in 1918–1921" that the first systematic statistics were published. They, too, were incomplete, but drawing upon more precise reports about 887 pogroms and 349 "excesses," the historian was able to present a sociological picture of the mass murder and larceny. Gergel distinguished between "excesses" (acts of anti-Semitic violence carried out by a single person, even if they had led to deaths of many people) and "pogroms" (acts of group violence). For the sake of simplicity, we will abandon that distinction and fold the relatively rare "excesses" into the general category of pogroms.

For half of the reliably verified 31,071 murder victims in 531 places, Gergel had access to a list that contained the sex and sometimes the age of those killed. These sources indicate that 76 percent of the victims were male, 3.5 percent under the age of eight, 19 percent between eight and twenty, 46.5 percent between twenty-one and forty, 15 percent were between forty-one and fifty, and 26 percent were older.

Gergel was familiar with the Jews' situation in Ukraine from his work as an observer for the Refugee Committee of the Soviet Red Cross during the pogroms. From his experience, he estimated the number killed at a very conservative 50,000 to 60,000. But he based his accounts of the perpetrators and chronology of the pogroms on the empirically reliable part of his data, and not suppositions.

According to Gergel, the army of the Ukrainian People's Republic under Petliura and the paramilitaries allied with the Ukrainian cause committed 40.1 percent of all pogroms and killed 53.7 percent of all victims. Monarchist and bourgeois White Russian forces were responsible for 17.2 percent of pogroms and 17 percent of those murdered. Fighters allied with the warlord Nikifor Grigoriev, who constantly switched sides, committed merely 4.2 percent of the pogroms but killed 11.2 percent of the casualties. Red Army troops killed only

2.3 percent of the victims but carried out 8.6 percent of the pogroms. The First Red Cavalry Army commanded by Semyon Budyonny was primarily responsible. The Polish army under the command of General Piłsudski was relatively disciplined, carrying out only 2.6 percent of the pogroms and causing 0.4 percent of the fatalities. The few troops under the command of Belarussian general Stanisław Bułak-Bałachowicz were only peripherally involved, carrying out 0.5 percent of pogroms and killing 0.7 percent of the victims. Free-ranging armed bands of rebels or deserters, whom we will refer to as "independents," were deemed responsible for 24.8 percent of pogroms and 14.8 percent of the Jewish murder victims. The average Jewish community suffered through 2.3 pogroms. The general governorate of Kyiv endured 2.9, and Chernihiv, Poltawa, and Cherson went through 5. The Jews of Chaschevat in Podolia endured 12 pogroms and those of Stavyshche (governorate of Kyiv) 14.

Gergel used his data to create an index by comparing the absolute number of the pogroms committed by each group with the average number of people murdered in each one. Ukrainian nationalists: 439 pogroms/average of 38 dead. Independents: 307/15. White Russian troops: 213/25. Red Army troops: 106/7. Paramilitaries: 52/67. Pogroms whose instigators were unknown: 33/1. Polish troops: 32/4.

Eighty percent of the anti-Jewish violence took place in areas where most Jews lived: the governorate of Kyiv (41.7 percent) and the Western Ukrainian-Polish border regions of Podolia (23.7) and Volhynia (16.3). In 12 percent of cases, the attackers murdered more than one hundred people in one pogrom location. More than a thousand were killed in the cities of Tetiev, Fastov, Chmelnyzkyj, and Kropywnyzkyj. There is no data on the number of rapes. Victims usually kept silent about what had happened to them, but there is no doubt that tens of thousands of Jewish women were subjected to sexual assault. The high point of terror visited upon Jewish communities came between May and September 1919. Half of all the violence between 1919 and 1921 happened during that period. As the Red Army and Polish troops began to advance, the anti-Jewish violence quickly receded.[34]

Gergel originally published his essay in Yiddish in Berlin, but it was also put out in English in 1951 in New York, twenty years after the author's death. The editorial notes pointed out that while the Ukrainian pogroms may have seemed limited compared with the six million Jews murdered in the Holocaust, they remained "a most important chapter in the story of the dissolution of East-European Jewry." More recent investigations have concluded that more than 100,000 Jews died in around 2,000 pogroms and individual acts of violence. The ground-breaking 2006 work by Lidia Miliakova, originally published in Moscow but cited here in the French edition, holds that most likely 150,000 Jews were killed and 200,000 injured, often crippled, and tens of thousands of Jewish women were raped. Some 300,000 Jewish children were left orphaned. In the 1920s the demographer Jakob Lestschinsky arrived at a similar number. He calculated that 125,000 Jews had been killed in Ukraine and 25,000 in Belarus.

On occasion, Heifetz identified an apparent connection between revolution and the pogroms. He wrote: "The Russian pogroms of the early 1880s corresponded to the revolutionary movement of the intelligentsia organized as 'Narodniki' (People's Friends), 'Zemlya i Volya' (Land and Freedom), and 'Narodnaya Volya' (Popular Will). Those in the beginning of our century, during the period of prerevolutionary unrest (1903–1905), corresponded to the great mass strikes in the south of Russia. Finally, the third pogrom wave corresponded to the outbreak of the first revolution itself at the end of 1905."[35] In late 1918, under the influence of gigantic, often successful national and social revolution, the fourth and by far and away most homicidal wave of anti-Jewish terror began.[36] As early as 1881, Narodnaya Volya activists greeted the pogroms as "the beginning of a social revolution" and accused Jews of invariably reproducing the "vices" and "tumors" of the ruling social order. Russian revolutionaries euphemistically characterized the pogroms as "flying sparks" that would unleash the revolutionary wildfire and for that reason were entirely welcome.[37]

We will ignore here the "documents" published in 1920 and 1927 by the nationalist Ukrainian government purporting to prove its pro-Jewish policies: there is considerable evidence that these were attempts to whitewash history.[38] The question of whether the Petliura regime in Kyiv willfully supported or merely tolerated the pogroms, hotly debated among some historians, is irrelevant here.[39] The important thing is that it offered no effective opposition—and it had good reason not to. Homicidal stealing from Jews and mass rape propped up Ukrainian troops' morale, reduced desertions, and alleviated the problem of recruitment, and they meant that soldiers didn't have to be paid as much. All this was greatly in the interest of the nationalist government in Kyiv. President Petliura and his commanders "knew only too well that there was no more reliable way of motivating the multitudes under their orders than permission to massacre Jews."[40]

Ukrainian Nationalist Bloodlust

Those were the general circumstances surrounding the outbreaks of violence. But what about the pogroms themselves: How did they proceed practically? What sort of internal logic did they follow?

Measured by what was to follow shortly, the first pogroms were relatively small. A good example is the violence in Ovruch in Volhynia, a city of 10,000 people, two-thirds of them Jews, in the governorate of Zhytomyr. No one there was particularly interested in politics. Amid all the pogroms Russian Jews had been forced to endure since 1881, Ovruch had remained peaceful. The first violence took place in December 1917. Angry at wartime inflation, Christian residents looted and destroyed some of the city's Jewish businesses. There were no attacks on Jewish homes, and no one was murdered.

That changed when Petliura's "freedom fighters" entered the city on December 25. Their commander, Ataman (Warlord) Kozyr-Zyrka, arrested the town's rabbi the next day, telling him: "I know that you are a Bolshevik, that all your relatives and all Jews are Bolsheviks. Know that I am going to destroy all the Jews in the city." Luckily for Jews, the Petliura militias were driven out of the city. But three days later, they returned and began a pogrom, in which seventeen people were killed. As his underlings were going about their bloodthirsty work, Kozyr-Zyrka ordered Jewish men to assemble in the public square and announced that he had "the right to destroy all the Jews and would do so if any one of them as much as touched the hair of a single Cossack." He demanded that Jews pay a hefty fine, and only after receiving it did he call off the orgy of terror.

The pogrom carried out by these Ukrainian People's Republic paramilitaries proved contagious. By the end of the civil war, Christian residents and militias had looted twelve hundred Jewish homes and killed more than one hundred people. (Pogrom initiators often invited Christian neighbors and farmers from surrounding areas to enjoy, take part in, and profit from the mass murder.) The official rationale may have been that the city's Jews were all Bolsheviks, but according to the 1921 report on the violence, the masses of Ukrainians involved would have accepted any reason. The pogrom eradicated differences in material wealth between Jews. Almost all ended up destitute.[41]

As part of the revolutionary pogroms of May 7 and 8, 1905, the Christian residents of Zhytomyr had already committed serious crimes of violence, in which twenty-nine Jews and one Christian, the university student Nikolay Blinov, were killed. (Blinov was murdered because he tried to help Jews.) Then on March 21, 1919, during the civil war, the Red Army left the city. The next morning, Petliura's men moved in and began five days of killing and pillaging. In the center of town, 317 Jews were murdered, as were many more on the outskirts—mostly elderly people, women, and children, since most of the young Jewish men had fled together with the Bolshevik troops. While the Ukrainian nationalist soldiers were mainly out to steal money and kill people, youths, building superintendents, and domestic servants plundered Jewish homes and businesses. The majority of Jews killed were poor. Jews with money were often able to save their lives by paying ransom. Given the massive lust for murder in the air, the number of dead remained relatively small. A disproportionate number of Christian families in Zhytomyr hid Jews, and a Red Army counteroffensive stopped the massacre on March 25.

Two days before, with the pogrom raging, Petliura visited the city together with a troop of farmers and had statements printed up saying: "We will defend all who don't want to become servants of Jews." Petliura was reported to have dismissed the mayor of Zhytomyr when he wanted to inform him about the homicides being carried out against Jews.[42]

Proskuriv (Proskurov): 1,600 Jews Murdered in Four Hours

Another one of Petliura's bands carried out a massacre in the small city of Pohrebyshche, a hundred kilometers southwest of Kyiv, on August 22, 1919. Eighteen hundred Jews lived there. Led by Ataman Zeleny, soldiers killed 375 of them. Afterward the chairman of the town's Jewish community there reported: "They carried out a pogrom in every sense of the word. They looted, raped and killed. They didn't want just what we owned. They wanted our souls. They dragged people up from their cellars and down from their attics in order to kill them. They spared neither young nor old. Among those killed were the ninety-year-old butcher Mazisuk and the one-hundred-year-old Binjomin Frenkel. They were beaten to death for 'Communist crimes.'"

Zeleny's troops carried out at least fourteen further pogroms in the region, killing at least 2,000 people. The Jews of the district capital, Trypillya, didn't escape the violence. In 2009, a pompous statue of Zeleny as a "fighter for the freedom of Ukraine" was erected there. Nearby there had long been a memorial site that in Soviet fashion remembered the joint Jewish and Communist victims of the civil war. It was turned into a museum for Ukrainian folklore.

On February 15, 1919, nationalist Ukrainian units committed a massacre on a new scale, one of the bloodiest in this period as a whole, in Proskuriv (Proskurov), about 240 kilometers east of Lviv. The city had 50,000 inhabitants, split evenly between Christians and Jews. Like in Ovruch, residents originally seem to have gotten along. Among the fifty members of the city council, twenty-four were Jews and twenty-six Christians. The mayor was Polish, as was the chairman of the city council.

Around ten days before the pogrom, Cossacks from the Ukrainian Republican Army occupied the city. Their leader was Ataman Ivan Semosenko, and they quickly overcame a rebellion by Bolshevist-leaning soldiers from the local garrison. Together with the Third Haidamak

Regiment, a paramilitary band of irregulars, Petliura's Cossacks then turned their attention to the city's Jews. Within a few hours they had butchered 1,650 people, orphaning 960 children. Polish and Ukrainian residents were spared their wrath.

Heifetz wrote a twenty-page summary of the testimony of eyewitnesses. It began: "The mass of the Jews had hardly heard of the Bolshevik revolt which had occurred in the barracks. Accustomed in recent times to all kinds of firing, they paid no particular attention to the shots which were heard that morning. It was Saturday and the orthodox Jews had gone early to the synagogue, where they prayed, and then, returning home, sat down to the Sabbath dinner. Many, according to established custom, after the Sabbath dinner, had lain down to sleep."

In the early afternoon, several hundred Cossacks rode in military formation to the Jewish quarter. They were led by a musical unit playing the song that was then and still is the Ukrainian national anthem, *"Szcze ne wmerla Ukrainy ni slava, ni volya"* (Glory and freedom are not yet dead in Ukraine). At exactly 2 p.m., they spread out in groups of five to fifteen. One eyewitness, Schenkmann, recalled: "With perfectly calm faces they entered the houses, took their sabers, and began to cut down all the Jews in the houses, without distinction of age or sex. They killed old men, women, and even nursing babies. They not only cut them down with the sword, but also thrust them through with bayonets. They resorted to firing only in case individuals succeeded in breaking out into the street. Then bullets were sent after them. When news of the beginning of the massacre spread among the Jews, they began to hide in attics and cellars, but the Cossacks dragged them down from the attics and killed them. Into the cellars they threw hand grenades."

The eyewitness report, cited by Heifetz, continued: "According to the testimony the Cossacks killed [Schenkmann's] younger brother on the street near the house, and then ran into the house and split the skull of his mother. The other members of the family hid under beds, but when his little brother saw his mother die he crept out from under the bed to kiss her body. The Cossacks started to cut down the boy. Then the old father could endure it no longer and also came out from under the bed, and one of the Cossacks killed him with two shots." Schenkmann himself somehow escaped unharmed.

A survivor named Marantz described how fifteen people were killed and four seriously wounded in a friend's home. When Marantz asked his Christian neighbors to help him dress the wounds of those injured, one woman lent him a hand while the others refused.

A Mrs. Grünfeld reported observing from her window as roughly twenty Haidamaka Cossacks stopped in front of the house across the street, which belonged to the Kashelev family. Four of them forced their way into the neighboring home of the Schiffmanns but emerged before long and cleaned off their bloody sabers in the snow. A short time later, it became known that they had massacred eight people.

An eyewitness named Spiegel told of having been on a visit with his brother to a family named Potekha, when he heard about the violence. Worried about his mother, he returned home and accompanied the elderly lady via back roads to some Polish acquaintances. But they turned her away, fearing for their lives if they took her in. When Spiegel returned to the Potekhas' house, Christian onlookers warned him against entering the building, because a massacre was going on. Concerned about his brother, he ignored their advice.

He found the entire family and his own brother dead in pools of blood. The family matriarch had been so badly mutilated that he could only identify her by her physical shape. "Near her lay the body of her son, hacked with saber-cuts and thrust through with bayonets. In the same manner her oldest daughter had been killed. The youngest daughter was also killed, and the middle one was lying severely wounded. A woman relative visiting them was also severely wounded. In the yard were two brothers Bressler and their aged mother. His brother was severely wounded, but still breathing, and died in his arms." Spiegel added, "Out of curiosity Christian neighbors came into the house, and I asked them to help me lay the wounded on beds, but they refused. Only one neighbor named Sikora rendered me some help. Two of the wounded died; the rest recovered, but remained cripples."

Such is the tenor of Heifetz's depiction of how 1,640 people were slaughtered in the space of less than four hours. The Cossacks' mission was murder. Their orders were not to rob or rape their victims. That was why they were so quick to carry out their butchery—and why civilians from Proskuriv had the chance to profit by stealing from those who had been killed. They were aided in their larceny by the macabre fact that the city's Jews, the vast majority of whom were Orthodox, had lit their lamps that Friday because they were forbidden to light fires or turn on electricity on the Sabbath. After the killing there was no one left to extinguish those lights, which guided Christian plunderers to Jewish homes, where they stole the effects of the deceased and desecrated their corpses. Ukrainian farmers had been hired to dig a mass grave, 64 meters long by 21 meters wide, at the cemetery. But here, too, locals stole clothing, pried gold fillings from the mouths of the dead, and cut off murdered women's fingers to get their rings. The dead weren't laid to rest until Monday.

The day of the massacre the Haidamak troops moved on to Felshtyn, twenty-five kilometers to the west of Proskuriv. Three days later, on February 18, 1919, they committed their next major atrocity. As had not been the case in the previous days, they raped a large number of women and looted and attacked 665 Jews, of whom 600 died immediately or soon thereafter. The dead represented a third of Felshtyn's Jewish population.[43]

Today there are almost no Jews living in this part of the world, although even as late as 1941, the terribly tortured Jewish community of Proskuriv, then part of the Soviet Union, had still numbered 14,518. But on July 7 of that year, German soldiers took the city. Before long, the occupiers had set up a forced labor camp for Jews from the towns and environs. Inmates were put to work building roads, a backbreaking task. The first mass shootings took place between August and November. Over the course of the following two years, Germans had 17,200 Jews from Proskuriv and the surrounding area murdered.[44]

The "Haidamaks"—A Ukrainian Ballad of Blood

In the days after the Proskuriv massacre, lone Jews, many of whom were on the move in fields, the forest, nearby villages and hamlets, continued to be killed.[45] Such murders, carried out spontaneously whenever soldiers happened upon Jews, were largely committed by the Third Haidamak Regiment.

The novelist Mikhail Bulgakov describes what this sort of roadside killing must have been like in his novel *The White Guard*, written in the early twenties. Bulgakov wrote:

On the night of February 2nd to the 3rd [1919], at the snow-covered approach to the Chain Bridge across the Dnieper two men were dragging a man in a torn black overcoat, his face bruised and bloodstained. A cossack sergeant was running alongside them and hitting the man over the head with a ramrod. His head jerked at each blow, but the bloodstained man was past crying out and only groaned. The ramrod cut hard and viciously into the tattered coat and each time the man responded with a hoarse cry.

"Ah, you dirty Yid!" the sergeant roared in fury. "We're going to see you shot! I'll teach you to skulk in the dark corners. I'll show you! What were you doing behind those piles of timber? Spy!"

But the bloodstained man did not reply to the cossack sergeant. Then the sergeant ran ahead, and the two men jumped aside to escape the flailing rod with its heavy, glittering brass tip. Without calculating the force of his blow the sergeant brought down the ramrod like a thunderbolt on to the man's head. Something cracked inside it and the man in black did not even groan. Thrusting up his arm, head lolling, he slumped from his knees to one side and with a wide sweep of his other arm he flung it out as though he wanted to scoop up more of the trampled and dung-stained snow. His fingers curled hook-wise and clawed at the dirty snow. Then the figure lying in the dark puddle twitched convulsively a few times and lay still.

An electric lamp hissed above the prone body, the anxious shadows of the two pig-tailed haidamaks fluttered around him, and above the lamp was a black sky and blinking stars.

As the man slumped to the ground, the star that was the planet Mars suddenly exploded in the frozen firmament above the City, scattered fire and gave a deafening burst.

After the star the distant spaces across the Dnieper, the distance leading to Moscow, echoed to a long, low boom. And immediately a second star plopped in the sky, though lower, just above the snow-covered roofs.

At that moment the Blue Division of the haidamaks marched over the bridge, into the City, through the City and out of it for ever.

Behind the Blue Division, the frost-bitten horses of Kozyr-Leshko's cavalry regiment crossed the bridge at a wolfish lope followed by a rumbling, bouncing field-kitchen . . . then it all disappeared as if it had never been. All that remained was the stiffening corpse of a Jew on the approach to the bridge, some trampled hay and horse-dung.

And the corpse was the only evidence that Petliura was not a myth but had really existed.[46]

The regiments took the name Haidamak from the depths—or perhaps abysses—of Ukrainian history. Haidamaks (also transliterated as gaidamaks) were fighters who, more than a century after the Proskuriv Revolt of 1648, launched a further bloody rebellion of peasants and Cossacks against the mainly Polish large landowners in the region in 1768. They murdered thousands of Jews along with aristocrats, Jesuits, and Catholic clergymen. Later these massacres of Poles and Jews were glorified as acts of heroism by the writer Taras Ševčenko, who is held in high esteem in Russia and Ukraine even today, in his ballad "Haydamaky" of 1841. Ševčenko wrote of a rich Jew, also called a Jew-swine, squatting and counting ducats, when a soldier pounds on his door and commands him to open it or be beaten. The troops break down the door anyway and whip the man viciously. His daughters are fetched, and they, too, are beaten and abused despite their entreaties and prayers. The blood of "Jews and Poles" is described as running under the door. The narrator says that if he had a thousand hands, he would strangle all the "vermin," and not a soul would remain alive in the town of Lysianka.[47] With next to no authorial distance, Ševčenko celebrates rape, robbery, and murder in the name of Ukraine—something most contemporary secondary literature prefers to ignore. He is still considered Ukraine's most important national poet. The same was true in the Stalinist era. "Haydamaky" was also published to great acclaim three times in Communist East Germany. In the Third Reich and afterward, Ukraine specialist Hans Koch, a self-declared historian and the man who organized Ukrainian collaboration with the Nazis, was among the leading Ševčenko admirers and imitators.[48]

The model for the 1768 murder of Jews Ševčenko found so worthy of praise was provided a hundred years earlier by Hetman Khmelnytsky, whom the German occupiers in spring 1918 promoted as a Ukrainian national hero. Ševčenko revered him as a spiritual and practical predecessor of the haidamaks he celebrated. In the Polish-Russian War of 1648–1653, Khmelnytsky's Cossacks had also carried out large-scale pogroms, killing tens of thousands of Jews. A full century later, the haidamaks emulated the murders carried out by the rebels under Khmelnytsky's command. For this reason, Simon Dubnow characterized the mass killings of 1918–21 as the "third haidamak eruption."[49]

In 1954, the Soviet government was very keen on consolidating Ukraine, which had been subject to such abuse by German troops during the Second World War, and encouraging a controlled, regional nationalism there. For instance, Khrushchev "gave" the Ukrainian Soviet Socialist Republic Crimea. This "gift" coincided with the three-hundredth anniversary of the 1654 Treaty that, at Khmelnytsky's request, rescued the Ukrainian Cossack state from Polish threat by making it a Russian protectorate. To mark the ceremonial occasion, celebrated in half Ukrainian-nationalist and half Russian-imperialist fashion, a special stamp commemorating Khmelnytsky was issued, new monuments were erected to Ukrainian national poets, thinkers, and heroes, and several cities were renamed, including Proskurov as Khmelnytsky. Ever since 1954, the city in which Ukrainian Cossacks murdered more than 16,000 Jewish civilians in 1918 is known by a name honoring the slaughterer Khmelnytsky as a Ukrainian liberation hero.

Enemies in War, Allies in Pogroms

To various extents, all the combatants in the war butchered and robbed Jews. The crimes of some groups may not seem especially grave because those groups controlled only a small amount of territory for short stretches of time, but the intensity of the violence was serious indeed. Taking part in it were everyone from White Russians loyal to the tsar to Ukrainians eager to escape Russian rule to anarchists aiming to destroy the state and dreaming of free associations of those who had been kept down and stripped of their rights. Many of the armed bands and mobs "were permanently changing sides," as Lidia Miliakova writes, and it was common for individual soldiers and whole divisions to go over to the enemy. Their leaders "were constantly concluding new, mostly fluid alliances, whose only common element was anti-Jewish pogroms."[50]

Anarchists, who fought for peasant self-rule and communist council freedom, were no less active in carrying out pogroms than Ukrainian nationalists. Under the pretext of class warfare, they stole whatever they could from Jews. Their leader, Nestor Machno, who fancied himself a cosmopolitan internationalist and lent his name to the Machnovshchina Partisan movement, gave his men free rein. His political ideas followed those of the virulent Russian anti-Semite and anarchist Mikhail Bakunin.[51] In 1908, Machno had aligned himself with the terrorist wing of the Russian populist *narodniki*.

For three years, Machno's men carried out pogroms in various places in the Mariupol and Donetsk districts. For example, on September 8, 1919, they entered Sofyevka in Yekaterinoslav province "under the black flag of the anarchists." There they robbed Jews, rich and poor, often down to the shirts off their backs, and raped and murdered the most unfortunate victims. Similar scenes were reported in the small cities of Khlebodarovka, Satichiye, and Nadioynaya.[52]

The troops of the warlord Nikifor Grigoriev were relatively few in number but particularly homicidal. In the First World War, Grigoriev had been a Russian army officer. In December 1918, he and his men joined up with Petliura's troops, but by February 1919 he was made a general in the Red Army. Then in May, he refused to follow orders and declared his independence, taking with him 15,000 heavily armed men, mostly peasants' sons from Southern Ukraine. He declared that he was pursuing a social revolutionary but also anti-Bolshevist, anti-

Jewish agenda. He called upon Ukrainians to throw off the yoke of the "Jewish servant" Lenin, to cleanse the country of Bolshevik commissars and "foreign elements," and to create a nationalist Ukrainian socialism. Within the space of weeks, Grigoriev's paramilitaries had carried out 148 pogroms. In the district capital Yelizavetgrad (later Kirovograd in the Cherson governorate), they killed more than a thousand Jews from May 15 to 17, 1919, alone. All in all, they butchered well over 5,000 Jewish people.[53]

Having temporarily gained ground, White Russian troops carried out a particularly large number of acts of violence against Jews when they were forced to retreat in late 1919. In the first phase of their advance in June and July, White Cossacks had only attacked isolated Jews, sometimes pillaging in cities or raping women. In the second phase, from August to October, looting Jewish quarters became routine, and many Jews were murdered. Still, the soldiers were more interested in larceny than anything else, so Jews were often able to deflect any homicidal intention with offers of money. But in the third phase, when the Red Army forced the White Russians to retreat in November and December, they began mass atrocities, taking out their frustration on the most defenseless people they encountered. White Russians may have only been responsible for a fifth of the pogrom murders in Ukraine, but they committed them within a very short span. Citing I. M. Cherikover, Oleg Budnitskii writes: "In this period, the Volunteer Army broke all records. Their pogroms were more intensive than those of the others, the number of victims was higher, and the violence was more widespread." In the small city of Fastov alone, paramilitaries under the command of General Anton Denikin killed more than one thousand Jews, most of them elderly people, women, and children, in August 1919.[54]

As mentioned above, soldiers from the First Red Cavalry Army under the command of General Budyonny also carried out murders and pogroms. Red Army war correspondent Isaak Babel recorded a number of cases. His accounts were first published in Moscow in 1926, earning the author the immediate enmity of Budyonny. From the Volhynian shtetl Berestchko, he reported how the Red Cossack troops he was accompanying rode into town. Shortly after arriving, they hung up posters on telegraph masts announcing that the Divisional War Commissioner Vinogradov would be holding a lecture that evening about the Second Congress of the Communist International. But before the talk came to pass, Babel witnessed the following scene: "Directly in front of my windows, several Cossacks were about to execute a gray-bearded old Jew for spying. The old man whimpered and kept squirming free. Then Kudrya from the machine gun unit grabbed the man by the head and put it under his armpit. The Jew fell silent and splayed his legs. Kudrya took out a dagger with his right hand and carefully stabbed the man to death, making sure he didn't get any blood on himself. Then he knocked on the boarded-up window. 'If anyone's interested, you can take him away,' he said. 'The path is free.'"[55]

Soldiers from the Sixth Division of the First Red Cavalry Army committed similar murders in September 1919 in Polonnoye in the district of Proskurov. An investigation into these crimes found cavalry soldiers turning not only against Jews, but some Communists: "In the days of the Sixth Division's retreat before Polish troops, the view took hold in several units: 'Let's cleanse the backward regions of Yids'; 'Let's do as our good old father Machno did'; 'Put down the Yids, the Commissars and the Communists!' The military and political leadership of the division didn't do anything at all to intervene against these slogans." The resulting pogrom was simply allowed to take its course. The report of the Extraordinary Investigative Committee of Revolutionary Military Soviets on the war crimes committed by its own Red Army troops continued: "The next day, Comrade Chepelev crossed through Polonnoye, where Red Army soldiers were still plundering. After dispersing them, he saw an orderly and the nurse Maria Chumakova of the Thirty-Third Regiment stripping the last items of value from a dead Jew. When the orderly fled, Chepelev shot him and arrested the nurse. But Chumakova succeeded in informing other soldiers that Chepelev had killed the orderly. They in turn shot Chepelev dead and acted as though nothing unusual had happened. No one informed on the murderer, although presumably the soldiers all knew him."[56]

In 1914, Jews owned 95 percent of all businesses and companies in Polonnoye. In 1917, soldiers from the regular army of the tsar killed 98 Jews in the city. After the Russians retreated, 25 Jews were conscripted to serve in the Ukrainian People's Republic army and were murdered by their fellow soldiers in their barracks. In the spring of 1919, Red Army troops carried out an initial pogrom, killing 8 Jews. In 1910, 15,257 Jews lived in Polonnoye. By 1923, there were only 5,080. During the First World War and the Russian civil war, the majority of Jews had fled the hotly contested city.

In 1939 there were still 4,171 Jews living in Polonnoye, accounting for 30 percent of the city's residents. In August 1941, German invaders shot 19 Jews as "Communist agents." On August 23, 113 more Jewish men were killed. On September 2, SS men, assisted by Ukrainian police, murdered 2,000 men, women, and children. A ghetto was established. The Germans forced 1,300 Jews, including some from surrounding areas, to do slave labor in a granite quarry. Meanwhile, "murder, robbery and destruction became everyday occurrences." June 25, 1942, saw the next mass executions, in which 1,270 Jews were killed. On January 9, 1944, Red Army soldiers liberated Polonnoye. Only eleven Jews had survived. Ukrainian families had hidden them, sometimes for money, but in all cases endangering their own lives.[57]

Hungarian historian and Holocaust survivor Peter Kenez describes the motivations of the pogrom initiators as follows: "It was . . . much easier to destroy the 'enemy' in a Jewish settlement than on a battlefield. Loot was the driving force and antisemitism, fanned by official propaganda, only justified the looting." The British journalist John Hodgson reported from White Russian headquarters: "The officers and the men of the army laid practically all the blame for their country's trouble on the Hebrew." And Heifetz concluded: "On the basis of exaggerated reports of 'the wealth of the Jews,' there developed among the peasants a feeling of envy and a desire for city products (manufactured goods, shoes), of which there was nothing in the Ukrainian village, rumor having it that the Jews in the larger centers enjoyed a superfluity of such things."

Just like the Ukrainian and Russian nationalists, Russian liberals, who had joined the umbrella Constitutional Democratic Party, kept close tabs on public opinion. At their party conference on November 3–6, 1919, in Kharkiv, they passed a resolution that can only be read in context as an incitement to carry out pogroms. It read: "The anti-Bolshevism of Jews is fraudulent. They're trying to save their own skins. Nothing else." A number of Russian Orthodox patriarchs also blamed Jews for causing Bolshevism. In so doing, they justified Christians' violating the sixth and tenth commandments. Other groups accused Jews of being members or servants of the bourgeoisie, financial speculators, and exploiters, and held them chiefly responsible for the suffering caused by five years of world and civil war.[58]

4

Minorities and Migrants

THE END OF FREE MOVEMENT

On the eve of the First World War, sociologists Eugen Doctor and Werner Sombart described the mass emigration of Jews as a release valve for the anti-Semitic pressure in Eastern Europe. At the same time, they predicted that this valve would soon be closed—and that the large Jewish minorities in Eastern Europe would be subject to even more discrimination. That was precisely how things turned out. No sooner had the Paris Peace Treaties of 1919 and 1920 been signed than the US radically throttled back immigration. A short time later, Australia, Canada, and other countries followed suit. That blocked paths out of Europe that many Jews had used. No longer did they have the option of escaping pogroms, revolution, and economic misery by fleeing abroad. They had nowhere to go. Just as Doctor and Sombart foresaw, the postwar situation of the so-called titular nations based on a single dominant ethnic group—Poland, Lithuania, Hungary, Romania, and as of 1933, Germany—encouraged hatred and pitiless state discrimination.

Public opinion in the US had also shifted since the First World War.

Revulsion at the ethnic hatred in tumultuous, impoverished Europe was mixed with fear that America would be forced to admit "human wrecks" instead of strong-bodied immigrants. In August 1920, the *New York Times* quoted the publisher of the *Jewish Daily News*, Leon Kamaiky, describing the situation and dreams of Polish Jews as follows: "If there were in existence a ship that could hold 3,000,000 human beings, the 3,000,000 Jews of Poland would board it and escape to America."[1] Statements like this even made their way into congressional debates. Within a few years, the prevailing opinion had come to hold that immigrants endangered American standards of living, imported poverty, caused the growth of slums, and exposed US workers to cutthroat wage competition. In addition, America at the time was suffering under the effects of demobilization, and the rapid mechanization of agriculture was driving hundreds of thousands of people into the cities in search of work.

The American Turnaround

The Emergency Quota Act of the summer of 1921 inaugurated a turnaround in American immigration policy, establishing strict ceilings on the number of people from European countries, Asia, Africa, and Australia allowed to enter. Congress had initially envisioned that the act would stay in force for three years, but clear majorities emerged for the permanent 1924 Immigration Law, which was expressly designed "to limit the immigration of aliens into the United States." The quotas from 1921 to 1924 were drastically reduced—to the detriment of Eastern and Southern Europeans far more than Northern and Western Europeans. Henceforth, ethnic considerations would limit the chances of Europeans as well Asians and Africans to move to the US. Further restrictions followed in 1929 and 1930.

Whereas from 1901 to 1910, 976,263 Jews, mostly from Eastern Europe, came to the US, from 1921 to 1925 that number was only 280,000; from 1926 to 1930, 55,000, and from 1931 to 1935, only 18,000. The effects of the new regulations are all the clearer when we examine individual years. In 1921, 119,000 Jews immigrated to the

US. In 1924, 10,000, and in 1932 only 2,700 Jews came. The figures are similar for all immigrants to the US. Between 1901 and 1910, 8.8 million Europeans relocated to the US, while between 1931 and 1938, a mere 375,000 arrived legally.

During the Great Depression, the US, Canada, and Australia almost completely closed what few small avenues of immigration still remained. In the spring of 1930, South Africa issued "the strictest of restrictions on immigration from Eastern and Southern European countries," and Guatemala, Peru, Argentina, and Brazil did the same. In 1936, the US relaxed the criteria for accepting Jews in reaction to the growing terrorization of Jews in Nazi Germany. As a result, 151,000 Jews were allowed to immigrate to the US between 1936 and 1942. They were almost exclusively from Western and Central Europe and accounted for 40 percent of all immigrants to the US during this period.[2]

As a rule, Eastern European Jewish emigrants passed through the Schlesischer Bahnhof train station (today's Ostbahnhof) in Berlin. The Aid Organization of German Jews maintained a kind of shelter for the people in transit, who encountered all kinds of problems and obstacles in their search for a new home. In December 1930, the Berlin newspaper *Abend* published an anonymous report on the lives and suffering of the people who slept in this large hall, calling this phenomenon "a piece of world history."

The author wrote: "A large space in the Schlesischer Bahnhof, in which trains arrive from Russia and Poland, Romania and the Baltic states. It's furnished simply and usefully. Signs in Yiddish, Russian and Polish say that visitors will be given as much tea as they want, shelter when necessary and, what is often more necessary, information and advice. The history of the Aid Organization of German Jews is the history of the European East." The author went on to list the Russian pogroms, discuss restrictive American immigration policies and their effect on European Jews, and mention the problems in the Berlin immigrants' hall. "Trains full of immigrants are announced and met at the station. There is a lot to do. Immigrants are given as much medical treatment as possible, and above all, malicious elements are kept away from the migrants. It's no accident that Schlesischer Bahnhof is a hive of pickpockets. A migrant enters the hall. Immediately an Aid Organization official is there to help, inquiring where he comes from and asking about his passport and papers and his wishes and worries, and then offering him a glass of tea. Much human misery passes through this hall in Schlesischer Bahnhof, for it is always the poor and oppressed who must leave their homeland to seek their uncertain fortune in the great wide world. But there is also much help offered here to protect these people in need."[3]

Many of the migrants in the 1920s got stuck in Bremerhaven and Hamburg because something was amiss with their visas or boat tickets, or the country they were headed to had just tightened up its immigration policies. "Innumerable individual and family tragedies of indescribable terribleness played themselves out. There were desperate struggles of uprooted people for a visa or at least a residency and work permit, hopeless tragedies of separation and migration in which women and children, aged and ill people are insolubly trapped." In its 1930 annual report, the head of the Aid Organization complained about the "rigid immigration policies" and increasing "disrespect for human rights and the duties of humanity." The volunteers did their best to "point the unfortunate victims of the postwar order to a destination that would give them the freedom and opportunity to better themselves, and to protect them from dissolution and downfall."

One consequence of the American closed-door policy was the increasing popularity of Zionism. Slowly but surely, more and more Jews under threat began to discuss emigrating to barely arable parts of Palestine. From January to April 1924, some 500 Jews a month left Europe, mostly Eastern Europe, for the territories under British mandate. That May the US cut back immigration quotas for a second time, and by August the number of Jews heading for Palestine shot up to 2,400. "Anti-Semitism in Europe and immigration restrictions in the New World have become the worst enemies of Arab Palestine and the best friends of Jewish Palestine," wrote Viennese Zionist Wolfgang Weisl in 1925.

Jews who had been made homeless bought land in Eretz Israel and began rebuilding their lives. Since the land would have to be transformed quickly, Weisl figured that Arabs would revolt, something he deemed "justified and in accordance with nature." Weisl predicted that it would not be possible to reach an amicable agreement because the situation was characterized by deep-seated "economic and economic-cultural conflicts that could not be solved by compromises and concessions." As the new arrivals brought with them typewriters, telephones, cinemas, electricity, and European-American forms of the economy, Arabs would be forced to give up ways of life they had maintained since the days of Abraham. In 1925, referring to the First World War, Weisl registered with delight that in the wake of "the greatest of all wars," the Jewish people were now returning to their land, "the Holy Land," after 1,800 years. Since 1919, the number of Jewish settlers in the territory of Britain's Palestinian mandate had more than doubled. By late June 1925, it was 128,000.[4]

Nationalist Two-Class System of Rights

Until 1914, along with foreign emigration, internal European migration lessened the impact of economic crises and structural transformation. But after the war, the possibilities of moving from densely populated, increasingly impoverished agricultural regions to rapidly growing industrial centers were very limited in the newly created nation-states of Eastern and Southeastern Europe. Jews and Christians alike found themselves abruptly cut off from former metropoles and economically prosperous areas because thousands of new borders within Europe destroyed the age-old routes of internal migration that had always compensated for social pressures.

With the demise of the old, monarchic states of Europe, Poles, who had previously been ruled by Germans, could no longer look for work in Berlin or the Ruhr Valley. The new borders cut off routes to Vienna, Chernivtsi, Budapest, and Trieste for the poor Jews of Eastern Galicia. Impoverished Lithuanian villagers could no longer do day labor in the textile factories of Łódź or the coal mines and steelworks of Dombrowa, industrial centers that had been part of tsarist Russia and produced goods for a gigantic empire stretching all the way to

Vladivostok. The results were bankruptcies, unemployment, and poverty. People could no longer move to other parts of the world or of their own native lands. Instead those countries demanded that whole segments of the population, who in their eyes were not part of the nation, be denaturalized to free up space for the suffering majority. As a consequence of such repression, hundreds of thousands of people tried to cross the new borders. But in doing so, they became economic refugees, undesirables, and stateless people. In 1933, some 70,000 Jews who weren't German citizens lived in Germany.

"In every hell there is an ultimate abyss, and the Austrian anti-Semites already talk gleefully about what they call 'tiger hunts,'" wrote Israel Zangwill in 1924. "In Romania, fascists are conspiring and threatening to eradicate the entire Jewish population. In unfortunate Hungary, where the economy teaches the virtues of patience, the Danube would be nearly crammed with Jewish corpses. In Poland, Jews risk their lives when entering a train carriage, and the most recent prank of this nouveau riche beggar of a country is that every [Polish] corporation has the right to exclude Jewish shareholders."[5]

The rulers of the unstable, large multinational states like Russia, Austria-Hungary, and the Ottoman Empire before the First World War may have given various ethnic groups unequal rights and responsibilities, but they never planned to simply drive them out. That abruptly changed with the rise of the new nation-states in the nineteenth and early twentieth centuries. There had always been moderate levels of friction between what was now defined as the national core and ethnic and religious minorities, and everywhere from the Baltic to the Aegean Sea, revolutionary nationalists ratcheted up that tension until it was unbearable.

This process took place in countries that had been materially ravaged and decimated and that lacked internal mobility, self-confidence, generally accepted constitutional organs, and economic prospects. The much celebrated overthrowing in 1917 and 1918 of old authorities, hierarchies, and conventions created a climate conducive to the springing up of hatred everywhere. The end of autocratically maintained power fanned the embers of anti-Semitism and violence because the newly constituted nations allowed a far greater radius of activity for nationalist chauvinism than the multinational monarchies had done. Moreover, democracy, nationalism, and socialism elevated different principles of equality, thereby rendering certain ethnic, linguistic, social, or religious categories unequal, depending on the focus. Jews could be discriminated against, expropriated, and hounded under all four.

The Zionist Leon Chasanowitsch paid attention to these connections when he documented the post-independence pogroms in Poland in 1919. He considered "the outbreaks of violence and massacres" not as acts of desperation and revenge of a "social class threatened with decline" but as "the first attempt by a nation that had been held down for half a century and now laid claim to rule to make use of its new-found freedom." It was the expression of intoxication of victory of "a popular element possessing the vices of both masters and slaves." Chasanowitsch's analysis ended on a depressing note: "we see before us the Jew-murdering Poland and seek in vain the better Poland that condemns and prevents such homicidal deeds."[6]

The omnipresent protectionism in this world of newly created nation-states was directed both internally and externally. Legislators and government administrators everywhere created a nationalistic, two-class system. The political project of the nation-states was to encourage the social and economic betterment of the ethnic majority and to create, as quickly as possible, a loyal middle class. Especially in times of crisis, it seemed logical to combine the rise of one group with the fall of others.

Such nationalist emancipation projects hit all minorities hard, whether they were Germans in Poland and Romania, Poles in Lithuania, Hungarians in Yugoslavia, or Lithuanians in Poland. Long before Germany began its "Aryanization" programs in 1933, robbing Jews of careers and assets to the benefit of the ethnic majority, other nations began Polishization, Latvianization, Lithuanianization, and Hellenization initiatives that disadvantaged resident minorities. For example, until 1918, Jews owned one-third of the major property in Austrian-controlled Bukovina. Jews and other minorities were the big losers when the region's new Romanian rulers reformed property laws in 1921. The economic discrimination against many minorities, including Jews, was not based on racist programs but on the positive desire to benefit the majority to the greatest possible extent. This aim became especially popular in the democratically conceived states. It tied the electoral majority of the populace to its new elites.[7]

"It is only natural that the world war, which marked the conclusion of the great period of global discovery, also put an end to freedom of migration," concluded the demographers Alexander and Eugen Kulischer, who themselves had migrated from Russia to Berlin after the Bolshevik Revolution, in 1931. "With the end of the double way out—founding new colonies and occupying new markets—states tried to reserve the basic necessities for survival for their own population.... As the great gates of the Atlantic and of the land of milk and honey, which depicted itself as a refuge for the world's poor and disadvantaged, have loudly slammed shut and are sealed off more and more hermetically, barriers have been erected on borders old and new in the form of restrictions on entry and permission to work. This means that, as in the old days, masses of people are piling up and pressing in at all of the closed and partly closed gateways, large and small, and explosive tensions are building in every nook and cranny."[8]

In reaction to such conditions, the peace treaties of 1919 and 1920 included provisions protecting the rights of national minorities. In late January 1918, for instance, the government of Poland, newly founded under German authority, solemnly declared: "The equality of citizens without regard to descent and confession ... will form the guiding principle of the state."[9] As the years leading up to the next world war would demonstrate, the governments and populations of the newly created nations of Europe tended to forget such declarations quite quickly. Provisions in treaties to protect minorities were soon revealed to be nothing but words.

Still, there were decisive differences. Minorities who had the support of a nation-state of their own could count on protection from "their" fatherland, to which they could always return if things became unbearable in their "host" countries. In fact the men who drew up the

Paris peace treaties reckoned with this sort of migration and a concomitant "voluntary" ethnic homogenization and assimilation under nationalist pressure. But Jews represented, in the words of Hannah Arendt, the "*minorité par excellence*."[10] They had no nation-state or army protecting their backs, nor any territory where they could flee or take refuge. In the Europe of 1920, there were around 7 million Jews in this situation: 3.2 million in what was then Poland, 2 million in the Soviet Union, 780,000 in Romania, 600,000 in Hungary, and 300,000 in the Baltic states. As of 1933, 500,000 mostly assimilated German Jews were added to the numbers of "undesirables" and stripped of their citizenship, and 350,000 Austrian and Czechoslovakian Jews suffered the same fate in 1938 and 1939.

ETHNIC HOMOGENIZATION SINCE 1923

After some vacillation, Greeks joined the First World War on the side of the Entente to fight against their archenemies the Turks and the Bulgarians. For that, Greece was handsomely rewarded at the Paris peace conferences. Greece was given Western Thrace, which had been part of Bulgaria since 1913, and it has held this territory, with the exception of 1941–44, ever since.

In addition, the nation creators in Paris promised their ally the greater part of European territory still in Turkish hands after the Balkan Wars, including the city of Edirne (Adrianople). For a few years, then, Greece extended all the way to the Black Sea. Turkey's only territory in Europe was a thin strip of land between the Dardanelles and the Bosphorus. The Aegean Islands were also ceded to Greece, albeit without the Dodecanese, including Rhodes, which Italy had seized in its war against the Ottoman Empire in 1912. The Turkish city of Izmir (Smyrna), on the Asia Minor side of the Aegean, and the surrounding area became Greek as well. Muslims represented a majority of roughly 60 percent in Izmir, but Christian Greeks, who were also numerous, had significantly more economic power.

Encouraged and supported by the British with arms, money, and military advisors, Greek troops had made the status of Izmir a fait accompli, occupying the city on May 15, 1919, and murdering at least a thousand Muslim civilians the day the troops marched in. But the goals of the Greek offensive, known as the *megali idea*, or "great idea," went much further. Unlike the adherents of the Greek monarchy, republican politicians in particular propagated the creation of a greater Greek empire stretching from Constantinople to the Asian coastlines of the Black Sea, which included a significant portion of the Turkish Aegean coast. In conjunction with Greece, British statesmen even eyed the possibility of taking Constantinople (Istanbul) away from the Turks.

With such war aims in mind, Greek troops advanced almost to Ankara in 1920, carrying out countless massacres of Muslims, before what the German-language Hungarian newspaper *Pester Lloyd* called their "insane project" met indomitable Turkish resistance. With the Greeks forced to retreat in June 1921, thousands of Greek civilians fell victim to Turkish reprisals. Greek politicians would later downplay their war of aggression as "ill-conceived," while the warmongering British prime minister David Lloyd George consoled them with warm words from the Lower House of Parliament on August 4, 1922, saying that Greek troops in Asia Minor had achieved more than any other army could have.[11]

Forced Exchange of Populations

The 1923 Treaty of Lausanne officially ended hostilities between the Ottoman Empire and the Entente. At the insistence of the League of Nations, which was established in 1920, the parties concerned had signed a preliminary treaty on January 30, 1923, agreeing upon an exchange of populations between Turkey and Greece. That treaty envisioned "unmixing" two "peoples," who were, to be more precise, adherents of different religions. Under the influence of Fridtjof Nansen, the League's high commissioner on refugees and prisoners of war, and after endless dillydallying, diplomats in Lausanne took a decision and forced through a quick "final peace arrangement." It featured something previously unknown in international law: the forced resettlement of minorities. At the start of the peace conference on December 1, 1922, Nansen had supported this drastic measure, arguing that the undeniable hardship it entailed would be less "than the hardship that would come about if nothing were done."

The peace negotiators assumed that "the suffering that will doubtlessly be caused will be offset by the advantages both countries will ultimately derive from a greater homogeneity of the populace and the eradication of old, deeply rooted conflicts." At the time, Greece had a population of 5 million. It faced having to accept around 1.5 million refugees and people forced to resettle from Asia Minor, Eastern Thrace, and Bulgaria. Three hundred thousand of them died in camps of hunger and disease before international help could arrive. Eighty percent of the refugees were women and children. A whole generation of men had died as soldiers during the war or had been killed as civilians.

In return, 350,000 Turks, chiefly from northern Greece, were transferred to those cities on the coast of Asia Minor where Greeks had lived for centuries. With religion being the decisive criterion, 20,000 so-called Cretan Turks, Muslim Greeks who spoke not a word of Turkish, were also forced to leave their homes. The same thing happened to tens of thousands of Muslim Albanians in northern Greece, which had been conquered in 1912. Turkish Christians were also forcibly resettled in Greece. Nansen spoke of "tribal comrades of one faith." Religion became such a central criterion because the Turkish delegation had absolutely refused to use the European categories of race or ethnicity but insisted that faith be the deciding factor for the transfer of populations and the protection of minorities. Exceptions to the forced resettlements were made for the Greeks of Constantinople and the Muslims of Western Thrace. But many of these people moved anyway to escape harassment by the Turkish and Greek sides.

People in these places had lived for centuries grouped according to professions and neighborhoods, traditions and religions, and had dealt with the affairs of their towns, cities, and regions jointly, if not always harmoniously. Following the war and the Treaty of Lausanne, they became mere pawns of nationalist politics. The members of a mixed commission that included supposedly neutral members from the League of Nations supervised the transfer of populations. They tried to mediate in cases of conflict such as that of the widow W. and her children. Her husband's family had been born Jewish but converted to Islam, and she herself came from an Islamic Greek background on her father's side and an Albanian one on her mother's side. Was her resettlement to Turkey legitimate?

Nansen arranged for the League of Nations to issue an international loan of 14 million British pounds to help the government in Athens build housing and create jobs for the new arrivals and fertilize arid land. In the end Nansen was satisfied with the job he'd done, announcing publicly that "what originally seemed to be a misfortune for the country has been transformed into a glorious success."[12] The Turkish government had to cope with resettling far fewer people, but faced the task of populating a number of villages and towns formerly occupied by Greeks. So it immediately began "bringing home" tens of thousands of Muslims from Bulgaria, Yugoslavia, Romania, and the Soviet Union. The nationalization and resettlement of minorities of Turkish descent, such as the Crimean Tartars, continued until the end of the twentieth century. In Greece, too, the national office for receiving and settling people of Greek descent became a long-term institution. After the upheavals of 1989, 100,000 Pontic Greeks were "repatriated in the motherland." These were people whose forefathers had lived in the lands around the Black Sea for centuries.

Representatives from Britain, France, Italy, the US, and the European states bordering on Greece and Turkey had participated in the Lausanne conference. With only one exception they all agreed to the forced resettlements—the American representative rejected the idea because it ran contrary to the American idea of the individual's right to life, liberty, and the pursuit of happiness. Britain's conservative foreign secretary, George Curzon, voted for the agreement while condemning the treaty as "a thoroughly bad and vicious solution, for which the world will pay a heavy penalty for a hundred years to come." Many of the delegates shared his opinion. But as ugly and out of step with conventional international law as the compulsory exchange of populations was, the politicians considered it a justifiable instrument in certain situations. Curzon himself characterized it as the quickest and most efficient way to bring the mass flight that was already progressing under control and to end the massive death toll among civilians and pacify the situation. The preliminary agreement about the exchange of populations in January led to the Greek-Turkish peace in Lausanne in the summer of 1923, which superseded the 1920 Treaty of Sèvres and called into question all the peace agreements of Paris.[13] Over the course of the twentieth century, more than fifty million people were displaced and forcibly resettled because of their ethnicity, language, social identity, or religion.

Policies of Ethnic Violence Begin to Spread

In 1927, the main representative of the German minority in Latvia, Paul Schiemann, warned against solving nationality conflicts by forcibly resettling people. He recognized the danger of exclusion inherent within the idea of national self-determination, which when carried to the logical extreme would lead to the "violent and brutal transplantation" of parts of the population from one state to another—"with all of its pernicious consequences."[14] For some years, European diplomats had considered the Treaty of Lausanne the absolute exception, one they had been forced to make by the pressure of circumstances in order to avoid the killing of hundreds of thousands of innocents in a relatively uncivilized part of the world. But gradually, an increasing number of political leaders and policy makers began to see the transfer of populations as a favored way of creating lasting peace in difficult configurations, of "unweaving" hostile ethnic groups and "replanting" them.

One of the pioneers of this school of thought was the German historian Karl C. Thalheim. In the 1930 edition of the *Archiv für Auswanderungswesen* (Archive for Emigration) journal, he identified a change in the politics of emigration proceeding in tandem with dramatically decreasing numbers of people leaving their homelands for abroad. "The flow of migrants around the world is less about liberal ideas of freedom than about state economic planning," he wrote. Thalheim announced that he would expand on such planning in a further edition, but although he apparently already had a basic outline in mind, it wouldn't appear until 1941.

In that same journal, another author soon expressed his outrage at the compulsory Greek-Turkish exchange of populations. "One and a half million people were driven from their homes and farms in the age of humanism," the author wrote. "They lost everything except what they could carry with them." Three years later, in 1933, the journal offered slightly different figures: "Two million people were 'pushed back and forth' because of a 'peace' document."

Officially, German intellectuals and diplomats of the 1920s and the first half of the 1930s rejected the Lausanne model. They considered it unthinkable since German minorities in other European countries numbered as many as eight million and, as a result of the territories Germany lost in the Treaty of Versailles, the country already had to accommodate roughly 800,000 people.[15] Hence Germany had always considered this example of semivoluntary or compulsory migration an injustice. In addition, the Great Depression hit Germany particularly hard. Thus, one didn't need to be a right-wing politician or voter to see the Germans as a "people without space"—to quote the title of a popular novel of the time. It was no accident that in *Mein Kampf*, Hitler promoted a course of first expanding "the area of the motherland" and only later merging "new settlers in the closest communion with the land of their origin."[16]

But hardly had the Third Reich been consolidated when the tone changed. By 1935, the following circumstance was noted approvingly in the *Archiv für Auswanderungswesen*: "The characteristic feature in terms of population policies of today's Greece is the basic homogeneity of its populace." In January 1937, the journal *Zeitschrift für Geopolitik*, which was keenly attuned to foreign policy and was published by the geographer and military general Karl Haushofer, printed an editorial note reading: "The great exchange after the end of the Greek-Turkish war was far too rarely appreciated by the public as a possibility and a model. It may have ripped millions of people from their homelands, but it also gave them new lands—a severe but clean solution to the minority question."[17] Haushofer was often cited as a major influence on Hitler's ideology of territorial expansion.

It didn't take long until the forced emigration of minorities, having now achieved international acceptance, was suggested as a way for states to get rid of their Jewish populations. In 1933, Romanian nationalist Gheorghe Cuza put forward Madagascar as the preferred place to achieve a "solution to the Jewish question." His suggestion attracted considerable opposition in the Romanian parliament, but not because his detractors disagreed with Cuza's aims. On the contrary they dismissed his suggestion as frivolous because France would never let its colony be used for this purpose. Still, that same year, former Romanian interior minister and later prime minister Octavian Goga campaigned with the promise that if he took power, a half a million Jews would be forced to leave Romania. That number represented two-thirds of Romania's Jewish population.

The activists of the Pan-Aryan Union in Vienna supported these sorts of projects and translated them to the global level in 1937, proposing that the entire world's Jewish population be sent to Madagascar. The 3.5 million inhabitants of the island, they thought, "could be resettled without difficulty to climatically and racially similar parts of the African mainland (Uganda, Mozambique)" and the depopulated island purchased "for an appropriate price" by Jews. The men drawing up these plans in Vienna described Madagascar as a "sufficiently large living and breeding area" with a healthful climate and unusually fertile soil. As a political precedent, they cited the Treaty of Lausanne, gushing that "the resettlement of both populations had been carried out within a few months and with no special friction," so that "no one could have objected at all to the uprooting of 700,000 Turks and 1,200,000 Greeks from their former historical surroundings." Based on this experience, there was every reason to believe that "the final solution to the Jewish question" could be completed.[18]

On August 15, 1938—a few months after Austria's annexation by Germany, in the immediate wake of the conference on refugees in Évian, several days before German troops entered Sudetenland, and in the middle of a rearmament boom that had led to a labor shortage—the directors of the *Archiv für Auswanderungswesen* declared that because Germany didn't have enough workers at its disposal, the country would soon have to decide whether to repatriate German émigrés. In reaction to an anti-Semitic incident, they noted: "It cannot be denied that since the world war, the extent and effects of ever growing migration of ever larger masses of people (we recall the massive migration of Greek, Turkish, Bulgarian, Armenian and Assyrian refugees as part of exchanges of populations) have consistently been underestimated."

In the next issue, the journal's editors published a translation of a speech by the Liberal member of British parliament Arthur Salter on how to solve the "Jewish emigrant question." Drawing on the example of Greece, Salter argued that Jewish refugees should be permanently settled in British colonies. The Greek experience, he claimed, had shown first that large numbers of refugees could be quickly resettled in new communities and second that government action was necessary to ensure the success of such resettlements.[19]

On August 6, 1939, amid German and Italian negotiations over the resettlement of some 200,000 Germans in southern Tirol, Switzerland's *Neue Zürcher Zeitung* newspaper ran an editorial on what it called "the modern migration of peoples." It wrote: "The resettlement measures in southern Tirol have directed attention to a problem that crops up constantly in the Balkans and Asia Minor. But because the populations concerned are more or less at a primitive level, the public hasn't paid them much mind." For instance, the paper wrote, people had barely noticed that in 1939 alone, 3,100 Turks from Romania and 11,290 from Bulgaria had "returned" to Turkey as part of a plan that the government in Ankara had been "programmatically" pursuing for years, guided by the "experience of the Greek-Turkish exchange of populations." The "positive effect" of this "bitter but promising beginning," the paper claimed, was that "both states have a more unified population" and relations between them had improved. Around the same time, Italian radio commented that a German-Italian agreement would solve the problem of the German population in Alto Adige (southern Tirol) "just as Greece and Turkey solved one of the thorniest minority problems of the postwar era in 1923." Hitler and Mussolini, the radio report continued, would now "resolve the southern Tirol question, albeit with far greater statesmanlike discretion."[20]

The Hellenization of Salonika: 1923–1943

The war Greece had so brashly declared on Turkey ended in disaster. By 1921 it was clear to the aggressors that they would lose the conflict and have to beat a costly retreat. With no hope of victory left, troop morale collapsed, and the desire to compensate by going after defenseless victims increased. In this frame of mind, Greek soldiers carried out a pogrom in Salonika in the summer of 1921, burning down a number of houses and murdering two hundred Jews and Muslims. A little later, in 1922, Prime Minister Eleftherios Venizelos issued unambiguous instructions for how to handle Greece's defeat: "Now that the idea of the largest possible Greater Greece has broken down, we can now only secure the borders of Greater Greece by making Macedonia and Western Thrace not only politically but also ethnically Greek."[21]

Life in Salonika fundamentally changed with the Greek-Turkish treaty on the exchange of populations in January 1923 and the subsequent agreement between Greece and Bulgaria the following year. As a result of those two deals, around 1.5 million destitute people needing resettlement arrived in Greece. But the government in Athens proved utterly incapable of giving the refugees, who mainly settled in the north, what they needed to be self-sufficient. Theoretically, the property of 350,000 expelled Muslims and Bulgarians stood at their disposal. But two-thirds of those assets had in fact been "strewn about" and seized by established Greeks before the refugees even got to the country.[22]

What was at the time the relatively generous loan of 14 million pounds organized by Nansen to resettle people in Greece was largely embezzled or used for other purposes. After the Athens government had spent most of the money and succeeded in getting advance payment of future installments, the creditors had had enough. "Greece is building a large and complicated organization that spends more annually on wages and general costs than it does on helping the settlers," wrote one observer, adding that the "gigantic administrative sums" stood "in no relation" to quality and performance.[23] Most refugees were simply left to fend for themselves and became dissatisfied and angry members of the proletariat. This climate of incompetence and corruption encouraged malevolent jealousy of Salonika's Jews, who had been living in the city for more than five hundred years. In the eyes of the ethnic Greek newcomers, Jews were foreigners who had no business being there.

For the city, the resettlement program meant that 100,000 Greeks from Asia Minor, Bulgaria, and Eastern Thrace arrived while 20,000 Muslims and Bulgarians departed. According to the 1928 census, 250,000 people, including 60,000 Jews, lived in Salonika. Whereas as recently as 1912 Greeks had only made up 18 percent of the city's population, they now represented a majority of 75.5 percent. By contrast, Jews, who had accounted for 60 percent of Salonika's inhabitants, now made up less than a quarter.

The result of the forced resettlements of 1923–24 was the Hellenization of Greece's newly acquired territories. If ten years previously Jews had been the connecting element between various groups within the population, they were now, after the disappearance of other groups, the final concrete "irritant" in a largely homogeneous but uncertain and miserably run national state.

"Jews Are Not Greeks"

Despite their decreased prominence, Jews still had considerable influence on the economy of Salonika and the Greek province of Macedonia.[24] That was something many Greeks wanted to change as quickly as possible. In 1919, they switched the official market day from Sunday to Saturday as a way of shutting out Jewish competition. In 1922 and 1923, the city administration forced all Jewish port workers to give up their long-term jobs to the benefit of Greeks. In 1923, two Jewish junk dealers were sentenced to death and executed in the face of protests for allegedly sabotaging the municipal telephone grid. In the summer of 1924, the Greek Parliament passed a law forbidding people to work on Sundays. Their intention was to economically damage the Jews and the Muslims still living in Western Thrace.

The justification for this measure went as follows: "No one wants to discriminate against anybody. With the proposed law, we are trying to improve our citizens' quality of life." To that end, the parliamentary deputies also decided to require that account books, contracts, bills, and other commercial paperwork be written in modern Greek, a language many of Salonika's Jews spoke not at all or poorly. The same law banned business signs and letterhead in Hebrew lettering. Step by step, the promoters of Greek nationalist interests reduced Jews' sphere of economic activity and subjected them to increasing harassment, thereby achieving their true end: making those affected ask whether they should emigrate.[25]

In 1924, Henry Morgenthau, then US consul in Salonika, described the effects of the state and social discrimination against Jews: "The well-to-do of the Jewish population of Salonica, who have always accepted heavy sacrifices in favor of the community and its institutions, are themselves absorbed in very serious economic problems. That which formed the rich class of our population has to a large extent emigrated as a consequence of the fire of 1917 or the economical situation of the town."[26] New anti-Jewish laws, the virulent anti-Semitism of Greek refugees, and finally the Great Depression prompted further waves of emigration. With most immigration to the US on hold, Salonika's Jewish émigrés often headed for France or Palestine, with the latter receiving more than 5,600 migrants between 1932 and 1938.

Since 1927, the right-wing extremist Greek National Union (Ethniki Enosis Ellas) had been gaining influence. Its members were mainly recruited from the uprooted Greeks who had been forcibly resettled and then abandoned by the state. On June 29, 1931, 2,000 members of this ultranationalist organization came together in the Jewish Campbell district, which had been built after the devastating fire of 1917, and launched a pogrom. They set buildings on fire, beat and injured Jews, and looted whatever they could get their hands on. Ultimately two Jews were killed, and 220 families left homeless.

The local press and leading politicians justified the violence, depicting Jews as rootless cosmopolitans and traitors with no national loyalties. In 1934, Prime Minister Venizelos, who had just lost a reelection bid, summed up the Greek resentment: "The Jews of Salonika are Jewish, not Greek patriots. They have closer connections to the Turks than to us. For that reason I will not allow Jews to influence Greek politics." Seven years before the German Wehrmacht invaded Greece, Venizelos scapegoated Jews as traitors who favored Greece's archenemy Turkey. To drive home his message he reiterated: "Jews are not Greeks and don't feel like Greeks."[27]

On January 24, 1933, Venizelos offered to stop his political party's vicious anti-Semitic campaigning if Jews would renounce the right to vote they had worked so hard for in the past. As far back as 1920, his ruling Liberals had restricted Salonika's Jews to voting in four special, separate polling stations "to protect Christians." Venizelos had lost that election, even though he had had votes from two of those polling stations declared invalid because of alleged irregularities. In slightly different forms, electoral manipulation to the detriment of Jews recurred in the 1923, 1926, and 1928 parliamentary elections.[28]

Venizelos and newspapers affiliated with his party accused Jews of undermining all of Greece's national endeavors. They printed headlines calling on people to "Beat the Jews!" and denigrated Salonika's Jewish population as "60,000 conspirators in the heart of the city" and a "dangerous and treacherous element."

"We have been too indulgent toward the Jews," declared the newspaper *Makedonia* in 1933. "The Jews are the enemies of Greece. They have declared war upon us and we shall accept their insolent challenge. We shall adopt the necessary attitude toward these odious foreigners, these accursed Jews. . . . We have already beaten them once. This time we shall exterminate them completely."[29] It's difficult to say what the newspaper meant when it wrote "We have already beaten them once," but it could have been a reference to the fire of 1917, which mainly affected the Jewish quarter.

Between 1913 and 1940, the Greek state constantly increased the tempo of Salonika's Hellenization. And the main political power behind this development came not from monarchist circles or the authoritarian general Ioannis Metaxas, who seized power in 1935. The politics of ethnic cleansing and the plan to strip Jews of their rights was part of the platform of the liberal-republican, pro-British Party of National Progress led by Venizelos, who served multiple terms as both prime minister and leader of the opposition. Despite everything, Jews who remained in Salonika succeeded in defending their economic advantages until 1941.[30] But then the Greek majority made up for lost ground and became determined to get rid of even the last of the city's Jews.

JEWS FLEE TO FRANCE

With the United States having closed its borders, many Europeans forced to emigrate dreamed of France. Some 70,000 Eastern European Jews and 15,000 from Greece and the French Maghreb settled in Paris during the 1920s. Together with those who had moved there before 1914, there were more newly arrived Jews in France than Jews who had been in the country long-term.

Compared to the rest of Europe, France was fairly welcoming toward the suffering and the displaced. Of 60,000 people who escaped Hitler's Germany in 1933, France accepted 25,000, more than 20,000 of them Jews. Large numbers of refugees followed in subsequent years, from the Saar region in 1935, from German-dominated Austria and Czechoslovakia in 1938 and 1939, and from Belgium in 1940, where thousands of Jews fled the approaching Wehrmacht. By the time Germany occupied France in the summer of 1940, 55,000 Jewish refugees from parts of Central Europe conquered or threatened by Nazi Germany had crossed the French border. Many of them traveled on to other countries. In the same period, some 20,000 Jews from Poland, Lithuania, Romania, and Hungary came to France.

All told, they were a minority among the masses of people who found refuge in France between the world wars. Tens of thousands of Armenians came from the Ottoman Empire and were followed by hundreds of thousands from Soviet Russia, Fascist Italy, and later Hitler's Germany and Franco's Spain. More than two million migrants also came to France from the Iberian Peninsula, Southeast Europe, and Poland. Between 1919 and 1940, 650,000 foreigners were naturalized, and most of the rest were registered and given residence permits. But some 10,000 lived in France illegally.

Eastern European Jews stuck out as particularly foreign. Poor and pious, they clung to their traditions, and spoke Yiddish or Ladino. How many there were, how many simply disappeared, how many managed to get to the US, and how many arrived to take their place—no one knows. But by 1940, it is certain that 50,000 foreign, mostly stateless Jews took advantage of the possibility, available in France since 1927, to become naturalized citizens in relatively uncomplicated fashion.[31]

Many French people felt threatened by this group's will to better their social lot. Their high visibility in Paris stoked anti-Semitism, especially during the Depression, which first became noticeable in France in 1931 and which still had not been fully overcome in 1940. While not typical of the majority of French, a 1936 pamphlet titled "L'Invasion juive" by the anti-Semite Henri-Robert Petit suggested a change in the public mood. Petit wrote: "Just look at how they parade around our boulevards with their hooked noses, fleshy lips and kinky hair, babbling Jewish jargon. Just look at all these Semitic examples who slunk out of their ghettos and have come to take away your homes and jobs and rob you of your money and your future. These Jews are the masters of our country—they rule France."[32]

As outbursts of resentment became more frequent, if rarely so virulent, the French government reacted with restrictive legislation. From 1934 onward, immigration offices coupled residence permits for asylum seekers with a prohibition on working. The change was made in part after pressure from the Socialist and Communist trade union associations. Artisans, small merchants, and self-employed people were even more hostile toward refugees, particularly Jewish ones. In June 1933, representatives from the chambers of commerce in Colmar and Metz characterized the latter as "veritable pustules on the body of our economy." In November of the following year, Lionel de Tastes, a member of parliament who had drifted right from the left-wing republican camp, demanded that "the many foreigners active as merchants in France" be subjected to closer examination since, in his eyes, many of them engaged in crooked business deals. Fears for their jobs among people who worked in traditional trades further fueled anti-Semitism.

In 1937, France closed its borders to all Jewish refugees who didn't have German passports, including Polish Jews who had lived for years in Germany, and on May 2, 1938, legislators allowed the government to deport all illegal immigrants to their countries of origin. On November 12 of that year, three days after the Night of Broken Glass (*Kristallnacht*) in Germany, the French government announced that it would construct holding camps for stateless refugees.[33] With large numbers of refugees of various types coming in from its fascist neighbors Nazi Germany, Mussolini's Italy, and Franco's Spain, otherwise liberal France felt compelled to take such a step.

When Socialist Léon Blum was elected prime minister in a Popular Front government in April 1936, explicit and latent anti-Semitic sentiment found a perfect polarizing figure. Blum was France's first Jewish head of government. He came from a wealthy family and appointed a number of Jewish ministers in both of the governments he headed between 1936 and 1938. Tolerated by the French Communist Party, he eased several of the restrictions upon refugees, gave legal amnesty to Jews who had fled Nazi Germany, and helped them obtain residence permits. Despite the continuing economic depression, Blum's government reduced the standard working week from 48 to 40 hours and instituted paid vacation and better pensions.

Right-wing nationalists excoriated Blum's two short-lived cabinets as the essence of Jewish-Bolshevist treason. As a wealthy socialist who enjoyed luxury, Blum perfectly fit the stereotype of the Jewish Bolshevist plutocrat. In *L'Action française* newspaper, he was depicted as an agent of alternately Berlin, Moscow, London, or New York's Jewish community, a traitor who would drive France to ruin, betray it to "international financial Jewry," or drive the country into the war Hitler so badly wanted and needed. The war, French nationalists argued, would be fought by non-Jewish Frenchmen at the expense of France and on behalf of Blum's brothers in faith, who were being persecuted in Germany. The Action Française accused Blum of following his "racial instincts and acting as an accomplice and sorcerer's apprentice pushing for France's demise."

On July 4, 1936, the right-wing extremist city councilman Louis Darquier de Pellepoix bemoaned that France would imminently be "sold down the river." Jews were everywhere, he complained, telling people that they should be on their guard against rootless and restive Jews and their international agents, who were driving France into political anarchy and putting it under the thumb of rapacious financial capital. The country, he warned, was on the verge of being "enslaved and stultified." In 1942, Darquier de Pellepoix would succeed the notorious Xavier Vallat as commissioner-general for Jewish questions in the Vichy government. Vallat had greeted Blum in the French parliament on June 6, 1936, with the words: "Your appearance, Mr. President, undoubtedly marks a historic caesura. For the first time, this venerable Gallic-Roman country will be ruled by a Jew . . . [a] sharp-tongued student of the Talmud."[34]

On February 17, 1942, Vallat got into a spat with Adolf Eichmann's deputy Theodor Dannecker, in which the former claimed to have been the first to become anti-Semitic. He wrote of that exchange: "I reminded [Dannecker] that I was old enough to be his father and that for that reason I had been an anti-Semite for far longer than he had. I told him that if he had the slightest inkling of France's political history before Germany's invasion (a comment to which he reacted defensively), then he would realize that I was known, rightly or wrongly, as the only consistently anti-Semitic parliamentary deputy."[35]

Protectionists Strip Jewish Immigrants of Their Rights

In France's case, the objections to Jews that had been gradually becoming more and more frequent since the turn of the century were based less on traditional stereotypes than on fears of what was perceived as uncontrolled immigration, augmented by the Great Depression and France's long-standing tendency toward protectionism. Exemplifying the anxiety were the protests of French medical and law students, doctors, and lawyers. They had long targeted foreign Jews who were studying in France or trying to get their qualifications recognized and become French citizens. This protest movement increasingly gained momentum. It is worth mentioning that as a law student, future French president François Mitterrand took part in the protests in 1935 and was a member of anti-Jewish, nationalist organizations.[36] (Later as a socialist leader of France, he avoided talking about France's partial cooperation with its German occupiers and the anti-Jewish laws that were decreed by the French government and enforced by a large number of French officials. He also made sure that the archives remained shut. His conservative successor, Jacques Chirac, was the first to break the silence.)

Since 1892, a detailed French law had regulated the conditions under which foreign candidates were allowed to take their medical exams and earn doctorates. Initially doctors' association representatives and medical students welcomed the strict formal standards, thinking it would be difficult for foreigners to meet them. When that proved not to be the case, steps were taken to make it harder and harder for foreign students to matriculate. Nonetheless, despite the obstacles, the proportion of Jewish students at French medical schools rose from 9 to 19 percent between 1900 and 1935.

Limits on the number of Jews allowed to study at universities in Hungary, Romania, and Poland during the 1920s, together with anti-Semitic harassment by German and Austrian students, had driven many of those discriminated against to move to France. A provision in France's immigration law of 1927 allowing those with a degree from a French university to receive French citizenship after only a year and to practice their professions without restrictions also drew people to the country. The provision was intended to further the cause of integration, but amid the economic crisis after 1930, it elicited protests from demonstrators demanding "*La France pour les Français!*" Over the course of the 1930s the French government and French legislators amended the law several times. Ultimately, people who were recently naturalized, *naturalisés de fraîche date*, were degraded to citizens with lesser rights.

These people were also called *métèques* after the Ancient Greek word *métoikos*, meaning resident foreigners without political rights.

In 1934, the French state imposed a ten-year moratorium on newly naturalized citizens working in the civil service or as lawyers. French doctors felt they were being given short shrift, although the previous year they had succeeded in getting a five-year ban imposed on new French citizens working in certain medical professions. In 1935, the government under French premier Pierre Laval instituted binding quotas for artisans and merchants. (Laval had begun his political career before the First World War as a socialist but had moved step by step to the right, entering into national-socialist terrain. For a few months in 1940 and from 1942 to 1944, he served as the head of the Vichy government.)

As was also the case in other countries, politicians, students, and representatives of various professions in 1920s France discovered what was often called the "academic proletariat," a growing army of potentially unemployed university graduates. Because state and religion were officially separated in France, the talk was seldom explicitly about Jews. But Jews were meant, for instance, when in March 1935 Victor Balthazard, the director of the Paris Medical Academy, warned: "In five years, there will be five hundred Romanian doctors living in our country and practicing in our cities. How many will there be in ten years, if we do not quickly ward off this danger?"

Balthazard had the religious affiliations of his Romanian students checked and found out that 377 of 436 were "*Israélites.*" It was no accident that he focused on Romania. More than seven decades previously, the French government had offered people from the nascent state of Romania special privileges, including the chance to study in France, because they were military allies who spoke a related language. Balthazard asked, "Was the French government thinking of legions of Jews in 1857 and 1866 when they granted Romanians special rights?" Balthazard strictly distinguished between mid-nineteenth-century Romanians and "Jews who today are Romanian citizens—or at least purport to be." One of his colleagues wrote to a medical journal: "We need to be frank and acknowledge that the matriculation limit is directed against Jews. Romania reserves its universities for students from the Romanian people. Others go wherever they can. Yesterday Romanians came, today come Jews who tomorrow will be French citizens (and doctors in France), and the day after tomorrow it will be the Bolshevists." On April 21, 1933, the French parliament ordered that in future a maximum of ten Maghreb or Romanian candidates would be allowed to study medicine per year. Otherwise foreigners were only admitted to medical departments if they had completed their high school education in France.

But in the mind of the French medical community these measures didn't offer sufficient protection against unwanted competition. On the contrary, they only amplified demands for further protection. In 1935, lobbyists for French doctors succeeded, despite a shortage of physicians in Algeria and the French colonies, protectorates, and mandate areas, in getting non-French doctors banned from working in those places. As a result, the number of foreign Jewish medical students was halved by the mid-1930s. Representatives of the medical guild also demanded that fewer foreigners be naturalized, arguing, "As a friend and advisor to French families, a French doctor has to have a French name, French sensibilities and a French heart."[37]

In 1919 some 150,000 Jews lived in France. By 1940, their numbers were estimated at 320,000. Only around a third came from families with French roots dating back to 1870 or earlier. Unlike Eastern European Jewish immigrants, the refugees who had arrived since 1933 from Central Europe were well assimilated into their native lands and had little contact with either the older French Jews or the Eastern European and Levantine immigrants. When the Wehrmacht marched into Paris on June 14, 1940, France's Jews lived in numerous separate groups, divided by geographic origin, social status, and political convictions.[38]

The number of Jews in France increased fivefold between 1890 and 1940, in contrast to Germany, where after 1900, despite the migration of Eastern European Jews, it remained constant and even declined slightly in the late 1920s. The rapid rise of anti-Semitism in republican France might thus be interpreted as a byproduct of the discrimination against and displacement of Jews in countries like Germany, Poland, Lithuania, Romania, and Hungary, which forced hundreds of thousands of poor and impoverished Jews to flee to France. The bans on Jewish immigrants instituted by overseas countries like the US also meant more Jewish refugees trying to get into France and more animosity toward them. Economic hardship and war only bolstered these trends.

The government in Nazi Germany followed these developments with satisfaction. In the memo "The Jewish Question as a Factor of German Foreign Policy," the German Foreign Ministry told all its foreign offices in January 1939: "The poorer and thus more burdensome the Jewish immigrant is for the country to which he goes, the more vigorous the host country's reaction will be, and the more desirable and effective for German propagandistic interests." Such immigration would "call forth the resistance of established populations," teach the citizens of other countries what "the Jewish threat" was all about, and create "a wave of anti-Semitism." Civil servants in Berlin considered other countries' criticism of Germany's "exclusion of Jews" a "transitional phenomenon" and an example of "misguided pity." The explicitly stated goal of German foreign policy and policy toward Jews was the "establishment of a Jewish reservation somewhere in the world, although not in Palestine."[39]

FORBIDDEN HATRED IN THE SOVIET UNION

During the Russian Civil War, nationalist Ukrainians and other groups justified the mass murder of Jews by claiming that they were killing communists and their henchmen. Soldiers from the Red Army also carried out pogroms, but they were far less frequent. Mostly they left Jews in peace. For this reason, hundreds of thousands of Jews joined the Soviets. It was their "one and only alternative," in the words of political scientist Zvi Gitelman, their only hope of escaping "total physical eradication." Historian Matthias Vetter describes the situation in similar terms: "Before Jews allowed themselves to be killed as purported Bolsheviks, they preferred to join the Bolsheviks." In a posthumous fragment, Isaak Babel speculated that specific psychological needs drove young Jews to seek out the Red Army: the "hunger for friendship and camaraderie" and the satisfying feeling of "protection and loyalty" among comrades. These, wrote Babel, were the "best of all human qualities," which Jews had been "denied for so long."[40]

In contrast to the nationalist, monarchist, and openly anti-Semitic forces marauding around in the Russian civil war, the Soviet state at least guaranteed Jews' physical safety and legal equality, if not the security of their property. In the wake of the Menshevik February Revolution of 1917, all the restrictions on Jews' residence, careers, and educational possibilities were done away with. The Bolshevik Revolution the following October continued this trend.

Because Jews rarely belonged to the revolutionary, politically privileged classes of workers and farmers, Bolsheviks thought they should be given new, normalized types of work. Individual artisans became industrial laborers, merchants became farmers, and upwardly mobile bourgeois became reliable state officials. With that and with the end of class conflict in a harmonized society of assimilated equals, Bolsheviks believed, anti-Jewish hatred would automatically disappear, having been cast upon the Marxist dung heap of history. That was Lenin's theory at least. He considered anti-Semitism a "repulsive remnant from the old days of serfdom" and "pitch-black ignorance," although with one qualification. "Among Russian Jews, as is also the case for all nations, there are kulaks, exploiters and capitalists," Lenin cautioned.[41]

Anti-Semitism may have been officially forbidden and punishable, but it was by no means overcome. It continued to exist in semi-concealment in the former Pale of Settlement—the Ukrainian and Belarussian parts of the Soviet Union, which were quickly occupied by German troops in 1941. Because Jews appeared as major and minor revolutionary leaders and executors of the Kremlin's will, prejudices that had become obsolete in the western part of the Soviet Union were replaced with more modern ones. For the first time, the age-old dissatisfaction with Russian central authorities was transferred to Jews and associated with the hatred of communism, which had been so destructive for so many people. The bogeyman of the "Jewish Bolshevist" was born and combined in the popular imagination with anti-Semitic stereotypes from the tsarist era.

The "Jewish Problem" of Too Much Success

Under the new political circumstances, Jews' social status quickly changed, albeit not in the "normalizing" sense Bolshevik authorities would have liked. Socialist regulations concerning property, the soon-to-be unprecedentedly bloated state apparatus, and the educational mobilization of a population considered backward swiftly altered the structure of the country. Moreover, the Soviet wielders of power fired, deported, displaced, or killed members of the old elite. Millions of people were suddenly called upon to use their brains rather than their proletarian fists. The state urgently needed capable heads to set up, manage, and rationalize the legal system, schools, businesses, administrative bodies, newspapers, and factories. Gentile proletarians, navy men, and farmers were rarely up to the job, no matter how enthusiastic they were about Communist ideas for the future.

According to party statistics from 1922, Jews represented 5.2 percent of the membership in Lenin's party—hardly a disproportionate figure. But the leadership was different. Jews made up as much as 30 percent of the workers and soldiers councils, which were elected in the beginning, and—most conspicuously—in the Central Party Committee. At the Leningrad City Conference of the Communist Youth Association on January 5, 1920, everyone who spoke was Jewish. Historian Mikhail Beiser writes: "Zinoviev held a speech about the current situation. Slosman read out a report from the city Komsomol committee. Kagan talked about political and organizational questions. Itkina greeted the delegates in the name of the workers, and Saks represented the Central Committee of the Komsomol." The birth name of Grigory Zinoviev, a close associate of Lenin, was recorded alternately as Hirsch Apfelbaum and as Ovsei-Gershon Aronovich Radomylsky.[42]

Compared with their Christian countrymen, Jews were better able to make use of the new opportunities. The still smoldering rubble of the old society opened up chances to get ahead, according to Yuri Slezkine, the likes of which had never before been seen anywhere in the world. At the beginning of the Communist regime, if not permanently, the Soviet leadership needed Jews because, as a 1926 brochure on fending off anti-Semitism proclaimed, they were "hard-working, flexible, inventive, adroit and alert." In previous years, Lenin had thanked the "Jewish element," calling it a "pool of a rational and literate labor force," whose mobilization had "saved the revolution at a difficult time."[43]

Since 1918, hundreds of thousands of young Jews in particular fled the shtetl. By 1939, 1.3 million of these people were living in cities that had been off-limits to them before 1917. In the initial years that followed, from 1918 to 1923, 72,000 moved to Petrograd (as of 1924, Leningrad) and Moscow. Whereas the Christian population was only gradually urbanized, by 1939, 87 percent of Soviet Jews lived in cities. During the short phase of Lenin's semiliberal New Economic Policy from 1921 to 1927, many swiftly made names for themselves. Freed from constraints, Jews in 1924 owned 75.4 percent of Moscow's apothecaries and perfumeries, 48 percent of its jewelry shops, and 54 percent of all stores selling manufactured goods. All in all, Jews owned 32 percent of Moscow's shops.[44]

In his book *The Jewish Century*, Slezkine illustrated the rise of this minority, comprising only 1.8 percent of the Soviet population, with a number of enlightening statistics. In 1939, 17.1 percent of all university students in Moscow were Jewish. The comparable figure in Leningrad was 19 percent, in Kharkiv 24.6 percent, and Kyiv 35.6 percent. Six percent of Jews graduated from an institute of higher learning, compared with only 0.6 of the general populace. That year, Jews accounted for 15.5 percent of all the Soviet citizens with higher educations. In absolute terms, their numbers were lower than Russians but higher than Ukrainians. Thirty-three percent of all Soviet Jews between the ages of 19 and 24 studied at a university, while only 4.5 percent of the remaining Soviet population that age did the same.

By 1939, 82.5 percent of all employed Jews working in Leningrad did so in offices. Only 3 percent of all Soviet nurses but 19.6 percent of

Soviet doctors came from Jewish families. In Leningrad, Jews accounted for 14.4 percent of all retail shop employees but more than 30 percent of all branch managers as well as 70 percent of the city's dentists, 56.6 percent of its apothecaries, 45 percent of its defense attorneys, more than 38 percent of its doctors, 31.3 of its writers, journalists, and publishers, and 24.6 percent of its musicians. Of all primary-school teachers, 1.8 percent were Jewish, as were 14.1 percent of all research-ers and university professors in the Russian Soviet Republic in 1939. Surveys in the republics in the former Pale revealed that 12.3 percent of teachers and 32.7 of professors in Ukraine were Jewish, while 8 and 26 percent, respectively, in Belarus were. Moreover, between 1935 and 1940, 34.8 percent of the new members of the Russian Writers' Asso-ciation in the Moscow chapter (85 of 244) were Jews.[45]

This high degree of upward social mobility was accompanied, as Soviet authorities desired, by a process of assimilation. Hundreds of thousands of Soviet Jews abandoned their religious and everyday traditions. As early as 1926, one-third of Jewish men married gentile women. New Jewish farmers even raised pigs to demonstrate that they had broken with obsolete religious prohibitions.[46] In the 1939 census, 54.6 percent of the Soviet Union's three million Jews listed Russian and not Yiddish as their native language. In 1926, only 26 percent had spoken Russian as their mother tongue. In 1937, less than 15 percent of Jews said that they were religious, compared with 47 percent of the total population. Some of the answers given in the surveys may have been tactical and thus less than accurate, but they still indicate a trend toward integration.[47] That trend was far more pronounced among young people who had left the former Pale in 1917 than those who stayed behind and would be subjected to German domination.

From Traditional to Soviet Anti-Semitism

Besides Jewish participation in the Soviet leadership, disproportionate numbers of cultural elites and state functionaries also came from their midst. This applies to both the civilian sectors of the state apparatus and the secret service and other repressive institutions.[48] As a rule, those who had moved up in society no longer saw themselves as Jews, but rather as Soviet citizens. If they spoke of Jews at all, it was as "the Jews" in the third person, as though they didn't belong to that group.

Countless gentile farmers, office clerks, and agricultural and factory workers saw things differently, as this sampling of sentiments documented by post-office censors in Leningrad demonstrates: "The Jewish dominance is absolute" (October 1924); "the whole press is in the hands of the Jews" (June 1925); "the Jews, for the most part, live extremely well; everything, from trade to state employment, is in their hands" (September 1925); "every child knows that the Soviet government is a Jewish government" (September 1925). In his diary in 1924, Mikhail Bulgakov caricatured a group of people he considered would-be writers as "stale, slavish, Soviet riffraff, with a thick Jewish admixture."

In August 1926, the government's agitprop division reported to the Secretariat of the Communist Party Central Committee: "The sense that the Soviet regime patronizes the Jews, that it is 'the Jewish government,' that the Jews cause unemployment, housing shortages, college admissions problems, price rises, and commercial speculation—this sense is instilled in the workers by all the hostile elements.... If it does not encounter resistance, the wave of anti-Semitism threatens to become, in the very near future, a serious political question."[49]

Since 1917, Anatoly Lunacharsky had served as the head of the People's Commissariat for Education. In 1929, Stalin removed him from that post and made him the Soviet ambassador to the League of Nations. After his death in 1933, his name was expunged from the history of the Bolshevik Party. In 1929, in his final political act, Lunacharsky had published a polemic titled "On Anti-Semitism." In it, the decorated, classically educated people's commissar used a battery of metaphors, allegories, and sentences draped in Marxist platitudes to make one central, critical point: under Stalin, Soviet anti-Semitism was on the rise.

Lunacharsky asked why anti-Semitism was finding "so much resonance"—preceded by the censor-mollifying phrase "among counter-revolutionary forces." Perhaps intentionally, he offered a much too optimistic view of the status of Jews in Western Europe. The true target of his words was the disingenuous image of increasingly harmonious and humane coexistence among the various Soviet peoples. In opposition to the Communist Party's whitewashing of social reality, he offered the frank diagnosis that, aside from "a number of idiots," anti-Semitism "played a serious role nowhere in Europe except Russia."

Lunacharsky stressed "the mercantile abilities" with which Jews had succeeded in sowing "the seeds of capitalism in countries with primitive, limited, peasant cultures." Far from condemning that as a mortal antisocialist sin, he added: "As the cleverest researchers into human development have put forward, the Jews contributed an extraordinary amount to progress." They played a "key role" in the development of "urban culture" and in suppressing "the backward, natural, subsistence economy," encouraging artisanship, trade, and the money economy. That was why they had attracted the "terrible rage" of the peasants and the nationalist lower and middle classes that evolved from the peasantry. These were constantly inciting the masses to "exterminate" the "foreigners," who were seen as "malicious competitors."

In Lunacharsky's historicist and materialist analysis, the Russian intelligentsia envied Jews because they passed tests with flying colors, rose up through the ranks "despite the greatest of barriers," and became "Jewish dentists, Jewish midwives and Jewish lawyers." By no means did the advent of Soviet Communism solve the problem of anti-Semitism. On the contrary, likely using the kulaks as stand-ins for the entire Russian peasantry, he wrote of "primitive, coarse, uneducated kulaks who had no connections whatever abroad and no talent for money." Pointing to a parallel example, he went on to discuss the "primitive elements" among the Turkmen, Kurdish, or Georgian peasants of the Caucasus. They were not envious of the success of Jewish merchants who, though absent from the region, "operated on a large scale elsewhere," but of the Armenians who traded there. In this instance, too, Lunacharsky asserted, agitators whispered in peasants' ears: "Why are you poor? Why are you suffering, farmer? Because you're being exploited by the Armenian, a foreigner. The devil knows too well where he comes from. He has a different faith, a different language and a different character. Strike him down!" Stalin came from humble circumstances in Georgia. His mother was a serf, his father a shoemaker, prone to violence, who had tried to make his way as a small-time producer with ten employees, but had been unable to balance his books and had eventually succumbed to alcoholism. Small wonder then that Stalin himself was anti-Semitic.

Ultimately Lunacharsky opposed Jewish assimilation, arguing that Jews should retain their own character and that a "Russian-Jewish marriage" should be concluded. At the end of his brochure and its warning, he cited remarks he claimed to have heard from Lenin and Maxim Gorky: "With great joy, we observe the enormous growth of Russian-Jewish marriages. This is the correct path. Our Slavic blood has always had a great deal of peasant malt: it is thick and copious but it flows somewhat sluggishly, and our whole biological rhythm is a bit rural. On the other hand, the blood of our Jewish comrades flows swiftly. For that reason let us mix our blood and in this fruitful mixture find the human type that carries within the blood of Jewish people like a precious, thousand-year-old wine."[50]

Yet all the proclamations and enlightening publications did not wipe out the anti-Semitism of those who were supposed to be turned into "new men" by a "conscious" political avant-garde. On the contrary, anti-Semitism grew in strength and spread to the state leadership in the 1930s. In 1926, Yuri Larin, the leading functionary responsible for Jewish issues, concluded with disappointment that "anti-Semitism has taken hold of broad masses of working people." In 1929, he wrote: "The difference between Soviet anti-Semitism and the prerevolutionary variant resides in the fact that before the revolution anti-Semitism was almost unknown among workers."[51] Old enmities drew fresh strength from new social circumstances.

Larin, born Mikhail Aleksandrovich Luria, came from Simferopol and was part of those circles that acted as if they had always been Russian. One of his tasks was to recruit Jews to establish agricultural colonies. At first he tried to pursue this in Southern Ukraine and Crimea, but was soon forced to give up after meeting resistance from Russian, Ukrainian, and Tartar natives. While constantly feuding among themselves, these groups were united in their hostility toward Jews. After the attempts to resettle Jews were quashed by the local rural populace, the ostensible revolutionary subject, the Soviet leadership decided to found a Jewish Soviet republic in the inhospitable region of Birobidzhan. The region was located in the far east of Russia, just before Vladivostok, near the Chinese border. Larin, who died in 1932, devoted all his energy to this project. But he acknowledged: "With its eternally frozen soil, swamps, insect plagues, floods, temperatures of minus forty degrees and cultural isolation," he wrote, Birobidzhan "was not a completely suitable place for such human material as city-dwellers who were trying out agriculture for the first time."[52]

In the end only a few thousand Jewish colonists were ever settled there—a historically insignificant number. Nonetheless, the plan remains remarkable for its similarities to other ideas from Western Europe about sending Jews to Palestine or Madagascar or other places as peripheral as possible to the West.[53]

The initial idea was to relocate one hundred thousand Jewish families, around half a million people, and to "re-forge" at least some of these intellectual and mercantile people into muscular farmers and perspiring tractor drivers. In 1926, authorities set the ambitious goal of transferring 20 percent of all employed Jews into agriculture. But by 1939, only 5.8 percent of Soviet Jews labored as kolkhoz (collective) farmers, compared with almost half the remaining Soviet population. There was only one successful transformation. As private trade largely disappeared, Jewish merchants became civil servants, branch directors, and the heads of state offices in charge of ensuring the populace was supplied with the necessities. In their role as administrators, they often took the blame for the shortages caused by the Soviet economy and for diversions of commodities from private consumption to the state industrialization program. In 1931, Belarussian communists complained that the only reason Jews were trained as specialists was that they were such lousy workers. In Crimean factories, new Jewish workers were first hassled because of their accents and then severely harassed because they "were always trying to get ahead."

Even more prone than workers to attacking Jewish colleagues

because of their greater intellectual flexibility were students, especially in Ukraine. A letter to the editor published in the summer of 1926 by the *Tschervonyj Step* newspaper read: "Who is being educated in our universities? A bunch of Jews. They wrote the entrance exams so that no farmer would be admitted. Everywhere you look, there are Jews. If we had a people's republic of Ukraine, this would not be the case." Apparently the author saw Petliura's short-lived Ukrainian nationalist state, including its frequent pogroms, as a preferable alternative to Soviet rule.

In 1926, Mosche Rafes, a prominent prerevolutionary Jewish socialist workers representative and later a functionary within the Jewish department of the Communist Party, summarized some of the anti-Jewish attitudes of his time: "Jews are more cultivated than Russians and push them aside everywhere. . . . They refuse to do simple labor. They aspire to positions of command and higher salaries." In August 1928, Larin talked with Moscow workers about what had become virulent anti-Semitism. He wanted to hear their perspective. They cited, along with the premodern stereotypes of Jews considering themselves a chosen people and practicing bizarre rituals, a litany of the same complaints. Jews "refused to do hard physical work," "pursued their careers," "forged their grades to gain admission to university," "were immediately given places to live," and "never had to stand in line." Overall, Larin was told, "the Jewish bourgeoisie has made itself comfortable in Moscow."

This sort of anti-Semitism was not accompanied by a fundamental critique of the Soviet system. On the contrary it can be seen as a specific form of identification with Soviet rule. This is reflected in observations passed back by the German consulate in Kyiv to Berlin in 1926: "Among the people it is often said that 'We want to get along with the Soviets, but without Jews.'" As Matthias Vetter determined, in the Soviet Union, too, Jews appeared as "the winners of modernization and a privileged nation that produced socially successful individuals, careerists and functionaries." Popular anti-Semitism lived on behind the veil of socialist equality. On the one hand, it picked up on anti-Jewish resentment from the tsarist period, and on the other, it functioned as a reaction to the confusion of the revolution as well as the massive "dawning of modern-ism in Russian history" and the existential crises that entailed. Draw-ing support from official policies of egalitarianism, employed Russians developed a "socialist anti-Semitism" that helped them cope with "col-lective feelings of inferiority" and disappointments concerning the revo-lution."[54] The masses of people who suffered from production shortages and limitations on consumption looked for and found scapegoats, and that was useful to the Soviet leadership in the 1930s.

The October Revolution had redistributed opportunities with little regard to people's wishes. Hundreds of thousands of Jews seized their chance. Consequently, to follow Slezkine, a "problem" arose in the Soviet Union of Jews' having too much success.[55] As in nondictatorial countries, the question in the Soviet Union became what should happen when better school policy made the majority—the other Soviet peoples and in particular the Russians—better educated, and those people began demanding the top positions.

To allow communist leaders to incorporate anti-Semitism, which seemingly could not be eradicated but which encouraged general social solidarity, into their own dogma, Lenin found it opportune to speak of a Jewish bourgeoisie or petit bourgeois deviations while dis-creetly pointing out the nonproletarian and nonagricultural roots of most Jews. Moreover it was entirely in keeping with Stalin's "theory" of socialism in one country to invent a new nationalism dominated by Russia. Although they were known as a nation within the Soviet Union, Jews did not have a clearly demarcated territory as others did. Thus they were also considered a minority connected across borders with Jews in the Western world in "cosmopolitan" and "Zionist" fash-ion. That situation would prove perilous.

It may have sounded harmless when Stalin proclaimed in 1930 that the October Revolution "fills the hearts of Russian workers with the feeling of revolutionary national pride." But the Soviet supreme leader was soon to narrow his definition of "nation," and he stopped talking about the conjoining of various nations into the Soviet union in favor of speaking of the Russian people. By 1936 at the latest, the feudal, Russian Orthodox, militaristic, and cultural legacy of Russia was being promoted as a source of confident patriotism. It extended from Peter the Great to Joseph Stalin, from the pro-Russian Ukrainian freedom fighter and butcher of Jews Bohdan Khmelnytsky to Budyonny's Red Cavalry, from Modest Mussorgsky's turgid national operas to patriotic Socialist Realism.

On February 1, 1931, *Pravda* declared that all the peoples of the Soviet Union were "Soviet patriots to the same degree" but that "the Russian people were the first among equals because of their outstanding [historical] role." There was no place for Jews in this cult of all things Russian. The injustice, violence, and pogroms that had been visited on them disappeared in the glare of sanitized national history. Ultimately, in late 1943, during the "Great War for the Fatherland," the Soviet leadership replaced the "Internationale," which had been the national anthem of the Soviet Union, with a new one. It began with the lines: "An unbreakable union of free republics / Great Russia has welded forever to stand." Jewish-Russian journalist Vasily Grossman interpreted this transition as a consequence of the Soviet victory in Stalingrad, which "gave Stalin the chance to openly declare an ideology of nationalism."[56]

In December 1932, the Soviet government introduced universal personal identity cards that contained information about the holder's nationality. Russian security services maintained files with identical data and passport photos. Whatever the original purpose of the ID cards may have been, the information allowed authorities to treat people of different nationalities differently. From then on, a glance was all that was needed to distinguish between a Russian and a non-Russian. People living within the Soviet Union who were members of other nations and who were thereby suspicious included Poles, Germans, Tatars, Greeks, and Koreans. Starting in the later 1930s, they were subject to systematic resettlement. Parallel to repressive programs of nationalization, there was also a strict Russification regime. Thousands of non-Russian schools and cultural institutions disappeared within a few months, and Soviet citizens who previously used the Latin, Arabic, or Hebrew alphabets were forced to write in Cyrillic. This was not only an instance of repression—it also manifested a will to modernize.

Initially the language a person spoke and the information he himself provided were sufficient to officially establish a person's nationality. But on April 2, 1938, a testing procedure came into force that was only acknowledged internally. Now a person's nationality was no longer determined by what he said but by his parents' ethnicity: "If one's parents are Germans, Poles, etc., the person being registered cannot be classified as Russian, Belarussian etc., irrespective of where they were born, how long they have lived in the USSR, or whether they have changed their citizenship etc." The edict explicitly stated that people's last names could be cited as reasons for reviewing that person's nationality.[57] That stipulation particularly, if not exclusively, affected people with names like Eisenstat, Gubelman, and Shapiro.

By 1938 almost all Yiddish newspapers and publishing houses were forced to close, just like the majority of Ukrainian, Belarussian, and Tatar ones.[58] It was the start of an era in which the Soviet terror apparatus used affiliations with "Bundism" (after the Jewish socialist party BUND), Jewish nationalism, and Zionism to decide whether undesirables would live or die. While some functionaries in this apparatus came from Jewish backgrounds, and state terror could theoretically strike anyone, those who were born Russians had the least to fear. If we consider the Soviet Union's tendency to think in black-or-white, friend-or-foe terms, the nationalist turn of the 1930s would have bolstered anti-Semitism even without any accompanying propaganda. While the nationalist-totalitarian movement in Western Europe increasingly adopted socialist elements in its political philosophy, the situation was reversed in the Soviet Union. Stalin increasingly stabilized the inherently unstable edifice of socialism with nationalist and pan-Slavic cement. German historian Jorg Baberowski calls 1937 the year of "social" and 1938 the year of "ethnic" cleansing.[59] Jews were subjected to both.

1936: Massive Terror and a Change of Elites

The prehistory to these developments was the conflict in the Soviet leadership of the late 1920s between the group around Stalin and the soon-to-be-defeated leftist opposition around Leon Trotsky, Lev Kamenev, and Grigory Zinoviev, who all came from Jewish families. Soviet propaganda may have stopped short of using Nazi language like "treacherous Jews" or "Jewish sub-humans," but otherwise the whole repertoire of anti-Semitic stereotypes was trotted out during the major show trials from 1936 to 1938. *Pravda* and *Izvestiya* wrote of "the venal Judases" around Trotsky, "the sellers of the people's blood," "the despicable hirelings of fascism," "the lascivious apprentices of the Gestapo," and the followers of "the paramount spy Judas-Trotsky" who were attempting to "sell our happy, liberated people into slavery."[60]

Born in 1904 in Galicia, Austrian-American journalist and writer Wilhelm Siegmund Schlamm (later William S. Schlamm) broke with Communist ideology in the 1930s after being a fervent adherent for fifteen years. The deciding event was the show trial of Zinoviev and others in Moscow in 1936. A short time later, he published a pamphlet titled "Dictatorship of Lies: A Reckoning," in which he analyzed the trial from a distance.

"Among other things it was a pogrom," he wrote:

> It was impossible to ignore the satisfaction with which the obviously Jewish names of some of the defendants—Moises Lurye, Nathan Lurye—were popularized beyond every objective necessity for internal Russian consumption. The message was that Jewish socialists in Europe should not be under any more illusions. On the street and in Russia's villages, there was plenty of wide-awake or soon to be awakened anti-Semitism. Josef Stalin was thoroughly aware of such impulses from below. From the very beginning, his robust private war against Trotsky had an anti-Semitic counterpoint—initially it was soft and in the background, then it became ever more coarse until in the end it was unmistakable. . . . From the top down, from the mouths of the court officials and the newspaper editorial boards, it wasn't necessary to say a single word. The effect from *below* was enormous and unambiguous: "Jews!" No, Stalin's supporters didn't verbally incite any anti-Jewish hatred. But it's unmistakable where their "educational

work" is headed, and they know full well which sensitive membranes of the Russian body politic need to be poked in order to achieve certain specific effects. They go into great academic detail to combat Trotsky and his friends' theory of perpetual revolution, but, especially with the addition of such figures of speech as were used at the trial, kolkhoz farmers interpret this foreign-sounding formulation to mean something else entirely and far simpler: "These Jews—they're always pushing unease, eternal haste and restlessness. That's Jews for you. But we've finally had enough. We want peace and quiet. We aren't rootless people made of air who can only feel at ease—it's well known—in endless quarrels and fights and Talmudic debating. We are Russian people, and Stalin is one of us."[61]

Schlamm's contemporary descriptions accord with what Khrushchev later said about the Stalin era. As the man responsible for building the Moscow Metro and other gigantic projects and later a member of the Central Committee, Khrushchev was in constant contact with Stalin in the 1930s. Khrushchev recalled that when Stalin was informed about things being amiss in Aircraft Factory Number 30, where Jewish managers and engineers apparently worked, he said: "We should give cudgels to the good workers in the factory so they can give these Jews a good beating after work." Such remarks could be easily misunderstood as commands, although according to Khrushchev the greatest care was taken not to cite Stalin since "as the [Soviet] leader and main theoretician he made sure that anti-Semitism never shimmered through in his writings and speeches." When he talked privately, Stalin had no such scruples: "In a familiar, exaggerated tone of voice, he would often imitate how Jews spoke. The imitation was on the level of idle talk by stupid, backward people who despised Jews and ridiculed their peculiarities. But Stalin had fun doing this, and he wasn't bad at it."[62]

The deportations and mass executions of the Great Purge from 1936 to 1938 were not directed against Jews per se but disproportionately affected this group compared to other Soviet nationalities. One reason was the general criteria by which victims were selected: non-proletarian social origins, previous membership in non-Bolshevik parties, and a nationality considered in some sense hostile. Taken together, these criteria applied more to the Jews who were part of the country's elite than to Russians. During the Purge, some 1.5 million people were taken into custody, of whom half were shot on false pretenses while the other half were sent to camps, where around 200,000 of them died. Among the victims of this so-called cleansing were hundreds of thousands of the Bolshevik old guard and "socially harmful elements," especially kulaks and members of certain ethnic minorities. State terror was even directed against employees of the NKVD, the main institution of Soviet persecution. In 1936, almost a third of NKVD officers came from Jewish families. By 1938, the figure was down to 4 percent.

Between 1934 and 1939, more than half a million, mostly young people, assumed positions of leadership in the Soviet state, forcing the party itself to become younger. In 1939, as historian Karl Schlögel writes, 80.5 percent of party members had joined after 1923, and a quarter only after 1938. Roughly half came from the working and farming classes, and "many moved into leading positions fresh out of university." In 1992, historian Oleg Khlevniuk summarized the effects of the Great Purge in a single sentence: "The party youth rose meteorically amid the mass repression, and that encouraged their submission toward the leader and their support for the repressions of the old guard." Jörg Baberowski concurs, writing that the hundreds of thousands of parvenus "were obedient because they owed everything to the death of the old guard."

The decisions that laid the groundwork for this had been taken at the Central Committee plenum in early 1937. In his opening speech, Stalin spoke about the elimination of the old party elite, and in his concluding address, he pointed out that in 1927 the party had only 9,600 members who had graduated college whereas in 1937 it already had 105,000.[63] The months of the Great Purge can be seen as the second time after the October Revolution that Soviet elites had been replaced. This was made possible by twenty years of forced educational reforms, and it was directed against those who swiftly and in great numbers had risen to lofty positions in the Soviet state: Jews.

The replacement of elites necessary for the functioning of the state went hand in hand with the Russian nationalization of the Soviet Union. Both fueled anti-Semitism, which had been, at most, suppressed by the state. This can be most clearly documented in the period in which inner conflicts should have receded, the years of the Soviet Union's defensive war against Nazi Germany's invasion.

On December 29, 1942, a man named I. Lev wrote to Ilya Ehrenburg from the industrial city of Sterlitamak in the southwestern foothills of the Urals: "The enormous rise in anti-Semitism in so many parts of the Soviet Union concerns me. Be it in streetcars, trains or in lines in front of shops, anti-Semitism oozes out of people's conversations: 'The Jews launder money,' 'Because of them the price of food is rising,' 'They avoid fighting at the front,' 'They keep us Russians down.'" During a train journey, a fellow traveler, an engineer at a munitions factory, had taken it upon himself to inform Lev that Jews "were, without exception, capitalist speculators and a parasitic tumor on the body of the state."

Also in 1942, an unnamed Jewish soldier wrote to Ehrenburg: "Why does everyone hate Jews? Everyone, everywhere." The author had special experience of what he described. For years, as a passionate Soviet, he had argued against older Jews' insistence that "A goy is always a goy." His comrades in the Red Army thought he was Russian. For that reason, he experienced unfiltered anti-Semitism "in its most horrible form" and was ultimately forced to admit that the old Jews had been right. If he identified himself as a Jew, when someone said something anti-Semitic, he would receive in answer what was meant as a compliment: "You can't be a Jew. Jews are all treacherous scoundrels." At a loss, the soldier asked what he should do amid this sea of resentment and hatred: "Should I wear a sign saying 'Jew' pinned to me?"[64]

Several years before Stalin's death, his successor Khrushchev told of witnessing a pogrom when he was twelve years old. It had taken place in October 1906 in the small mining city of Yusovka, which in 1924 was incorporated into Stalino, today's Donetsk. Following a rumor that "for three days you could do whatever you wanted to Jews," thousands of miners seized the opportunity and went on a spree of looting and murder. Khrushchev later recalled the "primitive mentality of the workers" and described how he and a friend had gone to the medical ward of the factory where injured and dead Jews had been taken: "A terrible sight awaited us. The corpses of Jews who had been beaten to death lay in long rows upon the floor."

Khrushchev said subsequently that the workers of his home city had "later come back to their senses." But in the mid-1960s, by then out of power, he wrote that "Unfortunately, the seeds of anti-Semitism remained in our system, and apparently there still isn't the necessary prevention and resistance."[65]

5

Discrimination, Disenfranchisement, Denaturalization

THE "LITHUANIA AWAKEN!" PROJECT

During the nineteenth century, Lithuanian was spoken in the Russian protectorates Kaunas and Vilnius, extending west into predominantly Polish and German places. Squeezed in between Russians, Poles, Germans, and Latvians, most of the poorly educated and impoverished Lithuanian speakers lived in villages. But in the cities, there were increasingly louder calls for a "national rebirth."

As was the case elsewhere, groups of free-thinking intellectuals, Catholic priests, writers, and politicians imported the nationalist idea from the West. By the 1880s, these elites standardized the Lithuanian language, documented Lithuania's impressive history, and spoke out against Russian and Polish cultural hegemony and political domination. The project was called "Lithuania Awaken!," and in the eyes of nationalist pioneers, Jews were the ones who stood most in the way of the economic and social emancipation of their small and universally threatened people. In an 1884 edition of the national-liberal journal *Aušra* (Dawn), one of the leading nationalists, the physician Jonas Šliūpas, warned: "Jews are bloodsuckers. They suck people dry while they are sleeping and leave them behind completely drained." As a remedy the author implored his drowsy compatriots to "enter into the productive trades." That, argued Šliūpas, was the only way out of their stultifying uneducated rural poverty toward a better life. (A national monument to Dr. Šliūpas still stands in today's Palanga.) In the same journal, other secular Lithuanians encouraged the people to overcome their own "laziness and insecurity" and imitate the Jews' mercantile spirit. Once mobilized, they would be able to stand up to the "Jewish foreigners," who like lice "ceaselessly bite at us," and to drive them, in the words of several nationalist agitators, "from the market towns and cities."

Conservative Catholic publications were every bit as eager to sound the alarm. Thanks to established institutional structures and the stature of priests, Catholic opinion-makers had particular influence on ordinary people. In 1891, a Catholic editor demanded that all priests explain to peasants that "we can live without this plague, the Jews," and to popularize the idea that "He who loves God will deliver us from the Jews!" In 1904, echoing the nationalists, Father Pranas Turauskas described Lithuanians' path to economic emancipation: "The Jews will soon quit Lithuania if we Lithuanians get more involved in trade, found individual and joint businesses, and exclusively buy from our own kind."

As in other countries, the idea was to use trade and consumer associations to undermine Jews and, if that proved insufficient, to employ violence. Otherwise, alarmists warned, Jews would turn Lithuania into the "Polish province of New Palestine." In 1905, during the revolutionary unrest and widespread pogroms in the Russian Empire, the conservative Antanas Staugaitis preached uncompromising severity. Anyone who supported the cause of Lithuanian national and social progress, he argued, had to frankly name those who were most impeding it and "point their finger at the Jews."

Toward the end of the First World War, the tiny nation-state of Lithuania was created. Hemmed in by its neighbors, the country had around 2.3 million inhabitants, including 168,000 Jews (7 percent) in 1930. In the absence of alternatives, Kaunas became the capital. Vilnius, which until 1795 had been the cultural and political, if never the ethnic center of the Grand Duchy of Lithuania, had been occupied by Polish troops in 1919 and annexed by the new Poland. There was no Lithuanian majority in any of the tiny state's few cities. Seventy-five percent of trade was in Yiddish-speaking Jewish hands, while 21 percent of merchants spoke Polish and only 4 percent Lithuanian. The same constellation applied to urban property ownership: 45.8 percent of city real estate was owned by Jews, 33.8 percent by Poles, 7.5 percent by Russians, 6.5 percent by Lithuanians, and the rest by other minorities.

Both Lithuanians and Jews welcomed the end of the Russian yoke, and they both resisted Poland's ambitions to impose its dominance. Compared with Poland and Romania, there had been very few instances of anti-Jewish violence in Lithuania. But the somewhat harmonious coexistence of different ethnic groups didn't last long. In 1924, the post of minister for Jewish affairs was done away with, and one year later, restrictions were imposed on the cultural autonomy of Jewish communities. As was the case in other newly founded national states, Lithuania's political leaders went on a mission to emancipate the titular state population materially and socially—to the disadvantage of other groups who were better off. With the agrarian reforms of 1922, 38,700 landless Lithuanians received fields, and 26,000 tiny farmers were given additional property. The land that was being so generously doled out had previously belonged to Polish, Russian, and a handful of German large estate owners. In this way, the state satisfied impoverished villagers' hunger for something better in their lives.

Lithuania for Lithuanians

Jews weren't affected by these confiscations of property. But they had other reasons to fear for their existence. From the nationalist perspective, they were blocking the access of Christian Lithuanians to the promising professions connected with the cities. To correct this perceived imbalance, the new Lithuanian government gave almost all the positions in the civil service to members of the majority population. In 1934, only 477 of 35,200 Lithuanian civil servants were Jewish. In 1936, in the capital, Kaunas, where Jews made up a third of the populace and paid one-half of all the taxes, only 11 of the city's 800 employees were Jewish.

Educational discrimination was less crass in Lithuania than in Hungary, Romania, or Poland, but the proportion of Jewish students nonetheless sank between 1922 and 1938 from 30 to 15 percent. This was the result of significant investments made in the Lithuanian educational system and tests requiring that students speak the new national language, Lithuanian. Jews often spoke good Polish, Russian, or German, but rarely knew Lithuanian, which had been of little use in urban life.

Nationalist students resolutely expressed their hostility toward their Jewish peers and called for a moratorium on admitting Jews to university. To cite one extreme example: In 1933 the proportion of Jewish students at the medical school at Kaunas's Vytautas Magnus University was fifty-six times that of Jews in the population at large. In 1934, enraged campus activists declared: "Because of our tolerance, many departments today look like neighborhoods in Tel Aviv and not like Vytautas Magnus University." The fraternity New Lithuania appealed to the state and Lithuanian society to support the "native" intelligentsia because "the outcome of the competition with the non-Lithuanian intelligentsia remains uncertain."

During the Great Depression, the Lithuanian government encouraged economic and social hostility toward Jews. In 1934, it banned them from being involved in forestry, transport, and the trade of tobacco, matches, coal, sugar, and, a short time later, flax. Public contracts were as a rule awarded to Christian bidders. The Association of Trade, Industry and Artisanship, founded in 1930, pursued the goal of "Lithuania for Lithuanians." Jews were barred from joining since their mere presence contradicted the purpose of the organization, which was to Lithuanianize the country's industry within five years—and the commercial sector even sooner. Although the government didn't adopt the association's program wholesale as the group desired, it did support it in a variety of respects. In 1923, around 75 percent of all trading companies belonged to Jews, but that number declined swiftly. By the end of the 1930s, 43 percent of domestic and 66 percent of foreign trade had been transferred to Christian Lithuanian hands. Starting in 1937, the Young Lithuania (Jaunoji Lietuva) organization fought for the goal of "Lithuanians playing the leading role in all areas of life." The government, for its part, promoted "economic independence" from Jews. It encouraged upwardly mobile young people to become hardworking entrepreneurs and not part of an "unproductive academic proletariat," and nationalist politicians promised to help them get ahead. The Association for National Protection did its best to promote anti-Semitism, with speakers attacking "destructive Jewish behavior." They demanded that "Jews be eliminated from the economy so as to support the position of Lithuanians" and exhorted the majority, "Let us stand together with our own kind in all areas of life!"

Lithuanians' economic and intellectual advancement and their urbanization were to be pushed at Jews' expense. Jewish sociologist Jakob Lestschinsky characterized the economic attacks by Christian Lithuanians on Jews as a gradual and "maliciously organized process of destruction." In his analysis he stressed social and economic motors: "The broader the social basis of anti-Semitism becomes, the more resolutely Lithuanians of various social classes, especially shopkeepers and artisans, laid claim to Jews' economic positions." The same charge could be leveled against Christian Lithuanian students, whose numbers increased fourfold between 1922 and 1932.

Two aspects of the Lithuanian example bear particular attention. First, modern hostility toward Jews was ideologically connected with the economic and social emancipation of the backward masses, who lacked formal education. Second, anti-Semitism gained strength in the "days of freedom" in 1904 and 1905 when Russian censorship and police violence were eased for several months amid revolutionary unrest. No sooner did the government in St. Petersburg reestablish control than violent anti-Semitism tapered off. After the end of Russian rule, with the start of national independence, it smoldered under the initial republican regime and then reignited under the populist, autocratic one that followed—with the new, clearly formulated goal of driving Jews from their economic positions.[1]

ROMANIA: HATRED OF JEWS AND THE WILL OF THE PEOPLE

The statesmen who negotiated the peace treaties in Paris in 1919 and 1920 more than doubled Romania's square area with the aim of making it an anti-Soviet and anti-Hungarian buffer state. They added to the existing Romanian territory Hungarian Transylvania (Siebenbürgen), large parts of Banat, Russian Moldova (Bessarabia), and Austrian Bukovina. According to a 1930 census, 728,000 Jews lived in the country, making up around 4.5 percent of a total population of 16 million people. Before the First World War, Romania had only had around 6.5 million people. Economically and socially, the short-lived and weak government of this newly patched-together Greater Romania faced serious challenges.

Although Romanian anti-Semitism remained virulent, in 1919 the new liberal-democratic order and the conditions imposed upon the country by the Peace Treaty of Paris-Trianon suddenly gave Jews improved educational opportunities. Romania's new circumstances may not have been clearly defined, but it was obvious that they fundamentally differed from the prewar era. Between the academic years 1921–22 and 1935–36, Jews represented 23 percent of students at the University of Iaşi, and in the departments of law, medicine, and pharmacy they represented, respectively, 20, 40, and 80 percent of those enrolled. Albeit at a lower level, the universities in Bucharest, Cluj, and Cernăuţi reflected similar ratios.

That didn't work for long. As early as 1920, students and government ministry officials came up with the idea of founding a special university in Chişinău, formerly Russian Kishinev, "in order to train a Romanian elite," since Russians and Jews made up the majority in the existing universities. Also in 1920, Romanian students in Iași set the editorial offices of the Jewish magazine *Lumina* on fire. In 1922, they ransacked the printing press of the publisher H. Goldner, which put out the Jewish newspaper *Opinia*. Further acts of violence followed, one after another. In general, Romanian nationalist activists and agents of the secret police suspected Jews of communist and freemason activities.

In Cernăuți in 1920, university directors approved a course in Hebrew but, following historical examples, demanded double tuition from students enrolled in it. At the University of Cluj in late 1922, students prevented Jewish classmates from taking part in medical classes. One year later, Christian students physically ejected their Jewish counterparts from the Institute for Anatomy at the University of Iași. They also demanded that Jews only be allowed to perform autopsies on "bodies of their own race," that the police be forbidden from entering campus grounds, and that those who had been convicted of acts of violence against Jews be released from prison. Police and officials in the justice system in Iași sometimes, but not always, intervened against right-wing nationalist violence. Leaders of anti-Semitic campaigns were occasionally arrested or kicked out of university. Their followers immediately protested against "the brutal intervention of the police" and demanded, sometimes in violent demonstrations, the immediate rescindment of "state repression measures."

On April 23, 1923, nationalist groups occupied the university in Iași, insisting that admission limits be imposed on Jews. The university's leadership suspended classes and, in a tactical, opportunistic move, hinted that a referendum would be held. At the same time, militant students in Cluj demonstrated against the rector of their university, Jakob Kacobovici, because he was Jewish. In December, the rector in Iași called in the army to put down recurring student attacks. Individual professors, including the abovementioned political scientist Alexandru Cuza, sympathized with the rebels. Others took a clear stand against anti-Semitic acts of violence. One of them was the law professor Dumitru Mototolescu in Oradea (Nagyvárad), who was promptly branded a "Jew-lover." In 1925, a number of classrooms at the University of Bucharest had to be evacuated because of anti-Semitic rioting. In 1926, the University of Iaşi temporarily suspended classes for the same reason. All in all, anti-Semitic activities were becoming more severe and their appeal was increasing. Nationalist and Christian students, who encouraged one another, came together to vandalize synagogues, deface Torah scrolls, and attack their Jewish fellow students in parks, on trains, or at universities themselves.

Murderers of Jews Become Popular Heroes

In October 1924, Corneliu Zelea Codreanu shot dead the police prefect of Iaşi, Constantin Manciu, who had been installed the previous year. Codreanu's sole motivation? Manciu had repeatedly ordered his officers to suppress anti-Semitic acts of violence. The trial of Codreanu began on March 17, 1925, in Focşani. Hundreds of sympathizers traveled to Iaşi to show solidarity with the defendant. On the streets, they celebrated the murder he had committed as a heroic deed and began to "truly incite people to attack the peaceful Jewish populace." As the police and soldiers looked on, they destroyed Jewish businesses, throwing their inventory out into the streets, and laid waste to synagogues. A Jewish senator named Sanilievici asked for a declaration from the government about its position toward the "wanton destruction of these villains." He received no answer.

The judges at Codreanu's first trial found him guilty, but the appeals judges said he had acted in self-defense and acquitted him. The appeal was held in late May in Turnu Severain. Hardly had he exited the courtroom than Codreanu headed home "like a victor" while "along the way, especially on the trains, Jewish travelers were insulted and physically attacked." After a demonstration, inspired by Professor Cuza and to show solidarity with Codreanu in Iaşi, university and middle-school students threw two Jewish girls, Manaia Wagner and Marca Rimer, from a moving train. Both were seriously injured. When their attackers arrived in Iaşi, they boasted about what they had done, driving in open cars through the city and gleefully bellowing "Long live Codreanu!" and "Down with the Jews!" In 1926, Nicolae Totu traveled from Iaşi to Cernăuţi and shot dead the Jewish student David Fallik. Under pressure from anti-Semitic student protests, the court that heard the case acquitted the murderer in February 1927. The verdict was upheld in 1930.

Like Codreanu before him, Totu was celebrated as a hero. Cuza was one of his attorneys, and Romanian interior minister and later short-term prime minister Octavian Goga praised his deed as "a defense of Romania, whose honor had been wounded." Goga accused Jews of treating Romanians "in the country of Stephan the Great" (Stephan II, ca. 1433–1504) as the English treated the people they colonized. When tens of thousands of Jews in Cernăuţi staged a memorial for Fallik, Goga told the country's parliament that the funeral train had been an "anti-Romanian demonstration." In September 1933, he paid his respects to Adolf Hitler.[2]

In the summer of 1925, Jewish parliamentary deputies Adolphe Stern, Yehuda Leib Zirelsohn, and Nathan Lerner addressed the dramatically changed situation: "This cowardly and barbaric attack [on the two girls] is nothing other than the repetition and fatal result of various similar directionless attacks, which have been going on throughout Romania for the past two years together with a whole series of assassinations, ransackings and incidents of Jewish students' being abused and driven from university." After Codreanu's acquittal, "the knights of the swastika" believed that they ruled the land, and set about terrorizing the Jewish population and threatening their lives and security.[3] In 1927, when Zirelsohn excoriated acts of violence against Jews in the Romanian Senate, the chamber's president ordered that his words not be recorded in the protocol. Zirelsohn resigned in protest.

Until his violent death in 1938, Codreanu led the right-wing extremist Archangel Michael Legion, which rose to become Romania's third-strongest political party in the 1930s. Totu also became one of its leaders. Most of the anti-Semitic students came from modest, often farming backgrounds, a source of insecurity they transformed into militancy. They tried to convince themselves that they belonged to an especially noble people, the unsurpassable Romanians. But behind their martial façade, their sense of intellectual inadequacy was apparent, as revealed in a pamphlet distributed by the Association of Christian Students on November 28, 1924. It read: "December 10 is the third anniversary of the day on which Romanian students took up the cause of matriculation limits in order to defend the nation against foreign interlopers. Privileged by superior material backgrounds and other favorable circumstances, they are striving to destroy us and dominate the Romanian nation. . . . We students who have become enlightened must defend our nation and not shy away from either hard work or personal sacrifice in our effort to free her from the foreigners' clutches and protect her from future interlopers."[4]

As summarized by historian Lucian Nastasă of the University of Cluj: "The anti-Semitic groups became stronger and stronger at the universities. They created an atmosphere of militant agitation and intimidation that continually led to violence, incited by organizations and parties like the Christian-Social League, the Romanian Action, the National Romanian Fascists, the Christian-National Defense League, the Archangel Michael Legion, the Everything for the Fatherland Association, the Iron Guard, etc." In the years 1919 to 1930, politicized students and professors who sympathized with them helped form the group who would later pull the levers of state power in the 1930s. As to why organized anti-Semitism attracted so many eager followers between the world wars, Nastasă writes:

Mainly, at least as an initial impetus, it was economically and socially motivated. Romanian Jews had proven long before what remarkably good competitors they were in the areas of the economy and the higher professions so crucial to modernity. That embittered Christian Romanians and stoked their fears of failure. . . . After the First World War, Romania nominally gave Jews equal rights, although only under pressure from international organizations. Ultimately, in 1923, the constitution guaranteed their full rights as citizens. Banking on these somewhat secure rights, Jews, who had been kept away from universities, seized their new opportunities en masse.[5]

The scenes playing themselves out at universities also colored Romanian school policy. In 1926, only 8.2 percent of those getting university-
qualifying high school degrees were ethnic Romanians. Here, too, Jews
were miles ahead. For that reason, in October 1926 in Cernăuți a commission with a majority of radical nationalists was convened. Students
who had passed written exams were subjected to an oral test. The
results spoke for themselves: "All the students at the Romanian high
school passed the test, while fifty-one out of sixty-eight candidates
from the Jewish school failed it, as did twenty-six out of twenty-nine
students from the Ukrainian school and ten out of fourteen at the
German school."[6]

Although Romanian law didn't bar them from the civil service, Jews
were rarely tolerated in it between the world wars—a situation similar
to that in Wilhelmine Germany from 1870 to 1918. That left well-
educated Jews with little option but to seek out niches in economic
life and nonguild professions in order to earn a comfortable living.
Within a few years, Jews held top jobs on newspapers, in publishing
houses, and in film companies; they also became well-respected doctors, apothecaries, and lawyers. By contrast, their risk-averse Christian
contemporaries settled for poorly paid civil-service posts. When they
did dare to compete for better positions, they were more prone to failure than their Jewish peers.

The strict autonomy of Romanian universities introduced in 1919
and 1920 allowed nationalist professors to become a powerful and
perennial force. When posts needed to be filled, they preferred to tap
their own. Among the student body, influential radical nationalist activists demanded the exclusion of the overachieving Jewish minority in
the name of democracy and equal opportunity. There were real problems underlying this conflict. Since 1919, Romania had been improving its school system and had fostered enthusiasm for education. But
a lack of economic progress, cronyism, and the Great Depression had
caused stagnation. This created an unemployed "intellectual proletariat" that demanded some sort of career prospects. Romanian university
graduates increasingly tried to enter the nonguild professions and soon

sought to get rid of the Jewish competition. Politically they followed their generation's party leaders who propagated a "moral renewal of society" and called for an end of those parties that obeyed the commands of a "Jewish camarilla operating in the shadows and ruling over the Romanian finance system."

225,222 Jews Become Stateless

In 1937, Professor Cuza became a member of the government led by Octavian Goga. Despite only holding office for forty days, Prime Minister Goga pushed through a great amount of anti-Jewish legislation. He had all newspapers belonging to Jewish publishers closed and encouraged the Romanianization of schools, public administration, and companies and private businesses. Most significantly, he introduced a law requiring a review of Jews' Romanian citizenship. Owing to this legislation more than 30 percent of Romanian Jews lost their rights as citizens by November 1939. In this fashion the Romanian government made 225,222 people stateless.[7]

At the time the writer and journalist Mihail Sebastian, who had been born in 1907 as Iosif Hechter, noted in his diary that members of the government had adopted the coarse vocabulary of the far right, including terms like "Jewish sow" and "triumph of Judas." The day after Sebastian jotted this down, on December 30, 1937, Romanian Jews were prohibited from working as journalists. On January 2, 1938, he wrote: "They took away my permission to practice my profession. Our names were printed in all the newspapers as though we were criminals." On January 7, Sebastian's friend, the banker Aristide Blank, predicted: "The only hope for Jews is the preservation of the Goga government. What comes after it will be infinitely worse." As it happened, the government was overthrown on February 10, but the anti-Semitic laws remained on the books, and Blank's prognosis would prove prophetic.

On March 17, 1938, the newspaper *Cuvântul* ran the headline: "Pseudo-Scholar Freud Arrested by National Socialists in Vienna."

The same paper claimed that a group of Jewish attorneys who had been physically attacked before a court building in Bucharest had been "fighting among themselves." On August 22, Sebastian visited his friend Marietta, "who was practically boiling over with anti-Semitism." To his face she heaped abuse on "the fat-bellied Jews and Jewesses with their jewelry," making exceptions for "around a hundred thousand 'reasonable' Jews," of whom he was presumably one. On October 1, 1938, after the Munich agreement ceded Czech Sudetenland to Nazi Germany, he noted: "A horrific age is brewing up before us. Only now will we learn what Hitler's pressure means."[8]

How the Nazis viewed conditions in Romania at the time may be seen in a German dissertation of September 1938. "The Jewish Question in Romania" was submitted by Hans Schuster at the University of Leipzig, and praised Cuza as someone "who had worked incorruptibly on the solution to the Jewish question for decades" before complaining, inaccurately, that the Goga/Cuza government's anti-Semitic measures had "never made it beyond paper." Schuster was more effusive in his praise for the radical, paramilitary Iron Guard and the leader of the Archangel Michael Brigade, the murderer Codreanu, for his desire to "create a new Romanian man as the one who will carry out all measures and programs" and to sensibly combine "the peasant and the Jewish questions." According to the ideas of the Guard, "all questions lead back to the Jewish one as the most important national problem, both in the economic areas of trade and industry and the social one of middle-class life." Indeed, the Romanians were "a people without a middle class." The foreign Jewish minority, he argued, had continued right up to the present day to hinder the establishment of the Romanian nation. He urged Romanian politicians to do more: "Thus far, despite all Romanian efforts, the Jewish question has been a problem that has not been overcome. It will also be the crux of Romanian national life in the future and attract the attention of those foreign countries with an interest in solving the international Jewish question."[9]

This generation of Romanian students stayed true to the sentiments they expressed between 1919 and 1925, later turning them into reality. Schuster was by no means the only one to praise the idea of creating a nationalist middle class in Romania at the expense of Jews. On July 26, 1940, in conversation with Hitler, Romanian prime minister Ion Gigurtu remarked that Romania had already begun with the "solution of the Jewish question" but that "there was no way it could proceed on to a definitive settlement without help from the Führer, who would have to execute a total solution for all of Europe."[10]

Encouraged by Hitler, the Romanian regime imposed further restrictions on Jews. On August 8, 1940, the few remaining Jewish employees were fired from the career civil service. On October 4, a decree nationalized all Jewish property and businesses in the country's heartland. The Romanian economics minister was empowered to appoint commissars to Romanianize larger businesses and corporations. On October 9, marriages between Jews and gentiles were forbidden. On October 14, another decree banned Jews from teaching at or attending public schools and universities. Anyone with a Christian mother and a Jewish father was also considered Jewish.

On November 12, Jewish laborers and clerks in both the public and private sectors lost their jobs. On December 4, Jews were barred from military service, hit with a special tax, and required to do compulsory labor. Back in June, after France had surrendered to Germany, Sebastian had noted: "The rational mind stops functioning and the heart feels nothing anymore." By January 1, 1941, he wrote: "If we are allowed to survive this year, we will perhaps be that much closer to the end of the tunnel."

But only three weeks later, it was already apparent that 1941 would be a darker year still. From January 20 to 24, the fascists organized into the Archangel Michael Legion, which had formerly been part of the government and enjoyed German support, and tried to take control of the Romanian army. This putsch was put down with a minimum of casualties among Romanians. A "great catastrophe," however, was visited upon Bucharest's Jewish districts. "No window remained unbroken, and no house, regardless of how small, escaped being plundered and set on fire," reported Sebastian on January 27. "Imagine the burning district on Wednesday night, when hordes of criminals simply shot down horrified people. All of this happened in a

wretched neighborhood, a ghetto for the poor. Modestly living tradesmen, small-time merchants, humble, hard-working people who were
barely able to earn their daily bread. Here in the ruins an old woman,
a wailing, naked child who seemed to be waiting for something. For
what? For whom? Long lines of people waiting to enter the morgue.
So many people have disappeared. So many bodies have not been identified. Today's edition of *Universul* is full of Jewish death announce-
ments. The cemeteries are full of fresh graves. And we still don't know
how many Jews were killed." By January 27, 121 murdered Jews had
been buried in Bucharest.[11]

On March 18, a law raised rents for Jewish tenants. Sebastian found
such legal anti-Semitic measures more frightening and humiliating than
the beatings and broken windows. A decree on March 27 nationalized
all state property owned and rented by Jews who hadn't served in the
First World War or been naturalized before August 15, 1916. Jews'
homes were to be given to teachers, officers, and civil servants. Sebastian asked himself: "What will follow the appropriation of property?
Perhaps the establishment of a ghetto. And then? All that's left will
be a pogrom." On March 28, Romanian newspapers celebrated the
appropriations initiative. On April 20, authorities began confiscating
Jews' radios. Sebastian lost his that very day, his most important point
of connection with the rest of the world. He watched as preparations
were made for war with the Soviet Union and bemoaned "a summer
that will be extremely difficult for us Jews—it can't be otherwise." The
repressive measures listed here and many others required the creation
of a new state authority: the National Center for Romanianization,
which took up its work on May 2, 1941.

It was not that the state was imposing anti-Semitic restrictions to
head off popular anger or distract attention from social problems.
Rather, the Romanian people used their right to assemble and demonstrate to demand such action. As was the case in other countries, gentile
students and university graduates—the avant-garde of the nationalist
drive to improve Romania's lot—led the protests and shaped them
politically. Protected by a democratic constitution, they founded totalitarian nationalist organizations.

On June 21, 1941, Romanian prime minister Ion Antonescu announced that his country had been engaged since the early morning hours in a "holy war for the liberation of Bessarabia and Bukovina and the destruction of Bolshevism." That day, a decree was issued requiring fifty thousand Jews who lived in the countryside to surrender their property and move to the cities. Police hung up two different posters in the streets. The first depicted Stalin as the "Butcher of Red Square," while the second showed a "Jewish sow" with *payot*, a yarmulke, and a beard, dressed in a red caftan and holding a hammer and sickle. The poster read, "These are the leaders of Bolshevism." On June 27, Bucharest newspapers ran headlines demanding "Jewish swine" be put in "labor camps." Officials ransacked Jewish homes, confiscating bedding and pajamas to equip military hospitals. In early September, they ordered the Jewish community in Bucharest to collect and hand over within two days four thousand beds, pillows, and blankets as well as twice that number of sheets and pillowcases.

In August, all male Jews in Bucharest between the ages of eighteen and sixty were required to report to police and register for forced labor. No sooner had these people been conscripted than the Romanian government demanded a ransom of 10 million lei. Some Romanians felt ashamed and tried to console their Jewish acquaintances and offer assurances that they had no part in the repressive measures. "The bad thing," Sebastian wrote, "is that no one has anything to do with it. The whole world finds it worthy of condemnation and is outraged, yet nonetheless everyone is a small cog in the anti-Semitic factory that is the Romanian state, with its offices, administrative authorities, newspapers, institutions, laws and measures. . . . And the masses celebrate. The shedding of Jewish blood and the humiliation of the Jew has always been the best amusement for the people."[12]

POLISH NATIONALISTS IN ACTION

At the 1815 Congress of Vienna, international diplomats created what came to be known as "Congress Poland," a truncated protectorate state under Russian control. They declared Warsaw the capital and the

Russian tsar the Polish king. The idea was to head off Polish desires for liberty while giving cities and communities limited autonomy. Within this framework, despite the occasionally harsh Russian military regime, Polish desires for freedom and Polish nationalism thrived.

Whereas since 1806 German nationalism had been directed against French domination, Polish nationalism primarily saw Russia as the enemy together with Prussia and Austria, who had all agreed to the division of Poland. In both Germany and Poland, the ideology of liberty was accompanied early on by xenophobia and hostility toward Jews. In 1818, as the pioneer of German nationalism Ernst Moritz Arndt was publishing one of his many works containing anti-Semitic passages, the Polish revolutionary nationalist Walerian Łukasiński brought on his own polemic on the Jewish question. In it he accused Jews living in Poland of "total decadence of character," hatred for everything Christian, and a proclivity toward deception and nontransparent dealings.[13]

After Polish rebellions against the Russian yoke were violently put down in 1830–31 and 1863, the Narodowa Demokracja (National Democracy) movement rose to become Poland's strongest political force at the start of the twentieth century. It pursued the goal of a unified, ethnically "pure" populist state and successfully put itself forward as the "defender against everything foreign," particularly everything Jewish. In 1912, National Democrats made anti-Semitism into a popular centerpiece of their platform. As a beginning, they organized a countrywide boycott of Jewish businesses and companies. In the flyers they distributed, they alternately denigrated Jews as threatening modernizers, as obstacles to Poland's path to economic prosperity, and as stubbornly "ossified" insisters on tradition who were incapable of assimilation. In general, Jews were cast as willing tools of the exploitative Polish aristocracy and especially the tsarist government, which was trying to Russify Poland with the help of its Jewish henchmen.

The ideologue Roman Dmowski became one of the National Democrats' leading figures. From 1917 to 1921, he was one of the most prominent founders of the Polish Republic, and a signatory to the

Treaty of Versailles that sealed Germany's abdication of territory to the new Polish state. Dmowski characterized Jews as a "major internal danger" and potential destroyers of basic Christian values. He never tired of warning his Catholic compatriots about Jews' purported ruthlessness and slyness, or what he called the "instincts and proclivities of the Jewish psychological type." He demonized the "foreign elements" that could "all too easily force on Poles their social, political and even artistic and literary perspectives" and were capable of "absorbing the majority intellectually and in part also physically." Proceeding from such assumptions, he demanded that the National Democrats "lead the struggle for the social liberation from Jewish influences." Dmowski thought that pronounced class conflicts could be overcome, but not the "cultural, economic and political antagonism" of peoples with opposing characters.[14]

In a 1903 article titled "Thoughts of a Modern Pole," Dmowski laid out what he didn't like about Jews—and Germans, for that matter. The Polish people, he complained, had missed the boat with modernity and industrial development and had been unable to exploit the markets opening far to the east. Consequently, on the one hand, there were people who had earned wealth through "initiative, entrepreneurship and personal energy," while on the other, thousands "had been forced to scale back their needs as they declined socially." In Dmowski's eyes, Jews were the primary beneficiaries of dramatic increases in productivity and trade in goods—not because they had swindled people or were part of a treacherous race, but because they were "free of traditionally Polish passivity." Dmowski was an early supporter of boycotting Jewish businesses, but he didn't consider this an anti-Semitic end unto itself. Rather, he hoped boycotts would jump-start a social movement that would awaken the Polish people's "healthy social needs" and help them "seize control" of economic positions for a still-to-be-created nationalist Polish bourgeoisie. Once this process had gotten going, it would become self-perpetuating, thanks to the "increase in active middle-class people who would try to take over commercial fields presently dominated by a foreign element."[15]

Narodowa Demokracja's emphasis on ethnicity, which Dmowski

helped bring about, set the tone for politics in the Polish Republic between the two world wars. It was considered perfectly legitimate to use the newly created state as a powerful agency on behalf of the majority—and to the detriment of all ethnic and religious minorities. All the way back in their 1903 party platform, Narodowa Demokracja had called for an end to the "predominance of the Jews in broad stretches of economic life."[16] In 1934, Dmowski interrupted his political retirement to publish his book *Przewrot* (Upheaval). Filled with anti-Semitic outrage, he blamed Jews for all of Poland's defeats and humiliation: "If there hadn't been so many Jews in Poland, there would have been no division of Poland, and the Prussian government wouldn't have celebrated any triumphs in the East." In the same breath, he described former British prime minister Lloyd George as a "Jewish agent," who in 1919 listened to the Jews whispering in his ear and so decided against giving Poland the city of Danzig and major portions of Silesia and East and West Prussia. Dmowski also expressed his respect for Hitler's policies of "getting rid of Jewish influence in Germany."[17]

Dmowski was one of the fathers of the modern Polish state reconstituted in 1918, but also one of the patriarchs of an aggressive Polish anti-Semitism that was modern insofar as it addressed contemporary crises and problems. Today he is revered in his homeland as a hero of Poland's national rebirth. Dozens of streets and squares bear his name, and in 2006 a hulking memorial to him was unveiled in downtown Warsaw.

Like the National Democrats, equally influential conservative Catholic leaders did not follow the tradition of holding Jews responsible for the Crucifixion. They adhered to new socioeconomically based stereotypes. In his 1912 manifesto *Poznaj Żyda!* (Know the Jew!), which ran through many editions and is still reprinted today, the widely respected author Teodor Jeske-Choiński merged the Jewish question with Catholic social teachings. In garish terms, he depicted how the "Jewification" of economic life created a "terrible, ruthless battle for existence" and made honestly striving individuals into playthings of selfish industrialism, capital, and speculative investment.

He contrasted these demonic forces with an admirably harmonious form of the economy that was "committed to Christian ethics," that "defended people," and that knew "no competition at the cost of other suppliers and sellers."

Jeske-Choiński called upon the Polish people to defend themselves and teach a brutal lesson to their supposed oppressors: "The Jews will reap what they have sown. In the battle for survival, fantasies about love and people's right to live their lives are obsolete. The Jews would be the first to laugh if they succeeded in halting the Poles' economic self-defense."[18] In fact since 1870, despite a myriad of Russian and Polish national restrictions, a disproportionate number of Jews had achieved success in academic positions or as entrepreneurs and bankers. In 1929, they still represented half of all Polish doctors, almost half of all Polish writers, artists, journalists, architects, teachers, lawyers, and engineers, and more than half of all chemists, mathematicians, and physicists.[19]

Discrimination Against Jews to the Benefit of Poles

Freed from the yoke of the powers that had divided the country, the new Polish republic constituted itself in late 1918. Head of state Józef Piłsudski and his troops succeeded in expanding eastward beyond the so-called Curzon line into disputed Lithuanian, Belarussian, and Ukrainian territories. The line, which forms today's eastern Polish border, had been proposed by British foreign minister George Curzon at the 1919 Paris Peace Conference and reflected the complex linguistic and cultural topography of Eastern Europe. With the exception of the Białystok district, it was also the line used by Hitler and Stalin when they divided up Poland in 1939. The Second Polish Republic, which was formed between 1918 and 1921, had 30 million inhabitants, but only two-thirds of them were Poles in the nationalist sense. The country was also home to 5 million Ukrainians, 3 million Jews, 2 million Germans, and 1.2 million Belarussians as well as groups of Lithuanians, Czechs, Hungarians, Ruthenians, and people of mixed heritage like the Kashubians and the Slonzaks (Czech Silesians).

As a military man, General Piłsudski was able to dramatically expand Polish territory in the three years after the First World War. As a politician, he had been one of the leaders of the Polish Social Democratic Party since 1893. In 1926 he staged a military coup against the legitimately elected but chaos-ridden Polish government. From that time on until his death in 1935, supported by the populist Sanacja (Recovery) movement he had founded, he ruled Poland in authoritarian fashion. Sanacja consisted of people who tended both to the political right and left. Together, their aim was to build a national, social-welfare-oriented consensus.

Jews had little to hope for from this newly founded republic. Most of their Catholic compatriots considered them disruptors of solidarity whose liberties were to be curtailed to the benefit of Poles.[20] To this end the new democratically elected Polish government went after Jewish schools, professional colleges, and Hebrew academies. Using a variety of pretexts, they limited the right of Jewish tradesmen to train apprentices, knowing full well that Christian tradespeople would not accept Jewish apprentices. The restrictions were aimed at keeping hundreds of thousands of young Jews from continuing to practice their fathers' trades, forcing them to emigrate. At the time, Jews represented around 10 percent of the Polish population, although they accounted for more like 22 percent of people living in cities. Eighty percent of all employed Jews earned their keep as tradesmen.

The Great Depression hit Poland in 1929 and was still being felt in 1939. Internally, it led to an increase in anti-Jewish activities and took on, in the words of one historian, "terrible dimensions" for Jews, who were effectively shut out of jobs in heavy industry. The broad-based textile economy was an especially important source of work, but Depression-era unemployment rates in that sector ran as high as 80 percent. By 1938, the Warsaw unemployment office only allocated work to Jewish women at two in the afternoon—and only after jobs had been given to all the Christian women seeking work that day.[21]

A high sales tax disproportionately affected Jews, who mainly lived from trade, artisanship, and small businesses or did regular jobs for bigger companies. Between 1927 and 1931, the Polish government's revenues from this tax increased by 80 percent, while agricultural work was entirely exempt from the tax, and property tax for farmers was kept low. In comparison to trade and manufacturing, the Christian farmers of largely agricultural Poland contributed only one-sixth of state revenues.

The German-Jewish Relief Organization listed other instances of intentional discrimination. Factories and companies owned by Christian Poles were "increasingly used by the public sector, and cartels were encouraged in an attempt to marginalize Jewish trade." Moreover, Christian merchants, factory owners, and cooperatives received "cheap credit from state institutions," whereas Jews were refused such loans. Meanwhile, the state took all the concessions it had granted to Jews for selling products like tobacco, salt, and alcohol and awarded them to "wounded military veterans, civil servants and military personnel." The timber trade remained completely in state hands, and with the assistance of the government, "Jew-free" monopolies were established. In its allocation of currency and import-export licenses, the state also helped organize the exclusion of Jews from more and more sectors of the Polish economy.

Despite repeatedly promising to do so, the government never relaxed the prohibition of working on Sunday. "Jews are forced to take two, and in winter two and a half days off, which of course makes them less competitive compared to non-Jewish merchants and artisans," noted the Relief Organization. Although no official restrictions existed, a tacit agreement excluded Jews from "everything from ministerial posts on down to mail delivery and train conductor jobs." Leading the campaigns and legal proceedings were nationalist, social-nationalist, and Catholic forces who nearly always cooperated with one another. Wherever debates arose about "the Jewish economic type," as they often did, socialists usually joined in as well. They too advocated the agenda of gentile cooperatives and the "battle against speculative investors."[22]

In 1936, social scientist Jakob Lestschinsky registered a decrease in the percentage of Jews in urban populations—perhaps because of non-Jews moving from the country or the incorporation of surround-ing rural areas into cities. In any case, Lestschinsky predicted "very dire" consequences for Jews: "The suburban populations absorbed into cities quickly acclimate to urban life and swiftly become intensive competitors in trade and commerce, further increasing the number of people looking to earn a living in ways the cities offered." Because Polish village populations were leaving en masse, "with the force of a power of nature," and there were not enough industrial jobs to go around, the battle for positions in the traditionally organized artisan trades, even the least lucrative, sometimes turned violent.

In 1934, after Poland had rescinded the guarantees of protection for minorities it had grudgingly issued in the Paris Treaty, Catholic clergy, journalists, parliamentarians, and the government pushed for legal and extralegal restrictions on Jews. Nationalists harassed Chris-tians who frequented Jewish shops, handing out lists with the names and addresses of Polish businesses and shops from which people were encouraged to obtain goods and services. Cutting off Jewish possi-bilities for earning a living amounted to an economic pogrom—"so intertwined in contemporary Poland with the physical one," as Lest-schinsky wrote in 1936, "that they can hardly be distinguished."

Historian Cornelius Groschel concluded: "The desire to economi-cally marginalize the Jewish population in the Second Polish Republic was part of the 'national modernization' of the Polish state," intended to mobilize in equal measure farmers, the self-employed middle classes, and civil servants. Economic and social-welfare goals were para-mount.[23]

"Ghetto Benches" for Jewish Students

Hardly had the Second Polish Republic been founded than Christian students vehemently demanded that universities be protected from being "permanently Jewified." The *Gazeta Warszawska* wrote on October 2, 1922, that the University of Cracow was "Jewified both intellectually and in terms of personnel." On April 21, 1923, national-ist students bombed the Cracow home of the internationally renowned

Jewish physicist Władysław Natanson, though the professor was unharmed.

At the time, Jews made up a quarter of student bodies. But in 1923, following Russian, Romanian, and Hungarian models, the Polish government drew up a law regulating admission to the country's universities on the basis of ethnicity. The draft legislation stipulated that students from religious and linguistic minorities could only be admitted in "the same proportion as the minority in question represented within the whole population." After a campaign by the Comité des Délégations Juives in Paris, the government decided at the last minute that it didn't need such a law. But limits on the numbers of Jewish students were gradually and tacitly imposed anyway—in contravention of the agreement to protect national and religious minorities Poland had agreed to in Versailles on June 28, 1919.

Of the 200 places for new students at Warsaw's medical school in 1923, only nine went to Jews. By contrast, Lviv's law school instituted what initially seemed to be remarkably liberal quotas: 60 percent of places were reserved for Poles, while 40 percent were allocated to Jews and Ukrainians. In the fall semester of 1925–26, there were 600 openings. But because only 220 Poles applied for them, the university president ordered that the number of spots be reduced, allowing only 145 Jews and Ukrainians. Cracow's medical school had been limiting the number of Jews since 1922. In the fall of 1925, 100 places were open, of which 13 were given to the 400 Jewish applicants. The dean denied that this amounted to a limit.

Other university heads came up with especially clever ways of keeping Jews from studying medicine. One was to make admission contingent upon "a sufficient number of Jewish corpses" being available for basic anatomy classes—as if the baptized dead couldn't bear to be dissected by unbaptized students.[24] Polish university administrators knew that for religious reasons Jews were far less likely than Christians to donate their bodies to science. They had copied this form of exclusion from their Romanian colleagues who in 1925 had pushed for a law that stipulated: "If Jewish hospitals don't provide sufficient corpses, Jewish students are prohibited from practicing on Christian bodies."[25]

By 1927, 9 percent of the students at Warsaw Polytechnic University, 8.3 percent at the Cracow Medical Academy, and 10 percent at that city's Institute for Pharmacology were Jewish. But many gentile students were unhappy even with such decreased numbers and demanded a total ban on Jews attending university. Also, as had already happened in Russia and Romania, gentiles soon called for "nostrification," a refusal to acknowledge academic degrees acquired abroad. "What do Jews do when they're not admitted to study in Poland?" asked nationalist student leaders. "Large numbers of them go abroad and can look forward afterward to a rosy career." Polish legislators were encouraged to close this loophole so that ambitious young Christians would be relieved of competition.[26]

The University of Lublin was made a Catholic institution. In Posen, previously part of Germany, Polish nationalist democrats summarily barred Jews from matriculating. The same thing happened at the University of Cracow, and only a handful of Jews were admitted to the Cracow School of Mining.[27] Professors also insisted on excluding women because they feared that "in this way Jewesses could gain access to Polish universities."

Intimidation of Jews increased throughout society in the 1930s, and universities were no exception. "Hardly a day passes without reports of Jews being assaulted in the streets, Jewish students being attacked in their universities and Jewish shop windows smashed," wrote the *Canadian Jewish Chronicle* in 1935. "On top of this violence the Jewish population is also confronted with a rapidly growing anti-Jewish boycott. . . . Refusal of the authorities to grant the anti-Semites' demand that Jewish students in the Warsaw Polytechnique Institute be segregated led to a riot during which nationalist students threw Jewish students out of windows. . . . More than a score of the anti-Semites were arrested." The majority of professors sympathized with the protesting students and had no objection to the latter's goals or their means of achieving them. University presidents and deans themselves ordered that Jews could only sit in special sections of lecture halls, so-called ghetto benches, in some cases banishing them to separate rooms entirely. During the 1938–39 fall semester, there were several major acts of violence in Lviv's two main universities. Three Jewish students—Karol Zellermayer, Samuel Proweller, and Markus Landsberg—were stabbed to death. Because Jewish students began defending themselves against the mounting violence, there were casualties on the other side as well.

Some faculty members did oppose the anti-Jewish violence. As early as 1919, Poland's leading linguist and enemy of narrow-minded nationalism Jan Nieczysław Baudouin de Courtenay criticized the restrictions. Educated in Prague, Leipzig, Cracow, and St. Petersburg, he taught at the University of Warsaw, where he publicly complained: "Today we are no longer guided by reason and concern for the general welfare, but by bestial hostility and 'racist' prejudice. Today we strive for the radical 'de-Jewification' of Polish society and the radical 'de-Jewification' of Polish science. In our revived state, this is considered evidence of the most stringent sort of 'patriotism.' Still, I consider this not just repulsive and disgusting, but worse, foolish and corruptive."

De Courtenay advised Zionist leaders and those who insisted on a legally protected, semiautonomous Jewish community in Poland to moderate their demands. He thought that claims to "national-personal and cultural autonomy" went too far because they insisted upon "autonomous institutions and administrative separation from the rest of the population." He argued that Jews had to accept the Second Republic's constitutional institutions, civil and criminal legal codes, as well as the state's right to raise taxes. Special Jewish schools should, however, be allowed state support and be under state supervision. "Those born Catholic and those born Jewish," wrote de Courtenay in a clear and elegant plea for liberalism, tolerance, and loyalty to the state, "must accept that they live on the same soil, within the borders of the same state."[28]

Another opponent, the Warsaw professor for philosophy and logic Tadeusz Kotarbiński, complained that Catholic clergy were inculcating young people with hatred of Jews. The so-called Jew parties—annual orgies of violence against Jews in November—were, as he pointed out, "normally kicked off with religious services."[29] Writer Kazimierz Brandys recalled similar scenes from his course in law at Warsaw University from 1935 to 1939. The son of a well-to-do assimilated Jewish family, Brandys had turned his back on religion and joined the Young Legion, which had been founded in the spirit of Piłsudski's authoritarian policies. He eventually left the organization, later writing: "At the meetings of the Warsaw chapter of the Legion, the speeches are scarcely distinguishable from the slogans of the fascist Falange. When one speaker criticized the anti-Semitic currents in the organization, saying 'My mother comes from a Jewish family,' he was greeted with mocking laughter. 'What am I doing here?' I asked myself, and turned in my membership card the very next day."

Brandys recalled that "Polish lawyers and doctors associations required proof of Aryan heritage" and that the Polish Education Ministry allowed universities to segregate Jews in lecture halls. Catholics were assigned to "even places," and Jews to "odd ones," with corresponding stamps in their student identification cards. Brandys was considered Christian. Together with other left-leaning fellow students, he remained standing against the wall "in protest at the bench ghetto." But the protesters were "always in the minority" and were "attacked by troops of brawlers every time." Meanwhile, the dean of the law school in Warsaw, Roman Rybarski, refused to let students involved in the protest take their exams. "That happened three months before one million Aryan Germans invaded Poland and one and a half years before the walls of the Warsaw Ghetto were built," Brandys recalled. In 1942, German occupiers murdered Rybarski at Auschwitz as a representative of Poland's nationalist intelligentsia.

Catholic National Anti-Semitism

In April 1933, the weekly newspaper of the southern Polish bishopric of Kielce, *Gazeta Tygodniowa*, offered an ambivalent analysis of the new regime across the border in Germany: "Hitler is Poland's enemy, but in the struggle against the moral corrosion caused by Jews, we have to admit he's right." Two days later, *Dzwon Niedzielny*, the Sunday paper of the bishopric of Cracow, seconded those thoughts: "Twenty-five professors, almost all of them Jews, have been stripped of their academic chairs in Germany. And they won't be the last. Only now do we realize how Jewified German academia was—and it's well known that we in Poland are suffering far worse!" The National Party's Germany expert, Stanisław Kozicki, and the Berlin correspondent for *Gazeta Warszawska*, Jerzy Drobnik, agreed that the "German-Jewish conflict was an internal private matter of the Reich," and Kozicki found warm words to praise the new German government for taking on Jews.[30]

In 1936, in an extreme exaggeration, *Dzwon Niedzielny* claimed that Jews owned 75 percent of all public real estate and 80 percent of all industrial facilities, did 85 percent of all trade, and received 90 percent of all private credit. "Must we accept this?" the paper asked. The answer given by these religious reporters and editors, who saw themselves as soldiers in the national vanguard, was absolutely not. They portrayed measures aimed at excluding Jews as acts of self-defense and argued in truly secular fashion: "Jews dominate most free trades. They control artisanship and are making advances in agriculture. They already control literary and artistic creation, and with the help of the press and radio they steer public opinion."

In 1938, the paper of the tiny bishopric of Tarnów, *Nasza Sprawa*, sought to stir up envy and hatred for the many Jews getting by as tailors. This was rarely a lucrative undertaking. Nonetheless, the paper pointed out that Kielce with its 58,000 inhabitants had 4,470 tailors' workshops, only a quarter of which were owned by Christian Poles. "Hundreds of thousands of Jews and their families are leading a comfortable existence," the paper concluded, thanks to Jewish domination of commerce, the skilled trades, and industry. In 1936 the newspaper *Niedziela* in the diocese of Częstochowa accused Jews of "spreading out" in Poland while forgetting that they were "not 'natives' but rather unwelcome guests."

As historian Viktoria Pollmann has shown, as a political goal the "de-Jewification of the Polish economy" enjoyed the complete support of the clerical and nationalist press. The 1938 "Week of Polishization of Industry, Commerce and Artisanship" began with a mass in Warsaw

Cathedral. Church reporters from *Gazeta Tygodniowa* reported on the proceedings with frank statements of hatred: "The Polishization of our unbelievably Jewified cities and towns is one of the most urgent questions of our lives and the slogan 'To each his own' one of our national commandments. . . . Only when millions of Poles can earn their daily bread in their own fatherland will prosperity grow in the country and we'll be rid of the plague that originated in those who have dragged our villages into ruination—the Jews. Only then will the most dangerous enemy—the enemy within—be defeated." To accelerate this process, the paper instructed its religious readership: "A good Pole doesn't spend a single złoty in a Jewish place of business."

Less stridently but no less insistently the head of Catholic Poland, Cardinal August Hlond, had called upon the faithful in a pastoral letter to boycott Jewish businesses: "From an economic perspective it is good to prefer one's own kind to others and pass by Jewish shops and market stalls." The cardinal had his letter read from Catholic pulpits throughout Poland in February 1936, providing millions of the faithful with a special variation on the commandment to love thy neighbor. "It's permissible to love one's own people more," he assured Polish Catholics. The cardinal condemned physical violence and conceded that there were many "pious, honest, just, charitable and generous" Jews, but that didn't negate the existence of a serious problem: "It is a fact that Jews fight against the Catholic Church, encourage free thinking and form the avant-garde of godlessness, Bolshevism and all revolutionary movements. It is a fact that Jews have a corrosive influence on morality and spread pornography with their publishing houses. It is true that Jews engage in deception, usury and slave trading."

In the fall of 1938, a *Gazeta Tygodniowa* author asked: "How can the country be de-Jewified?" His answer: "The Jews must be settled in uninhabited and nearly uninhabited places. Left to themselves, they could found a state of their own and no longer corrupt, demoralize or exploit anyone. With all their influence and wealth, it will be easy for them to find and, if necessary, purchase such a settlement area." The daily newspaper *Głos Narodu*, which had been owned by the archdiocese of Cracow since 1936, both criticized and expressed understanding for the Night of Broken Glass in Nazi Germany: "The Third Reich is about to burst the shackles Jews have put upon that country's economic and cultural life." Jews would have to leave Germany for good, the paper wrote, and recognize that "their hour of history was now at hand."[31]

Maksymilian Maria Kolbe, a Franciscan monk who was beatified in 1982, was born in Łódź but studied theology in Rome, where in 1917 he and some of his like-minded brothers founded the Catholic fundamentalist Knights of the Immaculata. The group dedicated itself to fighting secularism, free thinkers, and socialism. Kolbe himself formulated its statutes, which emphasized a series of self-imposed duties including "to try to change the minds of sinners, heretics, schismatics, Jews, etc. . . . and particularly freemasons and contribute to the salvation of all under the protection and mediation of the Immaculate Virgin."

In 1927, Kolbe founded the Niepokalanów monastery in the village of Teresin near Warsaw. There, together with several hundred lay brothers, he created the largest Catholic newspaper company in Poland. In 1936, after doing five years of missionary work in Japan, he resumed his duties at the head of the monastery and the company, which included putting out the daily newspaper *Mały Dziennik*. Founded in 1935 in the style of a modern tabloid, it was published with the express purpose of combating Jews, freemasons, and liberals.

In 1936, the paper attacked the nonreligious doctor Janusz Korczak, a Jew born Henryk Goldszmit, as a "free thinker, atheist and enemy of Catholicism." Korczak was then director of two orphanages, one for Jewish and one for Christian children, and the paper accused him of favoring the former because the Jewish orphans received additional tutoring. The journalists from *Mały Dziennik* considered it a "scandal" that "our children are put in the care of our enemy." They demanded the government put a stop to it, given that Korczak "is hostile to the Polish cause and undermines it."[32]

On November 9, 1938, the German diplomat Ernst vom Rath died after being shot by a Jewish teenager in Paris. *Mały Dziennik*, in an article titled "Lunatic Jews Not Satisfied with the Blood of a Third-Rate Civil Servant," characterized him as a "victim of Jewish brutality." The paper didn't mention the terrible pogrom—the Night of Broken Glass—that immediately commenced in Germany, merely noting: "It is to be expected that Chancellor Hitler will now push through the so-called 'final' policy against Jews."[33] One year later, Prelate Stanisław Trzeciak, one of the countless anti-Semitic clerics in Poland, justified Germany's treatment of Jews by writing: "Hitler derives his laws from the papal encyclicals . . . he is following the example of prominent popes."[34]

A 1938 article in the monthly magazine *Rycerz Niepokalanej*, which was founded by Kolbe in 1922 and for which he served as editor in chief and frequently wrote, offered the following words of praise: "In the battle against the front of freemasons, the church has found an ally: fascism. . . . Whenever you encounter people who minimize the destructive, demoralizing, antistate and antinational activities of the Jews, you can be certain that they are influenced by freemasonry, since freemasonry comes from Jewishness and serves its political ends." The same publication proclaimed in 1939 that Jewishness had eaten its way "like a cancerous tumor into the body of the people," adding: "It is tearing trade, industry, artisanship and even the land away from us."[35]

Those examples suffice to sketch out the extent of daily bias and hatred, although Catholic publications were surpassed in this regard by the younger wordsmiths of the National Party. One of them was the lawyer Michał Howorka, who in his 1934 book *Walka o Wielką Polskę* (Battle for the New Poland) demanded that Jews in Poland be left with no choice but to emigrate: "But first they must be made bankrupt. Only then should they emigrate. We cannot let them go until they have been turned into a pack of beggars. We can't afford to be sentimental. In our striving for victory over an enemy like this, we can't shy away from any sacrifice or effort. We cannot take account of any rights to property, civil rights or indeed life itself. We have to eradicate this tangle of Jews among us once and for all."[36]

After Germany invaded Poland, the German occupiers sent Kolbe and Howorka to Auschwitz, where they were murdered on August 14, 1941, and March 10, 1942, respectively, because they were members of the Polish nationalist intelligentsia. Korczak was sent as a Jew to Treblinka, where he was killed on August 7, 1942. He had refused offers by Christian Poles to help him flee the Warsaw Ghetto because he felt it his duty to accompany to their deaths the orphans with whom he had been charged. In Auschwitz, Kolbe had taken the place of a Christian fellow inmate with children who was to be executed in an act of reprisal. The man Kolbe saved, Franciszek Gajowniczek, survived the ordeal, dying in 1995 at the age of ninety-four.

HUMILIATED, IGNORANT HUNGARIANS

The peace treaty signed on June 4, 1920, in the Grand Trianon Palace in Versailles left behind a Hungary that was little more than a rump state, stripped of two-thirds of its territory and almost 60 percent of its population. The territories taken away consisted of places with non-Hungarian and mixed populations and areas settled by Hungarians, where they were now in the majority. Hungary was forced to cede large stretches of land to the newly formed states of Czechoslovakia and Yugoslavia as well as to newly enlarged Romania, while Burgenland was given to Austria. Of the 10 million inhabitants in these territories, some 3.3 million considered themselves Magyars in terms of language, heritage, and culture. Thus it was not without reason that most Hungarians considered themselves to be one of the biggest losers in the aftermath of the First World War.

After the collapse of Béla Kun's short-lived socialist Hungarian Republic of Councils in 1919, nationalists defamed Hungarian Jews collectively as traitors and Bolsheviks. Counterrevolutionaries killed some five thousand people, three thousand of them Jews. Yet political, social, and religious differences notwithstanding, almost all Hungarians could unite behind the slogan "*Nem, nem, soha!*" (No, no, never) to the terms of peace dictated to the country at Trianon. In his memoirs, writer Ephraim Kishon, who was born in Budapest in 1924 as Ferenc Hoffmann, described how Hungarians felt between the world

wars. He recalled as a student wistfully singing songs about reunit-
ing Hungary ("Oh my sweet Transylvania, we're prepared to die for
you"). In 1942, he even finished his course of study at the Budapest
Trade School with a test on the topic of "The heroic resistance of Hungary, the bulwark of Christianity and European culture, against the
Bolshevik hordes."[37]

Nationalistic and anti-Communist thinking in Hungary paved the
way in the 1930s for an alliance with Nazi Germany. Berlin achieved
for Budapest what it had only aspired to: a major revision of the Paris
peace treaties. Between 1938 and 1941, Hitler helped Hungary gain
significant stretches of territory to the detriment of Romania, Yugoslavia, and Slovakia, the state Hitler himself allowed to be created
on March 24, 1939. With Italy's help, the German Führer enlarged
Hungary from 93,000 to 172,000 square kilometers and increased the
population from 9 to 15 million people. Beginning in 1941, Hungarian troops fought side by side with their German allies against the
Soviet Union. Jewish Hungarians were forbidden to bear arms but
were deployed to build settlements or clear mines. Some 42,000 of
these Jewish "construction soldiers" died. In mid-July 1941, Hungary
deported 15,000 "foreigners," that is, Jews declared to be Polish, Slovakian, or stateless. They were murdered by German police battalions
in Kamianets-Podilskyi in what is now Ukraine in late August of that
year.[38]

As Switzerland's *Neue Zürcher Zeitung* reported on March 21,
1944, two days after the Wehrmacht invaded Hungary, Hungarians
determined to destroy the Trianon peace agreement had "permanently
trapped the country in the web of German war policies." It was only
at that point, late in the Second World War, that Germany needed to
apply moderate pressure to ensure the continued cooperation of conservative, nationalist forces in Hungary.

Up until then Hungary had remained a caste-oriented, reactionary state, dominated by paternalist large landowners and marred
by grotesque social inequalities. Yet although communists had been
kept down since the bloody suppression of the Hungarian Republic
of Councils and important parliamentary rights had been curtailed,

Hungary still had a variety of newspapers and political parties. They ranged from moderate social democrats to the oppositional liberal democratic Independent Smallholders, from the Agrarian Workers and Civic Party to the nationalist parties and the right-wing revolutionary and occasionally banned Arrow Cross Party. The conservative Renewal Party gained importance in the 1930s and increasingly influenced the political climate, despite being internally divided. Hungary's often rotating governments were essentially a club for national-liberal and conservative bigwigs who regularly quarreled among themselves and then came back together in new constellations. Hungary was a "special case," wrote historian Andreas Hillgruber in 1959, "in an era shaped by clashes between democratic, fascist and communist ideas."[39]

The personification of this special case was Miklós Horthy de Nagybánya, the monarchist former admiral of the Austro-Hungarian Navy who served as the regent of Hungary from 1920 to October 15, 1944. Horthy, who preferred to be addressed as "your excellency," decided over questions of war and peace and had the right to convene and dismiss the parliament and to send legislation back for further consultations twice before being required to sign it into law. In contrast to Hitler's Germany, Hungary was far freer and far less socially equitable. The old European emphasis on tradition by Hungary's thin upper class prevented an alliance of the lower classes, parvenu intelligentsia, and former elites of the sort Hitler so successfully forged.

Nonetheless, in the May 1939 elections, the fascist Arrow Cross Party, which while related to the National Socialists was more radical due to Hungary's premodern character, won twenty-nine parliamentary mandates, more than one-sixth of all seats available. In Budapest, it received over one-third of the vote—an impressive result considering that Hungary's electoral system favored the rich. Arrow Cross supporters fought for "a national workers' state" and the "liberation of man, soil, work and the [ethnically native] people," while agitating against the "yoke" of the "Jewish-Marxist plutocracy." They aimed to simultaneously overcome feudalism and capitalism and to emancipate workers, denigrated as "smelly proletarians," making them equal members of "a worker-friendly nation." The Arrow Cross Party represented a threat to the feudal order still running things in Hungary and gave a prominent voice to the lower classes, which had been kept indentured, ignorant, and poor.

A significant number of adherents of the Hungarian Communists, who were banned, found a new home in this explicitly anti-Semitic party. Its membership, platform, and influence explain three aspects of Hungarian society, then and later: the general social welfare benefits from anti-Semitic measures; the ease with which Arrow Cross supporters became reliable pillars in the new populist Communist regime after 1945; and the socially integrative, stubborn refusal after the Second World War to talk about the Holocaust.

Magyar-Style Anti-Semitic Equality

In 1920, Jews represented barely 6 percent of the Hungarian population but 51 percent of lawyers, 39 percent of engineers and chemists, 34 percent of journalists, and around 50 percent of doctors. This was no great surprise since between 1910 and 1930 the percentage of Jews over the age of twenty who had graduated from a university-track high school rose from 18.2 to 22.1 percent while it declined among gentiles from 4.3 to 4.1 percent. Jewish students also finished their university studies more quickly and got better marks. The prohibition on Jewish lawyers practicing in Hungary was only lifted in 1867. Thirty years later, according to one estimate, the sons of small-time Jewish merchants and artisans made up "30 to 50 percent of the educated 'new middle class'" in modernizing Hungary. These people had relatively high earnings and ensured that their own children were also well educated.

Soon after the suppression of the Republic of Councils, the new Hungarian government introduced matriculation limits on Jewish university students. The corresponding law came into force on September 26, 1920. It was passed by an overwhelming majority of the parliament and signed by Prime Minister Pál Teleki and Horthy. In the run-up to this legislative act, nationalist students had demonstrated in favor of it, and because the law initially applied only to new students, the demonstrations continued. The end result was that, to ensure ethnic transparency, "true Magyar" students were given a say in policy. From that point on, they sent delegates to matriculation commissions, who acted like equality commissioners, making sure that the number of Jewish students did not exceed what were seen as fair quotas.

In 1922, Alajos Kovács, a statistician and anti-Semite, calculated that Jews controlled 20 to 25 percent of the national income and assets in Hungary instead of the "proportional" 5.9 percent that was their due. This "terrifying" disproportionality, he insisted, needed to be corrected. But who would benefit? As historian Péter Tibor Nagy has demonstrated statistically, the interests of the Hungarian population as a whole were not, as is often claimed, made a priority. Nagy writes: "Rather, the restrictions on the numbers of Jewish students prioritized the interests of 210,000 middle-class Christian families over those of 60,000 similarly situated Jewish ones." Christians were afraid of competition from a Jewish minority that seemed able to rise up socially with the greatest of ease.[40]

The 1920 law bore the wordy, ostensibly harmless title "Regulation on Matriculation to the Universities, Technical University and Economic Faculty in Budapest and the Legal Academies." Its significant paragraphs don't mention Jews specifically. The law merely stipulates that "the proportion of matriculates who reside in the country and belong to individual races and nationalities are ideally to reach the proportions of the religions and nationalities concerned and at least nine-tenths of same."

The word "race" was not used for the sake of ethnic discrimination. Some individual, local acts of bias notwithstanding, Hungarian Jews who had converted to Christianity were still allowed to study without any restrictions. The law used the word so as not to distinguish between the Christian confessions. The intention was to deny practicing Jews access to middle-class educational opportunities and careers. This aim was supported by measures taken by the city administration of

Budapest, a city in which every fifth resident was Jewish. In 1920–21, 160 Jewish teachers were fired, a significant number of Jewish deans demoted to teachers, and Jewish professors were transferred from the trade academies to less prestigious people's schools.[41]

Both the League of Nations and Jewish organizations in Britain and France considered the matriculation restrictions a violation of the guarantees of minority rights in the Trianon treaty. In response to their protests, the Hungarian government claimed that it was trying to reduce the "intellectual proletariat" and ensure the "patriotic loyalty of future civil servants" and the "proportional" equality of opportunity between various nationalities. Before the restrictions, the government said, the proportion of Jewish students had reached an "intolerable" average of 34 percent; at the University of Pécs, it was 45.2 percent. By late 1921, the proportion of Jewish students had been brought down to an average of 11.3 percent, a two-thirds reduction, and by the 1935–36 fall semester that figure had fallen to 8 percent. As a consequence, thousands of Hungarian Jews who wanted to study at university in the 1920s and 1930s did so at Austrian, Italian, Czech, French, and (until 1933) German universities. In line with its basic aim, the Hungarian matriculation law improved gentiles' chances in the job market. By 1928, Jews represented around 19 percent of the well-educated people with jobs but 30 percent of the well-educated unemployed, the "intellectual proletariat." In Budapest the latter number was 38 percent.[42]

After an initial phase of shock and in response to international pressure, universities became more lax in enforcing the quotas, so that before 1940 the prescribed proportion of 6 percent Jewish students was never attained. The national-liberal Hungarian prime minister István Bethlen, who served from 1921 to 1931, declared ex post facto that he had always wanted to "revoke the numerus clausus [matriculation limits]"—but only when the "social situation in Hungary had been consolidated." Conversely, Hungarian anti-Semite István Barta, the author of a German-language book on the Jewish question, complained that "the smoldering racial protection movement had been condemned to impotence" by the successful tactics of the Jewish communities. Jewish leaders undertook a series of discreet interventions, and in 1928, the restrictions were in fact officially eased.[43]

In October 1932, the out-and-out anti-Semite Gyula Gömbös took over the government. The new prime minister came from the lower middle classes, had worked his way up to captain in the military, and had founded the Party for Racial Protection in 1924. Back then, the party had adopted illiberal slogans and demanded that matriculation restrictions be extended to include baptized former Jews. In 1925, he coorganized the International Congress of Anti-Semites in Budapest. As early as January 1921, in the newspaper *Szózat* (Wakening Call), Gömbös had formulated ideas that would find a broad echo in 1938: "I consider it necessary for the Hungarian government to contact the headquarters of the Zionists to arrange for the resettlement of hundreds of thousands of excess Jews with Hungarian citizenship. The fate of this people, which is dispersed throughout the world, must be decided in a way that guarantees the serenity of the other peoples." In a brochure written in German, Gömbös proclaimed: "Jews should only be allowed to assert themselves in any given area in relation to their numbers."

Despite these views, in his four years in power Gömbös didn't make existing anti-Jewish legislation more severe. On the contrary, probably at the urging of Horthy, he declared upon taking office that he had "rethought" his ideas on the Jewish question and would henceforth consider those Jews "who feel that they belong to the Hungarian national community as much my brothers as my Hungarian brothers." For historian Randolph Brahman, Gömbös's change of heart was purely tactical, while contemporary Hungarian anti-Semites saw the "power of Jewish money" at work, to which the prime minister had been forced to yield. Whatever the truth may have been, until Gömbös's early death in October 1936, Hungarian government policy quietly discriminated against Jews. Between the academic years 1932–33 and 1936–37, the proportion of Jewish university students dwindled from 12.5 to 7.4 percent. Meanwhile, Gömbös filled upper-level administrative military and governmental positions with people from diverse social backgrounds, lessening the influence of conservative elites and favoring what was sometimes known as "Young Hungary." The entry of the latter into state institutions was bad news for Jews. Among the newly promoted parvenus was Arrow Cross leader Ferenc Szálasi. His father was a career military man, who had never risen higher than junior officer, while his son made it all the way up to the rank of major in the Hungarian general staff.[44]

Gömbös's successor as prime minister, Kálmán Darányi, radicalized the government's anti-Jewish policies in a telling double move. On March 5, 1938, he banned the Arrow Cross Party while adopting on the same day part of its platform as official state policy. He didn't announce the reorientation in front of parliament, but rather in a partisan speech to workers in the industrial city of Györ. "Our government platform is dedicated to serving the welfare, health and culture of the lower classes, and I see this platform as embodying the idea of racial protection and national unity," Darányi told his listeners. "Jewry has succeeded in establishing itself in disproportionately large numbers in those areas of work in which it is easier to earn money. . . . The basic condition for the legal and systematic regulation of the Jewish question is that we create a socially equitable situation."[45]

Anti-Jewish Discrimination as an Act of Social Equity

Darányi, his followers, and most of his listeners understood social equity to mean that Jews would no longer have the right to freely choose what they did for work and that their proportion in certain job sectors would be limited to 20 percent. The government introduced corresponding legislation one month later, on April 8, 1939. It was called the "Law on More Effective Protection of Social and Economic Equity." Eighteen years after the law limiting Jewish matriculations, and despite Hungary's social and economic stagnation, parliamentary deputies still felt they had to help ambitious Magyar university graduates find suitably comfortable positions—to the detriment of Jews.

This interpretation of the situation is supported by the debates carried out in the upper and lower chambers of the Hungarian parliament. Tibor Eckhardt, the chairman of the Independent Smallholders

Party, justified his vote with the following argument: "Some time ago, before the draft of the Jewish legislation was distributed, I emphasized that the fundamental question was the proper distribution of income and wealth." Another deputy, inspired by the heat of class conflict, insisted that "the street sweepers are all Christians and the people sitting in the automobiles are all Jews." Mátyás Matolcsy rejected the draft legislation in the name of the National Peasants Party as being "far too mild." He demanded that "the Jews be pushed back to 5 percent" and "that key industries be nationalized and there be targeted comprehensive social-welfare reform policies, namely a radical land reform, as a supplement to the Jewish law, which only solves the problems of cities."

In the upper chamber of parliament, the deputy Zoltán Biró insisted that the law was directed not only against Jewish capital but also against the Jewish proletariat that had emigrated from Eastern Europe and that "sucked the money from and exploited the native populace in Eastern Hungary." Biró's colleagues Viktor Károlyi and János Teleszky found the law "compellingly appropriate for the end of preserving the social peace." After considering the legislation, parliamentary deputies voted it into law on May 29, 1938, by a large majority. Justice Minister Ödön Mikecz portrayed it as an act of "social equity."

With Jews representing only 6 percent of the Hungarian populace, many people found the 20 percent quota overly generous. But for those it affected, whether they were practicing or would-be doctors, lawyers, or engineers, or worked in the press, film, or theater, the limits were painful. The damage was all the greater because parliamentarians had also come up with clauses designed to additionally hem in the "unjust overrepresentation of Jews." For example, alongside the 20 percent quota, media companies weren't allowed to pay more than 20 percent of their total wages to Jews. In companies with more than ten employees, the 20 percent limit on Jews was calculated using only people working in "intellectually influential areas." At a newspaper, for instance, only journalists and editors counted, not bookkeepers, secretaries, porters, and typesetters. That further restricted the number of Jews in leading jobs.[46]

The anti-Jewish law of May 1938 was followed before the end of the year by another law directed at "the exaggerated influence of Jewry on the intellectual leadership of the country." It came into force on May 5, 1939, and aimed to provide a new foundation for "the beautiful edifice of hard-working Christian Hungary." That was how the newly appointed Prime Minister Béla Imrédy had put it on February 3. But Imrédy was a luckless figure. The anti-Semitism he helped promote turned around to bite him in the form of his Jewish great-grandmother. When this part of his ancestry was revealed, he was forced to resign after only a few weeks in office. Nonetheless, he remained politically active. In 1942 he demanded a "solution to the Jewish question" to be coupled with land reform and better social benefits for workers.[47] In 1944, Imrédy was an enthusiastic helper of the German occupiers. Two years later, a popular tribunal in Budapest sentenced him to death, and he was immediately executed.

With the second Jewish law, the quota of Jews in the professions listed above was reduced from 20 to 12 percent, and the reduction also applied to wages. Leading positions such as editor in chief, departmental head, and publisher had to be given to people of the Christian faith. From that moment on, Jews were no longer accepted as civil servants or state employees. Jewish judges and prosecutors were forced to retire within six months. Teachers and notaries were given a deadline of two years. For all institutions of higher education and secondary schools, strict matriculation limits of 6 percent were put in place. Because Jewish students already exceeded that limit, educational authorities reduced the percentage of newly matriculating Jewish students to a mere 1.4 percent for the 1939–40 fall semester. Thus what had been a limit now nearly amounted to an outright ban.[48] The 6 percent limit also applied to the awarding of commercial and trade licenses and public contracts given to Jewish-owned companies. To evade foreign complaints, in April 1939 Hungary quit the League of Nations.

A newly established government office with 600 employees supervised the law's implementation—German diplomats nicknamed it the "Jew Commissariat."[49] Employers were required to report twice yearly how many Jews they employed in intellectual jobs, and they were told how many Jews they would have to fire in the coming six months. The law also stripped most Jews of their right to vote just before the 1939 parliamentary and local elections. Since Jews had tended to vote for liberal parties, the measure favored conservatives and right-wing radicals. Moreover, the Hungarian interior minister was granted the authority to denaturalize all Jews who had gained Hungarian citizenship after July 1, 1914. The most ominous paragraph in the law came at the end. It empowered the government "to encourage the emigration of Jews" and issue decrees concerning their right to take their assets with them "for which normally laws would be required." These paragraphs in a democratically passed law enabled the government to summarily confiscate the assets of 725,000 Jews in 1944 and abet their "emigration"—in many cases, to Auschwitz.

Hungary's third Jewish law came into force in August 1941 and defined for the first time in the country's legal system the term "half-Jew." Following the lead of the 1935 Nuremberg Laws in Germany, children of mixed Jewish-Christian marriages were considered Jewish if they belonged to the Jewish cultural community. In the parliamentary debates about the law, deputies pursued two aims: refining Hungary's policies of segregation in order to, as Imrédy put it, encourage "the future exodus of Jews" and give the state a way to confiscate land without compensation from half-Jews. Amid these heated discussions, Béla Varga of the Smallholders Party argued for half of all Hungary's Jews to be forcibly resettled. He was not alone. As the former prime minister Bethlen summarized, "there was no speaker in parliament who suggested a solution other than the Jews' being forced to emigrate to a Jewish national state."[50]

At the same time the state launched a campaign to create a sort of commerce "that was unmistakably permeated by the Christian spirit." This entailed support programs for ambitious young Christians, including scholarships to attend trade schools, cheap lines of credit to set up businesses, and evening continuing education classes on everything from bookkeeping, customs law, and rail and ship tariffs to shop-window decoration and the use of advertisements. And encouraged by the help they had begun to receive in school, young Christians did indeed seek to "take the chances that the Jewish Law opened up for them." By mid-1941, Budapest city officials had stripped Jewish market sellers of their stalls, forty-five hundred grain dealers throughout the country had lost their concessions, and the situation was similar in all agricultural sectors. Drawing attention to these measures, Presidential Regent Horthy proclaimed: "We have implanted an interest in economic life and a proclivity for the free trades in our children and our young people. . . . I trust that our gifted race, which is capable of anything, can achieve everything."[51]

Hardly had Hungary regained Northern Transylvania from Romania after the Second Vienna Award on August 30, 1940, than the Hungarian government stripped Jews there of their rights, revoking trade licenses and issuing edicts about where they were allowed to run businesses and where not. Jews were also branded collaborators and profiteers of twenty years of Romanian rule, which had now been overcome. The tone of these initiatives is neatly conveyed by an article in the *Magyar Nép* (Hungarian People) newspaper on May 9, 1942, about the forced withdrawal of Jewish merchants from the city of Kolozsvár (Cluj): "Until now, the Grüns and Cohens have lorded over the main square. Romanian parvenus, the upper classes of the Romanian occupiers, were these shops' best customers. Elegant ladies from Romania proper came here to purchase silk and exquisite English fabric, fur coats, jewelry, snake-skin shoes—in short the finest and most fashionable things from anywhere and everywhere. While masses of Hungarians suffered want and privation, they weighed silk and gold."[52]

Until 1945, agriculture in scantly industrialized Hungary was based on the feudal estate economy, tiny landowners, serfs, farm maids, and seasonally employed day laborers. Poverty and sluggish industrialization led some 1.4 million of these people to emigrate to the US between 1900 and 1914. In 1937, the authors of a League of Nations report noted the extreme poverty of rural Hungarians compared with others in Europe. They kept themselves alive, the report stated, with "bread and paprika, paprika and bread, and on a good day maybe a little bacon." Estate owners still enjoyed the right to mete out corporal punishment and to approve or disapprove of marriages, determining how

Hungary's rural poor lived at the time. According to the 1930 census, some 2.3 million people existed in these conditions—almost a third of the entire Hungarian population.[53]

Against the backdrop of this notorious misery, both chambers of the Hungarian parliament repeatedly debated the issue of land reform, but the politically powerful aristocracy always succeeded in blocking any action. In 1938 a number of leading politicians jointly arrived at an idea of how to break the impasse by "enlisting Jewish land for the purposes of land reform." There are no precise statistics on how much land Jews possessed, but around 10 percent of all agricultural and forest lands were probably owned or leased by Jews. That expropriation was the subject of paragraphs fifteen and sixteen of the Second Jewish Law of 1939, which mandated "the exclusion of Jews from any possession of rural property," a move intended "to give new momentum to land reform" and "strengthen Magyar farmers."[54]

Hungarian land reform followed the maxim "Peace to peasant huts and palaces—war upon the Jews," as is evident from Prime Minister Pál Teleki's justification of it on February 22, 1939: "No government can be in doubt that property and land should make their way into Hungarian hands, safe hands, and not the hands of those who aren't connected with the land by any family tradition." Teleki's successor, Miklós Kállay, also stressed to parliament on March 19, 1942, his determination to "appropriate Jewish property without exception." After being interrupted by frenetic applause, he continued: "On the basis of the Racial Protection Law, I will enforce our claims upon this property. . . . I will also appropriate all forests that are in Jewish hands. . . . We can put the confiscated forest land to good use for our future settlement policies." This act of expropriation included not just land but everything on it, including livestock.[55]

Kállay was not just a puppet, carrying out the will of the Nazi regime; he was trying to maneuver Hungary out of its perilous alliance with the Third Reich. He considered his anti-Semitic policies as "proof" of his "independent way of acting" and claimed to be following venerable social-welfare-state goals. To qualify for acquiring and working the newly expropriated land, candidates had to be below a certain income level, have at least three children, or be an officially registered hero or victim of war.

Such was the demand for Jewish land that on September 6, 1942, the Hungarian parliament extended the expropriation of forests and fields to property owned by those defined the year before as half-Jews. A body called the Land and Soil Credit Institute was charged with distributing the stolen real estate and buildings. In 1943 it announced that it had achieved an "excellent balance," thanks chiefly to "compulsorily relinquished Jewish property." In 1944, the German-language journal devoted to the Hungarian economy, *Ungarischer Volkswirt*, offered fulsome praise: "This leading altruistic agrarian institute was able to develop an extraordinarily productive effectiveness." The body had succeeded in taking away more than 300,000 hectares of land from Jewish owners.

But the demands for "productivity" didn't stop there. Unsurprisingly, in October 1942, Kállay directed the public's covetous gaze to new sources of wealth and announced that he was levying a "special war contribution" upon Jews. This was merely a euphemism for another act of expropriation. And that wasn't the end of his attempts to provide for the Magyar population: "Among our social problems is that of housing, which is also organized in anti-social ways that particularly benefit the Jews. I am not yet in a position to describe precisely how we will proceed. But I intend to solve the housing question in this fashion."

Kállay had already sketched out Hungary's happy future, free of Jews, in a public speech the preceding April: "This question can only be solved by creating a tabula rasa. Jewry must be removed, deprived of the right to property and the use of Hungarian soil." He concluded his address with the words: "There is no other solution than the resettlement of 800,000 Jews out of Hungary." At that point, there were "minutes of thunderous applause throughout the monumental event hall," a newspaper reported. Another source quoted Kállay as saying that "the formal de-Jewification of economic life" was insufficient and that it was more crucial to "eradicate the Jewish spirit." Kállay said that he knew that "Jews would have to be excluded in stages, sooner rather than later, from the concerns of Hungarian life" and that there could be no other "final solution than the resettlement of the 800,000-strong heads of [Hungarian] Jewry." In Berlin, the Nazi leadership viewed such speeches with satisfaction: "Step by step, the solution of the Jewish question in Hungary is making progress."[56] But as a number of documents show, not everyone was satisfied by the level of progress. On April 16, 1943, Horthy told Hitler that "he [Horthy] had done everything that could be done ethically against the Jews, but there was no way to murder or otherwise kill them."[57]

Like Horthy, the advocates of Hungary's Jewish policy between 1920 and 1943 rarely contemplated the idea of mass murder. They formulated positive goals intended to create a peaceful, homogeneous, and strong nationalist state. Nonetheless, when the Wehrmacht occupied Hungary in March 1944, Germans were immediately able to exploit a nationalist climate that had been spreading since 1920. Increasingly draconian anti-Jewish legislation encouraged the general public's greedy willingness to help itself to the many things deported Jews left behind. The main thing was that the Jews disappeared. It was to achieve this end that civil servants and police officers from the Hungarian interior ministry closely cooperated with the commando led by Adolf Eichmann.

Years of debates about Jewish laws and the legislation itself had accustomed Hungarian society to "legal" forms of exclusion. The prohibitions on Jews studying at university and practicing the trades of their choice, followed by the partial expropriation of their property, allowed gentile Hungarians, in the words of postwar politician István Bibó, "to create an extraordinarily advantageous situation without any personal exertion, thanks to the state." The anti-Jewish measures had "the appearance of social reform" that allowed the majority to get behind them. In reality, however, the anti-Semitic policies propped up the old, long-decayed social order. Hungarian Jews were "subjected to increasingly targeted threats to their physical security" and ultimately deported. Playing a decisive social, if not political role in this process were the large number of active anti-Semites who cultivated smallminded resentments and the many people who enriched themselves with what Jews left behind in the second half of the Second World War. They justified their actions by asking: Hadn't the Jews always been "impertinent and demanding"? Hadn't their own "selfish interests" been first and foremost on their minds? Such were the observations Bibó recorded in a 1948 essay on the Jewish question in Hungary. The heading of the final section reads: "Our Responsibility for What Happened."[58]

6

Expulsion and Eradication

ÉVIAN: WHERETO WITH THE JEWS?

Upon the initiative of US president Franklin D. Roosevelt, international representatives came together for a conference on refugees from July 6 to 15, 1938, in the French spa town of Évian-les-Bains. The event was organized by American and British diplomats for the express purpose of discussing how the roughly 500,000 Jews left in Germany and Austria could emigrate from the Third Reich. The auspices weren't good. In the run-up to the conference, many of the thirty-two countries that participated took steps to hinder or block the mass arrival of Jews fleeing Austria after its annexation by Nazi Germany. German authorities were driving people across its borders and onto migrant ships without any money.

Before 1938, the year when the Nazi leadership radicalized its policy of expelling Jews from Germany, they had been leaving the country at a steady rate. Of the half million Jews who then lived in Germany, 135,000 had yielded to rising pressure by fleeing or legally emigrating. Thirty thousand went to other Western European countries, 15,000 to

North America, 21,000 to South America, 4,000 to South Africa, and 2,000 to the rest of the world. In addition some 20,000 Jews returned to countries in Eastern Europe, mostly Poland, from where they had originally come.[1]

The measures decided upon in Évian have been subjected to more than enough moral evaluation, and it is not my intention to criticize the individual nations and their initiatives. Ultimately, Roosevelt's rational and humane intentions were flouted by the machinations of Hitler's Germany. But it is worth investigating how the concerns and special wishes that preceded, accompanied, and followed the conference reflected the situation and prospects of the approximately four million Eastern and Central European Jews outside the Third Reich and the Soviet Union.

Top officials in the British Foreign Office who were charged with preparing the conference feared it might encourage other countries to follow Germany and Austria's lead and try to get rid of their own Jewish populations. No matter how little or how much was achieved in Évian, a May 1938 briefing for British foreign minister Lord Halifax made clear that "the question of the Jews in Central Europe will be raised sooner or later and can only be resolved comprehensively and perhaps radically." Organizers were afraid that a crackdown on Jews by Poland, Romania, and Hungary would unleash "a movement of population possibly involving several million people."[2]

When the US formally invited Romania to take part, Romanian foreign minister Nicolae Petrescu-Comnen reacted with delight, telling the US ambassador that he hoped the Jewish resettlement initiative would be "extended" to his country. One of the final acts of the Goga-Cuza government was to give an interview with the Nazi *Völkischer Beobachter* newspaper on February 9, 1938, in which Cuza detailed his vision for a strategic alliance with Hitler's Germany: "We have to force the Western democracies to choose between opening up new territories for Jewish immigration or accepting a violent solution to the conflict. It is difficult for us to constrain the people from carrying out pogroms, and those in Paris and London should be made to know that we won't always be able to do this. A decision must be taken quickly." In a more moderate tone, but ultimately pursuing the same goal, the next Romanian government drew up a memorandum that it presented to London on December 5, 1938. A Jewish state, it demanded, must be established in cooperation with Jewish organizations and be supported by "a decisive action" on the part of the Western powers to "quickly and thoroughly solve the Jewish question."[3]

On September 20, 1938, there was a remarkably cordial discussion between Polish ambassador Jósef Lipski and Adolf Hitler, in which a jovial Führer suggested that "the Jewish problem could be solved by emigration to the British colonies based on an agreement with Poland, Hungary and possibly Romania." Polish foreign minister Józef Beck recorded Lipski's answer: "On this score, I told [Hitler] that we would erect a magnificent monument to him in Warsaw, if he brought about such a solution."[4] At that juncture Warsaw had good relations with Nazi Germany because as part of the imminent German annexation of the Sudetenland, Hitler intended to toss Poland a territorial scrap, the Czech border town and transportation hub Český Těšín and the surrounding territory of Olsa. It was this prospective "pillage and destruction of the Czechoslovak state" that led Winston Churchill to describe Poland as having a "hyena appetite."[5]

Things would soon turn frosty again between Berlin and Warsaw as Hitler prepared for war against Poland. By the time Beck visited London on April 5 and 6, 1939, Germany had deported 17,000 Polish Jews living in Germany back to their "homeland," staged the Night of Broken Glass pogrom, destroyed the state of Czechoslovakia, forced Lithuania to cede the city of Memel (Klaipėda), and given Hungary much of Slovakia. In a communiqué on Beck's visit, the British government announced that it would sign a solidarity pact with Poland. Although it was hardly a priority, Whitehall publicly endorsed Beck's suggestion that "all international efforts to resolve the Jewish problem should also include the Jews of Poland." At the behest of Bucharest, Beck drew attention "to a similar problem in Romania," to which the British side declared that it recognized the difficulties at hand and was willing "at any time to consider suggested solutions with the Polish and Romanian governments."[6]

US diplomats had rejected similar ideas—at Britain's request—in the immediate wake of the Night of Broken Glass. But Poland's ambassador in Washington, Jerzy Potocki, quickly intervened. He considered it unjust that "the US directed its attention solely to refugees of Germany who were being terribly persecuted" while ignoring Poland's 3.5 million Jews. "The Polish government wants to get rid of them," Potocki said, "but they're not being mistreated." The following day, he met with the chief of the State Department's Western European Division and threatened that if Poland weren't treated the same as Germany on the question of Jewish emigration, it could come to numerous outbreaks of anti-Semitic violence.[7]

London diplomats trying to engineer a minimal consensus and only too aware of Poland, Romania, and Hungary's hard-line attitudes tried to keep those countries away from the Évian Conference—no mean feat. Appeals to members of the British Commonwealth and British colonies to play a constructive role fell on deaf ears, and some even refused to respond. Initially, only Australia agreed to send a delegate to Évian and declared itself willing to accept five hundred Jewish refugees a year. New Zealand, Canada, and South Africa declined to participate. "My own feeling is that nothing will help solving an international problem by bringing it to other nations," Canadian prime minister William Mackenzie Lyon King asserted. "We must be careful not to try to play the role of a dog in the manger, with our wide open spaces and our small population." He added, "We would have riots if we agreed to a policy that admitted [large] numbers of Jews." South Africa let it be known that it already had enough Jews and, with a general election approaching, would not do anything to facilitate further immigration.

During the conference itself, Australian trade minister Thomas W. White articulated what was probably running through many of the delegates' heads: "It will no doubt be appreciated also that as we have no real racial problem, we are not desirous of importing one." Afterward, while discussing the duties that could potentially result for the United Kingdom from the final conference resolution, Home Secretary Samuel Hoare protested that although he would do his best, "there was a good deal of feeling growing up in this country . . . against the admission of Jews to British colonies."[8]

Orderly Jewish emigration presupposed that German authorities would cooperate. But realistic British diplomats realized that Nazi Germany was pursuing two contradictory aims: to deport Jews once they had been rendered penniless and to use them as hostages to force concessions from the Western democracies. On April 26, 1938, Hermann Göring decreed that all non-Aryans would have to register their assets with tax authorities. The Foreign Office in London had no doubt that this requirement was intended to help the Germans gain control of Jewish wealth, even if the people being expropriated remained in the country. Those in power in Berlin, it was understood, intended to have Jews suffer, starve, and die—and that humanitarian objections would therefore be useless.[9]

Adding to the immediate difficulties in helping Europe's Jews was the general global political situation. Beginning in 1936, there were repeated uprisings in British-run Palestine against Jewish emigration. To head off further unrest, London gave in and throttled back the numbers of Jews moving to the Middle East. (Some 300,000 Jews had settled in Palestine since 1920, including around 40,000 who came from Germany as of 1933.) Spain was engaged in a civil war that was being stoked by Germany, Italy, and the Soviet Union, which presented a danger for British military and commercial ships passing through the Strait of Gibraltar. Italy possessed colonies in Eritrea and Somalia and, as of 1935, was expanding into Ethiopia. In 1937, Mussolini began an attempt to conquer Libya, while Japanese troops landed in China. All these conflicts relegated the Jewish question to secondary importance in London and Paris.

In order to secure the Suez Canal, which was so important strategically and economically, Britain had to reach a tenable understanding with Arab states and the Muslim world. Their loyalty was purchased with money and a refusal to allow the establishment of a Jewish state in Palestine. The British military and many British colonial authorities viewed geopolitical interests as more important than any considerations derived from the persecution of Jews in Germany, Austria, or elsewhere. At the time, several hundred thousand Jews lived in the British Empire, compared with eighty million Muslims.

THE CONFERENCE: A BEGINNING WITHOUT AN END

Leading US diplomats saw the unpredictable nations of Europe as a "topsy-turvy world" and were left shaking their heads at the Spanish Civil War, the quarrels over national minorities, and the European proclivity toward authoritarianism. Typical American sentiments at the time were: "The European pot is boiling again"; "The crises are succeeding one another with exhilarated tempo"; and "Stalin stands to profit by other people fighting, but not by fighting himself." There were concerned American reports about the pitiful state of the French Air Force and the gap between the British and German aircraft industries. Conversely, British leaders pressured their American partners to build huge warships. From Cologne, American general counsel Alfred W. Klieforth reported that ordinary people were fully behind Hitler since he gave them food, jobs, and national pride. German workers were happy to labor fifty-eight to sixty hours a week, Klieforth wrote, saying he had never seen the like of it in any other country. Those who were especially productive were given berths on cruises to Norway or the Canary Islands.[10]

Nonetheless, Roosevelt told advisors that it was time to tackle the Jewish problem in "Napoleonic" fashion. As his main advisor on refugee issues, James G. McDonald, made clear in a preliminary meeting in London, Roosevelt envisioned a large-scale settlement plan paid for in part by state and in part by private funds and goods. The US president's determination to act was fueled by his contempt for the hesitant, ineffective dillydallying of the League of Nations, and once he began to think in grand terms, he approved of extending the agenda at Évian to include Central Europe. He was also prepared to treat the anti-Semitic wishes and plans of the Polish, Romanian, Lithuanian, and Hungarian governments as legitimate. Roosevelt's loose talk on this score horrified London and Paris—which successfully shot down his ideas.[11]

But grand presidential aspirations notwithstanding, the suggestion McDonald made to his British colleagues was pragmatic and immediate: the United States was prepared to accept 27,000 Jewish refugees a year. That was the upper limit on the number of immigrants from Germany as a whole, and it was now to be reserved exclusively for German and Austrian Jews. That number could even be expanded slightly if returnees to Germany were taken into account. McDonald expected the states and colonies in the Commonwealth to offer similar quotas. He had no hopes of help from France, which he thought would use the conference to get rid of its own refugees. The subject of the costs of limited emigration was studiously avoided. Publicly, American and British negotiators demanded that German Jews be allowed to take some of their assets with them, but privately and realistically they acknowledged that the Nazi government intended to plunder their wealth and keep them as a class of helots.[12]

On March 19, 1938, Roosevelt announced that the conference would be held. A week later, Hitler answered with a speech broadcast live on the radio and printed in the *Völkischer Beobachter*: "I can only hope and expect that the other world, which has such deep sympathy with these criminals [the Jews], will at least be generous enough to convert this sympathy into practical aid. For our part, we are ready to place all these criminals at the disposal of these countries, if need be by putting them on luxury ocean liners." From that point on, in characteristically bad faith, the Nazi regime tried both to disrupt and use the conference for its own ends. In the weeks that followed it herded hundreds of destitute Jews across land borders and the Danube River into Czechoslovakia and Hungary.

A bit later, on the express command of SS and Reich Security Office leader Reinhard Heydrich in Vienna, 4,000 young Jewish men were arrested and severely mistreated. Half of them were taken to the Dachau concentration camp. Terrorizing Jews in this way was designed to outrage world opinion. It was a staged humanitarian catastrophe, thanks to which word of the humiliation, torture, imprisonment, and murder of Jews would get out, and Jewish organizations would be forced to put pressure on their respective national governments. Jewish defense associations and foreign states, the Nazis hoped, would then transfer large sums of hard currency to free the Jews who were being so badly mistreated. During the Night of Broken Glass pogrom of November 9 and 10, 1938, and the subsequent, unusually brutal internment of 25,000 Jewish men in concentration camps, Hitler used the same strategy of increasing the pressure on Jews to emigrate. On November 24, the SS newspaper *Das schwarze Korps* wrote that if Jews didn't disappear immediately, they would be "eradicated like criminals."[13]

The Nazi government, which had run up massive debts and was not considered creditworthy even within Germany itself, had a vested interest in continuing its unconstrained confiscation of Jewish assets. In 1938, Jewish wealth was estimated at eight billion reichsmarks—a considerable sum considering that Reich tax authorities only took in 17 billion reichsmarks from taxes, duties, and levies that year.[14] With this in mind, on the second day of the Évian conference, the German Foreign Ministry issued the following orders to its embassies in countries affected by the refugee question: "The question of whether Germany can ease its stance on the transference of capital in Jewish hands is to be answered in the negative since, especially after the war, a transfer of capital accumulated by Jews would be intolerable for Germany." In other words, by this point Germany had already decided to retain all the assets of Jews. Embassies were also told to insist that the Jewish question was "a domestic German problem exempt from all discussions."[15]

Hungary didn't send a delegation to Évian; Romania, Poland, and Greece were represented by observers; and Italy boycotted the conference. The event could not be held in Geneva, the home of the League of Nations, because Switzerland didn't want to further strain its already precarious relationship with Germany, so the neighboring French city was chosen as a substitute. Bern's own delegation didn't consist of any diplomats, but rather Immigration Police head Heinrich Rothmund. The Geneva newspaper *Journal des Nations* didn't mince words about the event, running a headline on its opening day that read: "*Voilà une conférence qui est morte, avant qu'elle soit née*"—behold a conference that is dead before it's even been born.

The conference began on July 8, 1938, with some sobering words from its chairman, Myron C. Taylor, who spoke of large-scale forced migration and the need for quick and effective results and long-term, comprehensive solutions. How these were to be achieved remained unclear. British representatives had been ordered to avoid using the word "Palestine" and to keep as much distance as possible from the many representatives of Jewish organizations who had traveled to Évian. It was equally taboo for American delegates to discuss the possibility of financial assistance from the states represented at the conference to fund emigration. French and British negotiators insisted that their US colleagues, whom they considered naïve, not even suggest that aid could be offered to refugees from Poland, Romania, and other Central European countries. That, the European diplomats asserted, would immediately make the governments in question increase pressure on their own minorities to emigrate, creating an inestimable problem for Western destination countries.

In their official statements, delegates recited statistics about how many refugees their countries had already accepted, suggesting that they had reached their limits. The German-language Jewish newspaper *Jüdische Rundschau* reported with obvious disappointment: "The representatives of these countries probably had no choice but to speak like this, and anyone who expected anything different was probably, as the conference joke had it, reading Évian from back to front [naively]." Non-Jewish newspapers were often more frank about the anti-Jewish bias the conference had to try to overcome. On July 11, the *Gazette de Lausanne* pointed out that many people believed Jews possessed "a far too powerful position for such a small minority" and that this was the cause of the "resistance to them, which in many places has become a general attack." The middle-class Catholic paper *La Libre*

Belgique asked just ahead of the conference on July 7: "Was it not said before the [First] World War that a tenth of all the gold in the world belonged to Jews?" By contrast, on July 14, a similar French newspaper, *La Croix*, stressed the need to heed Jewish cries for help: "We must not become complicit in a solution to the Jewish question that entails the erasure, the complete destruction of an entire people."[16]

As is to be expected from a conference of this sort, the delegates in Évian agreed upon the minimum, including the formation of the Intergovernmental Committee on Refugees, which had a modicum of authority to negotiate whatever it could between the Third Reich and Jewish organizations. As far as the assets of those forced to emigrate went, the delegates could hardly have been expected to achieve much in the way of future concessions from Germany. But internally, they spoke of forcing it to allow refugees to take 15 to 20 percent of their wealth with them.

The question of transferring wealth was a serious problem. By increasingly terrorizing Jews, the Nazi regime wanted to force western nations to quit boycotting German products and services in return for minor humanitarian concessions. Germany suffered from a lack of hard currency, and its ability to import raw materials and goods for its armament program was limited. Because the regime had racked up such enormous debts, the reichsmark was no longer accepted on foreign markets. For that reason, Jews who legally emigrated from Germany had to leave behind any jewelry, gemstones, artworks, gold, currency, and foreign securities they possessed. Jews who remained in Germany and Austria were required in the summer of 1938 with "the greatest haste" (Göring) to sell their valuables to the Reichsbank, for which they received next-to-worthless government bonds.[17]

Humanitarians who tried to buy Jews' freedom with currency sent to Germany or in return for bolstering German exports faced the moral dilemma of helping to build up Hitler's "war machine," as Joseph Tenenbaum put it on August 17, 1938, in a letter of alarm to the founding president of the World Jewish Congress, Rabbi Stephen Wise. Wise sought advice from his mentor, Louis Brandeis, who agreed with Tenenbaum and also warned that financial arrangements with

Hitler would be a fateful mistake for both Jews and the entire world. Three years later, in his introductory remarks at the Wannsee Conference, Heydrich spoke of how important it had been to protect Germany's currency reserves, adding that Jewish organizations abroad had provided 9.5 million dollars.[18]

Those who held power in Germany tried any way they could to acquire currency for armaments, including taking everything Jews owned and expelling them penniless across the country's borders. On December 6, 1938, four weeks after the Night of Broken Glass, during the first negotiations with the intergovernmental committee created at Évian, Göring gave a speech on the Jewish question to Nazi Gauleiter (local leaders) and other high officials. With an eye toward the pogrom, Göring praised "the positive side of the latest activities: that the emigration question has become acute and other peoples now see that Jews can no longer live in Germany." Financially, Göring said that, as he had told representatives of Jewish organizations, Germany neither could nor wanted to use its currency to help Jews leave the country. "There is only one way, I told them, namely that your racial comrades take out loans in hard currency with the help of those governments that support you—America and England being the two that primarily spring to mind." Göring demanded an end to foreign anti-German boycotts as well as "very extensive contributions," crowing, "How I use this money is my business."[19] He was referring to money for buying raw materials desperately needed by German arms factories.

The demand for orderly forced migration formulated in the final resolution in Évian had a pragmatic, humanitarian side, for which the US argued more or less alone. If America accepted some 30,000 Jewish refugees from Germany, that would represent only 0.2 percent of the country's total population. If Britain's global empire with its 600 million people did the same, the percent of refugees compared with the total population would be far smaller. And if all the other nations at Évian would pledge to accept a similar quota, just enough smaller not to cause major domestic political disputes, then 100,000 Jews from Germany and Austria could easily be accommodated. Within five years, a short period for major international projects, all of 500,000 people on whose behalf the conference had been called could be taken care of. The American government's goal was to steer the chaotic forced emigration of German Jews into orderly channels and to ensure it happened in regulated fashion. Despite all the difficulties, the tenacious American diplomats succeeded in getting conference participants to agree to a framework for further talks. And the US kept its promise. In 1939, the United States accepted 43,500 and in 1940 37,000 endangered European Jews.[20]

The American plan and conference chairman Taylor presumed that the German side would return to reason. But Hitler's regime was bent on war, trampling upon all attempts at diplomacy. From the German perspective, talks were only good for keeping adversaries in the dark for a few additional months. Germany was thus solely responsible for the failure of Évian.[21] With hindsight, we know that a preventive war against Germany would have been the preferable alternative. But how could politicians at the time, democratically elected and bound to defend constitutions and act according to the voters' will, have answered for and pushed through such a course of action?

WAR, ETHNOPOLITICS, AND THE HOLOCAUST

At the start of the Second World War, the German regime combined the propagandistic and predatory intentions of its Jewish policy and its overarching aims to "ethnically disentangle" many millions of people and conquer additional "German living space" in Eastern Europe. Hitler's speech of October 6, 1939, set the general direction: he announced the transfer of numerous German ethnic groups, in particular those who fell under Stalin's power after the German-Soviet Nonaggression Pact of August 24 and the German-Soviet Frontier Treaty of September 28, 1939. When 200,000 southern Tiroleans were included, Hitler was talking about a total of half a million people. In passing, he mentioned that the southeast of Europe was also "filled with unsustainable splinters of the German people." He was referring to the two million people of German extraction who were citizens of Hungary, Romania, Yugoslavia, Slovakia, and Bulgaria.

Hitler euphemistically described his plans as a "forward-looking ordering of European life," marking the start of a general "feeling of European security" thanks to remade "ethnographic relations." He understood this to mean, among other things, the "resettlement of nationalities," combined with a correction of national borders, so as to create "better lines of separation" between individual peoples not just in East-Central Europe but in "almost all Southern and Southeastern European states." In line with his duplicitous promises of peace, he claimed that the measures he proposed would be sufficient "to remove at least a part of the causes of conflict in Europe." Jews were one of these alleged causes of conflict—one that especially preoccupied the regimes of Eastern and Southeastern Europe and that Germany constantly stoked. "In this context," Hitler said, there had to be "an attempt to order and regulate the Jewish problem."[22] That was how he described mass deportations.

Hitler concealed his true intentions behind semimoderate words and from day one presented a sanitized picture of Germany's barbaric occupation of Poland. But one particular personnel decision gave outside observers a good idea of how and to what end the European resettlements directed from Berlin would proceed. On October 7, 1939, the day after his programmatic speech, Hitler named none other than Heinrich Himmler to execute "the ethnic sweeping out of corridors," as the initiative was known among Nazis. In preparation for this task, the head of the SS and the German police gave himself a third, grandiose title: Reich Commissar for the Consolidation of German Nationhood.

From that point on expulsion and resettlement projects would be tightly connected with acts of terror against Jews in the countries dominated by Germany. To structure his new task, Himmler created two new offices, both headed by Heydrich, who also controlled the Gestapo, the Security Police, and the Security Service. The first, the Central Immigration Office, was responsible for resettling Germans living abroad in the Third Reich. The second, the Central Office for Migrants (UWZ), took care of the mass expulsions and ghettoization of undesirables. The offices were supposed to work in tandem, importing and expelling hundreds of thousands of people. They were staffed with experienced SS functionaries, among them Adolf Eichmann, who up to the autumn of 1939 had been in charge of "Jewish emigration" in Vienna, Berlin, and Prague. He now returned full-time to Berlin to head the newly created department of "Emigration and Evacuation Matters," known as the IVD4 (later IVB4). His employees in branch offices, for example in Posen or Łódź, were part of the UWZ. From his headquarters in Berlin, Eichmann presided over the deportations first of Poles, then Serbs, Croats, Slovenes, and Jews.

The drive toward homogeneity covered the Germans outside Germany as well. In line with a treaty the Nazi leadership had signed with Italy in the fall of 1939, German-speaking Southern Tiroleans were to be resettled. They faced the choice of either returning to the Reich or being forced to Italianize. Only a small group who chose to remain resisted either alternative. In a pamphlet addressed to "fellow countrymen" and distributed in the region in late 1939, they wrote:

> You have been given the freedom to choose between your homeland [Tirol] and Galicia. . . . You are to live in huts from which Polish occupants have been driven and to work on farms from which the owner and their wives and children have been driven. Plopped down in the midst of hostile people, surrounded by Slovaks, Czechs and Polacks, with Russian Bolshevists very nearby, you are to be 'deployed' in the national struggle against Poland. You will be despised and hated as intruders by these people and ultimately driven from the country, since the wheel of fortune constantly turns, and in the not-too-distant future these people will demand that the houses and fields taken from them be returned. You, in turn, will be left with nothing and will be forced to wander. But where to? No one knows, least of all those people who are trying today to lure you from your homeland with unconscionable propaganda.[23]

Despite the evidence available to anyone who bothered to read the newspapers, Germany's ethnopolitical plans didn't elicit any negative response. Ever since the Greek-Turkish Resettlement Treaty of 1923, the pioneers of compulsory resettlement had been gaining followers. The tone Hitler had taken in his October 6 speech fit in with an already accepted political school of thought. Before the Second World War, Italy concluded a minor resettlement treaty with Yugoslavia and prepared the one that concerned Southern Tiroleans. Thanks to similar agreements, Yugoslavia, Romania, and Bulgaria had been "returning" members of their Muslim minorities to Turkey for years. The Munich Agreement of September 29, 1938, also included a passage about such "repatriations." The agreement forced Czechoslovakia to cede Sudetenland with its predominately German population to the Third Reich. The agreement had been signed by Hitler, Mussolini, and the prime ministers of Britain and France. Point Seven allowed for the exchange of minorities who after the dramatic shifting of borders found themselves living in the "wrong" country.[24] This clause was never invoked because Germany occupied the rest of Czechoslovakia a few months later.

Nonetheless, circles within the British government once again considered an exchange of populations as a way of pacifying the situation between Germany and Poland. On August 18, 1939, just two weeks before the start of the Second World War, the British Foreign Office asked its consul in Katowice whether he thought population transfers could end the conflict. No, he answered—the population was much too mixed. Nevertheless, a few days later, the British ambassador in Berlin, Sir Nevile Henderson, met with the Polish ambassador to Germany and proposed an exchange of populations to the German Foreign Ministry. Henderson considered it the only way to end conflicts between minorities and found the situation on the German-Polish border far simpler than that in Tirol. On August 27, Henderson reported by cable to London that Hitler had told him he was determined to end the "Macedonian conditions" on his eastern border. Henderson said he agreed, remarking that "the nationality idea being so strong today, the exchange of populations was a very useful solution."[25] But Hitler had lied throughout his conversation, claiming, for instance, that Germany was determined never again to enter into hostilities with Russia.[26]

As morally ambivalent as the British search for compromises with the Third Reich may have been, like the American efforts at Évian, blame for the failure of diplomacy falls squarely on Hitler, who was determined to take Germany to war. Five days after his talk with Henderson, Nazi Germany attacked Poland. The country would be divided, becoming the victim of ethnic policies that were from the very start connected with Germany's homicidal deeds. In November 1939, the man who ran the German general governorate of occupied central Poland, Hans Frank, announced: "The winter will be a hard one. If there's no bread for Poles, they shouldn't complain. . . . No kid gloves for the Jews. . . . The more who die, the better."[27]

GERMANY'S SOUTHEASTERN EUROPEAN ALLIES

Like Hungary, Austria, and Germany, Bulgaria was one of the losers of the First World War and had been forced to accept territorial losses. While Romania was among the victors in 1918, in 1940 it became the victim of Hungarian, Bulgarian, and Soviet redrawing of borders. Slovakia and Croatia only came into existence because of Germany's policies of violence. The common thread among these allies of Nazi Germany was they all had large national minorities that they wanted to get rid of, be it via organized exchanges of populations or expulsion into hostile neighboring states.

The Dream of Greater Bulgaria, Free of Foreigners

Until the Second World War, Bulgaria's 50,000 Jews had mostly lived inconspicuously among the general population of six million. Bulgaria had resettled people in exchange with Greece and had concluded a treaty with Turkey governing the number of Muslims, of whom there were several hundred thousand, to be "repatriated." In 1940, Bulgaria reached agreement with Romania over the division of the contested Dobruja region and an attendant resettlement program.

In response to German influence, but without any compulsion, the Bulgarian government made anti-Semitism an official state policy in 1940, bringing a "Law for the Protection of the Nation" before parliament. Deputies debated this legislation in two separate sessions and ultimately passed it. On January 23, 1941, the final law, signed by Tsar Boris III, came into effect. In one blow, Bulgaria's Jews lost nearly all their rights. They were forbidden from marrying Christians, were subject to forced labor instead of military service, needed police permission to change their place of residence, had no right to vote, were required to register their assets, were prohibited from buying property, and were admitted in only limited numbers to certain professions.

After Germany defeated Greece and Yugoslavia in April 1941, Bulgaria received the territorial gifts it had been promised by Berlin: Yugoslavian Macedonia (so-called Vardar Macedonia), Yugoslav territory around the city of Pirot, Greek Western Thrace, and parts of Greek Eastern Macedonia (Kavala Macedonia). Bulgarian troops marched into these places on April 21. Bulgarian prime minister Bogdan Filow, a classical philologist and archaeologist who had been educated in the German city of Freiburg, sent Hitler a telegram expressing his "deepest gratitude for the German army's liberation of Macedonia and Thrace."

In order to ease the financial burden of administering all this new territory, the Bulgarian government confiscated a quarter of Bulgarian Jews' declared assets in the summer of 1941. In May 1942, it expropriated 4,612 large- and small-scale Jewish businesses. On top of that, Jews were forced to build rail track and roads, and were made to wear special armbands. The government also issued decrees nationalizing Greek property in the Macedonian and Thracian areas it had acquired. By March 1942, it had seized 1,761 Greek businesses, including textile factories and shipyards, as well as the remaining assets of Serbs who had been driven elsewhere. These assets were auctioned off to Bulgarians.

The regime in Sofia wanted to Bulgarianize the "re-won territories" quickly. As troops were still marching in, the government said the "main task" would be to "cleanse them of the foreign population, including Greek and Serbian colonists, Jews, Turks, gypsies and Armenians." Montenegrins and Dalmatians were also targeted by the government plans.

For starters, the Bulgarian government expelled the Greek and Serbian "colonists," who had immigrated to the regions between 1913 and 1919 or who had been settled there strategically by their countries of origin for the sake of ethnic predominance. A government edict read, "The Serbian colonists must be forced to return to Serbia," while Greeks represented a bigger problem since they had originally been resettled from Asia Minor. Nonetheless, the Bulgarian state ordered: "The race principle applies not only to all Jews but to the Greeks and all other non-Aryans."

As a result, 26,450 Serbs were hounded from the Macedonian region of Skopje back to Serbia and at least 30,000 Greeks from Thrace to Greece. The citizenship law passed by the Bulgarian parliament in June 1941 for the "reliberated territories" stripped all non-Bulgarian residents of their civil rights. They were required to pay supplementary taxes and were marked for resettlement. Before 1943, this fate befell some 100,000 Serbs and an equal number of Greeks. Twenty-five thousand other Greeks were forced to move to the interior of Bulgaria.[28]

German officials, especially military ones, pressured the Bulgarians to slow down or cease the expulsions since they threatened the prospect for a peaceful German occupation of Serbia and Greece and increased the number of partisans. Germany was also keen not to place a burden on its relations with neutral Turkey, which explains the Bulgarian government's decision not to drive Muslims there. Sofia declared: "In consideration of the demands for an ethnically pure state, it is obvious the final solution of the Turkish question can only be the resettlement of Turks in Turkey on the basis of a bilateral treaty. But such a final solution is a question for the future. At the present time, it cannot be realized."[29] The situation was different with Jews. For them, Bulgaria's German allies offered a solution that seemed to have no negative side effects.

On February 22, 1943, Bulgarian Jewish Commissar Alexander Belev and Eichmann's envoy Theodor Dannecker reached an agreement, previously endorsed by the Bulgarian government, that more than 11,000 Jews would be "transported from the new provinces of Thrace and Macedonia to the eastern German territories."[30] In fact, they were taken one month later to Treblinka, where they were murdered. The Bulgarian government was responsible for rounding up these condemned people, locking them into train carriages, and bringing them to the port of Lom on the Danube River. Bulgarian settlers moved into the residences vacated by the Jews as part of an initiative to permanently Bulgarianize this territory. A short time later, the envoy of the commissariat on Jewish affairs in Macedonian Bitola, Georgi D. Džambazov, reported selling off the contents of the houses of almost 800 deported families: "With the departure of the Jews, on the basis of Edict Nr. 8655 on the liquidation of belongings of people of Jewish origin who have been taken abroad, the sales of what they left behind began. The quickest and most practical method turned out to be sales on site."[31]

As historian Jens Hoppe has shown, Bulgaria's treatment of Jews must be located in the "wider framework of its overall policy toward minorities," which focused on the "homogenization of the population through compulsory assimilation, expulsions (for example, of Greeks in the occupied territories) and even murder (for example of Jews in the occupied territories)."[32] But they drew a line at handing over Jews in the core of the country who mainly lived in the capital in Sofia. Germany's consul and its police attaché in Sofia were less than impressed. Indignant, they reported back to Berlin that because of shortcomings in worldview and on racial policy, the Bulgarian government didn't see the Jewish problem as "needing a solution." The measures they enacted in the annexed territories were only aimed at "mostly materialistic interests," which consisted of "assigning reliable Bulgarians to the property of deported Jews" and thereby "pacifying their demands."[33]

After the deportations of the 11,000 Jews from the annexed territories, the members of the Bulgarian Commissariat for Jewish Affairs began handing over Jews from Bulgaria proper to the Germans. Yet in 1943, after protests from the country's intellectual and religious elites, the government in Sofia refused to deliver up Jews who resided in the Bulgarian capital.

The reasons were pragmatic. In the winter of 1942–43, the Wehrmacht had been defeated in the Battle of Stalingrad, and German troops were heading toward capitulation in Northern Africa as well. That caused a political change of heart in Sofia, where government officials began to worry that further deportations of Jews could harm Bulgaria's postwar standing should Germany not prevail. It was this calculation that enabled the increasingly successful Allied campaigns against Hitler's Germany to save the lives of 50,000 Jews in central Bulgaria. The governments of Romania and Slovakia, who were also allied with Germany, were guided by a similar expediency.

Ethnic Policies in Hungary

Hungarian regent Miklós Horthy had long supported policies of ethnic violence, which he promoted as an instrument of ensuring peace, and he congratulated Hitler for his agenda-setting speech of October 6, 1939: "Your intention to resettle the German minority in their ancestral homeland solves a multitude of questions and prevents tensions. This excellent idea should be applied to other minorities." Horthy was thinking of the Germans, Romanians, Slovaks, Ukrainians, Serbs, Ruthenians, and Jews in his own country. He himself had already been a longtime adherent of radical resettlement programs. In 1934, he had told his Polish colleague József Piłsudski what he hoped would happen, should their mutual enemy, the Soviet Union, collapse: "In order to create peace and satisfaction for all time, the populations of various areas and nationalities could be exchanged."[34]

With the help of Germany and Italy, Hungary reacquired Northern Transylvania from Romania in 1941 and Voivodina, Bačka, and Prekmurje from Yugoslavia. But these annexations all brought with them not just expatriate Magyars, as was desired, but also several million people of undesirable nationalities into the Empire of the Holy Crown of Hungary. As a result, the number of Jews in Hungary increased from 400,000 to 725,000 from November 1938 to April 1941. The shifting of borders also meant that 220,000 Romanians left Northern Transylvania for Romania, which increased the pressure to find them jobs and places to live. Many Romanians chose to stay in Hungary, even though they were considered a foreign irritant.[35]

In 1943, when Horthy complained at a meeting with Hitler about the past incitement of unrest among 700,000 German-Hungarians by Nazi leaders, the protocol shows the two leaders quickly reaching agreement: "The Führer interjected that under the circumstances, the best solution would be to simply remove the Germans from Hungary. Horthy agreed strongly with this suggestion and drew attention to the recent exchange of Serbians and Hungarians." Germany, he said, needed a larger population while Hungary required additional living space for its own people. So Horthy said he would welcome it if "the Germans would be removed from Hungary."[36] On a much smaller scale during the war, Hungary arranged mutual resettlements with Croatia, Bosnia, and Serbia.[37]

Long before Horthy's meeting with Hitler, Hungarian representatives had repeatedly raised the topic of resettling Jews with their German partners. In late 1940, then prime minister Pál Teleki told Hitler "that the Jews will have to be removed from Europe as part of a peace agreement."[38] In early 1942, Major General József Heszlényi made German ambassador Carl August Clodius an offer to deport some "100,000 stateless Jews" across the Dniester River. In July, the Hungarian military attaché in Berlin, Sándor Homlok, reiterated the offer, phrasing it as a request. Eichmann refused. Such a "partial action," he said, would require an unjustifiable effort without "coming closer to a solution of the Jewish question in Hungary." In an off-the-record conversation with the editor in chief of the Hungarian newspaper *Pester Lloyd*, Döme Sztólay, Hungary's ambassador in Berlin, advocated deporting 300,000 Jews "to Russia"—later correcting that number down to 100,000 in response to a question from the journalist. The journalist insisted on knowing what the consequences would be for the deportees, whereupon Sztólay eventually admitted they would die.

On October 6, 1942, Baron László Vay—a leading official in the Hungarian Foreign Ministry, which was under the direct command of

Prime Minister Kállay—received Eichmann's henchman Dieter Wis-
liceny in Budapest and informed him that Hungary was prepared to
resettle 100,000 Jews from Carpathian Ukraine and Northern Transylvania to Germany. The second phase, Vay added, "would have to
include the flatlands [the Great Hungarian Plain] and finally the capital Budapest." On November 25, 1942, the general secretary of the
Transylvanian Party, Béla Teleki, suggested in parliament that Orthodox Jews living in what was again Hungarian Transylvania be resettled. Some 150,000 pure Magyars would find new homes there at the
same time.[39]

These proposals foreshadowed the order in which Jews would be
deported from Hungary in 1944, with the Yiddish-speaking Orthodox being the first to be taken away. These people lived primarily in
nationally disputed regions like Carpathian Ukraine and Northern
Transylvania. The Hungarian government wanted to get rid of them in
order to settle the new parts of the country, especially the cities, with
Magyars and to offer them better career chances and a better life at
the cost of those who had been deported. This is precisely what Hitler
had advised Horthy to do when the two met in Salzburg on April 16,
1943. The protocol of that meeting has Hitler saying that Hungary,
like Slovakia, "could house Jews in concentration camps." Hitler laid
out the advantages of such a course of action: "It would open many
opportunities to the children of the country by freeing up positions
occupied by Jews and allow the children of people to build résumés
previously closed off to them by Jews."[40]

The idea of enabling Christian Hungarians to better their social
lot at the expense of Jews had dominated public discussions in Hungary since the matriculation limits law of 1920, and it had only gained
momentum since 1938. The gas chambers of Auschwitz were not part
of what Hungarian politicians and ordinary Christians envisioned,
but stripping Jews of their wealth and deporting them to destinations
unknown certainly was. For that reason, it is not enough to speak of
Hungarian collaboration with Nazi Germany. There was a congruence
of interests. While Germans and Hungarians may have had differing

wishes and intentions, the result was the deportation of 423,000 Hungarian Jews with Hungarian permission to Auschwitz—370,000 were murdered there or in other camps. Hungarian officials stripped Jews of everything they owned, auctioning off their movable property to ordinary citizens and filling state coffers with the proceeds. They confiscated savings, insurance policies, and securities and nationalized real estate and businesses to be sold off later. All this proceeded without any great friction and in close cooperation with German occupiers.

In the months preceding Germany's conditional surrender on May 8 and 9, 1945, there was a parallel development in Hungary that spoke volumes about the continuities in the European politics of ethnicity. In March of that year, eastern Hungary had already been conquered by the Red Army. There, on March 15, in the provisional capital Debrecen, the Hungarian general Béla Miklós signed a decree ordering the confiscation of assets belonging to German Hungarians. Only the year before, on July 21, he had visited Hitler in his Wolf's Lair retreat in the wake of a failed assassination attempt and assured the Führer of Hungary's loyalty, listening without interruption to his lengthy digressions about the murder of Jews. Along with Miklós, the March 15 decree was signed by Agriculture Minister Imre Nagy, who would become the leader and principal martyr of the anti-Stalinist uprising in Hungary in 1956. The decree bore the title "Eradication of Large-Scale Property Ownership." It was also directed against aristocrats, but paragraphs four and five specifically targeted the 200,000 Hungarian citizens of German origin who were members of the minority organization Popular League of Germans in Hungary or who had "readopted their German-sounding family names."[41] Thus, in the spring of 1945, Hungarians used the same methods they had employed against Jews to impoverish German Hungarians in the east of the country. The final destination of these people wasn't Auschwitz, but the goals of the policy were familiar: ethnic homogenization, the need to accommodate Hungarians from North Transylvania, which was now again part of Romania, land reform, and the imperative of filling state coffers. At the same time, Hungarians in the west of the country, which was still under Wehrmacht control, were continuing to expropriate Jews. Soon, however, they would also change sides and confiscate the property of German Hungarians, too.

Hungary's first postwar civilian government was headed by the liberal democratic politician Zoltán Tildy, who became prime minister and then president. In 1948 the communists forced him to resign. In 1956, he became a minister of the rebel government. All the way back in 1938, his party, the Western-oriented, liberal-democratic Smallholders Party, which had been represented in the Hungarian parliament until 1944, had voted for the first Hungarian law sanctioning material discrimination against Jewish Hungarians. Their justification for doing so was to bring about the "correct distribution of income and wealth."[42]

The policy of ethnic cleansing extended across various Hungarian governments and forms of state. What President Regent Horthy had so fervently wished for in May 1944, the start of the deportations of Jews, became a reality between then and 1950: "After the war, every foreign race—be it the Jew, the Romanian, the Serbian, or the German—will have to leave the country since the Hungarians want to and must become the lords of this country."[43] After the Germans had been driven out, and following several transfers of populations with neighboring countries, Hungary became more ethnically "pure" than ever before.

Ethnic Policy in Romania

The resettlement of the German minorities from Estonia, Latvia, and eastern Poland in the winter of 1939–40 affected around 200,000 people. They came from Soviet-annexed areas of eastern Central Europe and were forced to leave their homes after the secret treaties concluded by the Soviet Union and Nazi Germany in September 1939. The resettlement of most of the Romanian Germans happened for different reasons and was part of the ethnic, national, and economic reordering Germany wanted to carry out in Southeastern Europe.

On June 28, 1940, the Soviet Union completed its annexation, sanctioned by Germany, of the Romanian provinces of Northern Bukovina and Bessarabia (Moldova). On August 30, 1940, Romania lost Northern Transylvania to Hungary and one week later Southern Dobruja to Bulgaria. To satisfy its allies Hungary and Bulgaria and its treaty partner the Soviet Union, the German government had severely infringed upon Romania's interests three times in succession. Nonetheless, Germany needed Romania for its oil reserves and grain exports, both of which were vital to the wartime economy. So Hitler promised to resettle Romanian Germans to Germany from those places where Romania's territorial losses had created a large number of migrants and refugees from what were now Hungarian, Bulgarian, and Soviet areas. Within a short time, the government had brought back to the Reich not just Germans from the Soviet areas but all those from the still Romanian Southern Bukovina and North Dobruja as well—all in all, 215,000 people. Almost all of them were to be resettled in occupied Poland, and their presence meant that Poles and Jews would be treated even more harshly.[44]

In Bucharest, Sabin Manuilă, a population researcher, led the ranks of the pragmatically oriented scientists in his field. In 1932 he published a study in which he suggested creating a state agency to "initiate an exchange of populations with Yugoslavia, Hungary, Czechoslovakia, Russia, Bulgaria and Greece" as a way of solving the problems of minorities in Romania.[45] From 1937 to 1947, he headed the Central Institute for Statistics, enjoyed direct access to those in power, and emphatically pleaded for the compulsory transfer of populations. In the summer of 1940, he founded an initiative to this end, using the same wording and justifications that Hitler had in his October 6, 1939, speech. Like the Führer, Manuilă claimed that the "transplantation" of millions of people would "end frictions that at present cause continual tension between states." In April 1941, he gushed about his great fortune in being able to help shape an epoch in which Romania's population problems would be permanently solved.[46]

In June and July 1941, together with the Wehrmacht, twelve Romanian divisions invaded the Soviet Union and retook Bessarabia and North Bukovina. That October, on the back of these victories,

Manuilă developed plans for a "comprehensive and compulsory forced exchange of populations."[47] He had been encouraged to do so by Romanian head of state Marshal Ion Antonescu in a personal conversation about "political population projects" on August 15. Antonescu had ordered the demographer to come up with a survey of the population and property in Bessarabia and Bukovina. Manuilă's data referred to Greater Romania in its 1939 borders, which included not just Bessarabia and Bukovina but also Northern Transylvania, now under Hungarian control. Romania hoped that most of this region would be returned, believing in Hitler and Göring's disingenuous assurance that they were willing, after victory was achieved in Eastern Europe, to review the conflict between Germany's two allies with a friendly eye toward Romania and to compensate Hungary with territory elsewhere.[48]

Manuilă suggested ceding several highly urbanized areas on the margins of Transylvania and Banat to Hungary and then carrying out a radical exchange of populations. "Politically, the time has come," he said, to create "a thoroughly homogeneous Romania." In an attempt to unite all patriotic sentiments, he envisioned "deporting all minorities with centrifugal leanings across the border." Later, the future Romanian state territory could be filled with pure-blooded Romanians from neighboring countries, and the external border of what he called "Romanian Romania, the eternal Romania," could be drawn so that "the political and ethnic lines would completely correspond" once and for all. According to his plan, the first step was to exchange large numbers of Serbs for a significantly smaller group of Romanians. Similar exchanges were to take place with Hungary, Bulgaria, and the German protectorates of Poland, Ukraine, and Russia.

After this stage, some 820,000 Siebenburg Saxons and Banat Swabians would remain in Romania, but in Manuilă's eyes there was no reason not to "repatriate" those Saxons and Swabians in a significantly larger "future Germany." Meanwhile, the Turkish government, as had been stipulated by treaty in 1936, would transfer 200,000 Tatars and Turks in phases to Anatolia. Between January 1, 1931, and July 1,

1938, 52,000 ethnic Turkish and Muslim emigrants had already left Romanian Dobruja for Turkey. The 1936 resettlement treaty, which took effect on April 1, 1937, envisioned that a further 35,000 families would leave Romania within the following five years, thereby freeing up 100,000 hectares of land for Christian Romanian farmers.[49] After Manuilă had made all his calculations and worked out a schedule, he turned to the topic of the 760,000 Jews in Greater Romania. They and the Roma, for whom he had no figures, were the subjects on the final, very brief point in his program, "Step Nr. 7." He wrote, cryptically: "The Jewish and gypsy questions are to be resolved in conjunction with the exchange of populations as a one-sided exchange." All told, Manuilă's ideas would have seen 5.4 million non-Romanians disappear from Romania, which amounted to 28 percent of the population, plus an unknown number of Roma. In return, 1.6 million expatriate Romanians were to be "pulled in."

Unlike for steps one through six, Manuilă didn't name any geographical destination for those to be resettled in step seven. What did he mean by "one-sided exchange"? While he and other bureaucrats adjusted the details of their ethnopolitical master plan in the late summer of 1941, the one-sided exchange of Jews was already under way in the form of deportation, ghettoization, and murder—even before steps one through six had begun in earnest. The reasons Manuilă gave for deporting Jews into oblivion were not racial or religious but materialistic. According to his statistics, the majority of Jews lived from trade, industry, and self-employed professions, and "this fact assures them a much higher standard of living than the middle classes of the country." The demographer was eager to break their "economic predominance." With their stores and banks, Jews "ruled over" the high streets while numerically far greater Romanians led wretched lives: "They live in side streets, are scattered through the fields and are public officials, servants and the like."[50]

In January 1941, Hitler had intimated to his Romanian allies that war with the Soviet Union was coming. Against this backdrop, on February 7, Antonescu told his cabinet of ministers what he intended for

EUROPE AGAINST THE JEWS, 1880–1945

Romania's Jews. Initially they would be put in ghettos and then, when the time was ripe, deported to territories "allocated to them on the international level." That was also the main thrust of Germany's Jewish policy in the months before the invasion of the Soviet Union. Upon victory in the east, the Jews would be deported to the most inhospitable parts of the Soviet Union. This, too, was what Manuilă meant by "one-sided exchange."[51]

On June 22, 1941, German and Romanian troops started waging war on the Soviet Union. That day Antonescu explained to the leader of the Farmers Party of Romania, Iuliu Maniu, that the country's grave structural problems could be solved "in their full breadth and complexity" as soon as the Jews had disappeared. Expropriating them would enable Romanian businesses and farmers to get the lines of credit they needed to modernize. Jewish personnel would be replaced, thus decreasing unemployment. All these things would be of "direct use" to Romanians and lead to "reforms . . . in the vital interest of our people."

Two weeks later, on July 3, Antonescu's deputy, Mihai Antonescu, told officers stationed in reconquered Bessarabia and North Bukovina that they were participating in a "historical moment" that had put the "ethnic cleansing" of the country on the agenda. At first, Jews would be put in labor camps and then be subjected, like other "foreign elements," to "forced emigration."[52] When he addressed the Romanian cabinet five days later, he expanded his ideas to Southern Bukovina in Romania proper: "The entire Jewish population must disappear from the villages and immediately turn over their profits. . . . Let's take this felicitous opportunity to get our hands on further agricultural properties, which we can then reallocate without running into problems with the owners as we did in 1940." The latter remarks referred to Soviet authorities' distribution of agriculturally useful land in the summer of 1940 to better politically integrate the rural poor during the year in which Bukovina and Bessarabia had been Soviet-annexed. A compromise needed to be found between the old and new landowners. Now the Romanian government figured that it could maintain psychological, social, and economic harmony in the country by using Jewish real estate, businesses, stocks of goods, inventories, and personal possessions.

Antonescu answered the question of what would happen to the people thus dispossessed in that same meeting with utter clarity: "Even if some of you traditionalists don't understand me, I am for the compulsory resettlement of all Jews away from Bessarabia and Bukovina. Likewise I am for the compulsory resettlement of all Ukrainian elements that no longer have any business being here. . . . Never in our history has there been a better opportunity for us—comprehensively, radically and in freedom to get rid of our ethnic shackles once and for all, and to nationally cleanse and renew our people."[53]

He issued the following call to the military officers and police leaders who had been invited to the meeting: "Be pitiless. Sweet-sounding, blurry, philosophical, humanitarian chatter has no place here." Now or never, the Romanian nation "had to be cleansed of all filth." Antonescu exhorted them: "If necessary, use your machine guns! From the very beginning, pay as little attention as possible to formalities." This was his way of attacking a "race" that he claimed "was striving for mastery everywhere." At this juncture, the 300,000 Jews in Romanian-occupied territories were probably foremost on his mind, and not Jews living in Romania proper. This homicidal speech was no doubt delivered in the name of the prime minister, who a few days before the onset of war had issued his own orders to the gendarmerie to kill village Jews "on the spot" in any newly conquered territories.[54]

During the first year of war, the Romanian police and army murdered between 150,000 and 180,000 Jews of all ages, mainly in reconquered areas and Transnistria. Many Jews from South Bukovina and the border town of Iași, in the east of Romania proper, also fell victim to the genocide. On June 29, 1941, it was the scene of a pogrom that cost 13,000 Jews their lives.[55] Goebbels considered Romania's bloodthirsty rigor a model for other countries. On August 19, 1943, the German propaganda minister noted in his diary: "Where the Jewish question is concerned, it is clear today in any case that a man like Antonescu has acted more radically than we have done thus far." Two days later, in Bucharest, a Romanian cavalry officer recounted over breakfast that "dozens, hundreds, thousands of Jews had been shot" on both sides of the Dniester River. "Although but a simple lieutenant," the man said, he had been allowed "to kill as many Jews as he wanted on orders or on his own initiative." The chauffeur who had brought him to Iași, the man added, had himself killed four Jews. All told, Romanian soldiers and police murdered at least 250,000 Jews between 1941 and 1944.[56]

On September 5, 1941, while large numbers of Jews were being murdered, Ion Antonescu issued instructions to his cabinet concerning future population policies in Bukovina and Bessarabia: "The complete clearing out [curățirea totală] of Jews and all others who have seeped into our midst, namely Ukrainians, Greeks, Gagauzes—all must be evacuated, one column after another." On February 26, 1942, he told his cabinet that he intended to "remove all the foreigners" from annexed Transnistria. Of the 2.3 million inhabitants of the region, only 8.3 percent spoke Romanian.

There was already a government agency in place for resettlement projects. In September 1940, Romania had created a precursor to what was later the Office for Romanianization, Colonization and Inventorization in order to organize a small-scale exchange of populations, agreed upon the previous month, with Bulgaria. One hundred and ten thousand Romanians had been forced to leave South Dobruja, and about half as many Bulgarians North Dobruja. After North Transylvania was once again made part of Hungary, around 200,000 Romanian-speaking refugees also arrived back in Romania. More followed when the Soviet Union annexed Bessarabia.[57] In this situation, the Romanian government enacted even more stringent anti-Semitic measures and laws. Germany's *Frankfurter Zeitung* reported retrospectively in 1943: "One by one, measures were enacted to target Jews' economic position. On October 5, 1940, the state was declared the legal owner and beneficiary of all Jewish land. Confiscated assets were primarily allocated to refugees from ceded territories. . . . In March the following year, urban property followed."[58]

As part of its demographic strategy Romania settled new arrivals in those places where Jewish property had been expropriated and where the Reich Commissar for the Consolidation of German Nationhood had evacuated 80,000 people of German origin from the Romanian heartland. In a short report about the "settlement work," a subordinate of Manuilă's later explained to an audience of German specialists: "The material element consisted of what were 260,000 hectares of fields, which thanks to the resettlement of Germans and expropriation of Jews passed into state hands."[59]

On December 4, 1941, the cabinet secretary Titus Dragoş took over the Office for Romanianization, Colonization and Inventorization. Before that, he had served as a general secretary in the Finance Ministry, where he was responsible for the Directorate for Refugees and Settlers, which expropriated Jews and placed Romanians in new homes. By May 1942, Ion Antonescu had ordered his interior minister to work with Dragoş to come up with a plan to "evacuate" all non-Romanians from South Bessarabia and to colonize the territory with "Romanian elements." On November 6, 1942, Antonescu demanded that the "theoretical, preliminary work" for this transfer of populations be accelerated and that all of Bessarabia, Bukovina, and especially Transnistria be included.[60]

In the end, not much came of Dragoş's efforts. In late 1942, the resettlement plans were dramatically cut back and put off until some indefinite point in the future. As was the case with Bulgaria, the Romanian government's course was changed not by any moral epiphany but by the military triumphs of the anti-Hitler coalition, especially the heavy defeats inflicted on German and Romanian troops on the eastern front in the winter of 1942–43. From this point on, the Romanian government moderated its use of terror and rebuffed requests from Berlin to deliver up to 300,000 Jews from the Romanian heartland. What's more, Jewish refugees from Poland and Hungary to Romania were also kept safe from German clutches.[61]

Deportation from Slovakia, Mass Murder in Croatia

Having been created as an independent state in 1939 by Nazi Germany, Slovakia remained dependent on Berlin's favor, and the German regime constantly interfered in Slovakian domestic affairs. But there were limits to the Slovaks' willingness to accept German "advice." Like Bulgaria and Hungary, Slovakia initially handed over Jews to Germany, but then unilaterally ended the deportations. Moreover, like Romania, Slovakia also offered Hungarian Jews protection in the summer of 1944.

In 1940, there were only 89,000 Slovakian Jews out of a population of 2.7 million. But in the spring of 1942, Slovakia's rulers decided of their own accord to send 60,000 of them to German "work camps." At the end of the year, after the deportations had taken place, a temporary, then a permanent moratorium was put in place. According to historian Tatjana Tönsmeyer, the government in Bratislava "ended its cooperation with the Third Reich" for two reasons. Respected representatives of the Catholic Church—a number of bishops together with Vatican diplomat Giuseppe Burzio—intervened on behalf of Slovakia's Jews, and Germany's lack of success in the war caused a change in popular opinion. While Slovakia's remaining 29,000 Jews were expropriated, they were otherwise largely left alone until the Wehrmacht occupied Slovakia for several weeks in late 1944.

Tönsmeyer cites the same motivations as in the other countries for the rapid denaturalization and expropriation of Slovakian Jews in 1940 and the urgent desire to deport this now penniless minority. Like elsewhere in southeastern Europe, she writes, "hostility toward Jews in Slovakia served as a common denominator in a society that had no idea how to deal with its modernization problems and the anxiety they engendered." Aryanization was carried out by Slovakia in the form of "social-welfare policies that took from the 'wealthy Jews' and gave to the 'impoverished Slovaks.'"[62] The synagogues in Bratislava survived the Second World War undamaged. The Orthodox one was torn down in 1961.

IN APRIL 1941, the Wehrmacht entered Belgrade. Six months earlier, the Yugoslav government, which had previously not been anti-Semitic, instituted broad matriculation limits regulating how many people of Jewish extraction could study at universities and other institutions of higher education. A few days before the law took effect, Jews were summarily expelled from educational institutions throughout Yugoslavia.[63]

Just as the Nazi government had split Czechoslovakia in 1938 and 1939, in 1941, with some help from Italy, it demolished the state of Yugoslavia. A much-diminished Serbia was governed by the military working with a regime of collaborators, and Germany, Italy, Bulgaria, and Hungary annexed significant stretches of Serbian territory. Croatia, on the other hand, was formed as a nominally independent vassal state and enlarged with parts of Slavonia and Bosnia-Herzegovina. It was ruled by the fascist Ustashe organization. Closely following German models, the Ustashe passed a series of Jewish laws in its first weeks in power. Six months on, it had the main synagogue in Zagreb demolished.

Of a total population of 6.6 million, Croatia contained 3.3 million Catholic Croats, 1.9 million Serbs, and 800,000 Muslim Bosnians, as well as German, Hungarian, Czech, Slovak, and Italian minorities, 40,000 Jews, and 25,000 Roma. On its own initiative, the Ustashe began a campaign of mass murder in which, according to historian Alexander Korb, the motif of ethnic cleansing emerged with "terrible clarity." More than 310,000 Serbs, some 26,000 Jews, and around 20,000 Roma fell victim to the genocide. By 1944, Croatian militias had displaced 240,000 surviving Serbs, who escaped with their lives but were rendered penniless. With the permission of the government in Zagreb, henchmen of Eichmann also deported an additional 6,650 Jews to German extermination camps.

As Korb has shown, the Croatian mass murderers were "by no means German marionettes" but rather people who acted "self-confidently and in their own interests." They pursued goals that "were clearly differentiated from those of the National Socialists" and tried to exterminate Jews and Roma to further their own large-scale political repopulation project. Valuables, whether they were left behind by Jews or Serbs, were redistributed by the state in the interest of economic renewal. "The stolen assets of minorities were set aside to strengthen the Croatian middle classes," writes Korb. Historian Philipp Ther adds that fields taken from Serbian farmers were used for modern forms of agriculture. In many villages, Croatians terrorized their neighbors of other nationalities with extreme brutality in the name of "improving the social standard and economic conditions of the community." Political loyalties and long-term, ingrained racist thinking played little or no role in all this.[64]

In Bulgaria, Hungary, Romania, Croatia, and Slovakia, all German allies, homicidal policies toward Jews were part of more broadly conceived projects of ethnic cleansing. They were also understood by social elites as a crucial element of forming the nation. They continued the practices of displacement, compulsory resettlement, and murder that had been common since the Balkan Wars of 1912 and 1913. The 1923 Lausanne Convention that had temporarily put a halt to the mass killings and refugee tragedies proved to have a hateful legacy insofar as it legitimized the exchange of populations and ethnic homogenization. In 1941, the Croatian regime elevated this treaty to its "guiding leitmotiv for the 'ethnic de-mixing' of the Balkans." That phrase also signified mass murder, as was shown in early 1943 when German special envoy Edmund Veesenmayer tried to exert a moderating influence on Ante Pavelić, the Croatian dictator, who answered: "The extermination and displacement of the Armenians in the Ottoman Empire made the later job of building up Turkey much easier."[65]

With war having desensitized people to mass violence, the German government provided to many southeastern countries an example of how to deal with Jews—by deporting them with an eye toward their murder. Whether in Zagreb, Bratislava, Bucharest, Budapest, or Sofia, elites and others increasingly began to believe that the war offered a unique chance to realize long-held plans for radical ethnopolitical action. Ion Antonescu was typical of many leaders when he said in the fall of 1941: "This is wartime, and a good time to settle the Jewish problem once and for all."[66]

THE ENEMY SOLVES THE JEWISH QUESTION

Germany's allies Romania and Croatia were directly involved in genocide against Jews. Under pressure from "Jew advisors" from German embassies, Bulgaria and Slovakia allowed parts of their Jewish populations to be transported to the death camps. The same is more or less true of Hungary, which spent more time as an ally of Germany than a nation occupied by it. Circumstances were different in France, Norway, Luxembourg, the Netherlands, and the Czech territory, which was known under Nazism as the Protectorate of Bohemia and Moravia, where Germany installed comparatively mild occupation regimes intended to encourage cooperation. State leaders in those countries differed as to how willingly they supported the German policy of deporting and exterminating Jews.

"No Appreciation for the Jewish Question" in Belgium

There were two notable exceptions to the voluntary participation in the Holocaust. The case of Denmark is well known. Thanks to its proximity to neutral Sweden, the ethical fiber of its royal family, the scarcity of German occupiers, and the efforts of a German diplomat determined to help, all 7,500 Jews in Denmark were saved in 1943. The situation in Belgium was different. This small, thickly settled part of Western Europe was governed by a German military administration, which relied on a council of state secretaries (Comité des Secrétaires-généraux) to organize the civilian aspects of Belgian life, while the elected government waited in London exile. Because Belgium was so close to the British Isles, the Wehrmacht deployed a great many soldiers in the country.

By the end of the occupation, German forces had succeeded in deporting around half of Belgium's 56,000 Jews, but Germans had to apprehend most of the victims themselves. In contrast to their French colleagues, Belgian bankers, notaries, and judges, who had access to information about accounts and property and commercial registers, refused to become complicit in the expropriation of persecuted people,[67] although there were isolated instances of Belgian police assisting German occupiers, especially in Antwerp in the Flemish part of the country. Historian Isa Meinen has detailed the significant differences between Belgium—where both government officials and the civilian population refused to cooperate—and France and the Netherlands. The head of the German military administration, the lawyer and honorary SS general Eggert Reeder, repeatedly had to report with regret back to Berlin that, unlike in France, the military administration in Belgium had to "force . . . political measures to be taken against Jews or carry them out itself." He complained that "the Belgian" had "no appreciation for the justice of the Jewish measures." Or as he telegraphed Himmler, "Appreciation for the Jewish question not very widespread here."

In May 1942, the military administration in Belgium ordered that all Jews wear Stars of David visibly on their clothing. Reeder wanted local communities to procure and distribute the yellow patches. But one week later, the conservative Catholic mayor of Brussels, Jules Coelst, categorically refused. In the name of all the nineteen mayors in the greater Brussels metropolitan area, he wrote to the head of the local commander's office: "It is not our place to debate with you whether the measures you have taken against Jews are appropriate. Yet it is our duty to inform you that you cannot demand that we participate in them. Many Jews are Belgian citizens, and moreover we cannot commit ourselves to enforcing an edict that so obviously runs contrary to the dignity of human beings, whoever they may be."[68]

In Belgium some 20 percent of deported Jews were apprehended with the help of local governmental offices or individuals. French police captured a far larger percentage of deportees on their own accord, and in the Netherlands, too, German occupiers found willing helpers, particularly within the state bureaucracy. During the first half of 1941, officials at the Dutch population registry drew up a "central registry of Jews and Jewish half-breeds." Their German superiors praised them as "loyal and even very diligent." The registry contained the names, addresses, and personal details of 160,820 people. Dutch government agencies also issued special Jewish identity cards featuring passport photos, fingerprints, and copies for residency offices. Dutch officials stamped the cards of full Jews with an upper case "J," of half-Jews with "BI," and quarter-Jews with "BII"—the "B" stood for bastard. On September 24, the superior SS and police leader responsible for the Netherlands, Hanns Rauter, sent a telegram to Himmler: "The new units of the Dutch police are performing well on the Jewish question and are arresting hundreds of Jews day and night."[69]

The extent of deportations to the death camps, then, was not solely determined by edicts from Berlin but was affected by the degree of state collaboration or resistance and by societal participation or refusal, as these figures show: more than 75 percent of Jews in the Netherlands went sent to death camps, 50 percent in Norway (out of 2,000), 45 percent in Belgium, 34 percent in Luxembourg, 25 percent in France, and only 2 percent in Denmark.

The Danger of Being a Foreign Jew in France

In the course of armistice negotiations in July 1940, after France's defeat by Germany, the two sides agreed upon how the country was to be administered. The French government, which continued to exist and was already led by Marshal Philippe Pétain, was responsible for the nonoccupied, southern part of France and enjoyed remarkable autonomy until late 1942. It also controlled the French administration in the occupied zone. For two years, the comparatively mild form of occupation there led many French officials, particularly in financial administration and the police, to act in the interests of the German occupiers. The German military commander and the German ambassador to France both resided in Paris, while the leaders of the French government were based in the southern spa town of Vichy. They no longer described their nation as the French republic, but rather as the French state. Coming from the nationalist right, many had advocated authoritarian forms of rule for quite some time and had admired Mussolini's success in Italy. Some even thought positively of Hitler. The Vichy government stripped Jews of their rights both in conjunction with the occupational authority and of its own accord. On July 2, 1941, it ordered the registration and on July 22 the expropriation of all Jews. Six months later, French officials had more or less confiscated everything Jews owned.[70]

One year earlier, on July 17, 1940, only a short time after it had been established, the Vichy government ordered that only those who could prove their fathers were French would be allowed to work for the state. Laws passed on August 16 and September 10 extended that restriction to the medical and legal professions. While the laws technically applied to anyone whose father was born abroad, they were only ever enforced against Jews. If we recall the vociferous protests by the corresponding professional organizations in the 1930s against allowing large numbers of Jews to practice law and medicine, then the rulers of the État Français were fulfilling demands that had been made long before the war in the République Française—ones which from the perspective of the protesters had never been adequately addressed.

Furthermore, on July 20, 1940, the Vichy regime created a commission to review and, in some cases, reverse, the 650,000 naturalizations that had taken place since 1927. This body harked back to the *commissions de triage* in Alsace-Lorraine in 1919 and 1920. The focus was on the tens of thousands of Jewish émigrés who had become French, and by 1943 thousands of them had been stripped of their citizenship. This meant that the Vichy regime could legally hand them over to the German occupiers to be sent to Auschwitz. Historian Michael Mayer has uncovered a telling detail that illustrates how far the Vichy regime was complicit in the Holocaust. On February 10, 1942, after the justice ministry and the commissariat on Jewish affairs had given their blessing, Pétain signed a law concerning the adoption of new names. It prohibited Jews from changing their names and established a commission to review all cases in which typically Jewish names had been changed since October 24, 1870.

Two years earlier, on October 4, 1940, a law had been passed allowing all foreign Jews to be detained without justification in camps. The Vichy government estimated that around 20,000 foreign Jews were living in France; a few months later, the same number of Jews were incarcerated. The law was intended to create a general acceptance for their deportation, with German assistance. To that end, the Vichy government's commissioner-general for Jewish questions, Xavier Vallat, declared in early 1942: "In normal times, the first partial solution consists of deporting all foreign-born Jews back to their countries of origin." But in times of war that wasn't possible, Vallat went on, since the countries in question had chosen to follow "the path of anti-Jewish policies."[71] It was thus up to the German occupiers to suggest to the Vichy government a solution commensurate with the unusual times. On July 2, as the Reich Main Security Office was about to commence deportations, Germany's ambassador in Paris, Otto Abetz, told his superiors in Berlin that, in his view, the French had no concerns about the "transport of 40,000 Jews from France to the Auschwitz camp." Nevertheless, he advised that mass apprehensions be carried out in such a way "that would increase the anti-Semitic sentiment that has been growing recently." As in Germany, the strengthening of anti-Semitic views in France "can largely be put down to the immigration of foreign Jews in past years." Therefore it would be "psychologically effective for the broad masses of the French people if the evacuation measures first affected those foreign Jews."[72] That is precisely what happened.

With considerable help from French officials and police, German occupiers were able to send 76,000 Jews from France to the death camps. More than 50,000 of them had never been or were no longer French citizens. Only a few survived. Just as was later the case in Hungary, French government agencies saw it as their duty to detain Jews, hold them in camps, and accompany and secure the transports as far as the French-German border. The cooperation worked extraordinarily well as long as most of those being deported were foreign Jews.[73]

Nevertheless, 225,000 of the approximately 300,000 Jews living in France at the time were saved. That was a high percentage compared with other countries conquered or subjugated by Germany. Many honorable French people, including Catholic clergy, nuns, and monks as well as communists, ordinary people, and individual officials, offered those under threat protection from their German and French persecutors. As Germany's military situation worsened after the Battle of Stalingrad, the cooperativeness of French civil servants and the Vichy regime declined. But hostility toward Jews and simple envy still were deadly threats, as two examples illustrate.

Albert Drach, a Jewish Viennese attorney who spoke with a pronounced German accent, survived the war in France thanks to forged identity papers. He later described an experience he had in the fall of 1943 in an overcrowded bus in the Maritime Alps near the Italian border. There he was verbally abused by "a couple of very young people . . . in the typical fashion of the country" as a "ridiculous métèque" (foreign intruder). Suddenly a German police officer stopped the bus and checked the passengers. "The door of our vehicle was opened from the outside," Drach related later.

> "Is everything okay?" asked a fat Prussian wearing gloves. "No," screamed the teenagers in the back, "there's a Jew here." The Prussian must have thought this was a joke. He grinned and shut the bus door, giving the signal for it to continue on. "Stop, stop!" yelled the young men. But the bus drove on. The young men kept on with their loutish behavior. In loud voices, they informed their fellow passengers that in their communities and elsewhere there were still Jews who should be apprehended and handed over.[74]

The other story comes from the world-renowned mathematician Benoit B. Mandelbrot, who was born in Warsaw in 1924 and came from a Jewish Lithuanian family. In 1936 he emigrated with his parents and brother to Paris, and in 1940 they fled to southern France. Zina Morhange, a friend of the family and a physician who had also come from Poland, was deported to Auschwitz because a colleague, "who simply wanted to get rid of the competition," turned her in. Morhange survived. The Mandelbrots remained undiscovered for two reasons. "We were fortunate that we didn't represent competition to anyone and didn't look like foreigners. My parents' systematic efforts at assimilation paid dividends. My brother and I sounded almost like native French boys, and we looked like them too."[75]

As was true with the populations, particularly elites, of other European states, most French people kept silent for decades about anti-Semitic collaboration with their German occupiers. After the Germans had been forced out of France in the fall of 1944, several interest groups immediately formed among those French people who had—innocently, they claimed—profited from what Jews had been forced to leave behind. The members of these associations demonstrated, chanted "France for the French," and did everything in their power not to restore to the Jews who returned their rightful businesses, companies, homes, and other belongings. In his 1995 novel *Quoi de neuf sur la guerre?* (What's the Latest from the War?) Robert Bober describes how difficult it was for the small numbers of returnees to get their apartments and houses back. Although they had injunctions in their hands and were accompanied by officers of the court and police, they were usually forced to retreat, business undone, in the face of "organized bands of people who had alarmed the occupants."[76]

All the files from the German occupation, and especially those of the French expropriation authority and the Finance Ministry, remained classified for half a century after the Second World War. Only at that point were they gradually released to the public. As of 2016 this process was still not complete.[77]

Citizens "of Luxembourgish Blood"

Shortly before being invaded by the Wehrmacht, all those states that hadn't enacted anti-Semitic laws and other measures did so. As was the case in France, the main justification was the perception that too many Jews displaced from elsewhere had been allowed to immigrate, legally or illegally. In the months before their respective German invasions, both Belgium and the Netherlands set up holding camps for such refugees.

As in France, the moderate anti-Semitism in Luxembourg before the 1930s intensified with the arrival of many immigrants and refugees. Of the 3,144 Jews who lived in this tiny country in 1935, 870 were citizens. Fears that the country was getting too foreign inspired the idea of scrapping Luxembourg's liberal citizenship law, based on the French model, and instituting the German idea of citizenship through blood. On March 9, 1940, two months before German troops marched in, the *loi sur l'indigénat luxembourgeois* was passed. Conservatives and socialists in parliament voted for this legislation, according to which "only those of Luxembourgish blood" could be citizens of the country.

This anti-Jewish law was inspired not by some sort of racist ideology but by simple fear of Jewish competition. A 2015 study commissioned by the Luxembourg government found: "Documented in numerous police files and articles in the right-wing extremist, Catholic and even liberal press, Jews were collectively accused of aiming to buy up whole segments of the Luxembourg economy. With cosmopolitan cleverness, it was alleged, they had also resorted to using hired proxies to achieve their ends." In May 1940, amid popular panic, the highest institution of civilian administration, the *Commission administrative*, began cooperating with Luxembourg's German occupiers. Officials were "invited" but not forced to persecute Jews, but they often enthusiastically took up this offer.[78]

Germans and Greeks Ghettoize Jews

In Salonika, the anti-Jewish measures enacted after the Wehrmacht's invasion on April 9, 1941, were applauded by a significant majority of the city's Greek residents. As a strategically important port, Salonika was put under German administration together with the Greek hinterland. Meanwhile Italian troops occupied the majority of Greece until Italy renounced its alliance with Germany in late summer 1943. Hardly had he arrived than the head of the German military administration reinstated the forbidden right-wing extremist National Union of Greece (Ethniki Enosis Ellados), which soon renamed itself the National Socialist Union of Greece (Elliniko Ethniko Sosialistiko Komma). For their part, Germans commandeered only the houses of Jews in Salonika, not Greeks.

In the months that followed, 48,000 refugees arrived from the parts of Northern Greece annexed by Bulgaria. They, too, were accommodated in houses where Jews had lived. Greek officials pushed for this to happen, and the local press began referring to Jews as "parasites." In the newspaper *Nea Evropi*, which supported Greek collaboration with Nazi Germany, the influential journalist Nikolaos Kammonas wrote a whole series of articles about the "diabolical depravity and poisonous treachery with which Jews built their financial and racial empire on the corpse of Macedonian Greece." On July 11, 1942, Salonika's German occupiers ordered 800 Jewish men to assemble in the city's Plateia Eleftheria (Liberty Square), where, watched by Greek police, they were humiliated all day in the scorching sun. In the end they were forced to register for forced labor. This action took place after consultations with—some say at the behest of—the Greek head of the general governorate of the province of Macedonia, Vasilis Simonidis. Many Greek residents watched the repugnant spectacle, unmoved or scornful.[79]

In December 1942, the mayor of Salonika succeeded where his predecessor had failed in 1917 and forced Jews to sign over ownership of the large Old Cemetery to the municipal government. Thirty-five hectares of inner-city real estate became available for construction. As early as August 4, 1930, and March 21, 1934, the Greek government had issued edicts on the basis of which the cemetery could be expropriated and destroyed, but its rightful owners had always prevented this from happening. Salonika city planners were first able to achieve their ends with German help. Today, the land is the site of Aristotle University, which had been planned as far back as 1917 but was only constructed after the Second World War.

The head of the German military administration, Max Merten, knew that the eradication of the cemetery would win points with the Christian Greek majority. In their eyes, writes historian Rena Molho, "the cemetery destruction represented a tabula rasa enabling Salonika's further Hellenization while for Jews it was a harbinger of the mass murder to come." With the visible destruction of the cemetery, the Christian majority was sending the Jewish community a clear message: your time is up.[80]

Indeed, no sooner had 500 city employees begun to dig up the cemetery's half-million graves than the first train rolled off to Auschwitz. The date was March 15, 1943. In the following five months, 43,850 Jews were taken from the city along with a further 2,134 from the surrounding German-occupied areas. Greek police, local administrators, and the Macedonia prefecture did all they could to assist in the deportations.[81] While the death trains were pulling out of the station, Greek merchants snapped up the businesses of their deported former competition. Jacques Stroumsa, a Jew born in 1913 in Salonika who also grew up there, remembered that it "served absolutely no purpose" to ask Christian families for shelter. Aside from a few rare exceptions, they refused.[82]

In the spring of 1944, German occupiers began to go after Jews in those Greek cities that had been under Italian military administration until the previous September. On March 25, the Jews of Patras were arrested by German soldiers and Greek police. Astro Alballa had left his home as a precaution and in hiding was able to observe telling scenes: "You could see people in the street taking everything they could carry from the homes of Jews."

That same day 1,850 Jews were detained in Ioannina and later deported. On May 27 the local newspaper *Ipeirotikos Kyrix* ran an article with the headline "Jewish Property." It describes widespread thievery: "More than two months ago the Jews were removed from Ioannina. Since then, various committees have met, and this and that has been heard. The broadest variety of plans has been discussed, but as this has been going on, Jewish property has continued to dwindle. We don't know how long this uncertain situation will carry on, but one thing is sure: if things proceed the way they're going, soon there'll be nothing left to distribute."

One of the few Jews who escaped capture by the Germans was Yushua Matsas. Like Alballa, he joined the Greek partisans and didn't resurface until the end of the occupation. While Greeks celebrated their liberation in October 1944, he felt like an unwanted foreigner despite having returned home: "We had difficulty finding a place to stay in our own homes. People had quartered themselves everywhere, and they took offense when we even asked if there was a room we could sleep in." Some of the goods looted from Jewish shops were still in a warehouse. But the leaders of the communist partisan organization ELAS only handed out 1 percent of them. "They gave every Jew present in the city some clothes and household items worth thirty gold sovereigns," recalled Matsas. Communist functionaries spirited the vast majority of these stolen goods off to Albania—as a reserve fund for the imminent Greek civil war.[83]

A short time later, British soldiers reached Ioannina. In their weekly report, they noted that deported Jews' assets were distributed to Greeks under the direction of the governor of Epirus Michalis Tsimbris. The Greeks who profited, speculated British troops, would probably not agree to return everything, and nothing was done to help Jews who had escaped deportation. In neighboring Preveza, portable Jewish belongings had been stored in warehouses, and a committee had been formed under the head official Aletras. It was an open secret, wrote the soldiers, that this committee was selling off things piece by piece and doing good business.[84]

On June 14, 1944, Germans transported 1,795 Jews from the island of Corfu to Auschwitz five days after they had been apprehended in a joint German-Greek action. Prefect Ioannes Komianos, Corfu mayor Spyridonos Kollas, and Police Chief Pericles Dedopoulos jointly proclaimed: "As has also been the case in the rest of Greece, Jews have been rounded up and are waiting to be sent to do forced labor. This measure has been welcomed by Corfu's upstanding native population. It will benefit our beloved, wonderful island. From now on, trade will be in our hands! Now we will harvest the fruits of our labor ourselves! How the supply of food and the economic situation will turn to our advantage! The entirety of Jewish property belongs to the Greek state and therefore to us all. The prefecture will take it over and administer it." In the community council, Kollas declared, "Our great friends the Germans have cleansed our island of Jews."[85]

Straight Talk from Italian and Spanish Diplomats

Everyone concerned knew what would happen to the Jews taken from Salonika. After the first deportations on March 15, 1943, following a conversation between the Italian consul, Guelfo Zamboni, and Merten, Lucillo Merci, an Italian liaison officer and translator, noted: "After all it is known that the Jews of Salonika are being sent to Poland. There, the physically fit among them are put to work, whereas the rest are

eliminated. In the end, the physically fit will also be liquidated." In the
wake of such reports, the Italian Foreign Ministry declared Jews living
in Greece to be Italian citizens and transported them to the Italian
occupation zone.

Nearly three weeks later, on April 6, Merci wrote: "The Germans
have transported around 20,000 Jews from Salonika to Poland."
During the deportations, which were carried out using cattle cars,
groups of 2,400 were watched over and herded onto the trains by
German and Greek police. "The Greeks break into the houses emptied of the deportees and loot anything they can get their hands on,"
Merci wrote. During the Greek Orthodox Easter festival on April 5,
a large puppet wearing a yellow Star of David was strung up next to
the White Tower, the city's main landmark. In Merci's interpretation,
Greeks had put it there "to imply that the turn of the murderers of
Jesus had come."[86]

Correspondence between Spanish diplomats also reveals how openly
people in Salonika talked about the mass murder of the city's Jews. Late
in the process, in June 1943, Federico Díez de Isasi, first secretary at the
Spanish embassy in Berlin, brought up the fate of Spanish Jews living in
Greece with the German Foreign Ministry. According to German notes
taken, Isasi said he understood why Jews were being interned but
rejected their deportation with the argument that Madrid "could never
agree to Spanish citizens being liquidated in Polish camps."[87] A short
while later, Spain's ambassador in Berlin, Ginés Vidal, approached
the Spanish foreign minister to inform him about the "tragic and final
consequences" for Spanish Jews if they were shipped from Greece to
Poland. At the same time, the junior embassy official Federico Oliván
wrote to the general director of foreign policy in the Spanish Foreign
Ministry, José María Doussinague, with the urgent message that inac-
tion would "automatically lead to the deaths" of those deported. "This
is the tragic reality," Oliván wrote, "before which we should not close
our eyes." He warned that after the war Spain could be held account-
able if "we wash our hands like Pontius Pilate, full in the knowledge
of what happens next—and abandon these people to their sad fate."
Under pressure from its diplomats in Berlin, the Spanish government

first tried to stall before slowly deciding that a surgical intervention was necessary. After a series of complicated detours, Madrid managed to rescue more than 500 Spanish Jews in Salonika from certain death.

The actual hero of this rescue was a man who acted vigorously in the background, Sebastián Romero Radigales, Spanish consul in Salonika and Athens. Initially he was accused of overreacting by his colleagues in Madrid. Undeterred, Radigales ignored orders to cooperate with German authorities. Unofficially, he sent a list with the names of all the endangered people to his colleagues in Spain's Berlin embassy and won over allies there. In 2014, the Yad Vashem memorial posthumously honored Sebastián Romero Radigales as one of the Righteous Among Nations.[88]

POLAND AND THE SOVIET UNION: GERMAN TERROR AND THE MURDER OF JEWS

In Poland and the Soviet Union, Germany pursued a scorched-earth policy involving daily arrests and executions and the systematic murder of religious leaders, lawyers, professors, Polish business leaders, and Soviet government workers. People were turned out of their homes, and hundreds of thousands of young men and women were arrested on market squares or in front of cinemas and then taken to Germany to perform slave labor. In short, people in these places were subjected to despotic cruelty and constantly had to fear for their lives, which undermined their morality and basic humanity.

Those hiding Jews in occupied Poland or the German-conquered part of the Soviet Union were risking their lives. Police official Bernhard Kaupp reported how his SS police battalion "de-Jewified" the village of Samary together with thirty-nine Ukrainian auxiliary officers on October 30, 1942: "All in all, seventy-four Jews were apprehended and executed. One Ukrainian family—a man, two women and three children—who harbored a Jewess living together with the family were also taken out and shot."[89]

In March 1942, the head of SS Einsatzgruppe C, Dr. Max Thomas, stationed in Kyiv, wrote, "cooperation with Ukrainian officials and the [Ukrainian] militia is generally good," and "in terms of mood the stringent measures taken against the Jews and the former party communists have had a positive effect." But Thomas also reported that his men had executed the mayor of Kremenchuk because he had "sabotaged the orders he had been given" by allowing "the leading local cleric Protejerej Romanskyj to baptize Jews and give them Christian Russian first names," which were then attested by the notary and entered into the registry of residents.[90]

When documenting the behavior of the Polish, Ukrainian, Russian, and Belarussian populations during the war, we need to keep in mind the boundless terror to which people were subjected. Likewise we should also remember those Poles, Ukrainians, Belarussians, and Russians who summoned the inner strength in an inhumane world created by Germans to shelter the persecuted. If they survived the war, they often thought it better not to inform their neighbors that they had helped Jews.

The courtyard between the library and the learning center at Yad Vashem is called Family Plaza. A huge raw iron sculpture there depicts the final steps taken by Nachum Freydovicz with three small children, two of them his grandchildren. Their story unfolded in 1943 in the Jewish ghetto of Grodno. Genia and Aaron Zandman learned that a "major action" was scheduled for the ghetto and realized they would have to hide. They and another family faced the barbaric decision of leaving behind three defenseless, tiny children, whose crying would have betrayed everyone hiding in the secret spaces of a vaulted synagogue basement. Genia Zandman's father, Nachum Freydovicz, encouraged by his wife, Tema, volunteered to stay behind with the children. He carried them in his arms to their deaths.

Felix Zandman was the only one of the Freydoviczes' grandchildren to survive the Holocaust. A Catholic couple named Jan and Anna Puchalski hid him and four other fugitives from the ghetto in the vicinity of Grodno. The couple themselves were desperately poor, starving, and had five children of their own to provide for. The Puchalskis kept their heads even when Germans raided their house and held out until the summer of 1944 when the Red Army liberated them and the people they sheltered. Why did they do this? Why risk their own lives in this fashion? "God gave you to us," Anna Puchalski told Felix Zandman. "I will not allow you to be killed. If we die, we die together. But you will survive, no question. You will stay here." Thousands of Europeans behaved in this way, including some Germans. Poles and Soviet people undoubtedly braved the greatest risk. In 1986 Jan and Anna Puchalski and their daughters Irena (married name: Bagińska), Grystyna (Maciejewska), and Sabina (Kazimierczyk) were recognized as Righteous Among Nations.[91]

Anti-Jewish Hatred Persists in War

In 1940, with help from the Catholic Church, the Polish government in exile quickly created a tight network of trusted agents and distributed a number of resistance pamphlets and flyers. Along with other sources, these publications yield insight into what Poles under German occupation thought about the Jewish question, which had been so hotly debated in prewar Poland.

On June 16, 1940, the Polish nationalist underground newspaper *Walka* (Struggle) published an article with the headline "General Governorate—paradisus Judaeorum." It contended that "the Jews are being clearly privileged by the anti-Semitic German racists," that they had "no reason to complain about the occupation," and that they served as spies helping Germans keep Poland under surveillance. In December of that year, the Jewish representative of the government-in-exile, Ignacy Schwarzbart, asked engineer Józef Podoski to fill him in on the situation of Polish Jews. Podoski had lived in Warsaw until the end of the previous September before making his way to London. He reported: "A great number of Poles from the intelligentsia, from the bourgeoisie and even the working classes have taken over Jews' positions in the economy. . . . In this form, despite the Polish hatred for Nazism and the Germans as occupiers, one Polish political goal has been reached: the strengthening of the Polish bourgeoisie." All in all, as Podoski summed it up, "the social strata concerned are tacitly satisfied with how things have turned out." He said he anticipated major conflicts should Jews demand their property back at some later point. Anti-Semitism, from which leftist parties too could never completely divorce themselves, would break out once again in even stronger form. Staggered, Schwarzbart recorded what Podoski had told him. His fears that "as far as Jews went, the Polish soul seems to have hardly changed at all" had been confirmed.[92]

On July 31, 1941, the farmers' newspaper *Placówka* (The Watch) wrote: "Today the Jews are weak and without influence. But when Poland is liberated, they will want to immediately tear down the ghetto walls and take back their factories and houses, which they only obtained via exploitation." Around the same time, the "Church Report from Poland for the Period June to Mid-July 1942," which was distributed by the government-in-exile, characterized the general situation as follows: "As far as the Jewish question is concerned, the Germans— alongside the great injustice they have done and continue to do to our country—have made a good start. They have shown us how to free the Polish populace from the Jewish plague and have pointed us down the path we should follow—of course less cruelly and brutally, but no less resolutely. It is undeniably a sign from Providence that the occupiers have taken it upon themselves to solve this burning question since the Polish people are too soft and unsystematic and would have never decided upon the powerful steps necessary in this matter."[93]

In January 1942, at a time in which Germans were getting the first gas chambers up and running, the Catholic-oriented magazine *Naród* (People) announced: "We insist that the Jews not be given back the political rights and property they have lost. In addition, in the future, they must all leave the country." *Naród* was published by the Christian Democratic Workers' Party, which was part of the Polish government-in-exile and advocated a federation of Slavic states. For the future treatment of the "extremely acute Jewish Question," they demanded: "We must cleanse all of Central and Southern Europe of the Jewish element, which amounts to removing some 8 to 9 million Jews."[94]

There were opposing voices. One of them, in the likewise Catholic-oriented newspaper *Pravda*, indirectly illustrated how common it had become for Poles not only to profit from but to participate in the mass murder of Jews. On May 5, 1941, the paper wrote:

> The immorality and barbarism that slaughter of Jews has caused among us has become an urgent issue. In many places (Kolno, Stawiski, Jagodne, Szumów, Dęblin) locals have taken part in the massacres. Everything must be done to combat this shameful scandal. The people must be made to understand that they are becoming the henchmen of Herod. They should be held up for condemnation in the underground press, and the executioners should be boycotted, threatened with severe legal punishment in the Free Polish Republic.[95]

On August 8, 1942, two thousand of the roughly four thousand Jews in the eastern Polish town of Szczebrzeszyn were to be rounded up and taken to the train station, where a train with fifty cars stood ready to make the short journey to the Belzec death camp. But the people condemned to death refused to obey orders to go to the local market hall. No one in the town believed these Jews were to be resettled in Ukraine. Many went into hiding. As the head physician at the town hospital, Zygmunt Klukowski, observed, German, Polish, and Jewish security officials, together with city employees, members of the Jewish council, and Jewish ghetto police, combed the town in search of them. While the search went on, city workers cleaned out the apartments where the Jews had lived and had their household effects and clothing taken to storehouses near the Rathaus. On top of that, wrote Klukowski in his journal, "a great many Poles, predominantly young men, eagerly helped search for the Jews."[96]

Klukowski managed to maintain a sense of humanity in the brutal conditions Germans had created. His diary entries depict how the terrorizing occupational authority made the community in general inhumane and how it exploited that condition. On February 23, 1941, he noted, as he had dozens of times about Polish colleagues, friends, and acquaintances from in and around Szczebrzeszyn: "Notary Henryk Rosinski died in the Dachau concentration camp. I have never in my life been in such a state of grief over the death of a friend, I cannot control myself; I cannot cover up my tears." On March 8: "A few days ago, another transport of evacuees arrived in Szczebrzeszyn, this time 200 persons. So far no group has had as many sick. I admitted more than twenty, mostly small children and very old people; three have already died." After sunset, hundreds of young people from Szczebrzeszyn would seek refuge in the forest so that they wouldn't be arrested in the German occupiers' nighttime raids and sent to Germany to do slave labor. "We are living like hunted animals," Klukowski wrote. "People are losing the energy to fight back . . . they are exhausted both physically and mentally."

On June 21, the day before Germany declared war on the Soviet Union, the hospital was told to prepare for "large numbers of wounded." Orders were issued to herd all sick Jews into two special buildings on the outskirts of town. Klukowski could only watch as a Polish police officer named Tatulinski was a "very active" participant in this action. By April 1942, trains full of Jews, first with twenty and later with fifty cars, were heading for Belzec. It was widely rumored that when they arrived, "some are killed with electricity, some with poison gases, and their bodies are burned." Now and again, one of the trains was forced to stop in Szczebrzeszyn station. "A young woman gave away a gold ring in exchange for a glass of water for her dying child," Klukowski recounted. "In Lublin, people witnessed small children being thrown through the windows of speeding trains. Many people are shot before reaching Belzec."

On May 8, 1942, "a real hell started" in Szczebrzeszyn. Gestapo officers brought in from Zamość and local German police stormed the ghetto. Polish police assisted them. "They shot people like ducks, killing them not only on the streets but also in their own homes—men, women and children, indiscriminately." German medical administrators strictly prohibited Polish doctors from treating injured Jews. Impassioned pleas to be allowed to help led to Gestapo troops storming the hospital and looking for Jews. "The way some Poles behave is completely out of line," Klukowski wrote at the end of his diary entry. "During the massacre some even laughed. Some went sneaking into Jewish houses from the back door searching for what could be stolen. Here is something different: the gestapo [*sic*] ordered the *Judenrat* [Jewish council] to pay 2000 złoty and 3lbs. of coffee for the ammunition used to kill Jews." Those in charge of Szczebrzeszyn could commit murder on any scale at will. They shot dead twenty elderly people at a construction site in broad daylight in the middle of the city. Their mass graves had already been dug a few days before. Six more Jews were subsequently shot dead, and then a young woman who had been caught without a yellow star. The killing went on day in, day out.

At around this time, the former teacher Leopold Rytko attempted to blackmail the widow of the dentist Nathan Bronsztein, who had been murdered. Rytko told her that if she didn't pay up, he would inform the authorities that she was a Jew, and she would be killed, too. Three weeks later, Rytko—"known as a gestapo informant"—was found dead at home. The Polish underground army (Armia Krajova) had struck. Gestapo troops immediately began to search for those who had taken vengeance. In the process, they shot a Mrs. Byk, Karol Turowski, and nine other Polish men. A number of men were taken into custody and sent to the city of Biłgoraj. "What will happen to them nobody knows," Klukowski noted. The daily terror hardened people's hearts. A bit earlier Klukowski had written: "Now when people meet on the streets the normal way of greeting is, 'Who was arrested? How many Jews were killed last night? Who was robbed?' These events are so common that, really, no one seems to care. Slowly you become accustomed to everything."

The final "so-called German displacement of Jews, in reality a liquidation of the entire Jewish population" began on October 21, 1942. The remaining Jews in Szczebrzeszyn were rounded up. Some were dragged from their hiding places, hand grenades were lobbed into basements, and more than four hundred Jews were shot to death that day at the Jewish Cemetery. The victims were largely elderly people, women, and children—young men hid out in the woods. There were posters throughout the city telling Poles that those who helped Jews would be executed, while those who betrayed them would be rewarded. This action involved not only German and blue-uniformed Polish police, but black-uniformed Polish security guards as well. Armed with sticks, they lashed out at defenseless people, herding them toward the cemetery. Polish men over the age of fifteen were forced to dig mass graves. As the Jews were being taken away, a large number of onlookers congregated, "laughing and even beating the Jews; others searched homes for more victims." While the massacre was taking place, other Jews were locked in a waiting train. They included a group from the neighboring town of Zwierzyniec. Just as in Szczebrzeszyn, Jews were killed in several hundred Polish cities and towns. After five days of mass murder, Polish plunderers seized what Jews had left behind. At the conclusion of the first of these hellish days, a shaken Klukowski noted: "You cannot even imagine the barbarism of the Germans. I am completely broken and cannot find myself."[97]

The situation of Jews in Poland remained extremely dangerous, as we can see from an order issued by one of the leaders of the Warsaw Uprising, Brigade General Tadeusz Pełczyński, on August 4, 1944, while he was fighting the Germans. After the insurgents had liberated several hundred Jews from a Warsaw camp, he commanded: "Make preparations for a provisional camp in which to accommodate all liberated Jews and other undesirable elements. Units will be issued orders so as to prevent possible abuse of Jews."[98] On the one hand, Pełczyński considered Jews undesirables; on the other, he considered it his duty to protect them from his Catholic countrymen.

Also Unwanted in the Soviet Union

Beginning in 1943, as Soviet troops started liberating the German-annexed parts of their country, many Jewish soldiers in the Red Army returned home. They later told what they had experienced. Civilian Jewish survivors, too, bore witness to how they were rejected. In total, around half a million Jews served in the Red Army, of whom 200,000 fell in battle or were murdered in German captivity, after being forced to drop their trousers and identified as Jews.

On May 28, 1944, the soldier Boris Fayvelis told Solomon Mikhoels about Jews who had gone into hiding in Simferopol on the Crimean peninsula. When they returned home after their liberation, they were greeted with "open hostility"—former neighbors had "plundered most of their property." Fayvelis cited the example of what happened to Dora and Rosa Aysenberg's families, who had miraculously survived, when they went home. Their neighbors, including a policeman named Grygory Ivanov, had stolen everything they owned, right down to their milk cow. Fayvelis complained to every Soviet institution he could think of in an effort to get the Aysenberg sisters and their half-starved children their cow back, but the authorities and courts of the Autonomous Soviet Socialist Republic of Crimea refused to help. Instead, they protected thieves and informants.

On July 22, the physician Israil Adessman wrote from Odessa to Ilya Ehrenburg: "After the German and Romanian cultural cannibals had been driven from Odessa, I could have halted the sun for joy. But in fact I'm practically choking here in an atmosphere poisoned by anti-Semitic propaganda. Everyone I know who has returned from the ghetto to Odessa can confirm that the Romanian-German plague has penetrated all of our Soviet institutions. Especially bizarre is the combination of anti-Semitism and an absence of Jews. Until recently, more than 200,000 Jews lived in Odessa. Today there are fewer than 200." Adessman had the impression that the few remaining Jews had "resurfaced from the underworld" to "ruin the mood [of the Russian majority] by their sheer existence," since Russians now feared they would lose the apartments and furnishings they had stolen.

That same summer, Blyuma Bronfin wrote a letter from the Ukrainian city of Chmelnik to her loved ones. "What can I tell you?" it began. "Riva, you ask where your sister Sura is. She's in the same place as my Mishunya, Beba, Isyunya and all our other relatives. They were killed on January 9, 1942. Six thousand Jews were murdered on this day." Bronfin was able to escape the Germans and flee to Romania. There she lived in "indescribable conditions" in a forced labor camp with 300 other Jews from Chmelnik. When she returned to the city, she was able to move back into her partially destroyed home, sharing it with a Russian woman who had purchased the house during the German occupation. Bronfin wrote: "Those who helped the Germans destroy us are still occupying their posts. . . . The city administration isn't taking care of us in the slightest. Thus far, they haven't given us any work, while our enemies find jobs everywhere. They're irritated that we're still alive. So you see, dear Riva, how 'good' we have it here. . . . Forgive me for writing such confused stuff after all we've been through. I can't write or speak anymore to tell you what it's like. My hands are trembling, and blood is running out of my eyes."[99]

7

The Return of the Unwanted

With help from a resistance group, a Greek Jew named Frederic Kakis was able to go underground in early 1943, and after German troops withdrew, he returned by boat to Salonika in the late autumn of 1944. Hardly had he arrived than he ran into thousands of pro-Communist demonstrators who were waving red flags and singing hymns to the legendary leader of the Bulgarian Communist movement, Georgi Dimitrov. An old man reassured the former exile: "You see these people? In a little while, when the British troops will come and start distributing food, these same people will shout 'Long live the King!'" And that's exactly what happened.

Together with his mother, who had also been rescued from the Nazis, Kakis sought out the houses his grandparents had owned. "What we found was shocking and devastating," Kakis recalled. The buildings were missing shutters and roofing shingles, yet families were living in the buildings nonetheless. "The Germans encouraged the local residents to take over any home belonging to Jews," he continued. "When we identified ourselves as the owners, we were greeted with hostility, and we were told that this was now their home and they were going to stay there. 'We were here first. You go away and find another place to stay.'"[1]

When the British historian Cecil Roth visited Salonika in 1946, he reported dejectedly: "Everywhere one could see traces of loot. I found a child in the street sitting on a synagogue chair carved with a Hebrew inscription; I was given a fragment of a Sefer Torah which had been cut up as soles for a pair of shoes; I saw carts in the cemetery removing Hebrew tombstones, on the instructions of the Director of Antiquities for the province, for the repair of one of the local ancient churches."[2]

The memories of the Jewish victims who survived the Holocaust show how brusquely gentiles showed them the door, not only in Salonika, but in Vienna; Vilnius; Oderberg, Czechoslovakia; and Eger, Hungary. Millions of Europeans had hoped that Jews would simply disappear, said nothing as people were deported, and profited from the things the deportees were forced to leave behind. As we have seen, the gentile populations in the countries occupied by Germany had also been harmed and traumatized and may have often not been fully in control of their actions. Nonetheless, everywhere Jews returned, they were rebuffed. The similarity of their stories illustrates a general truth: people were shocked when unexpected and unwanted Jews suddenly appeared on their doorsteps. Those who had taken possession of Jewish property believed that the former owners were dead. Indeed, they almost counted on it.

The Germans had laid the groundwork for such thinking in the period when they dominated the European continent. By distributing the belongings and property of Jewish deportees among local gentiles, the German masters made the latter complicit in their crimes, ensuring their silence and turning them into thieves and fencers of stolen goods. Hungarian archives still contain countless printed lists of articles of clothing, right on down to children's socks, transferred from Jewish to non-Jewish families in 1944, a year of extreme privation. Even the names of the individual families, both Jewish and gentile, are recorded. Only very few people were able to extricate themselves from material complicity in the genocide of Jews or to admit that they had treated the survivors unfairly.

In the days of liberation in 1944 and 1945, most surviving Jews didn't know that they were usually the only members of their families to have avoided the worst. They traveled under trying circumstances to the places they considered home, knocking on the doors of houses where they used to live and expecting a warm, perhaps even tearful welcome from their former neighbors and friends. They assumed they would find shelter, clothing, memories, human warmth, and, above all, information about what had happened to their parents, siblings, and children.

But what they encountered were desperate, war-battered people trying to make their way in the ruins of a devastated Europe—among them many small-time profiteers who had managed to secure a small advantage amid general chaos and death. They had moved into the homes of those deported, taken over their businesses, and divided up all their belongings, from the linen cupboards to the kitchen spoons. Those who returned, whose psyches were damaged in the worst possible ways, were greeted with obduracy, transparent excuses, greed, and, not infrequently, hatred. When they returned to their former homes, displaced Jews often quickly found out that they were, in fact, homeless.

VIENNA: HARD-HEARTED SILENCE

When German soldiers entered the Austrian capital on March 12, 1938, 190,000 Jews lived there. Only around 2,000 of them survived in Vienna until April 30, 1945, most thanks to the loyalty and courage of what Hitler called their "Aryan" wives. In the remaining months of 1945, some 3,000 survivors returned from the concentration camps. Exhausted and incapable of working, they "first needed to undergo a process of healing before they were strong enough to be employed again." That was how the leaders of the Israelite Cultural Community of Vienna described the situation in their "Activity Report for the Years 1945 to 1948."[3]

The difficulties were many. Aerial bombardments that March and artillery fire in April had badly damaged many buildings belonging to the Jewish community, including its archive and registrar's office. In the Jewish cemetery, 2,250 gravestones and 53 mausoleums had been destroyed. No sooner had the guns fallen silent than gentile Austrians began to style themselves as the first victims of the Nazi dictatorship, tacitly agreeing to keep mum about the past. In May 1947, the president of the Jewish cultural community, David Brill, wrote that "our homes and all that belongs to us are still in the possession of the thieves." Community leaders also failed to get the Austrian government "to take an interest in the return of our brothers from the countries where they found asylum," that is, the Viennese Jews wanted to come back, despite everything, to their former home city. Nevertheless, in April 1946 the elected leadership to the first provisional community tried to initiate a new beginning. As the report told, they "simply went about" rebuilding a new Israelite Cultural Community on the ruins of the old.

The first step was for the new board of directors to remove those functionaries who as members of the Eichmann-ordered Council of Elders of the Jewish Population had cooperated "all too willingly" with the Gestapo and the SS. The heads of the new community desperately looked for replacements, but "the reservoir from which one could draw was very small." Until 1938, Vienna's Jewish community had possessed and maintained dozens of schools, hospitals, old people's homes, libraries, orphanages, and food banks. Poor Jews had been given shelter, Jewish culture and rites had been preserved, and the community had a "well-trained and experienced apparatus" of six hundred officials and employees at its disposal. On March 12, 1938, all these things were shattered.

On that day, the overwhelming majority of Christian Austrians had voted to be annexed by the Third Reich, and many of them had celebrated the occasion with anti-Semitic acts of torment such as making Jews scrub sidewalks with toothbrushes and then dumping the dirty water over their heads afterward. "Rubbing parties" were what the Viennese called their civic-minded miniature pogroms.

After the social groundwork had been laid, Adolf Eichmann and his minions began their own systematic anti-Semitic work. Piece by piece, they chipped away at the corpus of the Jewish community until nothing was left but a shell emptied of both people and property. In support of its formal dissolution in 1942, those in power cited a 1890 decree by Emperor Franz Joseph setting out the legal requirements of the Israelite religious community.[4] In 1948, the reconstituted community's presidium accurately described this legal act as follows: "The law stipulated that a religious community could be dissolved if it is, for material reasons, unable to fulfill its duties. That was the case with the Israelite Cultural Community."

During the Night of Broken Glass pogroms of November 1938, the vanguard of rioters claiming to represent popular rage demolished ninety-four Viennese synagogues and places of worship. A mere accident spared the central community temple on Seitenstettengasse from complete destruction. The outside walls remained intact while the interior was "the very image of a heap of rubble." Amid the devastation and general need, Holocaust survivors succeeded in carrying out their first act of liberation. On April 2, 1946, the one hundredth anniversary of its establishment, they reconsecrated their temple. They inscribed in Hebrew the fourth verse of the one hundredth Psalm above its door: "Enter his gates with thanksgiving and his courts with praise."

The city had no rabbi. A community supervisor named Isidor Öhler stepped in to conduct services. Vienna Mayor Theodor Körner attended the ceremony, which was broadcast by Austrian radio throughout Europe and the rest of the world. In the subsequent memorial ceremony for the founders of the synagogue, the participants unveiled a marble tablet also containing a Hebrew inscription: "In memory of the men, women and children who lost their lives in the fateful years 1938–1945." On the first day of Passover, the community opened a kosher kitchen. A *mikveh* followed in 1946.

At the end of the first postwar year, 802 Viennese Jews who had emigrated to Shanghai in 1938 and 1939 were scheduled to return. The migration department of the cultural community was responsible for the extensive preparations. It worked together with a committee consisting of family members and friends of the Shanghai refugees. Together they had to overcome the bureaucratic concerns of the Austrian Interior Ministry and the "anti-Semitic-inflected resistance" of the Foreign Ministry. In the end, the director of the migration department, Michael Kohn, summarized the results of the campaign with low-key sarcasm: "We were able to get the Austrian government to declare its willingness to allow Austrian citizens to enter the country."

For its part, the Austrian government demanded subservience. Before they left China, the would-be returnees received a special form they had to sign in which they declared their loyalty to Austria. Only then did a member of the consulate from Vienna issue them travel visas. A mere eighteen months after the demise of the Third Reich, Austrians, the majority of whom had welcomed Hitler's Germany and driven out and helped murder Austrian Jews, now demanded written declarations of loyalty from the very people they had humiliated, robbed, and ostracized.

After those who remained determined to return to Austria had provided their signatures, they were put onboard two American troop transport ships, and several weeks later they set foot on European soil in Marseilles and Naples. From there, in the middle of winter, the repatriated Jews traveled in unheated cattle cars, with minimal provisions, to the border crossing at Tarvis, Austria. The trip took a week.

Friends and relatives of the returnees anxiously awaited their arrival, "heading to the border or spending days and nights in a state of constant readiness." By mid-February 1947, the wait was over. Mayor Körner went from cattle car to cattle car, greeting the returnees individually and telling them that "every single person was needed to rebuild the terribly devastated city."[5] The city housing authority, however, refused to provide these Austrians returning from Chinese exile with apartments and told community representatives that the returnees "could easily be accommodated in mass quarters."

In June 1947, a further 208 Viennese Jews arrived, unannounced.

They, too, had left Vienna in 1938 and 1939, heading for the Baltic territories or the Soviet Union. No sooner had the Third Reich, Romania, and Hungary launched their summer 1941 offensive against Russia than Soviet security forces arrested them as hostile aliens and transported them to the interior of the country, where they built a camp in Karaganda, Kazakhstan. There they dug coal and suffered through piercing cold in winter and pitiless heat in summer. Over the years, hundreds of thousands of people would disappear in Karaganda: Soviet criminals, alleged enemies of the state, Communist functionaries, deported Poles, Sinti, and Roma, Romanians, dissidents, those suspected of all manner of transgressions, German POWs, and German, Polish, Baltic, Russian, and Austrian Jews.

Alexander Solzhenitsyn described Karaganda as the biggest provincial capital in the "gulag archipelago." The Jewish prisoner Joseph Kuszelewicz from Belarus, who had fled the Holocaust and joined the Red Army, was suddenly arrested one day in 1946 and sent to Karaganda. At first he ended up in the camp train station. There, as he would later write, the deportees were divided up into various groups and sent on their way through seemingly endless corridors of barbed wire into the dismal, impenetrably laid out world of the camp proper, which stretched on for dozens of kilometers.[6]

Viennese Jews were among the relatively privileged prisoners. They weren't systematically murdered. Many of them died of malnutrition, frostbite, typhoid fever, dysentery, malaria, and tuberculosis, but their chances of survival were far higher than if they had fallen into German hands. In 1940, Menachem Begin, later Israeli prime minister, was taken from Soviet-annexed Lithuania to Siberia because the Soviet secret police considered him an "agent of British imperialism." Looking back many years later, Begin wrote: "Compared with the general, colossal catastrophe, my unhappy fate was insignificant. During this catastrophe, the Soviet Union unexpectedly provided Jews with inestimable help. I will always remember that, and no Jew has the right to ever forget it."[7]

On May 9, 1945, when the Jews in Karaganda learned of Germany's capitulation, they fell into one another's arms, weeping with happiness in the belief they were now free. They were wrong. The Soviet political commissions tersely informed them that their forced labor as vanquished German citizens had only just begun: "This is no day of joy for you. You will have to make up with your labor for what your people have done to the Russians."[8] The prisoners' torment would go on for almost two years.

In Vienna, the Karaganda Jews were sent to "several very poor-quality homeless shelters" with forty beds to a room. The housing authority was responsible for this. By the end of February 1948, it had only managed to find apartments for 17 percent of the 1,393 Jews who returned to the Austrian capital. Those figures testify to the disregard in which the Jews were held. We need to recall that under Nazi leadership, the city administration had given 50,000 apartments owned or rented by Jews to gentile Viennese from 1938 to 1942, thereby, as Hitler noted with satisfaction "solving the shortage of living space" in the Austrian capital. After the war the authority, which was headed by Social Democrats, didn't see anything wrong with allowing these people to continue living in the apartments. To its chagrin, the Jewish community was forced to acknowledge that the democratic political parties had refused to pass laws reversing "the National Socialist act of larceny."

Historian Walter Grab first returned to his native city in 1956, eighteen years after he was forced to flee Vienna as a nineteen-year-old. While there he visited the building he grew up in. Out of what used to be six renters, only the Czech former superintendent was still living in the building, albeit on the fourth rather than the ground floor. Grab rang the bell, and the former superintendent's wife opened the door. "Jesus, Mr. Grab has returned," she exclaimed. After a few seconds she invited him to come in, whereupon he took a seat in the living room and asked who used to live in the apartment. It was an architect named Theodor Giesskann. When he heard the name, Grab understood that all the furniture was the Giesskanns'. The wife explained that the Giesskann family had "disappeared somehow" and that "the Nazis had given them this lovely apartment and the furniture in it." Grab added: "At that point, a key turned in the door, and her husband, the former superintendent, stepped in." He immediately recognized the visitor and hissed to his wife: "Don't say a word!"[9]

In 1947 and 1948, at the start of the Cold War, the Soviets released most of their Austrian prisoners of war. The few Jews who had survived in the Austrian capital or had returned there now got to see how the Viennese government office treated former Wehrmacht soldiers. "Government officials began to adopt the strange position that the POWs were the returnees for whom everything had to be done and who could claim every sort of privilege, while our people were merely returning emigrants who had come back voluntarily, who shouldn't have done so, and who in any case had no claim to any special treatment," wrote Jewish community representatives. "They were helping Nazis or their enablers while our people were victims of Nazism—that's something they chose to forget."

By December 1947, the Israelite Cultural Community had twice as many members as it had eighteen months previously, just over 9,000 Jewish men, women, and children. Jewish religious life began to reawaken. In late April 1947, a requiem was held in the synagogue for Denmark's deceased King Christian X, who had helped save the lives of 5,000 Jews in his country in 1943. "If you introduce the yellow Star of David in Denmark," King Christian alone among the European heads of state said to his country's German occupiers, "I and the entire royal family will wear it, too, with pride and dignity." On June 8, the Vienna Synagogue held a memorial on the forty-third anniversary of the death of the father of Zionism, Theodor Herzl. On November 10, survivors came together to mourn the victims of the Night of Broken Glass and collected money for the "planting of an Austrian-style forest in Palestine." On December 6, the "large and enthusiastic congregation" turned out in droves for a service expressing gratitude that the United Nations had agreed to the founding of an independent Jewish state in Palestine.

GONE WITHOUT A TRACE IN VILNIUS

Since the partition of Poland in 1795, Vilnius had been part of the Russian Empire. Between 1914 and 1921, everyday life there was characterized by war, revolution, and battles between nationalities and pogroms. These were followed by economic crises and quarrels about minorities. In Vilnius, as in many other places, social upheaval destroyed the traditional coexistence and rivalries of city inhabitants of various nationalities: Poles, Lithuanians, and Jews. In the First World War, German troops had occupied the city; when they withdrew, it was briefly controlled by the Poles and then the Soviets. In the war that commenced immediately afterward, the Poles emerged with the upper hand. In 1939, as part of the Hitler-Stalin Pact, Vilnius again fell to the Soviet Union, and in the summer of 1940 it became part of the Lithuanian Soviet Socialist Republic. In 1941 it was conquered by the Wehrmacht. In the summer of 1941, some 8,000 of Vilnius's 220,000 Lithuanian Jews were able to flee to the center of the Soviet Union. Of those unable to run away, more than 200,000 were murdered. One hundred to 2,000 were able to go underground or survive as partisans in Lithuania.

One of them was Zahana Zuckermann-Stromsoe. In the fall of 2009, Israeli journalist Koby Ben-Simhon asked her for her opinion on the Quentin Tarantino film *Inglourious Basterds*, in which, in an inversion of history, Jews torture, beat to death, burn alive, and scalp Nazis. Zuckermann-Stromsoe found the film graphically violent and "really well done," adding, "It cheered me to watch Nazis begging for their lives and getting a bit of a taste of their own cruelty." Her own life had taken a very different course.

As a teenager she had survived the terror of the Vilnius ghetto and various camps. When Jews were forced on a death march, she begged in vain for her father's life, hid in a sewer canal, and was forced to listen to the tread of Nazi boots above her head—much as a Jewish family at the start of Tarantino's film does. "We were like rats," she recalled. "No one who hasn't been through the Holocaust can understand that, but that's the way it was." No sooner had she been liberated than she fled Europe as fast as she could. In Tel Aviv she started a new life and raised two children. In 2009, Zuckermann-Stromsoe took delight in her four grandchildren. "They are my true revenge," she said.[10]

Of the 60,000 Jews who had lived in Vilnius in 1939 and had been part of the city's character, several hundred reappeared in the summer of 1944. The returnees celebrated religious services in the badly damaged but still functional main synagogue. In accordance with the rules of their faith, they buried their desecrated and torn Torah scrolls. That fall, they opened a school and then a museum to exhibit the writings, pictures, and sculptures that the Jews of Vilnius, facing certain death, had buried or hidden behind walls so they would be preserved for posterity.

Other initiatives were blocked by the local populace. The Institute for Jewish Research (YIVO) was prevented from being reestablished, Yiddish newspapers and radio programs were banned, and the Jewish choir prohibited from singing in public. By the summer of 1945, 4,000 Jews were once again living in the city. A short time later the Soviet-Lithuanian city council ordered the provisionally restored synagogue torn down. The site was used as a parking lot until a kindergarten was built there in 1964. The Jewish school had to shut down in 1948. Historian Solomon Atamuk writes: "On June 10, 1949, the Ministerial Council of the Lithuanian Socialist Soviet Republic ordered the Jewish museum in Vilnius closed. Many of the objects exhibited were transferred to other Lithuanian institutions, but most Jewish books were taken to paper factories to be recycled. In 1950, Jewish institutions for children were shut."[11] Local functionaries argued that no one needed anything Jewish, including Jewish culture, because Jewish was not a nationality. Jewishness, they said, was "nothing."

At the same time, they changed the name of all streets recalling Vilnius's Jewish past. Gone from the map were Gaon Street, named after the greatest Jewish intellectual in the region, and Straszuna Street, one of the city's main commercial arteries, which commemorated Talmud scholar, cosmopolitan, and philanthropist Mathias Straszun. In 1952, city leaders in nearby Paneriai removed a memorial with a Yiddish inscription that remembered the 44,000 Jews who had been shot to death there.[12] Whereas over the years Lithuania suppressed all evidence of murdered Jews, in 1960 a huge memorial was built in the city of Pirčiupiai for 119 Christian Lithuanians killed in a German revenge massacre in June 1944.

In the late Stalin era, Jews were systematically defamed as treacherous cosmopolitans. In a show trial of Jewish doctors in Moscow in 1952, two prominent Lithuanian physicians were summoned before the court. Stalin's death in March 1953 brought a swift end to the proceedings and spared the alleged "murderers in white lab coats" any further consequences. To get a better handle on the public mood concerning Jews, agents of the Lithuanian secret service evaluated private letters gentile inhabitants of Vilnius sent abroad in this period. They recorded statements like these:

"Jewish barbers don't shave non-Jews as closely and try to poison them with cream."

"These Israelites want to strangle us. They have killed a number of excellent people. They're ripe for the gallows at the very least."

"Nothing good is to be expected from the Jews! The Germans didn't annihilate them for no reason. In this area, that was rational."

A Jewish citizen of Vilnius named E. M. Preissatshenko wrote: "I have no desire to go out into the streets. I imagine I will hear things like 'They killed too few of them!' Where will this end? It is a bitter blow for us Soviet Jews, responsible and loyal citizens of the Soviet Union, that we have to endure hostile looks just because we're Jews."

In the final twenty years of Soviet rule, more and more Lithuanian Jews emigrated to Israel and other countries in the West. A considerable number of state functionaries and gentile Lithuanians approved of this exodus. "Jews are leaving their apartments—now Lithuanians can move into them," one person was quoted as saying. "Jews are giving up their jobs—that creates new opportunities for Lithuanians!" Others were openly or secretly "simply satisfied that Lithuania is becoming 'Jew-free.'"[13]

RACHELA MARGOLIS, WHO was born in 1920, came from an affluent doctor's family in Vilnius. In 1943 she fled the city ghetto and joined up with partisans. After the German occupiers were defeated, a Polish neighbor returned to Margolis some documents that her father, since murdered, had buried in his garden. Margolis found her student ID card and the addresses of people to whom her father had entrusted family possessions before the Vilnius ghetto was established in 1941.

Although she expected the worst, the young woman contacted the putative caretakers of her family property. "People had gotten used to regarding Jewish property as their own and often didn't want to give it back," she recalled. "The Jew, hungry and homeless, was left standing there empty-handed. After all, he had no witnesses." One of the people Margolis went to see was an elderly woman who had been her father's nanny. Rachela immediately recognized some of her wealthy family's household effects but was given the brush-off: "I don't know you. No doctor ever left anything with me for safekeeping. Off with you!" As a former partisan, Margolis was able to get help from the police, whereupon the old woman blamed her failing memory. Margolis took a few things—to remember her murdered family by.[14]

After the end of German occupation, a Christian woman named Ona Šimaitė tried to help Jews recover their lost property but met with little success in Vilnius. "The people I asked were from various social classes, some were educated and some not, some were Lithuanians and some Poles, but they were all the same in one respect," she remembered. "They would only surrender belongings taken from Jews under great pressure or would categorically refuse my requests. I had to put up with a lot of abuse."[15]

The disregard of society at large was matched by that of the state. In October 1947, the World Jewish Congress in New York tried to prevent the destruction of the Old Jewish Cemetery in Vilnius, which dated back to the fifteenth century. Jewish representatives requested that the burial place be respected as a religious and historical site—as a *bet olam*, or "house of eternity."[16] Their entreaties moved no one. Between 1948 and 1950 the city administration had the cemetery plowed over and used the gravestones as construction materials. The now empty site was used for a monument to socialist progress in the form of a sports arena with an indoor swimming pool and a broad thoroughfare called Olympic Street. Synagogues still in existence were categorically denied the status of listed buildings, whereas a large number of Catholic churches enjoyed such protection.

The destruction of the Old Jewish Cemetery was welcomed by many of the city's Lithuanians and Poles. In 1924, while on a journey through what was then Poland, the German novelist Alfred Döblin had described the cemetery's "terrible dereliction." Pieces of brick were scattered around, and Polish soldiers rode and marched through the hallowed ground, using it as a shortcut between barracks. Now and then they would demolish a grave or chop down a religiously signifi-cant tree. "Soldiers were singing and suddenly there was a bleating," Döblin wrote. Curious, he walked over a hump topped with broken headstones. "From up there I could see a cow grazing below on the graves. Its dung was everywhere."[17] The cemetery had been disused since 1830, but it had almost certainly not been deconsecrated in accordance with Jewish law.

The New Jewish Cemetery, designed in the modern style, occupied a large stretch of land on the Neris River. Seventy thousand people were buried in it by 1960. At that point the city fathers—"acting in tacit concert with higher authorities"—also destroyed this final reminder of the Jewish past. They had the inscriptions sanded off the better qual-ity headstones and used them in various construction projects. They also combined the deconsecrated grounds with a neighboring park and allowed an open-air stage to be built there. Vingis Park opened in 1965 and remains a popular venue to this day, hosting events such as traditional Lithuanian folk-song festivals. The people of the city eradicated almost all traces of Jewish life that had survived the war. In 2014, Lithuania officially blamed the former Soviet authorities and began offering "professional guided tours of Jewish Vilnius."

DUPLICITY AND GUILT IN HUNGARY

Of the 440,000 Hungarian Jews deported to Auschwitz, approx-imately 340,000 were murdered in the gas chambers in early sum-mer 1944 and around 100,000 were forced into slave labor. In the final months of the Third Reich, more than 40,000 of the latter group were worked to death. In the fall and winter of 1944 and 1945, some 80,000 Hungarian Jews were made to go, mostly on foot, to Austria, where 20,000 of them died. After the end of the Second World War, 120,000 Hungarian Jews returned home—a large number compared to other countries.[18]

One of those who returned home was twenty-two-year-old Lilly Weisz, who later married and took her husband's name, Kertész. Like her father, grandfather, and great-grandfather, she grew up in the northern Hungarian city of Eger. She considered herself Hungarian until June 1944, when she and 1,620 other Jews were herded into a factory courtyard. That afternoon, Hungarian civil servants accompanied by Hungarian police appeared and "demanded that we hand over any money, jewelry and other valuables, although our baggage was searched anyway." The officials even confiscated people's wedding rings. The Jews were then physically searched and herded down the city's main road to the train station in the middle of the night. "There were lights on in the houses," Lilly remembered. "Dance music was playing in people's apartments. From their windows, the people of Eger watched the big event: the Jews were being taken away! A window was opened on the left, and a male, then a female voice bellowed out into the dark, stormy night: 'You won't be coming back!' I knew the people who lived in that apartment. I had visited them frequently, and they had always received me cordially. We didn't expect any apologies. But the fact that they treated us like this was deeply wounding."

Once they arrived at Auschwitz, Weisz was separated from her father, mother, and sister. She was sent on to the Neuengamme concentration camp in Germany itself, ending up in Bremen. There she was forced to clear rubble left behind by air raids. Shortly before the end of the war she was marched to Bergen-Belsen, where on April 15, 1945, a truck carrying loudspeakers broadcast the news of her salvation: "Here are soldiers of the British Army. You are now free. Tomorrow there will be food. The sick will be tended to. The healthy will be put in quarantine. You are free to go home. There's no need for panic. Everyone should stay in his place. Here are soldiers from the British army. Bergen-Belsen is liberated."

Lilly survived a serious typhoid infection, but thousands of others in Bergen-Belsen died of the disease. In late September she returned to her home country. In the courtyard of the Great Synagogue in Buda-pest, she learned that there had been no word from any of her family members. She then traveled to Eger, where she was given shelter by the Jewish relief organization Joint. The group had commandeered a stately villa, a former private sanatorium for sick women that had been run by Dr. Bela Kun. He and his entire family had been sent to the gas chambers at Auschwitz.

In the days that followed, Weisz had a look around her native city. Her family home, located directly next to a bridge, had been destroyed by Soviet troops. In the ruins she found some photographs. Joint didn't have sufficient funds to keep the twelve Jewish returnees sufficiently fed. "Day in, day out, there were either beans or potatoes, but it was never enough. There was never any meat, eggs or yoghurt." Lilly and the woman with whom she shared a room had no choice but to go to the vineyards and steal grapes. A watchman caught them, showering the two women with threats and abuse. They tried to explain their situation, telling him who they were. Without a word, the watchman dumped the grapes in Lilly's basket on the ground and covered them with soil. Then he pointed to the other side of the vineyard: "The sweet grapes are over there." He left, but not before turning around and adding: "In the morning, I'm the only watchman on duty."

Before they were deported, the Weisz family had entrusted two trunks full of their better clothing for safekeeping to two of their Christian neighbors. Lilly urgently needed shoes and things to wear, so she knocked on one of the neighbors' door. "Standing in the doorway, the woman said that she had nothing she could give me because the Russians had stolen everything," Lilly recalled. "She gave me a hostile look and shut the door in my face." Lilly repressed a sob, gathered her-self, and went to the other neighbor. "Thank God, you've returned," said this woman. Turning to her husband, she added: "Look at this, Joska, the older Weisz girl is back! Come on in!" The neighbor put out sponge cake and coffee and showed Lilly a photo album of pictures of her daughter, who had gotten married and now lived in Budapest. Finally, Lilly asked about her family's things. "It's hard for me to talk about this," the neighbor said. "You don't know what we've been through. First we were plundered by the Germans, then by the Russians. It broke my heart when they took away your things, too. I always liked your mother."

Lilly thanked the neighbor and left. Another woman had observed her coming and going and asked: "Did they say the Russians took everything away?" The Weiszes weren't the only family to give their belongings to the neighbor for safekeeping. "She boasted [about her good fortune] and how the Jews were never coming back," the other woman told Lilly, advising her to return to the neighbor's house. "Go back. Confront this thief!" the woman exhorted. "I swear her daughter still wears Mrs. Weisz's fur coat. If she doesn't hand over the coat voluntarily, report her to the police."

Disgusted by such coldheartedness and hypocrisy, Lilly set off back to her quarters. Along the way, she saw a movie poster. An elegantly dressed couple also stopped and stood behind her, examining it.

He: "Do you want to go to the cinema tonight?"

She: "No, I'd rather stay home."

He: "Fine."

She: "Besides the cinema is already full of Jews again. I just saw one at the bakery too. They're everywhere. There are more of them than we got rid of."

Back at the Joint shelter, Lilly was told that someone urgently wanted to speak with her. She didn't recognize the person's name, but she went to the address that had been left for her, where she found an older couple. They asked her to come into their apartment, even inviting her into the bedroom. There, she saw wardrobes, a dressing table, beds, night tables, lamps, rugs, and a sofa, all of which had come from the Weiszes' home. "The only things missing were the family photos on the wall," Lilly remembered. She burst into tears and fled to the kitchen. After sharing dinner, the couple traded embarrassed glances. Finally, the man began to speak: "The neighbors came and said that the Jews' furniture was being handed out."

The couple had seized the opportunity and gone to the Weiszes' home, where a government finance official had told them they could take whatever they wanted. "We walked through the rooms with a guilty conscience and asked what would happen, if the people who lived here returned," the man said. But the official told them: "No people lived here, just Jews. They won't be coming back." The couple acquired the complete furnishings of the bedroom at a discount price to be paid to the government. Lilly Weisz took a decorative pillow her mother had cherished and was happy. She later said that she was cheered when she met people like the watchman and the couple, who were open about the mistakes they had made. "It was the first night in Eger that I got a good night's sleep," she recalled about encountering the older couple.

A short time later, she learned that her entire family was dead. Her father, who was lame, had immediately been separated off to the left at Auschwitz, which meant the gas chambers. Her grandmother and aunts suffered the same fate. Lilly's brother, Gyula, had been in Budapest and thus not deported with the rest of the family. There, in October 1944, he had been executed by Hungarian fascists. Lilly's mother, Margret, and her younger sister, Judith, had been transferred from Auschwitz to an explosives factory in Lichtenau in western Germany. But they fell ill due to the inhuman working conditions there and were sent back to Auschwitz the same month Gyula was killed, where they too were gassed. Lilly's fiancé Gyuri Minkusz starved to death while being forced to labor for the Hungarian army sometime in the winter of 1944 and 1945.[19]

Because the Hungarian regime stopped assisting in the deportation of Jews in the summer of 1944, some 150,000 Hungarian Jews, mostly from Budapest, survived the war. A further 60,000 returned from German labor camps, and the same number came back from Austrian camps where they had been taken in the final months of the conflict. But an entire generation had been obliterated. Sixty thousand Jewish children had been deported to Auschwitz and murdered. In 1947, only 15,000 Jewish children lived in Hungary, the majority of them born after the war.

In 1946, several pogroms took place in Hungary. In the eastern Hungarian community of Kenmadaras, a mob attacked the secretary of the local Communist party because he was Jewish. He survived the attack, but two other Jews were murdered in the incident. Similar scenes played out in the northeastern Hungarian city of Miskolc. Here, too, people died. Leftist circles and others had called for an attack on robber capitalists and black-market and wartime profiteers, all of whom shared one characteristic—they were Jewish survivors of the Holocaust. Like other political parties, the Hungarian Communist Party encouraged such views: "In the past we were under the yoke of Jewish capital. In the present, nothing has changed. This must not be!" While the forms of propaganda and the strategies for justifying injustice may have varied, the ultimate aim was always to retain possession of stolen Jewish property. A popular joke at the time is all too telling. A Jew encounters a Christian, who asks him how he's doing. "That's a stupid question," the Jew responds. "I was in a concentration camp. Now I have nothing but the clothes on your back."[20]

FEAR AND TERROR IN POLAND

In the immediate postwar period, an estimated 600 to 3,000 of the Jews who returned to Poland or emerged from hiding were murdered. The following is a typically tragic story. Hania Piller was imprisoned at Auschwitz and liberated in Lower Silesia in February 1945. After walking home on foot, she ran into a former fellow inmate named Mrs. Berger. She had survived Auschwitz together with her son and was also headed home to the community of Brzeszcze, which was located only nine kilometers southwest of Auschwitz-Oświecim. Piller described what happened next: "It was a happy reunion. But some time later I heard something terrible. Mrs. Berger was killed in her own home by her Polish neighbors. I've never gotten over this tragedy. In the end, after everything she suffered during the war, after losing her entire family except for that one son, she was murdered by Poles."

What had happened? Brzeszcze, an industrial settlement with 3,500 inhabitants established around a coal mine, contained two flour mills, several farms, a distillery, and a small factory that manufactured medical supplies. Before 1939, a number of poor Jewish families lived there. Two stood out: the Finders owned the distillery, and the Bergers engaged in wholesale and retail trade. Most of the farmers and miners were in debt to the Bergers, who had given them credit for purchases. When the Germans rolled through town in September 1939, they deported all the 138 Jews there and confiscated their property. Only Mrs. Berger and her son Moishe-Munik survived. After they returned, the debtors feared they would be made to pay what they owed and that they would have to return everything they had stolen from the deportees. They murdered Mrs. Berger and her son out of greed.[21]

German soldiers and occupiers devastated Poland and parts of the Soviet Union in every conceivable way. The extent of the damage is documented in a report by an Anglo-American governmental commission in early 1946. It investigated the question of how many surviving European Jews could and wished to emigrate to Palestine. Commission members traveled to displaced persons' camps, Palestine itself, and all countries affected by German-led mass murder that lay outside the Soviet Union. The report's authors were shaken by the survivors' "indescribable suffering," adding, "It must also be understood that this happened in what were regarded as civilized communities."

Words, the commission found, could hardly do reality justice: "In the cold print of a report it is not possible accurately to portray our feelings with regard to the suffering deliberately inflicted by the Germans on those Jews who fell into their hands. The visit of our Sub-Committee to the Ghetto in Warsaw has left on their minds an impression which will forever remain. Areas of that city on which formerly stood large buildings are now a mass of brick rubble, covering the bodies of numberless unknown Jews. Adjoining the Ghetto there still stands an old barracks used as a place for killing Jews. Viewing this in the cold gray light of a February day one could imagine the depths of human suffering there endured. In the courtyards of the barracks were pits containing human ash and human bones. The effect of that place on Jews who came searching, so often in vain, for any trace of their dear ones can be left to the imagination."

The report also acknowledged the terrible psychological toll the Holocaust had taken upon those who lived through it:

> These Jewish survivors have not emerged from their ordeals unscathed either physically or mentally. It is rare indeed to find a complete Jewish family. Those who return to their old homes find them destroyed or occupied by others, their businesses gone or else in other hands. They search for relatives, frequently undertaking long journeys on hearing a rumor that one has been seen in another part of the country or in another center. Such was the system of the Germans that it is difficult for them ever to establish the death of their dear ones. They are faced also with very great difficulties in seeking the restitution of their property. . . . In Germany and in Poland, which was often described to us as 'the cemetery of European Jewry,' a Jew may see in the face of any man he looks upon the murderer of his family. It is understandable that few find themselves able to face such conditions.[22]

Within three and a half years, Germans murdered 72 percent of the Jewish population in the places they ruled, almost always with the passive or active support of local administrations, police, political parties, and ordinary anti-Semitic citizens.[23] Of the 352,559 Jews in Warsaw, only 6,000 survived; of the 17,840 Jews in Kielce, a mere 243. After the end of the Nazi horror, 80,000 of the 3 million persecuted Jews in Poland reappeared. Only 5,000 of them (a little less than 8 percent) were children under the age of fourteen. By comparison, in 1939, 30 percent of the Jewish population was under that age.[24] Moreover, nearly all the children of those who did survive grew up without grandparents. It is small wonder that in March 1947, the World Jewish Congress came to the conclusion that very large numbers of Jews had no desire to remain in Poland.[25]

CZECHOSLOVAKIA: OUT OF EUROPE AT ALL COSTS!

Ruth Huppert was born in 1922 in Ostrava, Czechoslovakia, the capital of the region of Moravia. Her father, Fritz, left her mother, and Ruth and her sister, Edith, grew up in part with their grandmother and their uncle Hugo's family. Hugo and Fritz were in the meat business in the suburb of Přívoz (Oderfurt). Starting out with a butcher's shop, they opened a buffet restaurant, a small chain of stores, and finally a meat-processing plant. Along the way, the family joined the upper-middle class with all that entailed: a nanny, piano lessons, an automobile, private schooling, and ski vacations.

In 1928 Ruth entered the Jewish People's School. There were eighteen boys and twenty-five girls in her class, which was led by a teacher named Grete Gross. The language of instruction was German—only a handful of subjects were taught in Czech. To ensure everything was done correctly, the regional school inspector I. Dworak visited the school once a year. In 1928, his report noted "everything found satisfactory." As of the school year 1936–37, the school principal was required to write his annual chronical in Czech.

On March 14, 1939, German troops occupied Moravia and the following day Prague. That June, the chronicle of the Jewish People's School stops abruptly. In his final entry, the principal noted: "Extraordinary circumstances have led to dramatic changes in the student body." Official statistics shed light on what he meant. The 187 pupils who began the school year in September 1938 were joined by 55 additional children in the first four months of German occupation. Obviously they had transferred from public schools to the Jewish People's School. In the same period, 91 of the 242 pupils left the school prematurely.

This means that within this time, 38 percent of the school's student body fled the region with their parents.[26]

Czechoslovakia's new German masters wasted no time in terrorizing Jews and confiscating everything they owned. In response, Fritz Huppert entrusted his most valuable possessions, his daughter's dowry, and other family things to his Czech apprentice Gustav, while handing over less valuable property to the Gestapo. After that, the family procured false identity papers and went underground in the village of Pozořice in southern Moravia. By October 1939, Adolf Eichmann had already deported 1,290 Jews from the Ostrava area to the Nisko region of occupied Poland. The deportations, he noted, were "primarily intended to gather experience in order to be able to evacuate larger masses."[27] In the summer of 1942, the Hupperts' true identity was discovered, and they were arrested and deported. Ruth alone survived—despite being sent to Theresienstadt and Auschwitz and being forced to undergo the death march to Taucha near the German city of Leipzig. There she hid in the forest until she was liberated by American troops on April 18, 1945.

In early 1938, the Jewish community of Ostrava had numbered 6,000 people. In the spring of 1945 there were only 2,954 Jews in the entire Moravia region. After trying to locate family members in Prague and then Pozořice, Ruth returned to Přívoz, proceeding directly to her uncle Hugo's house. She found it "deserted and plundered," later recalling, "The bare walls stared at me mockingly." She then started looking around for a room in the city, which was once again under Czech control. Ostrava's hotel owners had been good customers of her father's business and knew the family well, but all of them turned her away. "We are truly glad that you're back, Miss Huppert," she was told, "but we don't have a room for you because they're all occupied by the Russians."

Finally, she found shelter with the now aged midwife, a Miss Rutino, who had helped deliver her and whom she approached after chancing to meet her on the street. The next morning she went to the headquarters of the Israelite Cultural Community. "The closer I got, the more I hesitated, because I suspected what I would find," she recalled.

Ruth's worst fears were confirmed. There were no signs of any of her extended family.

Afterward, she visited her father and uncle's former apprentice Gustav. His family lived in a fine house, and they and the Hupperts had enjoyed good neighborly relations. "I was given a very cool reception, and I could see the disappointment in the family's faces that I had returned," Ruth remembered. "I was led into the living room, which contained all of our furniture. There, amidst my family's belongings, they told me to my face that the Russians had taken everything. It was an easy excuse for all concerned." Ruth proceeded on to her grandmother's house. It was occupied by strangers.

Dumbfounded and desperate, she left for Prague, where she married a man named Kurt Elias and witnessed the return of Jewish refugees from Poland who had snuck across the border without identity papers. The few survivors of the German death camps and execution squads had once again become the victims of persecution, afraid for their lives, after the pogroms that had erupted in liberated Poland. On July 4, 1946, in the town of Kielce, forty-two Jews were murdered by local anti-Semites. But that wasn't the only place where Jewish returnees were met with rejection and violence. As Ruth Elias later documented in her memoirs, when they inquired about their possessions, they were told, bitterly: "It's a shame that you weren't gassed. Why did you of all people have to return?"

Soon, Ruth recalled, tens of thousands of Jewish survivors had only one goal: Israel. They wanted "to leave Europe, which had caused us so much misery." In Naples, Ruth and Kurt Elias, together with 2,000 other émigrés, boarded the much-too-small steamship *Galilah*. In April 1949 they landed in Haifa.[28]

In 1939, 9,855,500 Jews lived in Europe. By 1945, that number was 3,833,000.[29] In the parts of Europe under German control, some 1.4 million Jews survived the Holocaust. Jews were more likely to have escaped being murdered in those places where German rule was for various reasons disrupted or constrained by governmental, social, or military forces. They included the Soviet Union, France, Hungary, Romania, Belgium, Bulgaria, Italy, Denmark, and Slovakia.

Between 1948 and 1951, 715,000 European Jews left for Israel, while 120,000 emigrated to North America. Six years after the end of the Second World War, more than half of the Jews who had escaped the German machinery of murder and lived outside the Soviet Union voluntarily left Europe.

Civilization and Its Breakdown

In 1808, at the dawn of the nineteenth century, the Jewish-German essayist Ludwig Börne advised future "historical researchers" that the motives for discriminating against and persecuting Jews "vary with the times." Börne was responding to the social and psychological aftereffects of upheavals and new prejudices that arose in his native city of Frankfurt am Main. For people at the time, the collapse of the Holy Roman Empire, the guilds, and the patrician system seemed like the end of the world. Within this context, Börne identified "envy and greed" as two increasingly strong motors of anti-Jewish resentment. He witnessed with his own eyes how the Jews of Frankfurt, liberated from the ghetto, elicited "the jealousy of the crowd" as "aristocrats of the trading class." Börne added: "[It is not] the extent of their wealth for which they are envied—Jewish merchants are not the richest ones in the city. But it was impossible to observe without irritation the speed and confidence with which they earned their money." Hardly had a new epoch of economic life begun than the enemies of Jews began using religion as "a pretense for hatred."[1]

Sixty years later, at the high point of the Industrial Revolution and the massive social realignments that were so painful for millions of people, secular anti-Semitism appeared as a force on the political stage. It directly addressed acute societal and economic problems, drawing from them its ultimately enormous destructive power.

Before the nationalist movements in Europe achieved political predominance, their theorists standardized national languages, codified national myths, folk tales, and legends, and selectively wrote down the narrative of a history understood in nationalist terms. Nationalists, who were usually in the political opposition and also considered themselves committed democrats, advocated compulsory education to combat widespread ignorance in the populace. They battled against the privileges of the aristocracy and the clergy. They supported the modern administrative state and demanded an independent judicial system, freedom of the press, free and secret elections, the creation of a robust national middle class, and better opportunities in life for everyday people. Europeans still enjoy their efforts today.

NATIONAL AND SOCIAL ASCENT

In the nineteenth century, nationalism blossomed as a romantic springtime of various peoples. In the twentieth, its ascendance set the tone for wars and revolutions that devoured countless human lives. As lawmakers, European nationalists dedicated themselves to the social emancipation of their own native groups. They also tried to expand the geographical boundaries of their "national soil," encouraging irredentist movements and violence against neighbors of other nationalities. The governments of newly founded states, or those that for nationalistic reasons had been either expanded or diminished, isolated themselves from one another. The reasons why are easily enumerated: mass impoverishment in the wake of the First World War, fear of revolution as of 1917–18, persistent brutality and fighting in disputed marginal areas, the end of legal emigration, and jingoism. Exacerbating the situation was the widespread suffering caused by the Great

Depression, which many countries still hadn't overcome by the start of the Second World War.

Wanting to help their people get back on their feet, the political leaders in the old and, in particular, the new nations supported restrictive tariffs and their domestic analogue—laws and decrees disadvantaging minorities, especially Jews. Such measures fit into broader social-nationalist policies such as Romanianization, Lithuanianization, Magyarization, Hellenization, Polonization, Czechization, and, relatively late, Aryanization. The idea of nationalization, a euphemism for expropriating what was owned by people branded as foreigners, harmonized well with the idea of the social-welfare state. It bridged divisions between socialists and social democrats, especially when it negated the property rights of "Jewish capitalists," "Jewish bankers," and "Jewish speculative investors." General battle cries like "*la France pour les français*" or "*Polska dla Polaków*" were all too often specifically directed against Jews. More and more, concepts like the national economy connoted that the entire economy rightfully belonged to an ethnically defined people, and that interlopers had parasitically enriched themselves by claiming the best parts of it. The logical conclusion from all this was to turn away Jewish refugees and force "foreign" Jews to emigrate, if need be by governmental pressure and the enlistment of popular rage.

In his 1979 *Handbuch der europäische Geschichte* (Handbook of European History), Theodor Schieder put forward a multistage model to illustrate the transitions between ethnocratic resettlement and mass murder of minorities. For Nazi Germany's "special population-policy methods," he identified the following sequence: 1) mandatory detention, 2) pressure to emigrate, 3) deportation, 4) forced resettlement in occupied territories conquered by Germany, and 5) physical destruction. Schieder had been complicit in Nazi policies. Forty years after he himself had drawn up plans for the resettlement of Poles and Jews, he acknowledged—self-critically, it seems—that the mass murder of Jews had been preceded by this multiphased "preliminary stage."[2]

Anyone wanting to analyze the political processes that led to mass murder should not skip over these preliminary stages, whose success or failure was decisive for what came next. In Athens, Brussels, Denmark, and parts of Italy, German occupiers failed in their efforts to arrest Jews and confine them in ghettos and camps because they lacked local support. But where local populaces and security forces cooperated, as they did in most places, all that was needed was German energy, encouragement, and authorization for people to commit previously unimaginable crimes.

Not everyone involved needed to participate in every stage. Modern division of labor was one of the defining characteristics of the Holocaust. That made it impossible for any one individual to see the entirety of what was happening, allowing people to look the other way. It diluted individual responsibility and lamed people's consciences, especially once the preliminary stages in Schieder's model had rendered Jews nearly invisible and isolated from everyday life. All too often, the jobs and belongings of those who were ghettoized, either locally or at some remove, were already being divvied up while they were still alive.

FROM DISCRIMINATION TO "DE-JEWIFICATION"

The spiritual fathers of the nationalist movements of Europe discovered anti-Semitism early on. Starting in the 1880s, in France it merged with powerful antirepublican, conservative currents, although it also appealed to some in the socialist camp. The overlap reflected a mutual interest in the protection of traditional French artisans, merchants, lawyers, and doctors. In Salonika, there was a drive to Hellenize what had not been a Greek city, and the Jewish majority was resented for the perceived favoritism they enjoyed under the Greeks' Ottoman Turkish archenemies. In Poland, leading proponents of nationalist democracy and the clergy propagated an anti-Jewish variant of economic protectionism and Catholic social teachings.

Beginning in 1930, after a brief internationalist phase, a Russian-accented Communism crystallized in the Soviet Union. Anti-Semitism, which had been suppressed for a good decade but never truly overcome, enjoyed a revival in socialist garb. With Jews having been allowed since 1917 to live anywhere in Russia, anti-Semitism took hold within segments of the population not previously susceptible to it. As was also true in the nonsocialist countries of Western Europe, not only did progress in education animate many millions of formerly uneducated citizens, it also stoked their hatred of Jews.

In class conflicts between the proletariat and the bourgeoisie, less mobile citizens rose up against the more inventive, talented, and successful in the name of justice and equality. It's no surprise, then, that the borders between socialist and nationalist collectivism remain permeable even today. Italy and Germany weren't the only places after 1918 where the two merged into one. Together the parties that ruled on the European Continent despised and attacked British liberalism. They worshiped the concept of the people and rejected individualism as a vestigial remnant of an epoch that had yet to be illuminated by the spirit of national solidarity.

Anti-Jewish slogans were an easy way to motivate masses of people, and they sat easily with the goal of national and social betterment. Once governments began protecting majorities against Jewish minorities, years of further discrimination were sure to follow. Jews denied the right to study at university or to sell tobacco and alcohol would soon be prohibited from practicing certain professions and then stripped in stages of their civic rights. From that point, it wasn't a huge leap for people to begin considering more drastic "solutions." Those who advanced such policies—for instance, the Polish nationalist-democrat Roman Dmowski or the Greek republican Eleftherios Venizelos—never envisioned mass shootings or gas chambers, but they did increasingly come to believe that their Jewish minorities should emigrate sometime in the foreseeable future.

Between the two world wars, nearly all Continental European countries pursued policies of isolationism and viewed neighboring states as enemies. In the same period Jewish minorities began to feel the full weight of deliberate state and societal marginalization. Romanian, Polish, Hungarian, Greek, and even French politicians began to speak more openly about forcing Jews to leave, promising members of their respective national majorities jobs, small-business opportunities, nicer places to live, successful medical and legal practices, and chances to become educated and have better futures.

As of 1933, Germany served as a radical example of how a Jewish minority could be dissimilated, and of how a mixture of naked violence and laws could be applied to undo all the advantages of Jewish emancipation within the space of weeks, months, or a few years. As early as April 1933, the Nazi regime was already hounding thousands of Jews from the public sector. In May 1935, Jews were barred from military service and the social respect it entailed, and that fall they were stripped of their rights as citizens. Together with anti-Jewish boycotts, dozens of laws and edicts discriminated against Jews to the benefit of the national majority, the much-vaunted German *Volk*. In 1938, the Third Reich, having incorporated Austria and other territories, assumed control of Jewish assets and drove tens of thousands of impoverished people out of the country.

Along with great numbers of refugees and displaced persons, the German regime succeeded in exporting the "Jewish question" to much of the rest of Europe, encouraging anti-Semitism in France, Belgium, Yugoslavia, Norway, the Netherlands, and Switzerland. This was a conscious strategy, as is evident from a pamphlet titled "The Jewish Question as a Factor in Foreign Policy in the Year 1938," which the German Foreign Ministry sent to its outposts abroad in 1939. One passage read: "The emigration of only around 100,000 Jews was sufficient to awaken foreign interest in, if not the understanding of many countries for the Jewish peril. We are able to calculate that the Jewish question will become a problem for international politics, if large masses of Jews from Germany, Poland, Hungary, and Romania are forced to move by increasing pressure applied by their host people."[3]

DEMOCRACY, REVOLUTION, AND JEW-HATRED

The social rise of the European masses bolstered rather than lessened anti-Jewish resentment. As historian Ulrich Wyrwa has shown in his comparison of pre-1914 German and Italian anti-Semitism, extremely limited voting rights in Italy basically ruled out the development of organized anti-Semitism. As of 1882, a mere 7 percent of the Italian populace enjoyed the franchise. "This deficit in terms of democracy benefited the predominantly bourgeois, literate and well-educated Jewish community," Wyrwa writes. "Anti-Semitic parties, whose political success in Germany was based to a large degree on the general right to vote for Reichstag deputies, would have had no chance in Italy."[4] Since 1871, all German men enjoyed the equal right to vote by secret ballot in Reichstag elections, although in Prussia a three-tier system continued to exist until 1918.

Wyrwa characterizes the historical situation as paradoxical, but in fact it was a harbinger of the rapid spread of anti-Semitism under democratic conditions in the period between the wars. Conditions for the racial segregation and ultimately homicidal hatred of Jews are not unique to authoritarian, totalitarian, or dictatorial states. Parliaments and governments in democratically organized nation-states also saw nothing amiss in following ethno-collectivistic doctrines. All too often, they operated according to the principle identified by sociologist Ulrich Beck: "Fundamental rights are nationally divisible—they can be accorded to everyone with the same nationality, the members of the *Volk*, and denied to all other human beings."[5]

One piece of evidence supporting Wyrwa's insight is the electoral reform introduced in 1896 in the royal Austrian regions of Bohemia and Moravia. It gave all adult males, with only marginal limitations, the right to vote. In so doing it "helped put anti-Semitism on the agenda," as historian Michal Frankl has shown. "Starting in the spring of 1896," he writes, "all Czech political parties mobilized their ranks whenever there were imperial council elections. In this phase of heightened activity, with its numerous events and press propaganda, the influence of anti-Semitism became increasingly apparent."

A group of radical young Czechs who called themselves Česká družina (Czech Following) formulated an early, typically national-socialist platform: state controls upon stock exchanges and high finance, nationalization of major industries, moderate taxes on modest earners, state assistance for small business people and farmers, and anti-Semitism. Česká družina leaders considered their fight against Jews as "not so much a national or racial . . . as above all an economic and social" struggle and demanded that "the gentile population be legally protected against Jewry."

The Česká družina never achieved any real significance, but its ideas did, as was evident at the conclusion of the election campaign in spring 1897. The democratic Young Czech Party won Prague with a decidedly anti-Jewish platform. Anti-Semitism had existed before, but as Frankl put it, the elections lent it a "new legitimacy" and organizational form. By late November/early December, there was serious violence against Jews in Prague and other cities. Those who carried out the pogroms looted and burned Jewish businesses and smashed synagogue windows. But as was true everywhere in Western Europe at the time, murder remained the exception. The public unrest, which resulted from this well-intentioned voting-rights reform, surprised the Austrian governorship. They declared martial law and threatened to shoot the rioters and strictly punish disturbers of peace. Within a few hours, the situation calmed down.[6]

According to Tomáš G. Masaryk, later the founding president of the Czechoslovakian Republic, there were many significant countercurrents in Czech Prague. Nonetheless, anti-Semitism remained an integral part of Czech nationalism. Frankl saw its general cause in the modernization of everyday life, and not in any persistence of medieval prejudice. "Resistance to basic liberal concepts of society and the free market" personified by the mentally agile Jewish minority, Frankl wrote, was "the central source" of Czech anti-Semitism. In retrospect, the 1867 law on Jewish emancipation and the extremely progressive expansion of the franchise in 1896 encouraged a nationalistic anti-Semitism. In other words, two major liberal reforms of the Hapsburg monarchy helped anti-Semitism take on a broadly effective organized form. Young Czech politicians were among the most influential anti-Semites as well as being of "the greatest service to the cause of Bohemian self-rule."[7] Anyone who thinks that modern anti-Semitism has nothing to do with aspects of political and economic progress will be unable to understand the ideology or plausibly describe its pandemic spread.

In 1906, the reformist, if not democratic Russian prime minister Pyotr Stolypin wanted to ease the anti-Jewish laws in autocratic Russia but was hindered by the opposition of ordinary people. When the journalist and Jewish activist Paul Nathan asked for his help, he responded, "We can't do this because the Russian people don't want this sort of change and we're afraid that if Jews are given fully equal rights, there will be new massacres."[8] Just a year before, in fact, revolutionary rebellions against the feudal powers in Russian-, Ukrainian-, and Polish-settled regions of the disintegrating Romanov Empire had all led to major pogroms.

The social background of the people who attacked, robbed, and murdered Jews in 1905 led the literary critic and philosopher Mikhail O. Gershenzon to some gloomy conclusions. He warned against the fashionable faith in the masses of uneducated workers and farmers shared by many Jewish socialist intellectuals. In 1905, as though anticipating the mass murder of Jews committed in the name of liberation between 1917 and 1920 within the collapsing tsarist empire, Gershenzon wrote: "With regard to our situation, it is not only impossible to 'melt into the masses.' On the contrary, we have more to fear from these masses than all the possible punishments of the state. We should praise and thank the government because ultimately only its bayonets and prisons stand between us and the rage of the people."[9]

Anti-Semitism reared its head in Hungary in 1920. Since their emancipation in 1867, Jews in Hungary had achieved significant economic positions and represented a major part of the bourgeoisie. While political groups before 1914 had claimed the Jews had usurped too many rights, after 1920 they had the chance for the first time to take political action in democratic conditions. At that point, such groups were able to privilege Magyars in the name of equity and to the detriment of successful Jews. Between 1920 and 1944, both houses of the Hungarian parliament passed many anti-Jewish laws by huge majorities. Those who voted against such legislation included deputies who considered certain laws not anti-Semitic enough.

Historian Michael Schwartz sees in the widespread policies of ethnic violence in the twentieth century "the entanglement of ethnic and social conflicts." Schwartz points out that ethnic-social political platforms had by 1920 already led to the genocide of Armenians and other cases of mass murder. Occasionally scholars have asserted that the various ethnic displacements of populations in twentieth-century Europe had nothing to do with the persecution of the Jews. "It would downplay the seriousness of the situation," argued one 2011 study, "to treat the ideology, planning and execution of National Socialist policies toward Jews as a case of 'ethnic cleansing.'"[10] As the preceding pages have shown over and over, however, this view is patently incorrect. The Holocaust was the most extreme example of the ethnic-cleansing phenomenon. While the Shoah cannot be solely explained as a product of any European-wide ethnicity-based political tendencies, such tendencies played an obvious role in the prehistory of the Holocaust. The hope of easily enriching oneself and quickly rising up the social ladder was a general motivation for twentieth-century ethnic violence and a significant contributor to the discrimination, persecution, and murder of European Jews. "The materialist distribution of wealth," Schwartz concurs, "was a decisive factor in gaining broad social acceptance of an ethnic cleansing, carried out primarily by elites for political reasons." It is perfectly legitimate to speak of a social revolution organized along ethnic lines to benefit ordinary people.[11]

Annexation of foreign territory did nothing to lessen the conflicts with minorities in Hungary and Germany, or, in 1941, in Romania and Bulgaria. On the contrary, those conflicts only increased. In the end, it was a relatively small step for the planners of state-mandated resettlement policies to view war as the great opportunity to use severe methods to solve self-created problems. Annexed territories became practice fields to try out expropriation and murder in the name of Germanification, Magyarization, Romanianization, Croatification, or Bulgarianization. Jews were only one unwanted minority among many. But everywhere they were the first to be expropriated and removed.

JEWS AS ENVIED ROLE MODELS

In his short excursus "The Stranger" from 1908, sociologist Georg Simmel investigated a number of theoretical questions that are relevant here. Simmel wrote about foreigners in general but also referred to the "classical example" of European Jews. For him, the "stranger" is a wanderer who encounters those fixed in one place, a free-floating cosmopolitan who meets those tied to a plot of land. But unlike wanderers who come today and go tomorrow, Simmel's stranger is a "person who comes today and stays tomorrow. He is, so to speak, the potential wanderer: although he has not moved on, he has not quite abandoned the freedom of coming and going." This stranger continues to view the native with distance, which makes him more independent. "He is freer practically and theoretically; he surveys conditions with less prejudice; his criteria for them are more general and more objective ideals; he is not tied down in his action by habit, piety, and precedent." The stranger is thus the "fundamentally mobile person."

In Simmel's description, strangers usually enter the lives of locals as traders and merchants. If the local economy is basically one of individual subsistence, merchants who occasionally offer products from faraway lands will not be an irritant. It is only with the advent of modernity that the stranger becomes a problem. The rapid division of labor in industrial production, which may involve cities, regions, states, and even continents, demands a swiftly expanding apparatus of intermediaries: transport companies, information connections, stock and commodities exchanges and brokers, lines of credit from banks, financial guarantees, and contracts. The stranger organizes this new realm of economic life. He is international and able to communicate with the entire world. He occupies many of the increasing numbers of new positions that require considerable intelligence, be they entrepreneurial, fixed-employment, or freelance.

The anti-Semitism that erupted so massively in Europe as of 1880 fits in well with this schema. As Simmel says, "Trade can always absorb more people than primary production; it is, therefore, the sphere indicated for the stranger, who intrudes as a supernumerary, so to speak, into a group in which the economic positions are actually occupied." But trade entails "unlimited combinations" and opens up new possibilities for economic success. "Intelligence always finds expansions and new territories, an achievement that is very difficult to attain for the original producer with his lesser mobility and his dependence upon a circle of customers that can be increased only slowly."[12]

In this period of general upheaval, the sedentary natives, who suddenly became the slow, relatively backward members of society, considered themselves unfairly disadvantaged. They reacted to the flexible strangers with a mixture of admiration and reserve, jealousy and animosity. It was precisely this incubator that yielded the anti-Semitic stereotypes we know so well. Jews were soon denigrated as rootless cosmopolitans while the settled residents were elevated into preservers of popular tradition, whose forefathers had cultivated the homeland with their hands since time immemorial, defending it against outside interlopers. This task was purportedly passed on as a legacy to younger generations.

In *The Jewish Century*, Yuri Slezkine doesn't refer to Simmel's model, but he does put forward a similar, if somewhat more nebulous distinction between what he calls Mercurians and Apollonians. In Greco-Roman mythology, Mercury (Hermes) was the god of messengers, merchants, intermediaries, and border-jumpers. Reducing Apollo to his little-known role in Cretan mythology, Slezkine depicts him as the god of shepherds and their flocks, holding a protective hand over the sedentary.[13]

We might object to Simmel and Slezkine that most Eastern European Jews lived in poverty, eking out livings as small-time traders, door-to-door peddlers, self-employed tailors, cobblers, smiths, or plumbers. Many lived hand to mouth and described themselves as possessing little more substance than air. Simmel, however, focused exclusively on the bourgeois, assimilated Jews of Germany, who assuredly were very different sorts of Jews. But in the present context we are concerned primarily with the historical juncture at the opening of the twentieth century, a period characterized by exceptional Jewish striving for social betterment. Simmel only touched on this topic, but his contemporary and fellow sociologist Werner Sombart explored it in depth. Again and again, Sombart stressed the point that although Jews started out from conditions equal to or worse than those of Christians, in Berlin and wherever else they were accorded economic freedom they succeeded in climbing the social ladder three to four times as quickly as Christians, who found themselves utterly overshadowed. Sombart found Jews in Germany on average "so much cleverer and more energetic than we are" that their exclusion from university teaching positions was justified. From the perspective of the economy, Sombert argued, it was lamentable that whenever there were two applicants, the "stupider" candidate, not the Jewish one, usually got the job. At the same time he approved of protective restrictions because otherwise "every single position as lecturer or professor would be occupied by Jews, baptized and not, which in the end makes no difference." This concluding remark illustrates the start of an anti-Semitism that went beyond religious confession. Like many people of his day, Sombart recognized that Jewish intellectual superiority by no means stopped when Jews converted to Christianity.[14]

The same rationale led the prominent nationalist historian Heinrich von Treitschke in 1879 to write anti-Jewish polemics. His often cited essay "Unsere Ansichten" (Our Views) focuses on the economic ambition of Jewish migrants, whom Treitschke pejoratively describes as a "horde of ambitious pants-peddling young punks . . . whose children and grandchildren they want to someday rule over Germany's stock exchanges and newspapers." Treitschke excoriated the "presumption" and nimble-witted dexterity of the Jewish parvenu, arguing that such qualities offended the "modest piety" and "old-fashioned, familiar willingness to work" of native Germans.[15]

This phenomenon was also evident in the other countries discussed in this book, whether the subject was the preponderance of Jews in the Lithuanian import-export trade or the high percentages of Jewish academy and university students; the number of Jewish tailors who established textile factories or merchants who ran flourishing trading businesses, turned tiny bookshops into major publishing houses, organized the construction of railroads or telegraph connections, or

developed banking and stock markets. In time, the envy of Jewish success turned into a hatred that was born of socioeconomic obstacles
and the resentment and depraved retaliations they engendered.

FROM MENTAL TO MATERIAL DIFFERENCES

At the start of the twentieth century, socialists and bourgeois discussed
how to encourage upward social mobility among the lower classes.
The goal was to open opportunities to the "talented and capable." In
1920, German political scientist Paul Mombert concluded with satisfaction that this "selection process" was the subject of intense political
and scientific attention since, ultimately, it was in the national interest
to find out "how upward mobility proceeded, what the decisive factors
were and who could climb the social ladder."

On the basis of empirical examples of gentile families within Germany, mostly over three generations, Mombert identified a tendency
to make transitions slowly: "As a rule, the rise or fall from one class
into another is completed by going through all the various levels of a
specific social class before the next generation enters the next one."
There was "a constant up and down" on the social ladder. In general, people sought to constantly better themselves, but setbacks were
also common, and sometimes the bottom dropped out. At first gentiles
were slow to strive for something better for themselves or their children, but with the demise of the old class system, the pace increased.
By 1920, Mombert concluded, striving was "an integral part of what
people today want."[16]

By the turn of the century at the latest, thanks not least to the
broad educational activities of social democratic parties, class structures had become fluid. German novelist Theodor Fontane described
this particularly well in his 1899 novel, *Der Stechlin*. It features a Pastor Lorenzen who can somewhat but not fully understand social democratic ideas. "The main opposition of everything modern to what is
old comes from people who no longer have to occupy the position in
which they were born," Fontane has his pastor say. "They now have
the freedom to use their abilities in all directions and in every area. It

used to be that people were an estate lord or a linen weaver for three hundred years. Now every linen weaver can be the lord of an estate someday." His advice on how to get through the new social ups and downs halfway intact: "Prefer the old as far as you can and go with the new as far as you must."[17]

The new conditions went hand in hand with a high degree of status anxiety. The desire of large numbers of people to educate and better themselves, which the state supported, was further encouraged during the First World War, in line with the saying, "Every soldier carried a marshal's baton in his knapsack." But millions came away disappointed. The general race for happiness created winners, losers, and people who achieved a lot but never made it to the top spots. That provoked hatred and envy for those in a recognizable group who were more successful.

But why did the aversion to Jews in Poland, Lithuania, or Romania increase so steadily when the majority of them were so obviously impoverished and disadvantaged? One explanation was put forward by the Marxist Zionist Ber Borochov in 1917. Borochov described the social situation of the Jewish and gentile segments of the population not as static but rather, like Sombart, as a dynamic process. In Borochov's view, modern capitalism pushed aside the Jewish artisans predominant in Eastern Europe, people who cut cloth, made shoes, or built furniture in tiny workshops. "Machinery is their greatest enemy," wrote Borochov. But Jews didn't react to this upheaval by attacking machinery or turning fatalistic. They adapted. Borochov described a "forcing out of Jewish workers that happened not suddenly, but as part of a long-term process of social regrouping." The introduction of steam-powered looms in Łódź and Białystok brought with it Christian rather than Jewish labor, and Jewish weavers there all but disappeared. The transition from hand to machine work generally entailed the transition from Jewish to Christian work. Jews emigrated, moved to big cities, or took the initiative by founding new industries.

Borochov saw mental reasons for the differences in behavior: "A Jew will decide to strike off on his own with limited resources and poor prospects for success in a way that a Christian would never dare to."

Jews began new businesses with little capital, while a Christian worker, even when he had a superior starting point, tended to remain "another man's servant for his entire life." Borochov concluded that "the human makeup of the Jewish working class is in constant flux," shifting far more swiftly than the Christian segment of the working class. With great determination, many Jews lifted themselves out of proletarian misery. They were succeeded in many jobs by other Jews who in turn emancipated themselves as quickly as possible from factory enslavement.[18] Gentile Socialists in Russian Poland observed the same pattern but viewed it negatively. In 1912 they cast doubts upon the revolutionary commitment of their Jewish class comrades because the latter "established themselves and became bourgeois" more quickly than Christian workers. The Socialists were suspicious of the speed with which Jews found ways and means of climbing the social ladder—and with which they left gentile proletarians behind.[19]

Far removed from any Marxist interpretations, Joseph Tenenbaum reached conclusions similar to Borochov's and, indirectly, to those of the Polish Socialists who repeatedly criticized "Polish sluggishness."[20] In his home city of Lviv, Tenenbaum observed: "The Jews mainly represent the urban middle-class, a category of people that in an exquisitely rural region like Galicia, where racial hatred runs strong, is not well-suited to alleviating the economically based conflict between town and country." Once large numbers of Galician peasants began moving to cities and encountering these sorts of Jews, the friction quickly increased: "[The farmer] arrives as *homo rudis*, as an uncultivated dunderhead, and runs into an intelligent, superior middle class with which he can hardly compete." Because the situation featured a clearly definable group of people who spoke and behaved differently and followed a different faith, Tenenbaum argued, the "envy born of competition" could take on much more acute form than in situations where the massive problems of social upheaval could not be projected onto a specific group. In a period of general urbanization, Jews were defamed as the ones "blocking" important avenues for earning a living in European cities.

Tenenbaum particularly emphasized two socioeconomic factors:

the increasingly hostile opposition between town and country that was unavoidable in the early stages of capitalist development and the dashed hopes of the first generation of Christian proletarians who had little choice but to move to the city, where because of their lack of education and sophistication they were condemned to fail. The result was an army of disappointed people who felt cheated of any chance to live happily. Moreover, many Poles' sense of national pride was wounded by the recognition that "Jewish hard work and Jewish initiative" had helped the country achieve a measure of prestige and economic might.[21] It was from this tension, analyzed by Börne, Simmel, Sombart, Borochov, Tenenbaum, and Slezkine, that modern anti-Semitism derived its energy. Twelve years before Simmel, Theodor Herzl had recognized "the upward class movement" of Austro-Hungarian Jews as a new source of enmity and contrasted this "entrepreneurial spirit" with the "stationary" work done by many gentiles. But the First World War socially activated those who survived it, often uprooting and forcing them to start anew and move forward. National majorities, encouraged and supported by their political representatives and governments, began to close the gap.[22]

WAR MADE GENOCIDE POSSIBLE

Along with the growing anti-Semitism in so many nations of Europe, another central precondition was required for genocide to occur: the Second World War and its furious destructive force. Germany bears sole responsibility for the war, as it does not for anti-Semitism per se. The Wehrmacht's pitiless, homicidal campaigns in Eastern Europe, the main area of Jewish settlement, dragged tens of millions of people into a vortex of privation, terror, and death. It made civilians into profiteers of the victims—and often enough into victims themselves. The demise of normal political structures of governance and organization, an end intentionally pursued by German occupiers, set the scene for plunder and murder.

The war was what lowered people's inhibitions against committing acts of violence, fueled their fantasies about internal enemies and traitors, and encouraged their covetousness of other people's belongings. It was in part the conditions created by war that paralyzed the consciences of so many Christians, so that thinking in brutal friend-enemy dichotomies and jaded shoulder-shrugging indifference to others' suffering became the norm. In the spring of 1942, when Goebbels wrote of the "extremely barbaric" procedure needed to bring about a final solution to the Jewish Question, he expressed gratitude for the necessary preconditions created by Germany: "Thank God, we have in war a whole series of possibilities that were off-limits to us in peace. These we must use."[23]

With the exceptions of Denmark and parts of Belgium, German executioners were able to exploit specific anxieties to encourage violence against Jews in all the countries they occupied or dominated. They picked up on people's long-standing wish for an ethnically pure national state or for the elimination of Jewish refugees or unwanted competition. The German overlords always tried to allow individual governments, national and local administrations, and certain segments of occupied populations to benefit from ghettoization and deportation of Jews. That helped them secure the assistance of local police units and administrators as well as the support or at least indifference of those populations. More than anything, however, the war waged so brutally by Germany augmented an already existing greed for the property of "foreigners." As a result, over and over, German occupiers pushed through the complete expropriation of Jews as a way to alleviate the misery they themselves had caused.

THE REWARDS OF CRIME

Did anti-Jewish measures and acts of violence make it easier or harder for Germany to occupy other countries? After all, the German conquerors needed to maintain control over vast stretches of territory with relatively small forces of their own. In his comprehensive 2011 study of the genocide of Jews in Lithuania, historian Christoph Dieckmann investigated this question. He concluded that the murder of Lithuanian Jews was used as a "means of encouraging upward social mobility" and that it accelerated the social and economic "reordering processes within a perennially poor society." The act of genocide was in keeping with the anti-Semitic, nationalist policies of social emancipation for the Lithuanian people that had been in place since the late nineteenth century.

Dieckmann interprets the expropriation of Jewish property during the war as a "policy of national-racist redistribution of wealth in society." Lithuanians were able to enrich themselves by stealing everything, portable or not, left behind by people who had been imprisoned in ghettos and murdered; this was a "major means of binding" German occupiers and Lithuania's gentile population. For Dieckmann, direct social and economic profit is the main explanation for the scant opposition to the murder of almost all of this small country's 220,000 Jews. He also concludes that the mass killing of Jews, carried out with the active assistance of the native population, made the German occupation of Lithuania "easier rather than more difficult."[24]

Collaboration isn't a fully adequate term for the interplay of native forces and occupiers. It is more accurate to speak of a coincidence of specific interests. Where Jews were concerned, this coincidence led to a level of popular and state cooperation that went far beyond the actions of individual traitorous Quislings. Today, memorial plaques in French schools memorialize Jewish students who were murdered in German death camps. They usually contain a statement that the children who were deported were arrested "*avec la complicité active*" of French police in the Vichy regime and then handed over to Nazi barbarians.

The Nazi regime wanted to "solve the Jewish question" in all German-occupied and -allied states and combined that aim with the idea of transporting Jews outside those countries for "work deployment." Germany's offer of "help" was accepted in many places. Indeed, it was viewed as a unique opportunity that had the additional advantage of allowing the political powers in the countries concerned to dilute their own responsibility or abdicate it entirely. Collaborators like French premier Pierre Laval talked about "work deployment" and "resettlement" for so long that they eventually believed in these things themselves.[25] And cooperation was made easier because occupation officers and representatives of the SS and the German Foreign Ministry offered material incentives when they pressed for Jews in occupied and allied countries to be deported. German occupiers were at pains to ensure that state coffers and national majorities in all these countries profited from the disappearance of an unwanted minority.

On October 15, 1941, the local German commandant of Kryvyi Rih in Ukraine reported that "the remaining Jews" were being shot by police forces, which included "the entire auxiliary police." The Ukrainian city administration had "confiscated Jewish homes, keeping the furniture for themselves or selling it to needy locals."[26] In the cities of Belarus, as historian Christian Gerlach has documented, German occupiers alleviated the housing shortage caused by their war in similar fashion: "As a rule, German military and civilian administrators left the former homes of Jews for the local government. . . . It was responsible for allocating them." The portable belongings of those who had been murdered were also used to benefit Belarussian and Polish people living in the area. Some were in such desperate need that they didn't think about the source of the goods they received, but "others accepted the massacre and the homes they were given with indifference or even approval [of their origins]."[27] In the middle of a cataclysmic war, the murder of millions of people allowed the governments of the countries affected by it to reallocate more than a million places to live, mostly in cities.

Against the wishes of the German occupation authorities in Belgrade, Hermann Göring decreed in early 1942 that Jewish assets were to be given to the Serbian state treasury "to provide financial assistance for the Serbian state budget, which has been heavily burdened by the costs of occupation." Around the same time, the 100 million francs French Jews had been required to pay to German occupiers were distributed to French gentiles whose property had been damaged by British air raids on Parisian rail facilities. The money was doled out by a specially formed *comité ouvrier de secours immédiat*.

German occupiers acted in much the same way during their brief African campaign in French Tunisia. After the port city of Tunis had been exposed to heavy British bombardment in the summer and fall of 1942, Security Police and Security Service commandos organized "immediate support for bombing victims," forcing Jews to pay a special levy of 50 million francs. As was the case in Paris, this stolen aid money was distributed by a special committee of locals to "families who have suffered damage, especially Muslims."

German occupiers offered similar immediate help to bombing victims in Budapest and Milan.[28] In occupied Poland, they deported hundreds of thousands of Jews to ghettos to make room for Poles who had been displaced by Germans in an attempt to Germanize the annexed western Polish provinces.[29] Businesses and workshops, furnishings, and clothing were sold to Poles by local Polish officials and mayors or handed out for free to displaced Poles, who had lost everything.

In Salonika, Himmler's Security Service intervened energetically in the summer of 1943 when the German military commandant tried to distribute the belongings of Jews deported to Auschwitz to members of the small local Bulgarian- and Romanian-language minorities. SS Hauptsturmführer Herbert Hösselbarth countermanded this as being "without a doubt politically and propagandistically unfavorable." The Greek government and local authorities, he said, had been promised that "Jewish assets would be put at the exclusive disposal of the Greek state for the purpose of benefiting Greek citizens."[30]

German occupiers handed out rewards everywhere, although never without keeping a portion of the booty for themselves.[31] Occupation authorities in various places confiscated bank accounts, securities, and life insurance policies. Local offices sold property and, insofar as they had not already been looted by neighbors, the contents of homes and workshops at bargain prices to natives. This participatory practice secured the passive support of millions of people in almost all the nations of Europe.

In his diary, Hungarian writer Sándor Márai, born Henrik Grosschmis in Košice in 1900, described the effects under even a mild occupation regime. In the winter of 1944–45, while fleeing the Red Army toward Budapest, he made a chance acquaintance. "On the road, a man joined me. He had fled from Lajosmizse. . . . I sought to reassure him that he'd be able to return home soon. In an addled voice, he murmured, 'I own two acres of Jew land. Do you think I'll get to keep it?'" This was how small-time profiteers from murder and larceny spoke about their spoils. Average, otherwise perfectly respectable people from all social classes derived benefits, large and small, from others' misery.[32]

And they did not want to give up those benefits. In the final months of the war, Czech president-in-exile Edvard Beneš announced in London that repatriating Jews would bring "difficulties" for his government. Ranking members of the French Resistance advised Charles de Gaulle in 1944 that he should not promise to bring deported Jews back to France, warning that it could damage his reputation.[33]

In 1947, the World Jewish Congress succeeded in getting the Polish government to extend the deadline for filing claims to assets by a year to December 31, 1948. But only a few survivors were able to make such claims. In the French occupation zone of postwar Germany, the French military government refused to restitute Jewish property in line with the regulations in the American zone because it was felt that the rules went too far and could stir up fresh anti-Semitism.[34]

GOEBBELS: "HE WHO SAYS A MUST SAY B"

Throughout Europe, including of course Germany, Nazi leaders had made as many people as they could into profiteers of Jewish persecution. Those who had participated in robbery, no matter how minor, said nothing when Jews were taken away to destinations unknown. Some people were happy to see the deportations. Those who had taken over the job of a deported office worker, a business or apartment, or borne off winter clothing or furnishings didn't as a rule protest against Nazi inhumanity. The only thing that interested such people was that the Jews were gone for good. The leaders of Nazi Germany counted on this effect. They knew only too well from their own experience of buying popular support by distributing the assets of German Jews that sharing such spoils shored up cooperation between occupiers, the people, and their political offices. It encouraged a bandit morality within a conspiratorial community from which it was very difficult to break free once people had taken the bait.

According to the wishes of the German military commandant in Paris, revenues from the sale of Jewish businesses and real estate were to go to "French state finances." Göring further ordered that the "economic participation of French buyers be prioritized." In this way France was to be "divorced from the Jewish world," as German ambassador Otto Abetz explained in Paris. He meant cutting the country's traditional ties to the Western democracies and binding it to Germany.[35]

Following Italy's example, in the winter of 1943–44 the Hungarian government tried to leave its ill-fated alliance with Nazi Germany. In response, the Wehrmacht subjected the country to a mild form of occupation on March 19, 1944. The Reich Commissioner for Hungary, Edmund Veesenmayer, changed only some of Hungary's political leadership and offered to help the new government address its "Jewish question." Six weeks later, on the orders of the Hungarian Interior Ministry, not the German occupiers, Hungarian police had interred 300,000 Jews in ghettos for immediate deportation to Auschwitz.

Goebbels watched what was happening from Berlin and felt a sense of triumph. "The Hungarians, in any case, will no longer break out of the logic of the Jewish question," he wrote. "He who says A must say B, and now that the Hungarians have started with Jewish policy, they won't be able to apply the brakes. At a certain point, Jewish policy drives itself. That's now the case with Hungary." Hitler added that "as the Hungarian example again shows . . . the advantages of anti-Semitism . . . are of a significance that shouldn't be underestimated." By involving the government in Budapest and above all the head of state Miklós Horthy as participants in mass murder, Hitler successfully bound Hungary to Germany so that its potential could be mobilized "to a major extent" for German interests.[36] Three years earlier, when the Reich Commissioner in Croatia, Edmund Glaise-Horstenau, had an audience with the Führer on April 14, 1941, he reported that the new Ustashe government needed money "because it wants to seek a solution to the Jewish question in Croatia as soon as possible." Hitler interjected,

"We can send them some experienced experts." But he rejected the idea of deporting Jews who had emigrated to Croatia after 1914. "The most money is with the other ones," he reasoned.[37]

Because the German conquerors shared their booty with the peoples they had subjugated, they lessened occupied people's willingness to resist, turning them into confidants and accessories. That helped the leadership persist in a ridiculously overambitious war, which they were ultimately able to extend to five years. Goebbels, Hitler, and their henchmen knew exactly what was meant by "He who says A must say B." They intentionally corrupted millions of people in the belief that at a certain point moral corrosion would become self-reinforcing. They made people callous and obedient.

The results of this mass complicity are evident in the whispered comments Fenyö Miksa (born Miksa Fleischmann) overheard in Budapest in the winter of 1944–45. Two deaconesses were talking about the people kept in the city's ghetto. Miksa wrote: "One of them said: 'It's completely certain that the Arrow Cross intends to do something terrible to the ghetto.' The other answered: 'I feel sorry for these poor people, but maybe it's good the way it is. This way they won't be able to take revenge.'"[38]

Nazi allies and German-occupied states had considerable leeway in refusing requests from Berlin to deport their Jewish populations, as examples from Bulgaria, Romania, France, Slovakia, individual European cities like Athens, and pre-1944 Hungary show. In those places, the national politicians didn't deliver up all their Jews, and there was little the Nazi regime could do about it. The reasons were twofold. First, the assimilated Jews of Athens, Sofia, Paris, Budapest, Bratislava, and Bucharest usually enjoyed much better protection than their Yiddish-speaking, traditional coreligionists. Second, the military successes of the anti-Hitler coalition made politicians who might have leaned toward complicity think twice. In most cases it was the increasingly successful prosecution of the war against the Wehrmacht, and not any moral qualms, that saved the lives of hundreds of thousands of acutely threatened Jews. It was only on April 29, 1943, after the German military had suffered painful defeats in Stalingrad and North

Africa, that the commissioner of Jews in the German Foreign Ministry complained: "In all of the Balkan countries, the negative attitude toward anti-Jewish measures has recently increased."[39]

GOOD ABETS EVIL

Everything that happens has prior factors and developments—prehistories—that can be viewed as potential causes, although the plausibility of such connections decreases the greater the time elapsed between a factor and an event. Moreover, depending on the perspective of the observer, the number and significance of relevant prehistories is open to debate. But there are some general truths. Few people today would dispute that the Holocaust was caused by a multiplicity of factors. And what made it singular is also beyond debate: the pitiless thoroughness with which six million people—in a brief period and across an entire continent—were killed because of their "ethnic origins."

It is correct to point out that the interplay of causes was what made such an unprecedented crime possible. But evaluated on their own, none of these individual causes is unique. Each one of them fits into the continuum of German and European history. This is most evident in the case of "modern" anti-Semitism, but it also applies to the other phenomena we have repeatedly encountered in the preceding chapters: jingoistic nationalism, anti-liberalism, friend-and-foe dichotomies, discrimination against minorities, the expropriation of alleged enemies of the people, heightened social and economic competition, general striving for social and economic betterment, utopian dreams of homogeneous societies, and the legal and morally caustic effects of foreign and civil wars. These mutually influencing factors all encouraged increasing radicalism, and anti-Semites from various countries eagerly learned from their peers.

The multiplicity of diverse prehistories leads to the question of *how* the individual elements combined, reacted to one another, and developed their explosive genocidal energy. When a tragedy occurs, a common reflex is to draw attention to chains of events. On their own, none of the individual events is causal; it's the combination, including factors that may appear entirely harmless, that produces a result. The catastrophe is analyzed, and those who come after try to minimize the risks of repeating history either by eradicating isolated culprits or averting their unpredictable interplay. Instead of chains of causality, we could also speak of contingent events. The Latin root of the word, *tangere*, means to physically touch. Most scholars use the term as a synonym for "possible" or "random." I understand the Holocaust to be a contingent event in the sense of a likely possibility, in the prehistory of which a variety of actors with various aims played a larger or smaller role. These protagonists sometimes interacted unconsciously or semiconsciously. In other respects they behaved in the full knowledge of what they were doing and why. Many couldn't suspect that their anti-Semitic rhetoric, incitement, and activities would help lead, years or even decades later, to Auschwitz. Even so, increasing numbers of Europeans between 1880 and 1939 came to wish that "the Jews" would disappear, and many of them did not shy from using violence. Others—perhaps most notably Theodor Herzl—recognized early on that persecution and bloodshed were a possibility and warned against it.

Anyone who aims to learn about the Holocaust in the preventative sense must insist on differentiated investigations of the prehistories that were the basis of this barbarity. It won't do to reduce the diverse forms of complicity to formulaic entities like the National Socialists, ethnic ideologues, and racist anti-Semites, or fascism, totalitarianism, and dictatorship, or even the dictator Hitler. Such labels serve the understandable longing to put maximum distance between ourselves and genocide. But they cover what we as human beings find so threatening in a layer of abstraction and explain nothing. Nor is it especially productive to trace modern anti-Semitism back to the centuries-old anti-Judaism of Christianity. Not even the anti-Semitic clerics of Poland referred back to this ideology. They, too, used contemporary economic and social arguments.

Insofar as gentiles in the first half of the twentieth century pressed for Jews to be partially or completely stripped of their civil rights or insisted they be shipped off to somewhere outside Europe, they were motivated by the same obsessive anxiety: the fear of a supposedly overwhelming power and the real intellectual and economic agility of a small, precisely delineable "foreign" group. Whether in Russia, Hungary, Poland, France, Greece, or Germany—everywhere the slow were pitted against the quick, the unimaginative against the lovers of ideas, the lazy against the industrious, the enviers against the envied. Under the pretense of equality and equity, the less educated tried to restrict the access of intellectually more nimble Jews to master appren-ticeships, academies, universities, and certain professions. For fearful laggards, the civil service in particular was a realm that offered profes-sional security, and thus was everywhere kept tightly closed to poten-tial Jewish colleagues.

With the end of the First World War, anti-Semitism became a polit-ical factor in most European countries. It primarily created a class-bridging sense of community, suffused with the national majority's envy and fear of failure. A secondary product of this lack of self-confidence was pompous claptrap about "genuine" Russians, Roma-nians, or Magyars, about the eternal values, the heroic grand deeds, and the historical sublimity of every so-called national people. One extreme example was the self-elevation of the humiliated German los-ers of the First World War into a "master race." In this sense, there was something real to "racial theory"—it helped majority titular peoples compensate for feelings of inferiority. Members of national majorities didn't really feel contempt for Jews as subhumans, even if that notion became commonplace in Nazi Germany. On the contrary, to stay with the metaphor, they admired and fought against superhumans. For that reason, in *The Jewish Century*, Yuri Slezkine doesn't analyze racial anti-Semitism at all. For Slezkine, Jews represented a "successful minority" in largely unsuccessful European nation-states.[40]

Jews' head start in terms of formal education and entrepreneurial spirit was already shrinking before the First World War and decreased notably thereafter. Everywhere, Christian majorities were beginning to catch up. Investment in schools and universities in both democracies and autocratic states was paying off. Urbanization, which put people in proximity to institutes of higher education and universities, also played a role.

In this situation, young artisans, salesmen, entrepreneurs, civil servants, academics, and workers' and peasants' ambitious sons sought to restrict opportunities for Jews or expel them from society entirely. The struggle for the rewards of modernity, which were always connected to performance, had begun in the 1880s and reached its zenith in the interbellum years. As the gap in education closed, the degree of friction between Jews and majority populations increased. A paradox? No, because only when those trying to bridge that gap had made a certain amount of progress did the elevated social status of those first out of the blocks appear attainable. Envy is born of social proximity, not of the distance between two cleanly separated groups whose material circumstances are different but fundamentally stable.

That leads us to a vexing conclusion, which I would like to present as a final thought for discussion, if not as an ultimate truth. Evil arises not only from evil but also from what is basically good. Well-intentioned educational policies and state-supported desires to lift the masses socially—both of which can be counted among twentieth-century Europe's great triumphs—served to increase hatred. The same is also true of the best political ideas and those most deserving of continuation: democracy, liberty, popular participation, self-determination, and social equality.

Arthur Ruppin, the sociologist and cofounder of the Hebrew University in Jerusalem, was thinking of just such positive social developments when he asserted in 1930 that "Jews are being confronted with rising Christian competition." The Christian majorities had learned from those they considered their enemies and woken up. "The mentality displayed by Jews today," Ruppin wrote, "is the mentality of gentiles tomorrow."[41]

The general drive for upward social mobility, which entailed so many fears and so much stress, insecurity, and possible disappointment for so many individuals, had stoked anti-Semitism since the nineteenth century. But it became especially strong in the politically, economically, and culturally turbulent 1920s and '30s. Seen from this vantage point, the greatest crime of the twentieth century, the Holocaust, is connected to the greatest achievement of the same epoch, namely, the social elevation of masses of people. Under the extreme pressure of the war, begun and led by Germany, what had moved civilization forward had also brought about its destruction.

BIBLIOGRAPHY

Abramson, Henry, *A Prayer for the Government: Ukrainians and Jews in Revolutionary Times, 1917–1920*, Cambridge, MA 1999.

Achim, Viorel, "The Romanian Population Exchange Project Elaborated by Sabin Manuilă in October 1941," in *Annali dell'Istituto storico italo-germanico in Trento* 27 (2001), pp. 593–617.

——, "Sabin Manuilă," in *Handbuch der völkischen Wissenschaft*, ed. Ingo Haar/Michael Fahlbusch, Munich 2008, pp. 397–402.

Adam, Magda, ed., *Allianz Hitler-Horthy-Mussolini. Dokumente zur ungarischen Aussenpolitik 1933–1945*, Budapest 1966.

ADAP = Akten zur deutschen auswärtigen Politik.

Akten zur deutschen auswärtigen Politik [ADAP], Serie D, vol. 5, Baden-Baden 1953.

——, Serie E, vol. 5, Göttingen 1978.

Alwart, Jenny, *Mit Taras Ševčenko Staat machen: Erinnerungskultur und Geschichtspolitik in der Ukraine vor und nach 1991*, Cologne 2012.

Aly, Götz, "Dafür wird die Welt busen: 'Ethnische Säuberungen'—die Geschichte eines europäischen Irrwegs," in *Frankfurter Allgemeine Zeitung*, 27 May 1995.

——, *"Endlösung." Volkerverschiebung und der Mord an den europaischen Juden*, Frankfurt am Main 1995.

——, *Rasse und Klasse*, Frankfurt am Main 2003.

——, *Hitlers Volksstaat: Raub, Rassenkrieg und nationaler Sozialismus*, Frankfurt am Main 2005.

——, *Warum die Deutschen? Warum die Juden? Gleichheit, Neid und Rassenhass*, Frankfurt am Main 2011.

——, *Volk ohne Mitte: Die Deutschen zwischen Freiheitsangst und Kollektivismus*, Frankfurt am Main 2015.

Aly, Götz, and Susanne Heim, *Vordenker der Vernichtung: Auschwitz und die deutschen Plane für eine neue europaische Ordnung*, Frankfurt am Main 2013.

Aly, Götz, and Karl Heinz Roth, *Die restlose Erfassung: Volkszahlen, Identifizieren, Aussondern im Nationalsozialismus*, Berlin 1984.

Anastassiadou, Méropi, "Salonique après 1912: La construction d'une ville néo-hellénique," in Esther Benbassa, *Salonique: Ville juive, ville ottomane, ville grecque*, Paris 2014.

Apostolou, Andrew, "'The Exception of Saloniki': Bystanders and Collaborators in Northern Greece," in *Holocaust and Genocide Studies* 14 (2000), pp. 165–96.

———, "When Did Greek Jews Become Greek?," in: *Yad Vashem Studies* 38, no. 2 (2010), pp. 205–18.

———, "Strategies of Evasion: Avoiding the Issue of Collaboration and Indifference During the Holocaust in Greece," in Roni Stauber, ed., *Collaboration with the Nazis: Public Discourse after the Holocaust*, Milton Park 2011, pp. 138–65.

Arendt, Hannah, *Elemente und Ursprunge totaler Herrschaft*, Munich 1991.

———, *Besuch in Deutschland*, Berlin 1993.

Arndt, Regine, *Leon Blum, ein jüdischer Franzose: Zur Bedeutung von bildhaften Vorstellungen für die antisemitische Propaganda in Frankreich während der 30er Jahre*, Hanover 1996.

Artuso, Vincent, *La "question juive" au Luxembourg (1933–1941): L'État luxembourgeois face aux persécutions antisémites nazies*, Luxembourg 2015.

Atamuk, Solomon, *Juden in Litauen: Ein geschichtlicher Überblick*, Konstanz 2000.

Babel, Isaak, *Mein Taubenschlag: Sämtliche Eräahlungen*, ed. Urs Heftrich and Bettina Kaibach, Munich 2014.

Baberowski, Jörg, *Verbrannte Erde: Stalins Herrschaft der Gewalt*, Munich 2012.

Bankier, David, ed., *The Jews are Coming Back: The Return of the Jews to Their Countries of Origin After WWII*, Jerusalem 2005.

Barta, Stefan, *Die Judenfrage in Ungarn*, Budapest 1941.

Bartusevičius, Vincas et al., eds., *Holocaust in Litauen: Krieg, Judenmord und Kollaboration im Jahre 1941*, Cologne 2003.

Baumgarten, Murray, Peter Kenez, and Bruce Thompson, eds., *Varieties of Antisemitism: History, Ideology, Discourse*, Newark 2009.

Benbassa, Esther, *Geschichte der Juden in Frankreich*, Berlin 2000.

Bendikaite, Egle, "Zwischen Anspruch und Wirklichkeit: Die Politik gegenüber den Juden in Litauen in der Zwischenkriegszeit," in Dittmar Dahlmann and Anke Hilbrenner, eds., *Zwischen grossen Erwartungen und bösem Erwachen*, Paderborn 2007, pp. 101–20.

Bendow, Josef; see Tenenbaum, Joseph.

Benz, Wolfgang, and Marion Neiss, eds., *Judenmord in Litauen: Studien und Dokumente*, Berlin 1999.

Bericht des Präsidiums der Israelitischen Kultusgemeinde Vienna über die Tätigkeit in den Jahren 1945 bis 1948, Vienna 1948 (Yad Vashem Library [YVL] 09088).

Berkson, Isaak B., *Theories of Americanization*, New York 1920.

Bibó, Istvan, *Zur Judenfrage: Am Beispiel Ungarns*, Frankfurt am Main 1990.

Biss, Andreas, "Geschäft mit dem Henker: Die 'Endlösung' in Ungarn," in: *Der Monat* 8 (1960), pp. 57–67.

Bober, Robert, *Was gibt's Neues vom Krieg*, Munich 1995.

Boeckel, Otto, *Die Verjüdung der höheren Schulen in Österreich und Deutschland*, n.p., 1886.

———, *Nochmals: "Die Juden-Könige unserer Zeit": Eine neue Ansprache an das deutsche Volk*, Berlin 1901.

Boeckh, Katrin, *Von den Balkankriegen zum Ersten Weltkrieg: Kleinstaatenpolitik und ethnische Selbstbestimmung auf dem Balkan*, Munich 1996.

Boldorf, Marcel, "Racist Parameters in the French Economy 1919–1939/44," in: Christoph Kreutzmüller, Michael Wildt, and Moshe Zimmermann, eds., *National Economies: Volks-Wirtschaft, Racism and Economy in Europe Between the Wars (1918–1939/45)*, Cambridge 2015, pp. 167–80.

Börne, Ludwig, *Sämtliche Schriften*, ed. Inge and Peter Rippmann, Düsseldorf 1964–1968.

Borochov, Ber, *Die wirtschaftliche Entwicklung des jüdischen Volkes*, Berlin 1920.

Bowman, Steven B., *The Agony of Greek Jews, 1940–1945*, Stanford 2009.

Braham, Randolph L., *The Politics of Genocide: The Holocaust in Hungary*, 2 vols., revised and enlarged edition, New York 1994.

Brandys, Kazimierz, *Warschauer Tagebuch: Die Monate davor, 1978–1981*, Frankfurt am Main 1984.

Bresslau, Harry, "Harry Bresslau," in Siegfried Steinberg, ed., *Geschichtswissenschaft der Gegenwart in Selbstdarstellungen*, Leipzig 1926, pp. 29–83.

Brill, David, *An die Judenschaft Wiens!*, Vienna 1947 (YVL 57-7186).

Broucek, Peter, ed., *Ein General im Zwielicht: Die Erinnerungen Edmund Glaises von Horstenau*. Vol. 3: *Dt. Bevollmächtigter General in Kroatien und Zeuge des Untergangs des "Tausendjährigen Reiches,"* Vienna 1988.

Budnitskii, Oleg, *Russian Jews Between the Reds and the Whites, 1917–1920*, Philadelphia 2012.

Bulgakov, Mikhail, *The White Guard*, London 1971.

Caron, Vicki, *Uneasy Asylum: France and the Jewish Refugee Crisis, 1933–1942*, Stanford 1999.

Case, Holly, *Between States: The Transylvanian Question and the European Idea During World War II*, Stanford 2009.

Cattaruzza, Marina, "Der 'historische Ort' der Vertreibungen im Europa des 20. Jahrhunderts," in Ralph Melville, Jiři Pešek, and Claus Scharf, eds., *Zwangsmigrationen im mittleren und östlichen Europa*, Mainz 2007, pp. 39–53.

Cattaruzza, Marina, Stefan Dyroff, and Dieter Langewiesche, eds., *Territorial Revisionism and the Allies of Germany in the Second World War: Goals, Expectations, Practices*, New York 2013.

Caumanns, Ute, and Mathias Niendorf, "Von Kolbe bis Kielce: Ein Heiliger, seine Presse und die Geschichte eines Pogroms," in Hans-Jurgen Bomelburg and Beate Eschment, eds., *"Der Fremde im Dorf": Überlegungen zum Eigenen und zum Fremden in der Geschichte*, Lüneburg 1998, pp. 169–94.

Chasanowitsch, Leon, *Die polnischen Judenpogrome im November und Dezember 1918: Tatsachen und Dokumente*, Stockholm 1919.

Chirac, Jacques, *Discours et messages: En hommage aux Juifs de France victimes de la collaboration de l'État français de Vichy avec l'occupant allemand*, Paris 1998.

Churchill, Winston S., *The Second World War*, vol. 1: *The Gathering Storm*, New York, 1948.

Claß, Heinrich (pseud. Daniel Frymann), *"Wenn ich der Kaiser war": Politische Wahrheiten und Notwendigkeiten*, Leipzig 1912.

———, *Zum deutschen Kriegsziel: Eine Flugschrift*, Munich 1917.

Clogg, Richard, *Greece 1940–1949: Occupation, Resistance, Civil War: A Documentary History*, Basingstoke 2002.

Codreanu, Corneliu Zelea, *Eiserne Garde*, Berlin 1941.

Cohen, Israel, *A Report on the Pogroms in Poland*, London 1919.

Committee of the Jewish Delegations, *The Pogroms in the Ukraine Under the Ukrainian Governments (1917–1920)*, London 1927.

Courtenay, Jan Nieczysław Baudouin de, "Der Antisemitismus und die Universitäten in Polen," in François Guesnet, ed., *Der Fremde als Nachbar*, Frankfurt am Main, 2009, pp. 354ff.

———, "Die polnische Staatlichkeit und die Juden in Polen," in François Guesnet, ed., *Der Fremde als Nachbar*, Frankfurt am Main 2009, pp. 344–53.

Dahlmann, Dittmar, and Anke Hilbrenner, eds., *Zwischen großen Erwartungen und bösem Erwachen: Juden, Politik und Antisemitismus in Ost- und Südosteuropa*, Paderborn 2007.

Delmer, Sefton, *Die Deutschen und ich*, Hamburg 1963.

Deutschland und Südosteuropa, ed. Arbeitswissenschaftliches Institut der Deutschen Arbeitsfront, Berlin 1940.

Dieckmann, Christoph, *Deutsche Besatzungspolitik in Litauen 1941–1944*, 2 vols., Göttingen 2011.

———, "'Jüdischer Bolschewismus' 1917 bis 1921: Überlegungen zu Verbreitung, Wirkungsweise und jüdischen Reaktionen," in Sybille Steinbacher, ed., *Holocaust und Völkermord: Die Reichweite des Vergleichs*, Frankfurt am Main 2012.

Dmowski, Roman, "Gedanken eines modernen Polen," in François Guesnet, ed., *Der Fremde als Nachbar*, Frankfurt am Main 2009, pp. 276–82.

Doctor, Eugen, *Emigration und Immigration: Ein Wort zur jüdischen Auswanderer-Not*, Berlin 1908.

Documents on the History of the Greek Jews: Records from the Historical Archives of the Ministry of Foreign Affairs, Ministry of Foreign Affairs of Greece, University of Athens, Department of Political Science and Public Administration, researched and edited by P. Constantopoulou and T. Veremis, Athens 1998.

Documents sur les pogromes en Ukraine et l'assassinat de Simon Petliura à Paris (1921–1926), Paris 1927.

Döblin, Alfred, *Reise in Polen*, Olten 1968 (original 1924).

Drach, Albert, *Unsentimentale Reise: Ein Bericht*, Munich 1990.

Drumont, Edouard, *Das verjüdete Frankreich*, 2 vols., Berlin 1889 (*La France juive*, Paris 1886).

———, *Les juifs contre la France: Une nouvelle Pologne*, Paris 1899.

Dublon-Knebel, Irith, ed., *German Foreign Office Documents on the Holocaust in Greece (1937–1944)*, Tel Aviv 2007.

Dubnow, Simon, *Weltgeschichte des jüdischen Volkes: Von seinen Uranfangen bis zur Gegenwart in zehn Banden*, vol. 10: *Die neueste Geschichte des jüdischen Volkes: Das Zeitalter der zweiten Reaktion (1880–1914) nebst Epilog (1914–1928)*, Berlin 1929.

———, *Mein Leben*, Berlin 1937.

———, *Weltgeschichte des jüdischen Volkes: Kurzgefasste Ausgabe in drei Banden*, vol. 3: *Die neueste Geschichte des jüdischen Volkes: Von der franz: Revolution bis zum Ausbruch des Weltkrieges*, Jerusalem 1938.

Duclert, Vincent, *Die Dreyfus-Affäre: Militarwahn, Republikfeindschaft, Judenhaß*, Berlin 1994.

Eaton, Henry L., *The Origins and Onsets of the Romanian Holocaust*, Detroit 2013.

Elias, Ruth, *Die Hoffnung erhielt mich am Leben: Mein Weg von Theresienstadt und Auschwitz nach Israel*, Munich 1988.

Embacher, Helga, *Neubeginn ohne Illusionen: Juden in Österreich nach 1945*, Vienna 1995.

Encyclopedia of Jewish Life Before and During the Holocaust, ed. Shmuel Spectator and Geoffrey Wigoder, introduction by Elie Wiesel, 3 vols., New York 2001.

Erben, Peter, *Auf eigenen Spuren: Aus Mährisch-Ostrau durch Theresienstadt, Auschwitz I, Mauthausen, Gusen III über Paris nach Israel: Jüdische Schicksale aus der Tschechoslowakei*, ed. Erhard Roy Wiehn, Konstanz 2001.

"Excerpts from the Salonika Diary of Lucillo Merci (Feb.–Aug. 1943)," compiled by Joseph Rochlitz, introduction by Menachem Shelach, in *Yad Vashem Studies* 18 (1987), pp. 293–323.

Faschismus, Getto, Massenmord, ed. Jüdisch-Historischen Institut Warschau, Berlin 1962.

Feszler, Ludwig, "Nachwuchs im Handel," in: *Ungarisches Wirtschafts-Jahrbuch* 18 (1942), pp. 292–98.

Fette, Julie, *Exclusions: Practicing Prejudice in French Law and Medicine, 1920–1945*, Ithaca, NY 2012.

Fink, Carole, *Defending the Rights of Others: The Great Powers, the Jews, and International Minority Protection, 1878–1938*, Cambridge 2004.

———, "Two Pogroms. Lemberg (November 1918) and Pinsk (April 1919)," in

Murray Baumgarten et al., eds., *Varieties of Antisemitism*, Newark 2009, pp. 151–68.

Fischer, Christopher J., *Alsace to the Alsatians? Visions and Divisions of Alsatian Regionalism, 1870–1939*, New York 2010.

Fleming, Katherine E., *Greece: A Jewish History*, Princeton 2008.

Fontane, Theodor, *Der Stechlin*, Berlin 1899.

Frank, Walter, *Nationalismus und Demokratie im Frankreich der dritten Republik (1871–1918)*, Hamburg 1933.

Frankl, Michal, *"Prag ist nunmehr antisemitisch": Tschechischer Antisemitismus am Ende des 19. Jahrhunderts*, Berlin 2011.

Friedländer, Saul, *Nazi Germany and the Jews*, vol. 1: *The Years of Persecution*, New York 1997.

———, *Nazi Germany and the Jews*, vol. 2: *The Years of Extermination*, New York 2007.

Friedmann, Tuvivah, *Theodor Herzl: "Konig der Juden,"* Haifa 1996.

Friedrich, Klaus-Peter, *Der nationalsozialistische Judenmord in polnischen Augen: Einstellungen in der polnischen Presse 1942–1946/47*, Marburg, 2003.

———, "Von der żydokomuna zur Lösung einer 'jüdischen Frage' durch Auswanderung: Die politische Instrumentalisierung ethnischer und kultureller Differenzen in Polen 1917/18 bis 1939," in Dittmar Dahlmann and Anke Hilbrenner, eds., *Zwischen grossen Erwartungen und bösem Erwachen*, Paderborn 2007, pp. 53–75.

Funke, Hajo/Hans-Hinrich Harbort, *Die andere Erinnerung: Gespräche mit jüdischen Wissenschaftlern im Exil*, Frankfurt am Main 1989.

Gergel, Nahum, "The Pogroms in the Ukraine in 1918–1921," in *YIVO Annual of Jewish Social Science*, vol. 6, New York 1951, pp. 237–52. (English version of *Di pogromen in Ukraine in di yorn 1918–1921*, in Yaakov Lestschinsky, ed., *Shriftn far ekonomik un statistik*, Berlin 1928.)

Gerlach, Christian, "Die Wannsee-Konferenz, das Schicksal der deutschen Juden und Hitlers Grundsatzentscheidung, alle Juden Europas zu ermorden," in *WerkstattGeschichte* 18 (1997), pp. 7–44, reprinted in Gerlach, *Krieg, Ernährung, Völkermord*, Hamburg 1998, pp. 85–166.

———, *Krieg, Ernährung, Völkermord: Forschungen zur deutschen Vernichtungspolitik im Zweiten Weltkrieg*, Hamburg 1998.

———, *Kalkulierte Morde: Die deutsche Wirtschafts- und Vernichtungspolitik in Weisrussland 1941 bis 1944*, Hamburg 1999.

———, *Extrem gewalttätige Gesellschaften: Massengewalt im 20. Jahrhundert*, Munich 2011.

———, *The Extermination of the European Jews*, Cambridge 2016.

Gerlach, Christian, and Götz Aly, *Das letzte Kapitel: Realpolitik, Ideologie und der Mord an den ungarischen Juden 1944/45*, Stuttgart 2002.

Gitelman, Zwi, *A Century of Ambivalence: The Jews of Russia and the Soviet Union 1881 to the Present*, Bloomington 2001.

———, *Jewish Identities in Postcommunist Russia and Ukraine: An Uncertain Ethnicity*, Cambridge 2012.

Glass, Hildrun, *Minderheit zwischen zwei Diktaturen: Zur Geschichte der Juden in Rumänien 1944–1949*, Munich 2002.

———, *Deutschland und die Verfolgung der Juden im rumanischen Machtbereich 1940–1944*, Munich 2014.

Godley, Andrew, *Jewish Immigrant Entrepreneurship in New York and London 1880–1914: Enterprise and Culture*, London 2001.

Goebbels, Joseph, *Tagebücher*, 24 vols., Munich 1993–2008.

Golczewski, Frank, *Polnisch-jüdische Beziehungen 1881–1922*, Wiesbaden 1981.

Gömbös, Julius (Gyula), *Für die nationale Selbstzwecklichkeit: Zwölf Reden des Ministerpräsidenten Julius Gömbös*, Budapest 1932.

Gröschel, Cornelius, *Zwischen Antisemitismus und Modernisierungspolitik: Die Bedrohung des jüdischen Wirtschaftslebens in der Zweiten Polnischen Republik (1918–1939)*, Marburg 2010.

Grossman, Wassili, *Leben und Schicksal*, Frankfurt am Main 1987.

Gruner, Frank, *Patrioten und Kosmopoliten: Juden im Sowjetstaat 1941–1953*, Cologne 2008.

Grusenberg, S. O., *Die Bedürfnisse der jüdischen Bevölkerung Russlands: Denkschrift, gerichtet an die Represantanten-Conferenz der Jewish Colonization Association in Paris, Oktober 1896*, Berlin 1898.

Guesnet, François, ed., *Der Fremde als Nachbar: Polnische Positionen zur judischen Prasenz: Texte seit 1800*, Frankfurt am Main 2009.

Halács, Agoston, *Arbeitsverfassung*, n.p. [Budapest], n.y.

Harvey, Allen David, "Lost Children or Enemy Aliens? Classifying the Population of Alsace After the First World War," in *Journal of Contemporary History* 34 (1999), pp. 537–54.

Hatschikjan, Magarditsch A., and Stefan Troebst, eds., *Sudosteuropa: Gesellschaft, Politik, Wirtschaft, Kultur: Ein Handbuch*, Munich 1999.

Hausleitner, Mariana, *Die Rumänisierung der Bukowina: Die Durchsetzung des nationalistischen Anspruchs Großrumäniens 1918–1944*, Munich 2001.

Heiden, Konrad, *Geschichte des Nationalsozialismus: Die Karriere einer Idee*, Berlin 1932.

Heifetz, Elias, *The Slaughter of the Jews in the Ukraine*, New York 1921.

Heim, Susanne, and Götz Aly, "Staatliche Ordnung und 'organische Lösung': Die Rede Hermann Görings 'Über die Judenfrage' vom 6. Dez. 1938," in *Jahrb. für Antisemitismusforschung*, vol. 2, Frankfurt am Main 1993, pp. 378–405.

Heine, Eric, "Allgemeine Ermächtigung und konkrete Eigendynamik: Die Ermordung der Juden in den ländlichen Gebieten Litauens," in Bartusevičius et al., eds., *Holocaust in Litauen* (2003), pp. 91–103.

Heinen, Arnim, *Rumänien, der Holocaust und die Logik der Gewalt*, Munich 2007.

Hemberger, Andreas: *Illustrierte Geschichte des Balkankrieges 1912–13*, vol. 1, Vienna 1914.

Herczl, Moshe Y., *Christianity and the Holocaust of Hungarian Jewry*, London 1993.

Herzl, Theodor, *Der Judenstaat: Versuch einer modernen Lösung der Judenfrage*, Zurich 1997 (original Vienna and Leipzig 1896).

————, *Alt-Neuland*. Leipzig 1902.

————, "Selbstbiographie," in: *Theodor Herzl: Ein Gedenkbuch zum 5. Todestage*, ed. Executive Branch of the Zionist Organisation, Berlin 1929, pp. 42–46.

————, *Briefe und Tagebücher*, vol. 2: *Zionistisches Tagebuch 1895–1899*, ed. Johannes Wachten and Chaya Harel, Berlin 1984.

Hettling, Manfred, Michael G. Muller, and Guido Hausmann, eds., *Die "Judenfrage"—ein europäisches Phänomen*, Berlin 2013.

Hilfsverein der Deutschen Juden, *Fünfter Geschäftsbericht (1906)*, Berlin 1907.

————, *Siebenter Geschäftsbericht (1908)*, Berlin 1909.

————, *Achter Geschäftsbericht (1909)*, Berlin 1910.

————, *Zwölfter Geschäftsbericht (1913)*, Berlin 1914.

————, *Siebzehnter Geschäftsbericht (1918)*, Berlin 1919.

————, *Jahresbericht für 1930*, darin: *Dreißig Jahre Hilfsverein der Deutschen Juden 1901–1931*, Berlin 1931.

Hillgruber, Andreas, "Deutschland und Ungarn 1933–1944: Ein Überblick über die politischen und militärischen Beziehungen im Rahmen der europäischen Politik," in *Wehrwissenschaftliche Rundschau 9* (1959), pp. 651–76.

Hillgruber, Andreas, ed., *Staatsmänner und Diplomaten bei Hitler*, 2 vols., Frankfurt am Main 1967, 1970.

Hitler, Adolf, *Mein Kampf*, 5th ed., Munich 1930.

————, "Rede am 6. Oktober 1939 in Berlin vor dem Reichstag," in: *Der großdeutsche Freiheitskampf: Reden Adolf Hitlers*, ed. Philipp Bouhler, vol. 1: *1. September 1939 bis 10. Marz 1940*, Munich 1943, pp. 67–100.

Hoensch, Jorg K., Stanislav Biman, and Ľubomir Liptak, eds., *Judenemanzipation, Antisemitismus, Verfolgung in Deutschland, Österreich-Ungarn, den Böhmischen Ländern und der Slowakei*, Essen 1999.

Hoffmann, Christhard, and Bernd Passier, eds., *Die Juden: Vorurteil und Verfolgung im Spiegel literarischer Texte*, Stuttgart 1986.

Hoppe, Jens, "Juden als Feinde Bulgariens? Zur Politik gegenüber den bulgarischen Juden in der Zwischenkriegszeit," in Dittmar Dahlmann and Anke Hilbrenner, eds., *Erwartungen*, Paderborn 2007, pp. 217–52.

Hugues, Pascale, *Marthe & Mathilde: Eine Familie zwischen Frankreich und Deutschland*, Reinbek 2012.

Hyman, Paula E., *The Jews of Modern France*, Berkeley 1998.

Ihrig, Stefan, *Ataturk in the Nazi Imagination*, Cambridge, MA 2014.

Ioanid, Radu, "The Pogrom of Bucharest 21–23 January 1941," in *Holocaust and Genocide Studies 6* (1991), pp. 373–82.

Istóczy, Viktor, *Die Wiederherstellung des jüdischen Staates Palästina: Aus den Reden Viktor Istoczy's, gehalten im ungarischen Abgeordnetenhause [1878] wahrend der Reichstage von 1872–1896*, Budapest 1905.

Ivkova, Rossitza, *Rettung und Mord in genozidalen Entscheidungsprozessen: Bulgarien 1941–1943*, Bielefeld 2004.

Jericho-Polonius, S., *China auf der Balkanhalbinsel oder rumänische Judenfrage*, Lemberg 1901.

The Jewish Minority in Hungary: The Hungarian Law No. XXV of the Year 1920 ("Numerus Clausus") Before the Council of the League of Nations, December 10 & 12, 1925, London 1926.

Judavics-Paneth, Lassare, *Pogrom-Prozesse,* 2 vols., Berlin 1911.

Die Judenfrage im preußischen Abgeordnetenhause: Wörtlicher Abdruck der stenographischen Berichte vom 20. und 22. November 1880, Breslau 1880.

Die Judenfrage in Rumänien: Eine Aktensammlung, vorgelegt dem Brüsseler Congress "pro Armenia" vom 17. u. 18. Juli 1902, Vienna 1902.

Die Judenpogrome in Russland, hrsg. im Auftrage des Zionistischen Hilfsfonds in London von der zur Erforschung der Pogrome eingesetzten Kommission, vol. I: *Allgemeiner Teil,* vol. II: *Einzeldarstellungen,* Cologne 1910.

Judge, Edward H., *Ostern in Kischinjow: Anatomie eines Pogroms,* Mainz 1995.

Jüdisches Lexikon, vols. 1–5, Berlin 1927, reprint 1987.

Kahan, Arcadius, "Notes on Jewish Entrepreneurship in Tsarist Russia," in Gregory Guroff and Fred V. Carstensen, eds., *Entrepreneurship in Imperial Russia and the Soviet Union,* Princeton 1983, pp. 107–18.

Kakis, Frederic J., *Legacy of Courage: A Holocaust Survival Story in Greece,* Bloomington 2003.

Kállay, Nicholas, *Hungarian Premier: A Personal Account of a Nation's Struggle During the Second World War,* Westport 1970 (original 1954).

Kaplun-Kogan, Wladimir Wolf, *Die Wanderbewegungen der Juden,* Bonn 1913.

Karady, Viktor (Victor), "Das Judentum als Bildungsmacht der Moderne: Forschungsansätze zur relativen Überschulung in Mitteleuropa," in *Österreichische Zeitschrift für Geschichtswissenschaft* 8 (1997), pp. 347–61.

———, *Gewalterfahrung und Utopie: Juden in der europäischen Moderne,* Frankfurt am Main 1999.

———, "Jews in Hungarian Legal Profession and Among Law Students from the Emancipation till the Shoah," in *Iskolakultura Online* 1 (2007).

Karady, Victor, and Peter Tibor Nagy, eds., *The Numerus Clausus in Hungary: Studies on the First Anti-Jewish Law and Academic Anti-Semitism in Modern Central Europe,* Budapest 2012.

Katz, David, *Lithuanian Jewish Culture,* Vilnius 2004.

Kendziorek, Piotr, "Auf der Suche nach einer nationalen Identität: Polnische Debatten um die 'Judenfrage,'" in Andreas Reinke et al., eds., *Die "Judenfrage" in Ostmitteleuropa, Historische Pfade und politisch-soziale Konstellationen,* Berlin 2015, pp. 249–387.

Kenez, Peter, "Pogroms and White ideology," in John D. Klier and Schlomo Lambroza, eds., *Pogroms: Anti-Jewish Violence in Modern Russian History,* Cambridge 1992, pp. 293–313.

———, "Pogroms in Hungary, 1946," in Murray Baumgarten et al., eds., *Varieties of Antisemitism,* Newark 2009, pp. 223–36.

Kerepeszki, Róbert, "'The Racial Defense in Practice': The Activity of the Turul Association at Hungarian Universities Between the Two World Wars," in Victor Karady and Peter Tibor Nagy, eds., *The Numerus Clausus in Hungary,* Budapest 2012, pp. 136–49.

Kertesz, Lilly, *Von den Flammen verzehrt: Erinnerung einer ungarischen Jüdin*, Bremen 1999.

Khrushchev, Nikita, *Khrushchev Remembers*, Strobe Talbot, ed. and trans., Boston 1970.

Kieffer, Fritz, *Judenverfolgung in Deutschland—eine innere Angelegenheit? Internationale Reaktionen auf die Flüchtlingsproblematik 1933–1939*, Stuttgart 2002.

Kishon, Ephraim, *Nichts zu lachen: Erinnerungen*, Munich 1993.

Klarsfeld, Serge, *Vichy-Auschwitz: Die Zusammenarbeit der deutschen und französischen Behorden bei der "Endlösung der Judenfrage" in Frankreich*, Nordlingen 1989.

Klier, John D., and Shlomo Lambroza, eds., *Pogroms: Violence in Modern Russian History*, Cambridge 1992.

Klocke, Helmut, "Gesellschaftliche Kräfte und ungeschriebene Verfassungswirklichkeit in Ungarn 1933–1938," in: *Ungarn-Jahrbuch: Zeitschrift für interdisziplinare Hungarologie 9* (1978), pp. 159–95.

Klukowski, Zygmunt, *Diary from the Years of Occupation: 1939–44*, Urbana 1993.

Koch, Hans, "Die Gegensätzlichkeit der Gefühle bei Taras Ševčenko," in *Jahrbücher für die Geschichte Osteuropas 1* (1953), pp. 302–20.

Kohn, Hans, *Das moderne Russland: Grundzuge seiner Geschichte*, Freiburg im Breisgau 1957.

Korb, Alexander, *Im Schatten des Weltkriegs: Massengewalt der Ustaša gegen Serben, Juden und Roma in Kroatien 1941–1945*, Hamburg 2013.

Kossert, Andreas, "Founding Father of Modern Poland and Nationalist Antisemite: Roman Dmowski," in Rebecca Haynes and Martyn Rady, eds., *In the Shadow of Hitler: Personalities of the Right in Central and Eastern Europe*, London 2011, pp. 89–104.

Kotowski, Albert S., *Hitlers Bewegung im Urteil der polnischen Nationaldemokratie*, Wiesbaden 2000.

———, "'Polska dla Polakow': Über den Antisemitismus in Polen in der Zwischenkriegszeit," in Dittmar Dahlmann and Anke Hilbrenner, eds., *Zwischen grossen Erwartungen und bösem Erwachen*, Paderborn 2007, pp. 77–100.

Kovács, Mária M., "The Hungarian Numerus Clausus: Ideology, Apology and History, 1919–1945," in Victor Karady and Peter Tibor Nagy, eds., *The Numerus Clausus in Hungary*, Budapest 2012, pp. 27–55.

Kreutzmüller, Christoph, Michael Wildt, and Moshe Zimmermann, eds., *National Economies: Volks-Wirtschaft, Racism and Economy in Europe Between the Wars (1918–1939/45)*, Cambridge 2015.

Krzywiec, Grzegorz, "'Progressiver Antisemitismus' im russischen Teil Polens von 1905 bis 1914," in Manfred Hettling, Michael G. Muller, and Guido Hausmann, eds., *Die "Judenfrage"—ein europaisches Phänomen*, Berlin 2013, pp. 127–42.

Kulischer, Alexander/Eugen Kulischer, *Kriegs- und Wanderzüge: Weltgeschichte als Völkerbewegung*, Berlin 1932.

Kulischer, Eugene M. (= Eugen), *Jewish Migrations: Past Experiences and Post-War Prospects*, New York 1943.

———, *Europe on the Move: War and Population Changes, 1917–47*, New York 1948.

Kuszelewicz, Joseph, *Un Juif de Biélorussie de Lida a Karaganda: Ghetto, Maquis, Goulag*, Paris 2002.

Ladas, Stephen P., *The Exchange of Minorities: Bulgaria, Greece and Turkey*, New York 1932.

Lagarde, Paul de, "Konservativ?" in: Paul de Lagarde, *Dt. Schriften*, Göttingen 1892, pp. 5–36.

Lagrou, Pieter, "Return to a Vanished World: European Societies and the Remnants of Their Jewish Communities, 1945–1947," in David Bankier, ed., *The Jews Are Coming Back*, Jerusalem 2005, pp. 1–24.

Lansing, Robert, *Die Versailler Friedensverhandlungen: Persönliche Erinnerungen*, Berlin 1921.

Lazare, Bernard, *Die Juden in Rumänien*, Berlin 1902.

Lemberg, Hans, "Nationale 'Entmischung' und Zwangswanderungen in Mittelund Osteuropa 1938–1948," in: *Westfälische Forschungen* 39 (1989), pp. 383–92.

———, "'Ethnische Säuberung': Ein Mittel zur Lösung des Nationalitätenproblems?," in *Aus Politik und Zeitgeschichte, Beilage zur Wochenzeitung das Parlament* (B 46/92), 6 November 1992, pp. 27–38.

Lemkin, Raphael, *Axis Rule in Occupied Europe: Laws of Occupation, Analysis of Government, Proposals for Redress*, Washington, DC, 1944.

Lenin, V. I., *Werke*, vol. 29, Marz–August 1919, Berlin 1970.

Lestschinsky, Jacob, *Bilan de l'extermination*, Brussels 1946.

———, "The Economic Struggle of the Jews in Independent Lithuania," in: *Jewish Social Studies* 8 (1946), vol. 4, pp. 267–96.

———, *The Jewish Migration for the Past Hundred Years*, New York 1944.

———, "Jewish Migrations, 1840–1956," in: Finkelstein, *Jews* (1960), pp. 1536–96.

———, *Das jüdische Volk im Neuen Europa: Die wirtschaftliche Lage der Juden in Ost und Zentraleuropa seit dem Weltkrieg*, Prague 1934.

———, "Die Umsiedlung und Umschichtung des jüdischen Volkes im Laufe des letzten Jahrhunderts, Teil II," in: *Weltwirtschaftliches Archiv* 30 (1929), pp. 123–56; also "Die Umsiedlung . . . Teil III" in: *Weltwirtschaftliches Archiv* 32 (1930), pp. 563–99.

———, *Der wirtschaftliche Zusammenbruch der Juden in Deutschland und Polen*, Paris 1936.

Lichtenstaedter, Siegfried (Dr. Mehemed Emin Efendi), *Kultur und Humanität: Volkerpsychologische und politische Untersuchungen*, Würzburg 1897.

———, *Die Zukunft der Turkei: Ein Beitrag zur Lösung der orientalischen Frage*, Berlin 1898.

———, *Das neue Weltreich: Ein Beitrag zur Geschichte des 20. Jahrhunderts: Psychologische und politische Phantasien*, vol. I: *Vom chinesischen Kriege bis zur Eroberung Konstantinopels*, Munich 1901.

————, *Das neue Weltreich: Ein Beitrag zur Geschichte des 20. Jahrhunderts,* vol. II: *Von der Eroberung Konstantinopels bis zum Ende Österreich-Ungarns,* Leipzig 1903.

Löwe, Heinz-Dietrich, "Die Juden im bol'ševikischen System: Zwischen sozialem Wandel und Intervention," in Dittmar Dahlmann and Anke Hilbrenner, eds., *Zwischen grossen Erwartungen und bösem Erwachen,* Paderborn 2007, pp. 137–65.

Lunacharsky, Anatoly, *Ob Antisemitizme,* Moscow 1929.

Lustiger, Arno, *Rotbuch: Stalin und die Juden: Die tragische Geschichte des Jüdischen Antifaschistischen Komitees und der sowjetischen Juden,* Berlin 1998.

Maelicke, Alfred, "Fortschreitende Entjudung Europas," in *Die deutsche Volkswirtschaft, Sonderteil "Konstituierung der europäischen Wirtschaftsgemeinschaft"* 17 (1942–43), pp. 1272–76; reprinted in Susanne Heim and Götz Aly, eds., *Bevölkerungsstruktur und Massenmord: Neue Dokumente zur deutschen Politik der Jahre 1938–1945,* Berlin 1991, pp. 152–64.

Mandelbrot, Benoit B., *Schönes Chaos: Mein wundersames Leben,* Munich 2013.

Manuilă, Sabin, *Ethnographische Studie über die Bevölkerung Rumäniens,* [Bucharest] 1938.

————, "Das Judenproblem in Rumänien zahlenmäßig gesehen," in: *Deutsches Archiv für Landes- und Volksforschung 5* (1941), pp. 603–13.

Marcus, Joseph, *Social and Political History of the Jews in Poland, 1919–1939,* Berlin 1983.

Margaroni, Maria, "Das 'viel ersehnte' Saloniki oder der griechische Antisemitismus und die Reaktion der Juden (1879–1914)," in Ulrich Wyrwa, ed., *Einspruch und Abwehr: Die Reaktion des europäischen Judentums auf die Entstehung des Antisemitismus (1879–1914),* Frankfurt am Main 2010, pp. 251–68.

Margolis, Rachela, *Als Partisanin in Wilna: Erinnerungen an den jüdischen Widerstand in Litauen,* Frankfurt am Main 2008.

Marr, Wilhelm, *Der Sieg des Judenthums über das Germanenthum: Vom nicht confessionellen Standpunkt aus betrachtet,* Bern 1879.

————, *Der Judenkrieg, seine Fehler und wie er zu organisieren ist (Antisemitische Hefte, Nr. 1),* Chemnitz 1880.

Matolcsy, Matyas, *Die landwirtschaftliche Arbeitslosigkeit* (= Ungarisches Institut für Wirtschaftsforschung, Sonderheft Nr. 6), Budapest 1933.

Matsas, Michael, *The Illusion of Safety: The Story of the Greek Jews During the Second World War,* New York 1997.

Mayer, Arno J., *The Furies: Violence and Terror in the French and Russian Revolutions,* Princeton 2000.

Mayer, Michael, "'Die französische Regierung packt die Judenfrage an'": Vichy-Frankreich, deutsche Besatzungsmacht und der Beginn der 'Judenpolitik' im Sommer/Herbst 1940," in *Vierteljahrshefte für Zeitgeschichte 58* (2010), pp. 329–62.

————, *Staaten als Tater: Ministerialburokratie und "Judenpolitik" in NS-Deutschland und Vichy-Frankreich: Ein Vergleich*, Munich 2010.

Mazower, Mark, *Salonica, City of Ghosts: Christians, Muslims and Jews, 1430–1950*, New York 2004.

Meinen, Insa, *Die Shoah in Belgien*, Darmstadt 2009.

Melville, Ralph, Jiři Pešek, and Claus Scharf, eds., *Zwangsmigrationen im mittleren und östlichen Europa: Volkerrecht, Konzeptionen, Praxis (1938–1950)*, Mainz 2007.

Meron, Orly C., *Jewish Entrepreneurship in Salonica 1912–1940: An Ethnic Economy in Transition*, Brighton 2011.

Messmer, Matthias, *Sowjetischer und postkommunistischer Antisemitismus: Entwicklungen in Russland, der Ukraine und Litauen*, Konstanz 1997.

Messner, Reinhold, ed., *Die Option: 1939 stimmten 86% der Südtiroler für das Aufgeben ihrer Heimat. Warum? Ein Lehrstück in Zeitgeschichte*, Munich 1989.

Meyer, Ahlrich, *Das Wissen um Auschwitz: Täter und Opfer der "Endlösung" in Westeuropa*, Paderborn 2010.

Miliakova, Lidia, ed., *Le livre des pogroms: Antichambre d'un génocide, Ukraine, Russie, Biélorussie 1917–1922*, Paris 2010 (more extensive Russian first edition, Moscow 2006).

Modras, Ronald, *The Catholic Church and Antisemitism: Poland 1933–1939*, Chur 1994.

Mojzes, Paul, *Balkan Genocides: Holocaust and Ethnic Cleansing in the Twentieth Century*, Lanham 2011.

Molho, Rena, *Salonica and Istanbul: Social, Political and Cultural Aspects of Jewish Life*, Istanbul 2005.

Mombert, Paul, "Die Tatsachen der Klassenbildung," in *Schmollers Jahrbuch* 44 (1920), pp. 93–122.

Motzkin, Leo, *La campagne antisémite en Pologne: Troubles universitaires, Question du "numerus clausus," Boycott économique, Attitude des tribunaux*, Paris 1932.

Müller, Uwe, "The Meaning of Land Reforms for the Constitution," in Christoph Kreutzmüller, Michael Wildt, and Moshe Zimmermann, eds., *National Economies*, Cambridge 2015, pp. 181–95.

Münz, Wilhelm, *Die Judenmetzeleien in Russland: Ein offener Brief an die regierenden Fürsten und Staatsoberhäupter der Kulturwelt*, Breslau 1906.

Nagy, Peter Tibor, "The First Anti-Jewish Law in Inter-war Europe," in Victor Karady and Peter Tibor Nagy, eds., *The Numerus Clausus in Hungary*, Budapest 2012, pp. 56–68.

Nansen, Fridtjof, *Betrogenes Volk: Eine Studienreise durch Georgien und Armenien als Oberkommissar des Völkerbundes*, Leipzig 1928.

Nastasă, Lucian, "Anti-Semitism at Universities in Romania (1919–1939)," in Victor Karady and Peter Tibor Nagy, eds., *The Numerus Clausus in Hungary*, Budapest 2012, pp. 219–43.

Nathan, Paul, *Die russische Revolution und die Juden*, Lecture of 5 December 1906 (privately printed).

Nathan, Paul, Elkan Adler, and Bernhard Kahn, *Bericht über das Balkanhilfswerk*, Berlin 1913.

Negură, Ion, "Das Siedlungswerk von 1942 in Rumänien," in *Raumforschung und Raumordnung* 7 (1943), nos. 1–2, pp. 62ff.

Nolte, Ernst, *Der Faschismus in seiner Epoche*, Munich 1963.

Nossig, Alfred, *Materialien zur Statistik des jüdischen Stammes*, Vienna 1887.

Oltmer, Jochen, *Migration und Politik in der Weimarer Republik*, Göttingen 2005.

Opfer, Bjorn, "Der Wahn vom homogenen Großreich: Die bulgarische Nationalitätenpolitik im besetzten Makedonien während des Zweiten Weltkrieges," in *Zeitschrift für Genozidforschung* 6 (2005), no. 1, pp. 42–71.

Pacholkiv, Svjatoslav, "Zwischen Einbeziehung und Ausgrenzung: Die Juden in Lemberg," in Binnenkade, Alexandra, et al., *Vertraut und fremd zugleich: Jüdisch-christliche Nachbarschaften in Warschau, Lengnau, Lemberg*, Cologne 2009, pp. 155–216.

Pan-arische Union (Weltbund der arischen, arianisierten und affilierten Völker in Wien), ed., *Zusammenschluss der Arier oder Zusammenbruch des Altertums und der christlichen Kultur*, Vienna [1937].

Paugam, Jacques, *L'âge d'or du Maurrassisme*, Paris 1971.

Petit, Henri-Robert, *L'Invasion juive*, Paris 1936.

Petrow, Nikita, "Die Kaderpolitik des NKWD während der Massenrepressalien 1936–39," in Wladislaw Hedeler, ed., *Stalinistischer Terror 1934–41: Eine Forschungsbilanz*, Berlin 2002, pp. 11–32.

Picker, Henry, *Hitlers Tischgespräche im Führerhauptquartier*, Stuttgart 1976.

[Pinsker, Leo], *Autoemanzipation! Mahnruf an seine Stammesgenossen von einem russischen Juden*, Berlin 1882.

Plaut, Joshua Eli, *Greek Jewry in the Twentieth Century, 1913–1983: Patterns of Jewish Survival in the Greek Provinces Before and After the Holocaust*, Madison 1996.

Pohl, Dieter, "Ukrainische Hilfskräfte beim Mord an den Juden," in Gerhard Paul, ed., *Die Täter der Shoah: Fanatische Nationalsozialisten oder ganz normale Deutsche?* Göttingen 2002, pp. 205–34.

Pollmann, Viktoria, *Untermieter im christlichen Haus: Die Kirche und die "jüdische Frage" in Polen anhand der Bistumspresse der Metropolie Krakau 1926–1939*, Wiesbaden 2001.

Poznanski, Renée, "French Apprehensions, Jewish Expectations: From a Social Imaginary to a Political Practice," in David Bankier, ed., *The Jews Are Coming Back*, Jerusalem 2005, pp. 25–57.

Proskurover Relief Organization, ed., *Khurbn Proskurov; tsum ondenken fun di heylige neshomes vos zaynen umgekumen, in der shreklikher shkhite, vos iz ongefirt gevoren durkh di haydamakes 1919*, Newark 1924.

Reifer, Manfred, *Der hundertjährige Kampf um die Judenemanzipation in Rumänien (1825–1925)*, Breslau 1925 (an offprint of *Monatsschrift für Geschichte und Wissenschaft des Judentums*, Jg. 1925, vol. 7, pp. 426–44).

Report of the Anglo-American Committee of Enquiry Regarding the Problems of European Jewry and Palestine, Lausanne, April 20, 1946; London 1946.

Richter, Klaus, "'Ein Schatten über dem ganzen Land': Wirtschaftliche Emanzipation und die 'Judenfrage' in Litauen 1883–1914," in Manfred Hettling, Michael G. Muller, and Guido Hausmann, eds., *Die "Judenfrage"—ein europäisches Phänomen*, Berlin 2013, pp. 321–44.

Righini, Eugenio, *Antisemitismo e semitismo nell'Italia politica moderna*, Milan 1901.

Rosenberg, Alfred, *Der staatsfeindliche Zionismus aufgrund jüdischer Quellen*, Hamburg 1922.

Rosenfeld, Max, *Die polnische Judenfrage: Problem und Lösung*, Vienna 1918.

Rother, Bernd, *Spanien und der Holocaust*, Tübingen 2001.

Rudorff, Andrea, "Maksymilian Kolbe," in *Handbuch des Antisemitismus: Judenfeindschaft in Geschichte und Gegenwart*, ed. Wolfgang Benz, vol. 2,1, Berlin 2009, pp. 434ff.

Rülf, Jsaak, *Drei Tage in Jüdisch-Russland: Ein Cultur- und Sittenbild*, Frankfurt am Main 1882.

———, *Die russischen Juden: Ihre Leidensgeschichte und unsere Rettungsversuche*, Memel 1892.

Ruppin, Arthur, *Die Juden der Gegenwart: Eine sozialwissenschaftliche Studie*, Berlin 1904; substantially revised second edition, Berlin 1911.

———, *Die sozialen Verhältnisse der Juden in Russland*, Berlin 1906.

———, *Der Kampf der Juden um ihre Zukunft*, vol. 2: *Soziologie der Juden*, Berlin 1931.

Russische Greuel, *Die Juden-Verfolgung in Russland*, ed. Russisch-jüdischen Comité (Nathan Mayer von Rothschild), Berlin 1882.

Die russischen Judenverfolgungen: Fünfzehn Briefe aus Süd-Russland, Frankfurt am Main 1882.

Salter, Arthur, "Zur Lösung der Frage der Flüchtlingswanderungen: Eine englische Stimme zur Lösung der jüdischen Emigrantenfrage," in: *Archiv für Wanderungswesen und Auslandskunde* 10 (1938/39), pp. 139ff.

Sanders, Ronald, *Shores of Refuge: A Hundred Years of Jewish Emigration*, New York 1988.

Schechtman, Joseph B., *European Population Transfers 1939–1945*, New York 1946.

Schickert, Klaus, *Die Judenfrage in Ungarn: Jüdische Assimilation und antisemitische Bewegung im 19. und 20. Jahrhundert*, second edition, Essen 1943.

Schieder, Theodor, ed., *Das Schicksal der Deutschen in Ungarn* (= Dokumentation der Vertreibung der Deutschen aus Ost-Mitteleuropa, vol. 2), Dusseldorf 1956.

———, "Europa im Zeitalter der Weltmächte," in *Handbuch der europäischen Geschichte*, vol. 7, no. 1, Stuttgart 1979, pp. 1–351.

Schiemann, Paul, "Rede v. 25. 7. 1928 in Wien," in: *Die Wiener Tagung des Verbandes der deutschen Volksgruppen in Europa (Bericht)*, in *Nation und Staat* 1 (1927/1928), pp. 893–95.

Schlamm, Willi (Wilhelm Siegmund, later William S. Schlamm), *Diktatur der Lüge: Eine Abrechnung*, Zurich 1937.

Schlögel, Karl, *Berlin, Ostbahnhof Europas: Russen und Deutsche in ihrem Jahrhundert*, Berlin 1998.

———, *Terror und Traum*. Moscow 1937; Munich 2008.

Schoeps, Julius H., "'Das Urteil wird öffentlich verkündet werden . . .': Der erste Dreyfus-Prozeß im Spiegel von Theodor Herzls Pariser Korrespondenz," in *Das Jüdische Echo* 43 (October 1994), pp. 99–108.

Schuster, Frank M., *Zwischen den Fronten: Osteuropäische Juden während des Ersten Weltkrieges (1914–1919)*, Cologne 2004.

Schuster, Hans, *Die Judenfrage in Rumänien*, Leipzig 1938.

Schwartz, Michael, *Ethnische "Säuberungen" in der Moderne: Globale Wechselwirkungen nationalsozialistischer und rassistischer Gewaltpolitik im 19. und 20. Jahrhundert*, Munich 2013.

Sebastian, Mihail, *"Voller Entsetzen, aber nicht verzweifelt": Tagebücher 1935–44*, ed. Edward Kanterian, Berlin 2005.

Seligsohn, Julius L., *Israel: Die Einwanderung nach USA*, Berlin 1940.

Ševčenko, Taras, *Der Kobsar*, 2 vols., Moscow 1951.

———, *Meine Lieder, meine Träume: Gedichte und Zeichnungen*, Berlin-Kiev 1987.

Silagi, Denis, *Die Juden in Ungarn in der Zwischenkriegszeit, in Ungarn—Jahrbuch 5* (1973), pp. 198–214.

Silberner, Edmund, *Sozialisten zur Judenfrage: Ein Beitrag zur Geschichte des Sozialismus des 19. Jahrhunderts bis 1914*, Berlin 1962.

Simmel, Georg, *Soziologie: Untersuchungen über die Formen der Vergesellschaftung*, Leipzig 1908.

Singer, Isidor, *Presse und Judenthum*, 2nd ed., Vienna 1882.

Singer, J. (Isidor), ed., *Briefe christlicher Zeitgenossen über die Judenfrage*, Vienna 1885.

Slezkine, Yuri, *The Jewish Century*, Princeton 2019.

Smoliakovas, Grigorijus, *Die Nacht, die Jahre dauerte: Ein jüdisches Überlebensschicksal in Litauen 1941–1945*, Konstanz 1992.

Sokolow, Nahum, *Ewiger Haß auf ein Volk der Ewigkeit*, Warsaw 1882.

———, *Geschichte des Zionismus*, Vienna 1905.

Solonari, Vladimir, "An Important New Document on the Romanian Policy of Ethnic Cleansing," in *Holocaust and Genocide Studies* 21 (2007), pp. 268–97.

———, *Purifying the Nation: Population Exchange and Ethnic Cleansing in Nazi-Allied Romania*, Baltimore 2010.

Sombart, Werner, *Die Juden und das Wirtschaftsleben*, Leipzig 1911.

———, *Die Zukunft der Juden*, Leipzig 1912.

Stach, Reiner, *Kafka: Die frühen Jahre*, Frankfurt am Main 2014.

Stang, Knut, *Kollaboration und Massenmord: Die litauische Hilfspolizei, das Rollkommando Hamann und die Ermordung der litauischen Juden*, Frankfurt am Main 1996.

Stauber, Roni, ed., *Collaboration with the Nazis: Public Discourse after the Holocaust*, London 2014.

Stavroulakis, Nicholas P., *The Jews of Greece*, Athens 1997.

Stone, Jules, *The Numerus Clausus in the Universities of Eastern Europe*, Birmingham 1927.

Streit, Georgios, *Der Lausanner Vertrag und der griechisch-türkische Bevölkerungsaustausch*, Berlin 1929.

Stroumsa, Jacques, *Tu choisiras la vie: Violiniste à Auschwitz*, Paris 1998.

Šukys, Julija, *"And I burned with shame": The Testimony of Ona Šimaitė, Righteous Among the Nations: A Letter to Isaac Nachman Steinberg, Search and Research: Lectures and Papers* 10 (Yad Vashem, 2007).

Szinai, Miklos, and Laszlo Szűcs, eds., *The Confidential Papers of Admiral Horthy*, Budapest 1965.

Szöllösi-Janze, Margit, *Die Pfeilkreuzlerbewegung in Ungarn: Historischer Kontext, Entwicklung und Herrschaft*, Munich 1989.

Tausig, Franziska, *Shanghai-Passage: Flucht und Exil einer Wienerin*, Vienna 1987.

Tenenbaum, Joseph (Josef Bendow), *Der Lemberger Judenpogrom: November 1918–Jänner 1919*, Vienna 1919.

———, *Economic Antisemitism: A Review of Political and Economic Conditions of the Jews*, New York 1931.

Thalheim, Karl C., "Gegenwärtige und zukünftige Strukturwandlungen in der Wanderungswirtschaft der Welt," in *Archiv für Wanderungswesen* 3 (1930), pp. 41–47.

———, "Die menschlichen Wanderungen in Krise und Neuaufbau der Weltwirtschaft: Vortrag, gehalten vor der Deutschen Weltwirtschaftlichen Gesellschaft in Berlin am 28. November 1941," in: *Nachrichtenblatt der Reichsstelle für das Auswanderungswesen* 24 (1942), notebook 12, pp. 186–88.

Ther, Philipp, *Die dunkle Seite der Nationalstaaten: "Ethnische Säuberungen" im modernen Europa*, Göttingen 2011.

Thomas, Louis, *Alphonse Toussenel, socialiste national antisémite (1803–1885)*, Paris 1941.

Told (Berthold Baruch Feiwel), *Die Judenmassacres in Kischinew: Mit einem Weiheblatt von E. M. Lilien*, Berlin 1903.

Tolstoi, Iwan, *Der Antisemitismus in Russland*, Frankfurt am Main 1909.

Tonsmeyer, Tatjana, "Kollaboration als handlungsleitendes Motiv? Die slowakische Elite und das NS-Regime," in *Kooperation und Verbrechen: Formen der "Kollaboration" im östlichen Europa 1939–1945*, ed. Christoph Dieckmann et al., Göttingen 2003, pp. 25–54.

Traşcă, Ottmar, and Rudolf Graf, "Rumänien, Ungarn und die Minderheitenfrage zwischen Juli 1940 und August 1944," in Ralph Melville, Jiři Pešek, and Claus Scharf, eds., *Zwangsmigrationen im mittleren und östlichen Europa*, Mainz 2007, pp. 259–308.

Treitschke, Heinrich von, *Ein Wort über unser Judenthum*. Separatabdruck aus dem 44., 45. u. 46. Bd. der Preuß. Jahrbücher, 4. verm. Aufl., Berlin 1881.

Troebst, Stefan, "Antisemitismus im 'Land ohne Antisemitismus': Staat, Titularnation und judische Minderheit in Bulgarien 1878–1993," in *Hausleitner, Mariana, Monika Katz, Juden und Antisemitismus im östlichen Europa*, Berlin 1995, pp. 109–26.

Trotzki, Leo, *Die Balkankriege 1912–13*, Essen 1996.

The Ukraine Terror and the Jewish Peril, ed. Federation of Ukrainian Jews, London 1921.

Ungvári, Tamas, *The "Jewish Question" in Europe: The Case of Hungary*, New York 2000.

Ungvary, Krisztian, *Die Schlacht um Budapest. 1944/45: Stalingrad an der Donau*, Munich 1999.

Varga, László, "Ungarn," in W. Benz, ed., *Dimension des Völkermords: Die Zahl der jüdischen Opfer des Nationalsozialismus*, Munich 1991, pp. 331–51.

Verbrechen der Wehrmacht: Dimensionen des Vernichtungskrieges 1941–1944, Exhibition catalogue ed. Hamburger Institut für Sozialforschung, Hamburg 2002.

Die Verfolgung und Ermordung der europäischen Juden durch das nationalsozialistische Deutschland 1933–1945 [VEJ], vol. 2: *The German Reich: 1938–August 1939*, Susanne Heim, ed., Munich 2009.

———, vol. 4: *Polen: September 1939–Juli 1941*, Klaus-Peter Friedrich, ed., Munich 2011.

———, vol. 5: *West- und Nordeuropa: 1940–Juni 1942*, Katja Happe, Michael Mayer, and Maja Peers, eds., Munich 2012.

———, vol. 7: *Sowjetunion mit annektierten Gebieten I: Besetzte sowjetische Gebiete unter deutscher Militärverwaltung, Baltikum und Transnistrien*, Bert Hoppe and Hildrun Glass, eds., Munich 2011.

———, vol. 8: *Sowjetunion mit annektierten Gebieten II*, Bert Hoppe, ed., Berlin 2016.

———, vol. 9: *Polen: Generalgouvernement, August 1941–1945*, Klaus-Peter Friedrich, ed., Munich 2014.

———, vol. 14: *Besetztes Südosteuropa und Italien*, Sara Berger et al., eds., Munich 2017.

Vetter, Matthias, *Antisemiten und Bolschewiki: Zum Verhältnis von Sowjetsystem und Judenfeindschaft 1917–1939*, Berlin 1995.

Vishniac, Roman, *Verschwundene Welt*, Munich 1983.

Weidlein, Johann, ed., *Der ungarische Antisemitismus in Dokumenten*, Schorndorf 1962.

Weinberg, Robert, "Workers, Pogroms, and the 1905 Revolution in Odessa," in *Russian Review* 46 (1987), pp. 53–75.

Weinert, Erich, *Gesammelte Werke: Nachdichtungen*, Berlin 1959.

Weisl, Wolfgang, *Der Kampf um das Heilige Land*, Vienna 1925.

Welter, Beate, *Die Judenpolitik der rumänischen Regierung 1866–1888*, Frankfurt am Main 1989.

Whyte, George R., *The Dreyfus Affair: A Chronological History*, London 2006.

Wildt, Michael, ed., *Die Judenpolitik des SD 1935 bis 1938: Eine Dokumentation*, Munich 1995.

Winock, Michel, *Nationalisme, antisémitisme et fascisme en France*, Paris 2004.

Wirtschaftsjahrbuch des Pester Lloyd: Ungarns Volkswirtschaft 1943, Budapest 1944.

Wischnitzer, Mark, *To Dwell in Safety: The Story of Jewish Migration since 1800*, Philadelphia 1948.

World Jewish Congress [WJC], *Short minutes of office committee meetings*, January 2, 1946–April 9, 1948.

———, *Memorandum to the United Nations Special Committee on Palestine*, [New York] 1947 (YVL 02855).

Wyrwa, Ulrich, "'La questione ebraica': Der Begriff 'Judenfrage' in der italienischen Sprache und die Juden in der neueren Geschichte Italiens," in Manfred Hettling, Michael G. Muller, and Guido Hausmann, eds., *Die "Judenfrage"— ein europäisches Phänomen*, Berlin 2013, pp. 181–202.

———, *Gesellschaftliche Konfliktfelder und die Entstehung des Antisemitismus: Das Deutsche Kaiserreich und das Liberale Italien im Vergleich*, Berlin 2015.

York-Steiner, Heinrich, *Die Kunst, als Jude zu leben: Minderheit verpflichtet*, Leipzig 1928.

Zandman, Felix, *Never the Last Journey*, New York 1995.

Zangwill, Israel, *Die territoriale Lösung der Judenfrage*, Vienna 1907.

———, *Ist der Zionismus tot?—Ja!*, Berlin 1924.

Zeltser, Arkadi, ed., *To Pour Out My Bitter Soul: Letters of Jews from USSR, 1941–1945*, Jerusalem 2016.

Zielenziger, Kurt, "Die Auswanderung der deutschen Juden seit 1938," in *Population. Journal of the International Union for the Scientific Investigation of Population Problems*, December 1937, pp. 81–95.

Zobel, Andreas, *Frankreichs extreme Rechte vor dem Ersten Weltkrieg unter besonderer Berücksichtigung der "Action française": Ein empirischer Beitrag zur Bestimmung des Begriffs Präfaschismus*, Berlin 1982.

Zola-Prozeß vor dem Schwurgericht vom 7. bis 23. Februar 1898 und der Dreyfus-Kampf in Frankreich, Chemnitz 1898.

Zweig, Stefan, *Die Welt von Gestern: Erinnerungen eines Europäers* (Stockholm 1942), Frankfurt am Main 1970.

NOTES

INTRODUCTION

1. Zangwill, *Territoriale Lösung*, pp. 5ff.
2. Brandenburgisches Landeshauptarchiv, Rep. 35H KZ Sachsenhausen, 3/7.
3. Letter 16 December 1938, cited in VEJ 2/203.
4. Kieffer, *Judenverfolgung*, p. 351f.
5. Glass, *Deutschland*, pp. 59ff.
6. Friedländer, *The Years of Extermination*, xxi.
7. Gerlach, *Wannsee-Konferenz*. Emphasis added.
8. Goebbels, *Tgb.*, II/3, pp. 557–63, 27 March 1942, entry.
9. Gerlach, Aly, *Kapitel*, pp. 325–34, 344–54.
10. Glass, *Minderheit*, pp. 20–23.
11. Arendt, *Elemente*, pp. 424, 435.
12. Marr, *Judenkrieg*, pp. 29–31; Marr, *Sieg*, pp. 3, 33, 45ff.; Boeckel, *Verjudung*; Boeckel, *Nochmals*, pp. 6–9; *Judenfrage im preussischen Abgeordneten-hause*, pp. 137ff.

1: PROPHETS OF FUTURE HORRORS

1. Cited in Schoeps, *Urteil*, p. 107.
2. There are many different published versions of Herzl's short manifesto, so no page numbers will be given for quotes from this work. English translations of the manifesto differ radically from the German original.
3. Hilfsverein, *Geschäftsbericht*, p. 35.

4. See Herzl's utopia, *Alt-Neuland*.

5. Pinsker, *Autoemanzipation*.

6. Cited in Heiden, *Geschichte*, pp. 66ff.

7. Herzl, *Briefe und Tagebücher*, pp. 58ff., 65, 117ff.

8. Cited in Herzl, *Selbstbiographie*, pp. 42–46.

9. Weisl, *Kampf*, p. 20; *Jüdisches Lexikon*, IV, 1, 700.

10. Zweig, *Welt*, pp. 126ff.

11. Lagarde, *Konservativ?*, p. 34.

12. Istóczy, *Wiederherstellung*, pp. 1–13.

13. See, for example, Nossig, *Materialien*, pp. 24–27.

14. Claß, *Kriegsziel*, pp. 6, 50–52; Claß, *Kaiser*, pp. 30–38, 74–78.

15. Cited in Slezkine, *Century*, pp. 159–60, 165.

16. Budnitskii, *Russian Jews*, p. 18.

17. Lestschinsky, *Migration*, pp. 1565ff.; Kaplun-Kogan, *Wanderbewegungen*, pp. 113–30.

18. Sombart, *Zukunft*, pp. 16–27.

19. Hilfsverein, *Geschäftsbericht*, pp. 14ff.

20. Cited in German translation in Hilfsverein, *Geschäftsbericht*, pp. 113–17.

21. Sombart, *Zukunft*, pp. 16–32.

22. Told, *Judenmassacres*, p. 102.

23. Hilfsverein, *Geschäftsbericht*, pp. 140ff.; Doctor, *Emigration* (1908).

24. Singer, *Presse und Judenthum*, pp. 6–8.

25. Lichtenstaedter, *Kultur*, pp. 6, 31, 164.

26. Lichtenstaedter, *Zukunft*, pp. 7, 14, 25ff., 29.

27. Lichtenstaedter, *Weltreich, Teil 1*, pp. 22ff., 88–95.

28. Aly, *Rasse*, p. 19.

29. Lichtenstaedter, *Weltreich*, vol. 2, pp. 23, 41ff., 59–70, 102ff., 108–10.

30. Dubnow, *Leben*, p. 124.

31. Schlögel, *Berlin*, p. 218.

2: THE SLUGGISH VERSUS THE AMBITIOUS

1. Singer, ed., *Briefe*, pp. 103–5, 191–93; Carl Vogt, "Zur Judenfrage," "Noch etwas über Barbarei," "Noch etwas zur Judenfrage," *Frankfurter Zeitung*, 4 December 1880 (no. 339), 31 December 1880 (no. 366), 6 February 1881 (no. 37).

2. On Virchow und Bamberger, see Aly, *Warum*, pp. 36ff., 47, 95; on Börne, Aly, *Volk*, p. 40.

3. Righini, *Antisemitismo*, pp. 23ff., 125–31, 350ff.

4. Dubnow, *Weltgeschichte*, vol. 10, pp. 256ff.

5. Wyrwa, *Questione*, pp. 193–95.

6. See Hilfsverein, *Geschäftsbericht*, pp. 105ff.

7. Judavics-Paneth, *Pogrom-Prozesse*, p. 18; *Russische Greuel*, pp. 9–11.

8. Dubnow, *Weltgeschichte*, vol. 10, pp. 137–39.

9. *Russische Greuel*, pp. 5–14, 21ff.; Rülf, *Russische Juden*, pp. 24ff., 31.

10. Told, *Judenmassacres*, pp. 92ff.

11. Tolstoi, *Antisemitismus*, pp. 62ff.

12. Hilfsverein, *Geschäftsbericht*, p. 96.

13. Ruppin, *Verhältnisse*, pp. 1–66; Kohn, *Russland*, pp. 65ff.

14. Godley, *Entrepreneurship*, pp. 71ff.; Slezkine, *Century*, p. 117; Sombart, *Zukunft*, p. 21.

15. See *Judenpogrome in Russland*.

16. Ibid., part 2, pp. 5–24; Judge, *Ostern*, pp. 20–23, 129.

17. Münz, *Judenmetzeleien*, pp. 4ff.

18. Slezkine, *Century*, p. 159.

19. Weinberg, *Workers*, p. 53n2, pp. 53–75.

20. Nathan, *Russische Revolution*, pp. 18, 26.

21. Hilfsverein, *Geschäftsbericht* (1907), pp. 74–76, *Geschäftsbericht* (1910), p. 24.

22. See Zangwill, *Lösung*, pp. 36ff.

23. Report by *Pester Lloyd* from St. Petersburg, 6 April 1910.

24. Judge, *Ostern*, p. 129; Slezkine, *Century*, p. 116.

25. Statistics from 1 January 1886; see Grusenberg, *Bedürfnisse*, p. 33.

26. Ruppin, *Juden*, p. 128.

27. Sombart, *Zukunft*, pp. 18ff.

28. Tolstoi, *Antisemitismus*, pp. 68–73; Nossig, *Materialien*, p. 85.

29. Ibid., pp. 78–83.

30. See Slezkine, *Century*, p. 158.

31. *Judenpogrome in Russland*, pp. 97–133 (A. Linden, "Der permanente Pogrom gegen die russischen Juden: Rechtsbeschrankungen").

32. Dubnow, *Leben*, pp. 53ff.; Ruppin, *Verhältnisse*, pp. 52–57.

33. Rülf, *Jüdisch-Russland*, pp. 14, 86, 96.

34. Kahan, *Notes*, p. 111; Budnitskii, *Russian Jews*, pp. 31ff.

35. Hilfsverein, *Geschäftsbericht* (1914), p. 73.

36. Welter, *Judenpolitik*, pp. 53ff.

37. Lazare, *Juden*, p. 32; Jericho-Polonius, *China*, pp. 15, 60ff.

38. Lazare, *Juden*, pp. 34–37, 67.

39. See *Judenfrage in Rumänien*, pp. 5–7.

40. Jericho-Polonius, *China*, pp. 61–87; Lazare, *Juden*, pp. 35–40, 45–54, 67–71, 86; Hilfsverein, *Geschäftsbericht* (1907), pp. 20–22; Reifer, *Kampf*, pp. 14ff.; Trotzki, *Balkankriege*, "Die Judenfrage" (1913), pp. 457, 462ff.; Motzkin, *Campagne*, pp. 18, 184.

41. Zola, "*J'accuse*," tr. and annotated by Shelley Temchin and Jean-Max Guieu, Georgetown University, 2001, https://faculty.georgetown.edu/guieuj/others /IAccuse/Jaccuse.htm.

42. Zobel, *Extreme Rechte*, pp. 95ff.

43. *Zola-Prozess*, pp. 1–16; Dubnow, *Weltgeschichte*, vol. 10 (1929), pp. 232–42, 245; Whyte, *Dreyfus*, pp. 418ff.

44. See Frank, *Nationalismus*, p. 600.
45. Paugam, *L'âge*, pp. 20–22, 127–34.
46. Duclert, *Dreyfus*, pp. 143–45.
47. Dubnow, *Weltgeschichte*, vol. 10 (1929), pp. 226ff.
48. See Frank, *Nationalismus*, p. 316.
49. Benbassa, *Geschichte*, pp. 168ff.
50. Drumont, *La France juive*, p. 517; Winock, *Nationalisme*, p. 130.
51. Thomas, *Precurseurs*, pp. 15–18.
52. Silberner, *Sozialisten*, pp. 12–82; Zobel, *Extreme Rechte*, p. 81; Benbassa, *Geschichte*, p. 175.
53. See the summary in Boldorf, *Parameters*.
54. Ibid., p. 87a; Nolte, *Faschismus*, p. 87.
55. Zobel, *Extreme Rechte*, pp. 30–32, 39, 99–101; Benbassa, *Geschichte*, pp. 176ff.
56. See Silberner, *Sozialisten*, pp. 70–74.
57. See Frank, *Nationalismus*, p. 319.
58. Hyman, *Jews of Modern France*, pp. 122–35.
59. Benbassa, *Geschichte*, pp. 170ff.
60. Margaroni, *Saloniki*, pp. 251–53.
61. See Meron, *Entrepreneurship*, p. 36.
62. Ibid., pp. 29–31; Bowman, *Agony*, p. 21; Boeckh, *Balkankriege*, p. 357.
63. Meron, *Entrepreneurship*, pp. 257–73.
64. Nathan, *Balkanhilfswerk*, pp. 4, 22–24; Hilfsverein, *Geschäftsbericht* (1914), pp. 66–72; International Commission, *Balkan Wars*, pp. 79ff.; Mojzes, *Genocides*, p. 34; Trotzki, *Balkankriege*, pp. 307–9.
65. Hilfsverein, *Geschäftsbericht* (1910), p. 38; Troebst, *Antisemitismus*, pp. 111–16.
66. Meron, *Entrepreneurship*, pp. 218, 36ff.
67. Ibid., pp. 21, 218.
68. Margaroni, *Saloniki*, p. 259.
69. Fleming, *Greece*, pp. 16ff., 35; Plaut, *Greek Jewry*, pp. 28–31; Matsas, *Illusion*, p. 16; Dubnow, *Weltgeschichte*, abridged edition, vol. 3 (1938), pp. 325, 418, 526, 611; Dubnow, *Weltgeschichte*, vol. 10 (1929), pp. 271ff., 480–82; Margaroni, *Saloniki*, pp. 258–61; Fink, *Defending*, pp. 58ff.; Molho, *Salonica*, pp. 219–21.
70. See Hemberger, *Balkankrieg*, pp. 382–90.
71. "Saloniki und seine heutige Bedeutung," *Deutsche Levante-Zeitung*, February 1, 1914 (see also January 1 and December 15, 1913).
72. See Boeckh, *Balkankriege*, p. 237.
73. See Meron, *Entrepreneurship*, p. 31; Fleming, *Greece*, p. 75.
74. Molho, *Salonica*, p. 229.

3: PEACE, CIVIL WAR, POGROMS

1. Lansing, *Versailler Verhandlungen*, pp. 70–79.
2. Bendow (Tenenbaum), *Judenpogrom*, pp. 10, 17; Döblin, *Reise*, pp. 199ff.
3. Lansing, Robert, English original: http://www.fulltextarchive.com/pdfs/The -Peace-Negotiations.pdf, p. 193.
4. Fink, *Defending*, pp. 164ff.
5. *Documents* (1998), introduction; *Jüdisches Lexikon* (1927), "Saloniki" and "Griechenland."
6. Hitler, *Kampf*, p. 356 (tr. Michael Ford: https://www.pdfdrive.com/adolf-hitler -mein-kampf-ford-translation-d18759118.html); Rosenberg, *Zionismus*.
7. Arendt, *Besuch*, p. 43.
8. Bresslau, "Bresslau," pp. 73ff.
9. Unless otherwise indicated, see Harvey, *Lost Children*.
10. Hugues, *Marthe*, pp. 92–97, 101ff., 112, 144.
11. Aly, *Volksstaat*, p. 261.
12. Cattaruzza, *Historischer Ort*, p. 47.
13. Oltmer, *Migration*, pp. 91ff.
14. Fischer, *Alsace*, pp. 131–36.
15. Mayer, *Staaten*, pp. 76, 137–40; Mayer, *Regierung*, pp. 356–60.
16. Picker, ed., *Hitlers Tischgesprache*, pp. 285ff.
17. Aly and Heim, *Vordenker*, pp. 120–31, 396.
18. Delmer, *Die Deutschen*, p. 669.
19. Cohen, *Report*, pp. 7ff., 11–20; Mission of the United States to Poland: Henry Morgenthau Sr., Report, 3 October 1919, https://en.wikisource.org /wiki/Mission_of_The_United_States_to_Poland:_Henry_Morgenthau,_ Sr._report.
20. Cohen, *Report*, p. 8; Golczewski, *Beziehungen* (1981), pp. 31–33.
21. Hilfsverein, *Geschäftsbericht* (1919), pp. 13–15; Golczewski, *Beziehungen*, pp. 197ff.; Pacholkiv, *Einbeziehung*, p. 187.
22. If not otherwise indicated, see Bendow, *Judenpogrom*.
23. Pacholkiv, *Einbeziehung*, pp. 186, 204.
24. Ibid., pp. 191, 188.
25. Ibid., pp. 192, 187.
26. See Schuster, *Fronten*, p. 433.
27. Chasanowitsch, *Judenpogrome*, p. 5.
28. Schuster, *Fronten*, pp. 437–44; Miliakova, ed., *Livre*, pp. 427–32.
29. Morgenthau, see note 19; Fink, *Pogroms*, pp. 153–55; Schuster, *Fronten*, pp. 445–48; Miliakova, ed., *Livre*, pp. 432–34.
30. Mayer, *Furies*, p. 520; Budnitskii, *Russian Jews*, pp. 217–74.
31. Jens Jessen, *Kiew*. "Michail Bulgakows 'Weiße Garde' als ukrainisches Lehrstuck," *Die Zeit*, 9 December 2004.
32. Heifetz, *Slaughter*, p. 21.
33. See Dieckmann, *Jüdischer Bolschewismus*, p. 69.

34. Gergel, *Pogroms* (1928–1951), pp. 237–51; Heifetz, *Slaughter*, pp. 84–89, 203–7; Vetter, *Antisemiten*, pp. 54–57; Abramson, *Prayer*, pp. 113–26.

35. Heifetz, *Slaughter*, pp. 1ff., 175–80. https://archive.org/stream/slaughter ofjewsi00heifuoft/slaughterofjewsi00heifuoft_djvu.txt, chapter 1, section 2.

36. Miliakova, ed., *Livre*, p. 31. On the number of pogrom victims, see Vetter, *Antisemiten*, pp. 54–57; Dieckmann, *Jüdischer Bolschewismus*, pp. 59ff.

37. Silberner, *Sozialisten*, pp. 277ff.

38. Among the misleading "documentary" works are: *Die Lage der Juden in der Ukraine: Eine Dokumentensammlung*, ed. Ukrainian Press Service; Wladimir Lewitzkyj and Gustav Specht, *Berlin* (1920); and *Documents* (1927).

39. For example, Abramson, *Prayer*, pp. 134–40.

40. Dubnow, *Weltgeschichte*, vol. 10, p. 526.

41. Heifetz, *Slaughter*, pp. 185–200; *Ukraine Terror*; Vetter, *Antisemiten*, p. 33.

42. Miliakova, ed., *Livre*, pp. 137–43; Heifetz, *Slaughter*, pp. 44–48.

43. Heifetz, *Slaughter*, pp. 208ff., 227–34; Proskurover Relief Organization, *tsum ondenken*; Miliakova, ed., *Livre*, pp. 107–37, 427–32; Dubnow, *Weltge-schichte*, vol. 10, pp. 526–29.

44. *Encyclopedia of Jewish Life*, vol. 2, p. 1028.

45. Heifetz, *Slaughter*, p. 212.

46. Bulgakov, *Guard*, based on a translation from the Russian by Michael Glenny (1971), chap. 20.

47. See Ševčenko, "Haydamaky."

48. Alwart, *Ševčenko* (the author studiously avoids the topic of Jews); Koch, *Gefühle bei Ševčenko*.

49. S. M. Dubnow, *Tret'ia gaidamachina* (1923), cited in Budnitskii, *Russian Jews*, p. 220; Dubnow, *Weltgeschichte*, vol. 10, p. 526. See Jawen Me-zula, "Schilderung des polnisch-kosakischen Krieges und der Leiden der Juden in Polen wahrend der Jahre 1648–1653: Bericht eines Zeitgenos-sen" (1863).

50. Dubnow, *Weltgeschichte*, vol. 10, p. 13.

51. Silberner, *Sozialisten*, pp. 270–77.

52. Miliakova, ed., *Livre*, pp. 252, 415–18; on anarchist pogroms: http://kehilalinks .jewishgen.org/colonies_of_ukraine/pogroms/ukrainianpogroms.htm (15 December 2015).

53. Miliakova, ed., *Livre*, pp. 13, 43; Heifetz, *Slaughter*, pp. 178, 243–48.

54. See Budnitskii, *Russian Jews*, p. 219.

55. Babel, *Taubenschlag*, pp. 282ff., 843ff.

56. Miliakova, ed., *Livre*, pp. 382–84.

57. http://jewua.org/polonnoe (12 January 2016).

58. Kenez, *Pogroms*, pp. 303–7; Heifetz, *Slaughter*, pp. 8ff.; Vetter, *Antisemiten*, p. 49.

4: MINORITIES AND MIGRANTS

1. *The New York Times*, 17 August 1920; see Sanders, *Shores*, p. 382.
2. Hilfsverein, *Jahresbericht* (1931), pp. 26–28; Lestschinsky, *Migration*, pp. 8, 15, Table IA; Wischnitzer, *Safety*, p. 289, Table I; Seligsohn, *Einwanderung*, pp. 11ff.
3. Hilfsverein, *Jahresbericht* (1931), pp. 28–32.
4. Weisl, *Kampf*, pp. 126–38, 274–77.
5. Zangwill, *Zionismus*, pp. 483ff.
6. Chasanowitsch, *Judenpogrome*, p. 14.
7. Hausleitner, *Rumänisierung*, p. 151; Muller, *Land Reforms*.
8. Kulischer, *Kriegs- und Wanderzüge*, pp. 201ff.
9. See Rosenfeld, *Polnische Judenfrage*, p. 182.
10. Arendt, *Elemente*, p. 433.
11. "Aus der Vorgeschichte der Orientkrise," in *Pester Lloyd*, 9 November 1922; Ihrig, *Ataturk*, p. 11.
12. Nansen, *Betrogenes Volk*, pp. 21–27.
13. Streit, *Lausanner Vertrag*; Ladas, *Exchange*, pp. 338–47; Lemberg, *Entmischung*, p. 386.
14. Schiemann, *Wiener Tagung*, pp. 894ff.
15. Kulischer, *Europe*, p. 175.
16. Thalheim, *Strukturwandlungen*, pp. 41–47; "Austausch," in *Archiv für Wanderungswesen* 3 (1930), pp. 114ff.; "Die griechische Flüchtlingswanderung," ibid., 5 (1933), pp. 124ff.; "Flüchtlingswanderung. Griechenland," ibid., 7 (1935), pp. 138ff.; Hitler, *Kampf*, p. 741. English translation by Michael Ford, London, 1939, p. 500.
17. *Zeitschrift für Geopolitik* 14 (1937), p. 53.
18. Hausleitner, *Rumänisierung*, pp. 254, 328; *Pan-arische Union*, p. 16.
19. Salter, *Lösung*.
20. See Schechtman, *Population*, p. 53.
21. Fleming, *Greece*, p. 87.
22. Schwartz, *Säuberungen*, p. 407.
23. G. B. Ducas, "Griechenland," in *Wirtschaftsdienst*, 20 February 1931, no. 8.
24. Meron, *Entrepreneurship*, pp. 37ff.
25. Fleming, *Greece*, pp. 84–87; Molho, *Salonica*, pp. 233–36; Stavroulakis, *Jews*, pp. 54ff.
26. See Meron, *Entrepreneurship*, p. 57.
27. Mazower, *Salonica*, p. 382; Apostolou, *Jews*, p. 213; Anastassiadou, *Salonique après 1912*; Molho, *Salonica*, pp. 229–39.
28. Molho, *Salonica*, pp. 231–33, 236ff.
29. Summary by the Jewish Telegraphic Agency of the campaigns in Salonika's liberal press beginning in May and continuing into June 1933. http://www.jta.org/1934/01/25/archive/venizelos-demands-jews-surrender-greek-suffrage.

30. Plaut, *Greek Jewry*, pp. 52–54.

31. Mayer, *Staaten*, p. 208; Hyman, *Jews*, pp. 137–59.

32. Petit, *L'Invasion*, p. 3; see Mayer, *Staaten*, p. 23.

33. Mayer, *Staaten*, pp. 24–26; Caron, *Asylum*, pp. 21–26.

34. See Arndt, *Léon Blum*, pp. 55–65.

35. See Mayer, *Staaten*, pp. 242ff.

36. Fette, *Exclusions*, p. 52.

37. Ibid., pp. 24ff., 41ff., 44–51; Caron, *Asylum*, pp. 29–32, 40, 66.

38. Benbassa, *Geschichte*, pp. 187–91, 204ff., 207ff.; Hyman, *Jews*, pp. 120–22, 137, 153.

39. Memorandum, Auswärtigen Amt, 25 January 1939 (Schumburg), ADAP, Serie D, vol. 5, pp. 780–85.

40. Vetter, *Antisemiten*, pp. 58ff.; Gitelman, *Century*, pp. 64–74; Babel, *Taubenschlag*, p. 682.

41. Lenin, *Werke*, vol. 29, pp. 239ff.

42. Slezkine, *Century*, pp. 169–73.

43. Ibid., p. 224; N. Semasko, *Kto i počemu travit evreev*, pp. 8–16. See also Vetter, *Antisemiten*, p. 172; for Lenin, see Slezkine, *Century*, p. 224.

44. Vetter, *Antisemiten*, pp. 96, 98; Slezkine, *Century*, p. 218.

45. Summarized in Slezkine, *Century*, pp. 224–26. The Soviet leadership soon decreed a number of restrictions, which, while not significantly preventing Jews from advancing, did hinder them. During the 1920s Jews were largely excluded from the preparatory courses at the *Rabochiy fakultet*, or "Workers' Faculty," necessary to qualify for many higher posts. There were also quotas reserved for "native" nationalities at the Soviet Union's universities. In 1923–24, Jews made up 47.4 percent of all students at universities in Ukraine, but by 1929–30 that figure was down to 23.3 percent—although some of the decline may have been due to the expansion of education in general. Nevertheless, Jewish university students clearly outperformed their peers, and by 1939, a decade later, their numbers had quadrupled, going from 22,518 to 98,216. But they represented only 11.1 percent of students as a whole. A new gentile elite was being cultivated.

46. Gitelman, *Century*, p. 96.

47. Grüner, *Patrioten*, pp. 28 ff.; Löwe, *Juden*, pp. 143, 159.

48. On the proportion of Jews in the higher ranks of Russian security services, see Petrov, *Kaderpolitik*, pp. 12ff.; Slezkine, *Century*, p. 236.

49. See Slezkine, *Century*, p. 244.

50. Lunacharsky, *Ob Antisemitizme*, pp. 12–15, 17, 24, 29, 46ff. Thanks to Jochen Krüger for the translation of the final quotation. See Slezkine, *Century*, p. 182.

51. Larin, *Evrei i antisemitizm w SSSR*, p. 247; see also Vetter, *Antisemiten*, p. 145.

52. Larin, *Evrei i antisemitizm w SSSR*, p. 184; see also Lustiger, *Rotbuch*, p. 79.

53. Vetter, *Antisemiten*, pp. 242–45.

54. Dates and quotes from ibid., pp. 148–60.

55. Slezkine, *Century*, p. 262.
56. Gitelman, *Jewish Identities*, p. 85; Grossman, *Leben*, p. 695.
57. See Slezkine, *Century*, p. 283.
58. Gitelman, *Jewish Identities*, pp. 83–85.
59. Baberowski, *Verbrannte Erde*, pp. 342–54.
60. See Vetter, *Antisemiten*, pp. 297ff.
61. Schlamm, *Diktatur*, pp. 96ff.
62. Khrushchev, *Khrushchev Remembers*, p. 267.
63. Schlögel, *Terror*, pp. 264ff., 570–75, which includes the quote from Khlevnyuk; Baberowski, *Verbrannte Erde*, p. 355; Petrov, *Kaderpolitik*; Khrushchev, *Khrushchev Remembers*, pp. 19ff.
64. Zeltser, ed., *My Bitter Soul*, pp. 166ff., 171ff.
65. Khrushchev, *Khrushchev Remembers*, pp. 271–74.

5: DISCRIMINATION, DISENFRANCHISEMENT, DENATURALIZATION

1. See Richter, *Schatten*, pp. 321–40; Lestschinsky, *Economic Struggle*, pp. 267–96; Dieckmann, *Besatzungspolitik*, pp. 97–105, 128ff.; Bendikaite, *Anspruch*, pp. 101–20; Dubnow, *Weltgeschichte*, vol. 10, p. 538.
2. See Hausleitner, *Rumänisierung*, p. 167, 192, 254; Eaton, *Origins*, pp. 58ff.; *Jüdisches Lexikon*, vol. 1, column 367.
3. Reifer, *Kampf*, pp. 26–29; Hausleitner, *Rumänisierung*, p. 167; from an anti-Semitic perspective, see Codreanu, *Garde*.
4. See Nastasă, *Anti-Semitism*, pp. 219–43.
5. Ibid., pp. 219–20.
6. Hausleitner, *Rumänisierung*, pp. 163–66.
7. Heinen, *Rumänien*, pp. 53ff.; Hausleitner, *Rumänisierung*, p. 332.
8. Sebastian, *Entsetzen*, pp. 202ff., 207, 211, 222, 226, 247, 264.
9. Schuster, *Judenfrage*, pp. iii–viii, 233–36. Schuster's dissertation was supported by the German Research Society. After the Second World War he was domestic politics editor for the *Süddeutsche Zeitung* from 1960 to 1970, then a member of the executive editorial board until 1976, when he reached retirement age. He was often hailed as a major liberal journalist, something he indeed gradually became after 1945. In 1967 and 1968 he was one of my teachers and mentors at the German Journalism Academy.
10. Hillgruber, ed., *Staatsmänner*, vol. 1 (1967), p. 171.
11. Sebastian, *Entsetzen*, pp. 408ff., 413–15, 427ff.; Ioanid, *Pogrom*, pp. 373–81.
12. Sebastian, *Entsetzen*, pp. 451, 457ff., 474ff., 499f, 502, 515, 524ff., 529; Glass, *Minderheit*, p. 17f; Glass, *Deutschland*, pp. 54–57, 91–93.
13. Kendziorek, *Suche*, pp. 286–89.
14. Ibid., pp. 335–51.
15. Dmowski, *Gedanken*, pp. 276–82.
16. Gröschel, *Antisemitismus*, pp. 49ff.
17. Kotowski, *Hitlers Bewegung*, p. 78; Kossert, *Founding Father*, pp. 98–101.

18. Kendziorek, *Suche*, pp. 328–33; Krzywiec, *Antisemitismus*, pp. 127–29.

19. Marcus, *Social History*, p. 67.

20. For a well-written and -researched overview, see Gröschel, *Antisemitismus*.

21. Vishniac, *Verschwundene Welt*, pp. 65, xxif; Lestschinsky, *Zusammenbruch*, pp. 51ff.

22. Hilfsverein, *Jahresbericht*, pp. 59–62; Dubnow, *Weltgeschichte*, vol. 10, p. 536; Gröschel, *Antisemitismus*, pp. 101, 105–107.

23. Gröschel, *Antisemitismus* (2010), pp. 409 ff., 431–33.

24. Hilfsverein, *Jahresbericht*, pp. 59–62; Gröschel, *Antisemitismus*, pp. 389, 404ff.

25. Reifer, *Kampf*, p. 31; Nastasă, *Anti-Semitism*, pp. 232ff.

26. Friedrich, *Żydokomuna*, p. 71.

27. Stone, *Numerus Clausus*, pp. 8ff., 17–19; Motzkin, *Campagne*, pp. 127–31, 141–86; Pollmann, *Untermieter* (2001), p. 248.

28. De Courtenay, *Antisemitismus*, pp. 354ff.; de Courtenay, *Staatlichkeit*, pp. 344–53.

29. Gröschel, *Antisemitismus*, pp. 388–401, *Canadian Jewish Chronicle*, 22 November 1935, p. 149; Brandys, *Warschauer Tagebuch*, pp. 150–56.

30. Pollmann, *Untermieter*, p. 377; Kotowski, *Hitlers Bewegung*, pp. 75ff.

31. Quotes from church press, see Pollmann, *Untermieter*, pp. 174–76, 291, 295ff., 298ff., 356ff., 385.

32. *Mały Dziennik*, 7 January 1936, see Modras, *Catholic Church*, pp. 66ff.

33. *Mały Dziennik*, 9–11 November 1938; see ibid., p. 302.

34. Kotowski, *Polska*, p. 95.

35. *Rycerz Niepokalanej*, 1938, pp. 224–230; also see Modras, *Catholic Church*, p. 72; Caumanns and Niendorf, "Kolbe bis Kielce," p. 175; Rudorff, "Maksymilian Kolbe," pp. 434ff.

36. Kotowski, *Polska*, pp. 84–98.

37. Kishon, *Lachen*, pp. 40ff.

38. Case, *States*, p. 185.

39. Hillgruber, *Deutschland*, p. 653; Szollosi-Janze, *Pfeilkreuzlerbewegung*, p. 109.

40. Karady, *Gewalterfahrung*, pp. 134–40; Karady, *Judentum*, pp. 348–50, 353; Kovács, *Numerus Clausus*, pp. 39–41; Nagy, *Anti-Jewish Law*, p. 65.

41. Karady, *Jews*, pp. 42–46.

42. Karady and Nagy, eds., *Numerus Clausus*, pp. 12, 14, 17–19; *Jewish Minority*, pp. 14–19, 39–41.

43. Barta, *Judenfrage*, pp. 161ff., 166; Weidlein, ed., *Antisemitismus*, p. 33; Herczl, *Christianity*, p. 46; Silagi, *Juden*, p. 201; Braham, *Politics*, pp. 30ff.; York-Steiner, *Kunst*, pp. 390, 407ff.; Karady, *Gewalterfahrung*, p. 142ff.

44. Gömbös, *Selbstzwecklichkeit*, p. 45; Weidlein, ed., *Antisemitismus*, pp. 38, 44; Barta, *Judenfrage*, p. 166; Braham, *Politics*, p. 52; Kovács, *Numerus Clausus*, p. 48; Klocke, *Kräfte*, pp. 168–73.

45. Weidlein, ed., *Antisemitismus*, pp. 52ff.

46. Ibid., pp. 52ff., 74, 77, 79ff., 87, 91, 105–7; Schickert, *Judenfrage*, p. 240; Silagi, *Juden*, pp. 213ff.; Varga, *Ungarn*, p. 332; *Deutschland und Südosteuropa*, p. 32.

47. Weidlein, ed., *Antisemitismus*, pp. 108ff.; *Transocean-Europaexpress*, 25 November 1942.

48. Karady and Nagy, eds., *Numerus Clausus*, p. 19.

49. Report, Jagow to Auswärtiges Amt, 29 January 1943, PA AA R 29792, Bl. 599.

50. Weidlein, ed., *Antisemitismus*, pp. 121, 124, 132ff.

51. Feszler, *Nachwuchs*, pp. 292–98.

52. Case, *States*, pp. 177, 183; on the overwhelmingly pro-Hungarian attitudes of Jews in the nationally disputed territories, see Ungvari, *Question*, pp. 98–101.

53. Matolcsy, *Arbeitslosigkeit*; Halacs, *Arbeitsverfassung*, pp. 179–82; *Deutschland und Südosteuropa*, p. 27.

54. *Wirtschaftsjahrbuch*, p. 184.

55. Barta, *Judenfrage*, p. 185; Weidlein, ed., *Antisemitismus*, pp. 110ff., 139ff.

56. Kallay, *Premier*, pp. 75ff.; Weidlein, ed., *Antisemitismus*, pp. 143ff., 149ff., 158; *Ungar: Volkswirt* 12 (1943), issue 2, pp. 11, 13 (1944), issue 2, p. 9; Maelicke, *Entjudung* (1943), pp. 1272–76.

57. Hillgruber, ed., *Staatsmänner*, vol. 2 (1970), pp. 245ff.

58. Bibo, *Judenfrage*, pp. 25–35.

6: EXPULSION AND ERADICATION

1. Zielenziger, *Auswanderung*, p. 95.

2. Draft (Roger Makins) for Halifax, 23 May 1938; see Kieffer, *Judenverfolgung*, p. 192.

3. Telegram (Gunther) to State Department, 13 April 1938; *Völkischer Beobachter,* 9 February 1938; see Kieffer, *Judenverfolgung*, pp. 222ff., 353.

4. See Kieffer, *Judenverfolgung*, p. 349.

5. Winston Churchill, *The Gathering Storm,* p. 311.

6. See Kieffer, *Judenverfolgung*, p. 448.

7. Diary of J. P. Moffat, entries 18–19 November, 31 December 1938, Houghton Library, Harvard University, MS AM 1407, vol. 40, 41, 1938 I, II, Film 95.

8. See Kieffer, *Judenverfolgung*, pp. 192–95, 237ff., 253. From http://www.annefrankguide.net/en-CA/bronnenbank.asp?aid=291525; Hoare from Laurence Rees, *The Holocaust: A New History*, p. 129.

9. Memorandum of instructions (Makins, Mallet), 15 June 1938, see Kieffer, *Judenverfolgung*, pp. 200, 202.

10. Moffat, entries from 13/19/21/22 May and 2/20/23 September 1938.

11. Ibid., 25 March 1938.

12. See Kieffer, *Judenverfolgung*, pp. 205ff.

13. "Lagebericht der Abt. II 112 des Sicherheitsdienstes für 1938"; see Wildt, ed., *Judenpolitik*, pp. 194–205; "Juden, was nun?," *Das Schwarze Korps*, 24 November 1938.

14. Aly, *Volksstaat*, pp. 54–66.

15. Memo (Weizsäcker), 8 July 1938, to eleven German embassies, ADAP, Serie D, Bd. 5, p. 753.

16. Account of Negotiation (Taylor), 20 July 1938, see Kieffer, *Judenverfolgung*, pp. 235ff.; *Jüdische Rundschau*, 12 July 1938; Newspaper quotes from Friedländer, *The Years of Persecution*, pp. 269ff.

17. Aly, *Volksstaat*, pp. 54, 57.

18. Wannsee conference protocol.

19. Heim and Aly, *Staatliche Ordnung*, pp. 385ff.

20. Kulischer, *Jewish Migrations*, p. 51.

21. See Kieffer, *Judenverfolgung*, pp. 233., 294ff., 318ff.

22. Hitler, *Reden*, 6 October 1939.

23. See Messner, *Option*, pp. 246ff.

24. Lemberg, *Entmischung*; Ther, *Dunkle Seite*, p. 108.

25. See Lemberg, *Ethnische Säuberung*, pp. 30ff.

26. Hitler to Henderson, 25 August 1939, ADAP, Serie D, Bd. 7, pp. 233–35.

27. See *Faschismus*, p. 244.

28. Opfer, *Wahn*, pp. 46–49; Lemkin, *Axis*, pp. 189ff.; Schechtman, *European Population*, pp. 416ff., 419; Kulischer, *Europe*, p. 265. The figures given in the literature vary wildly.

29. See Ivkova, *Rettung*, pp. 178–84. The author provides vague time references but detailed source information for her documents.

30. German edition, Landesarchiv Berlin, B Rep. 039–01/342, Bl. 87.

31. Report to the Commissar for Jewish Affairs, 20 April 1943; see VEJ 14/183.

32. Hoppe, *Juden Bulgariens*, p. 250.

33. Polizeiattaché der dt. Gesandtschaft in Sofia to RSHA ("Judenabschub aus Bulgarien"), 5 April 1943; PA AA R 100863, Bl. 178–83.

34. Horthy to Hitler, 3 November 1939; Horthy to Piłsudski, 10 October 1934, Szinai and Szucs, eds., *Confidential Papers*, pp. 332ff, 346.

35. Schechtman, *European Population*, pp. 430ff.

36. Hillgruber, ed., *Staatsmänner*, vol. 2, p. 262 (17 April 1943); Weizsäcker, 20 April 1943, about a similar conversation with Szojay, PA AA R 29792, Bl. 178. Weizsäcker considered the idea "somewhat oppressive."

37. Schechtman, *European Population*, pp. 436–39.

38. Hillgruber, ed., *Staatsmänner*, vol. 1, p. 348 (20 November 1940).

39. See Gerlach and Aly, *Kapitel*, pp. 79ff.

40. Conversation between Hitler and Horthy, 16–18 April 1943, ADAP, Serie E, Bd. 5, pp. 621–40.

41. Schieder, ed., *Dokumentation*, vol. 2 (1956), p. 37E.

42. See Weidlein, ed., *Antisemitismus*, p. 77.

43. Gerlach and Aly, *Kapitel*, pp. 430–33.

44. Aly, *Endlösung*, pp. 167, 255–61.
45. Manuilă, *Politica de populacie a statului şi problema minorităcilor etnice*; see Traşcă/Graf, *Rumänien*, p. 260.
46. See Achim, *Romanian Population*, pp. 599ff.
47. Ibid., pp. 609–17; Achim, *Manuilă*, pp. 397–402; Solonari, *Purifying*, pp. 75–94.
48. Glass, *Deutschland*, pp. 149, 202.
49. Manuilă, *Studie*, p. 32; *Zschr. f. Geopolitik* 14 (1937), p. 53.
50. Manuilă, *Judenproblem*, pp. 612ff.
51. Aly, *Endlösung*, pp. 268–79.
52. See Hausleitner, *Rumänisierung*, pp. 288, 377; Heinen, *Rumänien*, p. 55.
53. Protokoll der Ministerratssitzung, 8 July 1941; see VEJ 7/284.
54. Directive by I. Antonescu to gendarmes on the "cleansing of the country," 17–18 June 1941, see VEJ 7, p. 64.
55. Ibid., p. 69.
56. Goebbels, *Tgb.*, II/2, p. 269, 19 August 1941; Sebastian, *Entsetzen*, p. 532.
57. Solonari, *Document*, p. 279.
58. "Rumäniens Kampf gegen die Juden," *Frankfurter Zeitung*, 22 July 1943.
59. Negură, *Siedlungswerk*, pp. 62ff.
60. Solonari, *Document*, pp. 268–97.
61. Glass, *Deutschland*, pp. 161, 175–81, 268.
62. Tönsmeyer, *Kollaboration*, pp. 49–52.
63. *Službene Novine Kraljevine Jugoslavije*, Nr. 229-LXXX-A v. 5. 10. 1940; letter by Mirko Fuks, 22 October 1940, protesting his eleven-year-old daughter's immediate expusion from school, VEJ 14/84.
64. Korb, *Schatten*, pp. 78, 206, 432–38, 443; Ther, *Dunkle Seite*, pp. 145–47.
65. See Korb, *Schatten*, pp. 174ff.
66. Report by US envoy Franklin M. Gunther, 4 November 1941; see Friedländer, *The Years of Extermination*, p. 227.
67. Aly, *Volksstaat*, pp. 231ff.
68. Meinen, *Shoah*, pp. 23, 25ff., 28, 40; VEJ 5/193.
69. Aly and Roth, *Erfassung*, pp. 64–67; VEJ 5/82, 12/81.
70. VEJ 5, pp. 48ff., Dok. 5/271, 5/273, 5/275.
71. Mayer, *Staaten*, pp. 30, 32, 35–37, 307ff.
72. See Klarsfeld, *Vichy-Auschwitz*, p. 392.
73. Mayer, *Staaten*, pp. 278–80.
74. Drach, *Unsentimentale Reise*, p. 206.
75. Mandelbrot, *Chaos*, p. 90.
76. Bober, *Neues*, pp. 135–39. The associations of those who had "Romanized" Jewish property had resonant names: Association française des propriétaires des biens aryanisés; Association des administrateurs provisoires de France; Association nationale intercorporative du commerce de l'industrie et de l'artisanat; Renaissance du foyer français; Fédération des locataires de bonne foi; Union des commercants, industriels et artisans français.

77. See Gilles Morin, "Vichy: Les archives sont-elles vraiment toutes accessibles? Elles étaient déjà presque ouvertes. Pourtant, l'arrêté publié en décembre 2015 est un 'tournant démocratique.' Explication," in *L'Histoire*, no. 427, September 2016, pp. 27ff.

78. Artuso, *La question juive*, pp. 93ff., 223ff.

79. See Dublon-Knebel, ed., *German Documents*, p. 239.

80. Apostolou, *Jews*, p. 215; Molho, *Salonica*, pp. 63ff.; Anastassiadou, *Salonique*, p. 102; on Kammona's retrospective transcriptions of Yom Tov Yakoel, VEJ 14/207; letter military administration, Saloniki, 18 October 1942, VEJ 14/217.

81. The figures on the number of people deported range from 45 to 450 to 48,533; see Bowman, *Agony*, pp. 83–92.

82. Matsas, *Illusion*, p. 289; Stroumsa, *La vie*, p. 136.

83. Matsas, *Illusion*, pp. 191ff., 202ff.; Plaut, *Greek Jewry*, pp. 70–72.

84. "Wochenbericht einer brit. Propagandaeinheit für die Zeit v. 22.–29. 11. 1944 über die soziale Lage in der Region Epirus," see VEJ 14/303.

85. Matsas, *Illusion*, p. 292; Clogg, *Greece 1940–1949*, p. 103; Apostolou, *Strategies*, pp. 138ff.

86. *Excerpts from the Salonika Diary of L. Merci*, pp. 303–13.

87. See Dublon-Knebel, ed., *German Documents*, pp. 412–14.

88. See Rother, *Spanien*, pp. 225ff.

89. See VEJ 8/216.

90. See VEJ 7/446.

91. Zandman, *Never the Last Journey*, pp. 75–79, 88ff.; Yad Vashem Arch., Righteous, 3466.

92. See VEJ 4/126, 208.

93. See VEJ 4/318, 319.

94. See Friedländer, *The Years of Extermination*, p. 385. For a host of other sources, see Friedrich, *Judenmord*.

95. See Friedrich, *Judenmord*, p. 314.

96. See VEJ 9/121. This version of Klukowski's diary is translated directly from the original Polish and contains sections left out of the English version cited below.

97. Klukowski, *Diary*, pp. 139ff., 156ff., 159, 191, 195–97, 219–23.

98. VEJ 9/121, 293.

99. Zeltser, ed., *My Bitter Soul*, pp. 205–15, 223–25.

7: THE RETURN OF THE UNWANTED

1. Kakis, *Legacy*, pp. 229–31, 238.

2. Cecil Roth, "The Last Days of Jewish Salonica," *Commentary*, 1 July 1950, pp. 49–55.

3. See "Bericht des Präsidiums" (1948); Brill, "An die Judenschaft" (1947); Liste der Israelit. Kultusgemeinde "Aus den Konzentrationslagern nach Wien

zurückgekehrte Juden," October 31, 1945, YVL 95–2247F. The rest of this section is based on these accounts.

4. Law of 21 March 1890, *Reichsgesetzblatt fur die im Reichsrathe vertretenen Königreiche und Länder*, Vienna, pp. 109–13.

5. Tausig, *Shanghai*, pp. 139–54; Embacher, *Neubeginn* (1995), pp. 123–32.

6. Kuszelewicz, *Juif* (2002), p. 10.

7. Cited in Messmer, *Antisemitismus* (1997), p. 444.

8. Herbert Rosenkranz, eyewitness testimony, February 1965, p. 20; Mircia Rosenkranz, eyewitness testimony, January 1967, p. 17, Yad Vashem Arch. 0.3, 2751, 3358.

9. Funke, Harbort, *Erinnerung* (1989), Sp. 141ff.

10. Ben-Simhon, "Schön ist die Rache in Gedanken," in *Berliner Zeitung*, 19 November 2009.

11. Atamuk, *Juden*, pp. 217ff.

12. Smoliakovas, *Nacht*, pp. 16, 28; Messmer, *Antisemitismus*, pp. 447ff.

13. Atamuk, *Juden*, pp. 220, 250.

14. Margolis, *Partisanin*, pp. 232ff.

15. Cited in Šukys, *Shame*, p. 72.

16. WJC, Short Minutes, 31 October 1947.

17. Döblin, *Reise*, p. 147.

18. Gerlach and Aly, *Kapitel*, pp. 19–117, 127–48, 186–239, 259ff., 295ff., 409ff.

19. Kertesz, *Flammen*, pp. 174–202.

20. Kenez, *Pogroms* (2009), pp. 232–34.

21. Report H. Brenner, born Piller, 10 August 1992, Yad Vashem Arch. 0.3/6661; www.jewishgen.org/yizkor/oswiecim1/osw417.html, p. 429 (November 2015).

22. *Report of the Anglo-American Committee* (1946), pp. 12ff.

23. Lestschinsky, *Migrations*, pp. 1565ff.

24. Lestschinsky, *Bilan de l'extermination*.

25. WJC, Short Minutes, 31 March 1947.

26. Handgeschr. Chronik der Volksschule der israelit: Cultusgemeinde Mahrisch-Ostrau, 1899–1939, YVL 99–0970F.

27. Note by Eichmann, 6 October 1939, VEJ 4/18.

28. Elias, *Hoffnung*, pp. 249, 273–76, 299–310. Peter Erben, who also grew up in Moravian Ostrau, described similar experiences, See his *Spuren*, pp. 81–85.

29. WJC, Memorandum (1947).

CONCLUSION: CIVILIZATION AND ITS BREAKDOWN

1. Börne, *Schriften* ("Stattigkeit," 1808), vol. 1, pp. 27ff., 59.

2. Schieder, *Europa*, p. 11; Aly, *Volk*, pp. 168–200.

3. Memo, Auswärtigen Amts, 25 January 1939 (Schumburg), ADAP, Serie D, Vol. 5, pp. 780–785.

4. Wyrwa, *Konfliktfelder*, p. 374.

5. Ulrich Beck, *Macht und Gegenmacht*, pp. 338ff.; see Schwartz, *Säuberungen*, p. 627.

6. Stach, *Kafka*, pp. 172–77. In Czechoslovakia, Poland, Russia, Hungary, and France, anti-Semitism often went hand in hand with anti-Germanism.

7. Frankl, *Prag*, pp. 183–85, 200ff., 284–88.

8. Nathan, *Russische Revolution*, pp. 18, 26.

9. Budnitskii, *Russian Jews*, pp. 36–40.

10. Ther, *Dunkle Seite*, p. 161. See also the final chapter of Schwartz, *Ethnische "Säuberungen,"* pp. 623–46, which features much clear and better differentiated arguments than Ther.

11. Schwartz, *Säuberungen* (2013), pp. 634–37.

12. Simmel, *Soziologie*, pp. 685–91. English translation: https://www.infoamerica.org/documentos_pdf/simmel01.pdf.

13. Wolf[gang] Aly, *Der kretische Apollonkult*, pp. 44–48.

14. Sombart, *Zukunft*; Sombart, *Juden*.

15. Treitschke, "Ein Wort über unser Judenthum" (1879), pp. 2ff. This essay is sometimes translated into English as "The Jews Are Our Misfortune."

16. Mombert, *Tatsachen*, pp. 95, 116, 118. See also *Sozialer Auf- und Abstieg im Deutschen Volk: Statistische Methoden und Ergebnisse*, ed. Bayerisches Statistisches Landesamt (1930).

17. Fontane, *Stechlin* (1899), pp. 35, 355ff.

18. Borochov, *Entwicklung*, pp. 7, 16ff.

19. Slezkine, *Jahrhundert*, pp. 129–32; Golczewski, *Beziehungen*, p. 234.

20. Pollmann, *Untermieter*, p. 356.

21. Bendow (Tenenbaum), *Judenpogrom*, pp. 6–8.

22. Biss, *Geschäft*, pp. 58ff.

23. Goebbels, *Tgb.*, II/3, pp. 557–63, entry of 27 March 1942.

24. Dieckmann, *Besatzungspolitik*, pp. 1532ff.

25. Meyer, *Wissen*, p. 74.

26. See *Verbrechen der Wehrmacht*, p. 155.

27. Gerlach, *Kalkulierte Morde*, pp. 677, 680.

28. See Aly, *Volksstaat*, pp. 245ff.

29. For an example, see Aly, *Endlösung*, pp. 257–60.

30. Hoselbarth to Bevollmachtigter des Reiches für Griechenland Altenburg, 17 June 1943; see also VEJ 14/267.

31. For more details see Aly, *Volksstaat*.

32. Ungváry, *Schlacht*, pp. 348ff.

33. Bankier, ed., *Coming Back*, pp. viii–xi; Lagrou, *Return*, p. 8; Poznanski, *Apprehensions*, pp. 28ff., 48ff.

34. JWC, short minutes, June 18, July 11/29, December 18, 1947, March 8, 1948.

35. See Aly, *Volksstaat*, p. 244.

36. Goebbels, *Tgb.*, II/12, pp. 199, 232, entries of 27 April and 4 May 1944.

37. Broucek, ed., *General*, p. 90.

38. See Ungvary, *Schlacht*, pp. 348ff.

39. Von Thadden, 29 April 1943, see Dublon-Knebel, *German Documents*, pp. 338–40.
40. Slezkine, *Century*, p. 368.
41. Ruppin, *Soziologie der Juden*, pp. 53–56.

ACKNOWLEDGMENTS

My thanks and respect go to the authors of the many important studies and documentation since the epochal years 1989–90, including *The Persecution and Murder of the European Jews by Nazi Germany, 1933–1945*, abbreviated in the notes as VEJ, for which I served as coeditor for five years. As of 2017, ten of the sixteen planned volumes had appeared. This project, and the way in which my colleagues so naturally included different European perspectives, reinforced my decision to write this book.

I wrote large portions of this book in the library at Yad Vashem. My special gratitude goes out to the always helpful and friendly people who work at this memorial and research institution. I discussed my drafts with friends in Berlin, Vienna, Tutzing, and Jerusalem, and particular gratitude is due to Yehuda Bauer among many others. Israeli historians have long included the broader European context in their analyses of the Shoah.

I would also like to acknowledge my elegant English translator, Jefferson Chase, and wonderfully insightful and keen-eyed editor, Sara Bershtel at Metropolitan, together with the publisher's staff, for helping to bring my work to a wider international audience.

INDEX

ABOUT THE AUTHOR

GÖTZ ALY is the author of *Hitler's Beneficiaries* and *Why the Germans? Why the Jews?*, among other books. One of the most respected historians of the Third Reich and the Holocaust, he has received the National Jewish Book Award, as well as Germany's prestigious Heinrich Mann Prize, the Ludwig Börne Prize, and the Geschwister Scholl Prize, among numerous other honors. His books have been translated into thirteen languages. He lives in Berlin.